Meditation

FOR

DUMMIES®

3RD EDITION

Meditation FOR DUMMIES® 3RD EDITION

by Stephan Bodian

Foreword by Dr. Dean Ornish, MD
Author of *Dr. Dean Ornish's Program for Reversing Heart Disease*

WILEY

John Wiley & Sons, Inc.

Meditation For Dummies®, 3rd Edition

Published by
John Wiley & Sons, Inc.
111 River St.
Hoboken, NJ 07030-5774
www.wiley.com

Copyright © 2012 by John Wiley & Sons, Inc., Hoboken, New Jersey

Published by John Wiley & Sons, Inc., Hoboken, New Jersey

Published simultaneously in Canada

Library of Congress Control Number: 2012944671

ISBN 978-1-118-29144-3 (pbk); ISBN 978-1-118-33179-8 (ebk); ISBN 978-1-118-33399-0 (ebk); ISBN 978-1-118-33509-3 (ebk)

Manufactured in the United States of America

10 9 8 7 6 5 4 3 2 1

WILEY

About the Author

Stephan Bodian has been practicing and teaching meditation for more than 40 years. As the founder and director of the School for Awakening, he offers workshops, intensives, retreats, and classes devoted to meditation, self-inquiry, and spiritual realization. His most recent book is *Wake Up Now: A Guide to the Journey of Spiritual Awakening*.

When he's not writing or teaching, Stephan practices an approach to counseling and mentoring that guides people in using a blend of psychological insight and meditative reflection for inner exploration and healing. A licensed psychotherapist, he's available for phone or Skype consultations worldwide through his website, www.stephanbodian.org.

Stephan first became interested in meditation in high school when he came across the word Zen in a novel by Beat writer Jack Kerouac. After studying Asian philosophy at Columbia University and doing graduate work at Stanford, he went off to a Zen monastery in the mountains near Big Sur, California, where he shaved his head and spent long hours following his breath. Ordained a monk in 1974, he eventually became director of training at the Zen Center of Los Angeles and resident teacher at a small Zen center in San Diego before putting aside his robes in 1982 to pursue a master's degree in psychology — and a more ordinary life.

From 1984 to 1994 Stephan was editor-in-chief of Yoga Journal, an award-winning magazine devoted to yoga, meditation, and holistic health. In addition to Zen, he has practiced and studied insight meditation, Tibetan Buddhism, and Advaita Vedanta. His other books include *Timeless Visions, Healing Voices; Living Yoga* (with Georg Feuerstein); and *Buddhism For Dummies* (with Jon Landaw), a comprehensive, user-friendly introduction to one of the world's great spiritual traditions.

Stephan is also the author and narrator of a series of meditation-based audio programs: *Mindfulness Meditation*; *Freedom from Stress;* and *Stay Happy.* Produced by Mental Workout and offered online through the iTunes store or www.mentalworkout.com, these programs are available as apps for iPhone, Android, and Nokia platforms and as web-based applications.

For more information on Stephan's workshops, retreats, classes, and phone counseling and mentoring sessions, visit his website (www.stephanbodian.org).

Dedication

This book is dedicated to the great meditation masters and teachers in every culture and age, who continue to show us the way through their wise and compassionate example; and to you, dear reader: May the practice of meditation bring you the peace, health, and happiness you seek!

Author's Acknowledgments

I'd like to express my appreciation to the colleagues, teachers, and publishing professionals who contributed to the creation of this book. First, to the good folks at Wiley, including Acquisitions Editors Tammerly Booth, Mikal Belicove, and Michael Lewis, and Project Editor for the first edition Melba Hopper; and to my agent, Carol Susan Roth.

Special thanks to: Dean Ornish, M.D., whose pioneering research has helped to change the face of modern medicine, for so graciously providing the foreword; technical advisor Eleanor Criswell, Ed.D., professor of psychology at Sonoma State University, who has generously supported and critiqued my work over the years; and Rick Shiner, old friend and recording engineer extraordinaire, for producing and providing original music for the CD. Thanks also to Shabda Kahn, Thomas Keating, Rami Shapiro, David Orme-Johnson, and David Black, whose insights helped inform certain sections of this book.

I've had the inestimable good fortune to study with some great meditation teachers, whose guidance and instruction helped make this book possible. Deep bows to Shunryu Suzuki Roshi and Kobun Chino Otogawa Roshi; to Chogyam Trungpa Rinpoche and Drubwang Tsoknyi Rinpoche; to my beloved "root teacher," Jean Klein, who pointed directly to the heart of meditation; and to Adyashanti, friend and mentor, through whose loving words and lucid presence the Buddha finally awakened to itself.

I would also like to thank the other Western writers and teachers whose work has inspired and informed this book: Joan Borysenko, Pema Chodron, Jon Kabat-Zinn, Jack Kornfield, Joel Levey, Stephen Levine, Byron Katie, and Suzanne Segal.

Publisher's Acknowledgments

We're proud of this book; please send us your comments at http://dummies.custhelp.com. For other comments, please contact our Customer Care Department within the U.S. at 877-762-2974, outside the U.S. at 317-572-3993, or fax 317-572-4002.

Some of the people who helped bring this book to market include the following:

Acquisitions, Editorial, and Media Development

Project Editors: Heike Baird and Susan Hobbs

Acquisitions Editor: Michael Lewis

Copy Editor: Jessica Smith

Assistant Editor: David Lutton

Editorial Program Coordinator: Joe Niesen

Technical Editor: Lisa Ernst

Editorial Manager: Carmen Krikorian

Editorial Assistant: Rachelle Amick

Art Coordinator: Alicia B. South

Cover Photos: © iStockphoto.com / Angelika Schwarz

Cartoons: Rich Tennant (www.the5thwave.com)

Composition Services

Project Coordinator: Katherine Crocker

Layout and Graphics: Jennifer Creasey

Illustrator: Pam Tanzey

Proofreader: ConText Editorial Services, Inc.

Indexer: Estalita Slivoskey

Publishing and Editorial for Consumer Dummies

    Kathleen Nebenhaus, Vice President and Executive Publisher

    Kristin Ferguson-Wagstaffe, Product Development Director

    Ensley Eikenburg, Associate Publisher, Travel

    Kelly Regan, Editorial Director, Travel

Publishing for Technology Dummies

    Andy Cummings, Vice President and Publisher

Composition Services

    Debbie Stailey, Director of Composition Services

Contents at a Glance

Table of Contents

Foreword

*T*he title of this book is a little misleading because learning to meditate was one of the smartest decisions I ever made.

Meditation is power. Whatever you do, meditation can help you to do it better.

For example, my colleges and I demonstrated, for the first time, that the progression of even severe coronary disease often can be reversed when people go on my program of comprehensive lifestyle changes. Although many people believe that this program is based primarily on diet, meditation is actually an equally important part of it.

So — why meditate?

In *Meditation For Dummies*, 3rd Edition, Stephan Bodian helps dispel many of the most common misconceptions about meditation.

Many people view meditation as:	*In fact, meditation is:*
Boring	Interesting
Esoteric	Familiar
Ascetic	Sensual
Unproductive	Extremely productive
Difficult	Natural
Wimpy	Powerful

Meditation is the practice and process of paying attention and focusing your awareness. When you meditate, a number of desirable things begin to happen — slowly, at first, and deepening over time. As I describe in *Love & Survival*:

First, *when you can focus your awareness, you gain more power.* When you concentrate any form of energy, including mental energy, you gain power. When you focus your mind, you concentrate better. When you concentrate better, you perform better. You can accomplish more, whether in the classroom, in the board room, or in the athletic arena. Whatever you do, you can do it more effectively when you meditate. It is for this reason that spiritual teachers and texts often caution that one should begin the practice of meditation only in the context of other spiritual practices and disciplines that help develop compassion and wisdom to use properly this increased power.

Second, *you enjoy your senses more fully*. Although people sometimes view or use meditation as an ascetic experience to *control* their senses, meditation also can *enhance* your senses in ways that your profoundly sensual. Anything that you enjoy — food, sex, music, art, massage, and so on — is greatly enhanced by meditation. When you pay attention to something, it's a lot more enjoyable. Also, you don't need as much of it to get the same degree of pleasure, so you are more likely to enjoy without excess.

When you keep a wall around your heart to armor and protect it from pain, you also diminish your capacity to feel pleasure. When your life is in a continual rush, you may miss exquisite pleasures that exist from moment to moment. Attention spans get shorter. The need for stimulation continually increases just to feel *anything*. Meditation increases awareness and sensitivity; as such, it can be an antidote to numbness and distraction.

Third, *your mind quiets down and you experience an inner sense of peace, joy, and well-being*. When I first learned to meditate and began getting glimpses of inner peace, this experience changed my life. It redefined and reframed my experience. Before, I thought peace of mind came from getting and doing; now, I understand that it comes from *being*. It is our true nature to be peaceful until we disturb it.

This is a radically different concept of where our happiness and our well-being come from. In one of life's great paradoxes, not being aware of this truth, we often end up disturbing our inner peace while striving to get or to do what we think will bring that same peace to us.

Fourth, *you may directly experience and become more aware of the transcendent interconnectedness that already exists*. You may have a direct experience of God or the universal Self, whatever name you give to this experience.

Meditation is simple in concept but difficult to master. Fortunately, you don't have to master meditation to benefit from it. You just have to practice. No one ever really masters it completely, but even a few steps down that road can make a meaningful difference. It is the *process* of meditation that makes it so beneficial, not how well you perform.

In my research studies, most of the participants reported much greater difficulty practicing mediation than exercising our maintaining their diet. Why? You have to eat; it's just a question of what you eat. Meditation, on the other hand, is not part of most people's daily routine or experience. Exercise is more familiar to people, and also there is a macho quality to exercise — you're out there really doing something, whereas meditation still has what some of our research participants at first called the "wimp factor." From outward appearances, it looks as if you're not doing anything when you meditate. In fact, meditation is a powerful, active process.

There are many different types of meditation. It is found in all cultures and in all religions all over the world — because it works. Truth is truth. Whereas the forms vary, certain principles almost always are found.

This attitude of paying attention can help transform everything we do into a form of meditation. Whatever we do with concentration and awareness becomes meditation.

As the editor of *Yoga Journal* for many years, Stephan Bodian has had the opportunity to become familiar with many different approaches to meditation and yoga. He has distilled the best of these here and gently leads you step by step to discover a form and style of meditation that works best for you.

Meditation For Dummies, 3rd Edition. Smart. Very smart.

Dean Ornish, MD
Founder, President, and Director, Preventive Medicine Research Institute
Clinical Professor of Medicine, University of California, San Francisco
Author, *Love & Survival* and *Dr. Dean Ornish's Program for Reversing Heart Disease*

Foreword © 2012 by Dean Ornish, MD

Introduction

Everyone seems to want to know how to meditate these days. From anxious teens to their overwhelmed parents, harried construction workers to hurried executives, retired baby boomers to unemployed Gen Xers, more and more people are seeking solutions for the stressful, time-urgent, overstimulated lives we lead. Because the Internet can't provide satisfying answers to all of life's questions, people are turning in increasing numbers to time-honored practices like meditation for proven remedies to life's inevitable ills.

Indeed, according to a recent government survey, more than 10 percent of adults in the United States meditate regularly. That's tens of millions of people! Why do they bother? Because it works. Whether you're seeking greater focus to get your job done more efficiently, less stress and more peace of mind, or a deeper appreciation of the beauty and richness of life, the simple practice of sitting down and turning your attention inward can do wonders for your body and your mind.

The truth is, you can learn the basics of meditation in five minutes. Just sit in a comfortable position, straighten your back, breathe deeply, and rest your attention on the coming and going of your breath. It's as simple as that! If you do it regularly, you'll find that it won't be long before you're feeling more relaxed and enjoying life more. I speak from personal experience: I've been practicing meditation and teaching it to others for more than 40 years.

Simple though it may be, meditation also has tremendous subtlety and depth, if you're interested in pursuing it further. It's a lot like painting: You can buy your materials, take a few lessons, and have fun applying paint to paper. Or you can attend classes at your local education center or community college, specialize in a particular medium in art school, and make painting a central part of your life. In meditation, as in art, you can keep it simple — just get up every day and sit quietly for five or ten minutes — or explore the subtleties to your heart's content. It all depends on your needs, your intentions, and your level of interest and passion.

About This Book

When I began teaching meditation, I was always hard-pressed to come up with a single book that taught the basics, provided a comprehensive overview of techniques and practices, and offered guidance in going deeper. Global surveys generally ignore the nuts and bolts — what to focus on, how to sit, what to do about your crazy mind, and so on. Books that teach you how to meditate tend to offer just a few techniques. And those that show you how to explore the rich inner world of meditation often have a sectarian spiritual perspective that limits the breadth of their presentation. (In other words, you'd have to be a Buddhist or a yogi or a Sufi to know what they're talking about.)

Unlike those other books on meditation, *Meditation For Dummies,* 3rd Edition, covers all the bases. If you're looking for simple, easy-to-follow meditation instructions, you can find state-of-the-art guidance here that's filled with helpful tips from seasoned meditators as well as time-honored wisdom from the great teachers of old. If you want to get an overview of the meditation field before you zero in on a particular method or teaching, you can catch a glimpse of the primary approaches that are readily available these days. If you've been meditating in a particular way and want to expand your horizons to include other techniques, you'll be pleased to discover that this book features dozens of different meditations for a variety of purposes. They're drawn from a range of sources and traditions. And if you just want to understand why other people meditate — for instance, your partner, your friends, the guy in the office next to yours — and why you may want to join them, jump on board! You can read through whole chapters on how meditation makes you happier (and healthier), what science has learned about the physical and psychological benefits of meditation, and how you can get the most from meditation.

As a special bonus, this book includes instructional tracks, which are available on the CD accompanying this book or online (if you're reading a digital version). With these tracks, I guide you step by step through ten of the most powerful and effective meditations described in the book. When you've had your fill of reading and want something more experiential, you can sit down in a comfortable position, pop in the disc, and let my voice lead you effortlessly through the complete meditation process, from start to finish. What could be more accessible and user-friendly than that?

This book is many things at once: an instructional manual, a survey course, and a guidebook for deeper exploration. Feel free to read it from cover to cover if you want or just browse until you find the chapters that appeal to you. Throughout the book, you find meditations and exercises you can experiment with and enjoy. Some of them are also offered on the CD, so you can discover how to practice them directly without referring to the text.

The best thing about this book, in my humble estimation, is that it's fun to read. Meditation doesn't have to be a dull or somber affair. Quite the contrary: The whole point of meditating in the first place is to lighten up and experience more peace and joy in your life. So forget those stereotypes of the enigmatic Zen monk or the reclusive navel-gazer! You can find out everything you ever wanted to know about meditation and enjoy yourself in the process.

Conventions Used in This Book

I use a few conventions in this book to help your reading go smoothly:

- ✔ When I want to make a topic crystal clear, I break the essential points down into bulleted lists (like this one), so you can follow them easily without getting lost in a sea of excess verbiage.

- ✔ Just as a piece of music may begin with a few opening phrases known as a *prelude,* most meditation instructions in this book begin with a similar directive — to sit quietly, close your eyes, and take a few deep breaths. When you're accustomed to this prelude, you can naturally begin with it each time you meditate.

- ✔ The first time unfamiliar terms and phrases appear, they're set in *italics* and accompanied by a brief definition.

- ✔ **Bold** text indicates keywords in bulleted lists and highlights the action parts of numbered steps.

- ✔ Web addresses are set in `monofont` so you can easily spot them.

What You're Not to Read

Here and there throughout this book I've sprinkled sidebars (text in gray boxes), which offer extra information, such as stories, examples, explanations, and assorted meditations. Though they're fun to read and intended to spice up the book, they're not essential. So if you're in a hurry to get to the meat of the matter (or the yogurt, if you're a vegetarian), feel free to skip over them — and come back later if you're so inclined.

Foolish Assumptions

When I wrote this book, I made a few assumptions about you, dear reader, that I thought I should share with you before we begin:

- ✔ You're intrigued enough by the topic of meditation to pick up this book, but you haven't yet discovered how to meditate. Or if you have, you still feel the need for more guidance.

- ✔ You want less stress and more happiness and peace of mind, and you're willing to devote a little of your precious time to achieve it.

- ✔ Because you can't afford to spend long hours meditating in a monastery or ashram, you want instruction that you can put to use right now at home or at work.

✔ You don't live on a desert island or in some isolated part of the globe; instead, you inhabit the ordinary world and confront the usual stresses, pressures, and responsibilities that most people face.

If these assumptions apply to you, you're definitely in the right place!

How This Book Is Organized

Although I designed this book so you can read it cover to cover — some people still do that, don't they? — I also made sure that you can find what you're looking for easily and quickly by breaking it up into different parts. Each part covers a different phase of your encounter with meditation.

Part I: Getting Acquainted with Meditation

If you don't know a thing about meditation, you probably want to start here. You discover what meditation is (and isn't), where it comes from, why you may want to practice it, what science has learned about it, and how you can use meditation to reduce your stress, improve your health, and enhance your feelings of peace and well-being.

Part II: Getting Started

This part begins by introducing you to the devious workings of your own mind (in case you haven't already noticed) and explains how you can prepare for meditation by adjusting your attitude. Next, you find out how to sit (or lie) down and work with your mind by following my easy-to-follow, step-by-step instructions. I include a separate chapter on all the little details that most meditation books take for granted, such as how to keep your back (more or less) straight without getting uptight and what to do with your eyes and hands. I also include a chapter on preparing your body for sitting. I round out the part with powerful practices for opening your heart with love and compassion.

Part III: Troubleshooting and Fine-Tuning Your Practice

After you start meditating regularly, you'll find that questions and even problems arise from time to time. You may wonder how to put all the pieces together in a way that's uniquely suited to your needs. Or you may encounter distractions you don't know how to deal with, such as recurring fantasies or difficult emotions. (Or you may ask, "How can I possibly get my mind to stop playing the same Black-Eyed Peas song over and over?") This part covers the fine points and hot spots of practice.

Part IV: Meditation in Action

It's one thing to calm your mind and open your heart in the privacy of your room but quite another to practice meditation throughout your day, in the presence of your boss (or your clients), your partner, your kids, and the person in the car in front of you. This part shows you how to extend the benefits of meditation to every area of your life, from sex to stress-reduction to spirituality. If you're primarily interested in healing your body or mind or performing more effectively at work or play, this part includes a chapter that shows you exactly what you need to know. And if you're fascinated by the wonders of spiritual unfolding, you'll be glad to see the chapter devoted to spirituality.

Part V: The Part of Tens

I tend to gravitate to the end of a book first, which is why I love lists like these. In this part, you find answers to the most frequently asked questions about meditation and a collection of the best all-purpose meditations.

Part VI: Appendixes

If you're not sure what to do when you finish this book, you want to find out more about a particular technique or approach to meditation, or you just want to contact other people to meditate with, check out the annotated list of meditation organizations, centers, and books in Appendix A. In Appendix B, you find instructions on how to use the CD as well as a list of all the tracks. *Note:* If you're using a digital or enhanced digital version of this book, please go to http://booksupport.wiley.com for access to the additional content.

Icons Used in This Book

Throughout this book, I use icons in the margins to draw your attention to particular kinds of information. Here's a key to what those icons mean:

For direct personal guidance in practicing the meditations marked by this icon, just put down your book, cue up the CD, and follow my lead. (Or, if you're using a digital version of this book, you can download the tracks online and pop them on your portable media player.)

When you see this icon, prepare to stop what you're doing, take a few deep breaths, and start meditating. It's your chance to savor the real thing!

If I haven't said it before, I should have — it's important information that bears repeating.

This wise guy shows you where to look for musings of a more philosophical nature.

If you want your meditations to be easier and more effective, follow these tidbits of insider advice.

People have been meditating for thousands of years. Here's some of the cool stuff they've discovered, in the form of an anecdote or story.

Where To Go from Here

After you know the lay of the land (see the section "How This Book Is Organized"), your next step is to decide where to go. Remember that you don't have to read the book sequentially, from cover to cover — you can pick it up anywhere your interests lead you. I've written it intentionally with just such an approach in mind.

If you're drawn to a more theoretical discussion of the philosophical, historical, and scientific background of meditation, by all means start with Part I, in which I discuss meditation's history, its health benefits, and its positive effects on the body and brain. But if you're eager to get to the nitty-gritty and can't wait to sit down and start practicing, you may want to head directly for Part II, which provides everything you need to know to meditate effectively.

After you've been practicing for a few weeks or months, you can return for a refresher course and fine-tune your meditation by reading in Part III about the various difficulties and obstacles that may arise as well as about strategies for developing and expanding your practice. And if you have particular areas of interest, such as spirituality, healing, or performance enhancement, you can find what you're looking for in Part IV. Feel free to browse, meander, and read whatever strikes your fancy!

Finally, I would love to hear from you. To get in touch with me, check out my website at www.stephanbodian.org, or send an e-mail to info@ stephanbodian.org.

Part I
Getting Acquainted with Meditation

The 5th Wave   By Rich Tennant

©RICHTENNANT

"Okay, your posture's very good. Now relax, concentrate, and slowly let go of your cell phone."

In this part . . .

You find out everything you could possibly want to know about meditation to get you interested, motivated, and, ultimately, started.

Did you realize that meditation has an illustrious multicultural history? That regular practice offers dozens of scientifically proven benefits, from reduced stress and lower blood pressure and cholesterol levels to greater empathy and enhanced creativity? Or that meditation not only relaxes and uplifts you, but actually grows and changes your brain for the better in lasting ways? Well, read on!

Chapter 1

Embarking on Your Meditation Journey

In This Chapter

▶ Climbing the mountain of meditation

▶ Finding picnic spots and lesser peaks along the way

▶ Checking out the major meditation techniques

▶ Knowing what you'll see when you get to the top

▶ Developing concentration, receptive awareness, contemplation, and cultivation

The great thing about meditation is that it's actually quite simple. Just sit down, be quiet, turn your attention inward, and focus your awareness. That's all there is to it, really (see the sidebar "Meditation: It's easier than you think"). Then why, you may be wondering, do people write so many books and articles about meditation — including detailed books like this one? Why not just offer a few brief instructions and forget about all the verbiage?

Say, for example, that you're planning to take a long trip by car to some picturesque location. You can just jot down the directions and follow them one by one. After a few days, you'll get to where you want to go. But you'll enjoy the trip more if you have a travel guide to point out the sights along the way. And you may feel more secure if you carry a troubleshooting manual to tell you what to do when you have problems with your car. Perhaps you'd like to take some side trips to scenic spots or even change your itinerary entirely and get there by a different route or a different vehicle!

In the same way, you can consider the practice of meditation to be a journey of sorts — and the book you hold in your hands to be your travel guide. This chapter provides an overview of your trip, offers some alternative routes to your destination, explains the basic skills you need to know to get you there, and points to some detours that may advertise the same benefits but don't really deliver.

Meditation: It's easier than you think

Meditation is simply the practice of focusing your attention on a particular object — generally something simple, like a word or phrase, a candle flame or geometrical figure, or the coming and going of your breath. In everyday life, your mind is constantly processing a barrage of sensations, visual impressions, emotions, and thoughts. In general, when you meditate, you narrow your focus, limit the stimuli bombarding your nervous system — and calm your mind in the process.

For a quick taste of meditation, follow these instructions. (For detailed audio instructions, listen to Track 2. Or, for more complete meditation instructions, see Chapter 7.)

1. **Find a quiet place and sit comfortably with your back relatively straight.**

   If you tend to disappear into your favorite chair, find something a bit more supportive.

2. **Take a few deep breaths, close your eyes, and relax your body as much as you can.**

   If you don't know how to relax, you may want to check out Chapter 7.

3. **Choose a word or phrase that has special personal or spiritual meaning for you.**

   Here are some examples: "There's only love," "Don't worry, be happy," "Trust in God."

4. **Begin to breathe through your nose, and as you breathe, repeat the word or phrase quietly to yourself.**

You can whisper the word or phrase, *subvocalize* it (that is, move your tongue as though you're saying it, but don't say it aloud), or just repeat it in your mind. If you get distracted, come back to the repetition of the word or phrase. (If you have difficulty breathing through your nose, by all means breathe through your mouth instead.)

As an alternative, you can rest your attention on your breath as it comes and goes through your nostrils, returning to your breathing when you get distracted.

5. **Keep the meditation going for five minutes or more and then slowly get up and go about your day.**

How did you feel during meditation? Did it seem weird to say the same thing or follow your breath over and over? Did you find it difficult to stay focused? Did you keep changing the phrase? If so, don't worry. With regular practice and the guidance of this book, you'll gradually get the knack.

Of course, you could easily spend many fruitful and enjoyable years mastering the subtleties and complexities of meditation. But the good news is, the basic practice is actually quite simple, and you don't have to be an expert to do it or to enjoy its extraordinary benefits.

Getting an Overview of How the Journey Unfolds

No doubt you picked up this book because you're searching for something more in life — more peace of mind, more energy, more well-being, more meaning, more happiness, more joy. You've heard about meditation and you wonder what it has to offer.

Being an adventurous sort, I like to think of meditation as a climb up a mountain. You've seen snapshots of the summit, and from the bottom you can barely glimpse the summit through the clouds. But the only way to get there is up — one step at a time.

Different paths up the same mountain

Imagine that you're getting ready to climb a mountain. (If you live in the Netherlands or the midwestern United States, get out your *National Geographic* for this one!) How are you going to get to the top? You could take some climbing lessons, buy the right gear, and inch your way up one of the rocky faces. Or you could choose one of the many trails that meander up the mountain and take a leisurely hike to the summit. (Of course, you could always cheat and drive your car, but that would ruin my metaphor!)

Although they all end up at the same place, every trail has its unique characteristics. One may take you on a gradual ascent through forests and meadows, whereas another may head steeply uphill over dry, rocky terrain. From one, you may have vistas of lush valleys filled with flowers; from another, you may see farmland or desert.

Depending on your energy and your motivation, you may choose to stop at a picnic spot en route and while away a few hours (or a few days) enjoying the peace and quiet. Hey, you may enjoy that one spot so much that you decide not to climb any farther. Perhaps you'd rather climb one of the smaller peaks along the way instead of going the distance to the top. Or you may prefer to charge to the summit as quickly as you can without bothering to linger anywhere.

 Well, the journey of meditation has a great deal in common with climbing a mountain. You can aim for the top, or you can just set your sights on some grassy knoll or lesser peak halfway up the slope. Whatever your destination, you can have fun and reap the benefits of just breathing deeply and exercising muscles you didn't even know you had.

People have been climbing the mountain of meditation for thousands of years in different parts of the world. (For more on the history of meditation, see Chapter 3.) As a result, topographic maps and guidebooks abound, each with its own unique version of how to make your way up the mountain and its own recommendations for how to hike and what to carry. (To get a sense of the range of meditation materials available, just check out the shelves of your local bookstore or library or scan the website of your favorite online book source.)

Traditionally, the guidebooks describe a spiritual path involving a set of beliefs and practices, often secret, that have been passed down from one generation to the next (see the sidebar "Meditation's spiritual roots"). In recent decades, however, Western researchers and teachers have distilled meditation from its spiritual origins and now offer it as a remedy for a variety of 21st-century ills. (For more on the benefits of meditation, see Chapter 2. For more on meditation research, see Chapter 4.)

Although the maps and books may describe the summit differently — some emphasize the vast open spaces, others pay more attention to the peace or exhilaration you feel when you get there, and some even claim that there's more than one peak. I happen to agree with the ancient sage who said: "Meditation techniques are just different paths up the same mountain."

Here are a few of the many techniques that have been developed over the centuries:

- Repetition of a meaningful word or phrase, known as a *mantra* (see Chapters 3 and 14)
- Mindful awareness of the present moment (for more on *mindfulness,* see Chapters 7 and 17)
- Following or counting your breath (see Chapter 7)
- Paying attention to the flow of sensations in your body (see Chapter 7)
- Cultivation of lovingkindness, compassion, forgiveness, and other healing emotions (see Chapter 11)
- Concentration on a geometric shape or other simple visual object
- Visualization of a peaceful place or a healing energy or entity (see Chapter 18)
- Reading and reflecting upon inspirational or sacred writings (see Chapter 14)
- Gazing at a picture of a holy being or saint
- Contemplation of nature
- Chanting praises to the Divine

Throughout this book, you find opportunities to experiment with many of these techniques as well as detailed guidance in the practice of one in particular — *mindfulness* — beginning with your breath and then extending your meditation to every moment of your life.

The view from the summit — and from other peaks along the way

SPIRITUAL STUFF

When you reach the summit of the meditation mountain, what do you see? If you can trust the reports of the meditators and mystics who have climbed the mountain before you, you can declare with some confidence that the top of the mountain harbors the source of all love, wisdom, happiness, and joy. Some people call it spirit or soul, true nature or true self, the ultimate truth, or the ground of *being* (or just *being* itself). Others call it God or the Divine or the Holy Mystery, or simply the One. There are nearly as many names for it as people who experience it. And some spiritual traditions consider it so sacred and powerful that they hesitate to give it a name.

As for the *experience* of reaching the summit, seasoned meditators use words like *enlightenment* (from ignorance), *awakening* (from a dream), *liberation* (from bondage), *freedom* (from limitation), and *union* (with God or *being*).

Meditation's spiritual roots

Although many ordinary folks are meditating these days (including, quite possibly, people you know), the practice wasn't always so readily available. For centuries, monks, nuns, mystics, and wandering ascetics preserved it in secret, using it to enter higher states of consciousness and ultimately to achieve the pinnacle of their particular paths.

Highly motivated laypeople with time on their hands could always learn a few techniques. But the rigorous practice of meditation remained a sacred pursuit limited to an elite few who were willing to renounce the world and devote their lives to it. (See Chapter 3 for more on the history of meditation.)

How times have changed! From Beat Zen in the '50s and the influx of Indian yogis and swamis in the '60s to the current fascination with mindfulness, meditation has become mainstream, and its practical benefits are applauded in every medium, both actual and virtual. (For some of the websites devoted to meditation, see Appendix A.)

Meditation has been studied extensively in psychology labs and reduced to formulas like the Relaxation Response (a simple technique for diminishing stress). Yet it has never entirely lost its spiritual roots. In fact, the reason why meditation works so effectively is that it connects you with a spiritual dimension, which different commentators give different names, but I like to call simply *being*.

An old saying likens all these words and names to fingers pointing at the moon. If you pay too much attention to the finger, you risk missing the beautiful moon, which is the reason for pointing the finger in the first place. Ultimately, you need to experience the moon — or in this case, the summit — for yourself.

Of course, you may have no interest in lofty states and experiences like enlightenment or union. Perhaps you bought this book simply because you want to reduce your stress or enhance your healing process or deal with your emotions. Forget about the Holy Mystery — a little more clarity and peace of mind would suit you just fine, thank you very much!

Well, the truth is, you're going to follow the same path no matter how high up the mountain you want to go. The basic instructions remain the same, but you get to choose your destination. Among the most popular stopping places and promontories en route to the summit are the following:

- ✔ Stronger focus and concentration
- ✔ Reduced tension, anxiety, and stress
- ✔ Clearer thinking and less emotional turmoil
- ✔ Lower blood pressure and cholesterol
- ✔ Support in kicking addictions and other self-defeating behaviors
- ✔ Greater creativity and enhanced performance in work and play
- ✔ Increased self-understanding and self-acceptance
- ✔ More joy, love, and spontaneity
- ✔ Greater intimacy with friends and family members
- ✔ Enhanced feelings of happiness, contentment, and subjective well-being
- ✔ Deeper sense of meaning and purpose
- ✔ Glimpses of a spiritual dimension of being

As you can see, these way stations are actually major destinations in their own right, and all of them are well worth reaching. (For more on the benefits of meditation, see Chapter 2.) You may be quite content to stop halfway up the mountain after you've reduced your stress, improved your health, and experienced greater overall well-being. Or you may feel inspired to push on for the higher altitudes that the great meditators describe.

The taste of pure mountain water

To elaborate on this mountain metaphor a bit, imagine that a spring at the summit gushes forth the pure *water of being* and never runs dry. (Depending on your orientation, you may prefer to call it the *water of grace* or *spirit* or *unconditional love.*) Those who make it to the summit get to dive into the pool that surrounds the spring and immerse themselves completely in the water. In fact, some even merge with the water and become identical with *being* itself. (Don't worry. You won't merge if you don't want to!)

But you don't have to climb all the way to the top to enjoy the pure *taste of being.* The water flows down the mountain in streams and rivulets and nourishes the fields and towns below. In other words, you can taste *being* everywhere, in everything, because *being* is the essence that keeps life going at every level. Until you start meditating, though, you may not know what *being* tastes like.

When you meditate, you get closer to the source of the water and learn how to recognize its taste. (Depending on their personalities and where they are on the mountain, people use different terms to describe the water's taste, such as *calm, peace, well-being, wholeness, clarity,* and *compassion.*) It doesn't matter where you're headed or where you stop on your way up the mountain; you still get to dip your hands in the water of *being* and taste it for yourself. Then you can begin to find the taste of *being* wherever you go!

Discovering the treasure in your own house

In the Jewish tradition, they tell a story that has its counterparts in all the world's great meditative teachings. Simon, a simple tailor, fantasizes night and day about the great treasure he will one day find when he leaves his little village and his family home and ventures forth into the world. Late one night, with a few belongings on his back, he sets off on his travels.

For years, Simon wanders from one great city to another, making his living mending clothes, searching for the treasure he knows belongs to him. But all the people he asks about the treasure have problems of their own and are unable to help him.

One day he comes upon a psychic known far and wide for her extraordinary abilities. "Yes," she says, "there is indeed a vast treasure that belongs to you and you alone." Hearing this, Simon's eyes light up with excitement. "I will tell you how to find it," she continues, giving Simon complex directions that he meticulously records.

When she comes to the end of her instructions and describes the very street and house where this treasure is allegedly buried, Simon can't believe his ears. For this is the very home he had left years before when setting out on his quest.

Quickly he thanks the psychic, stuffs the directions in his pocket, and hurries back in the direction from which he came. And lo and behold, much to his surprise, he does indeed find a vast and unfathomable treasure buried beneath the hearth in his own house.

The point of this story is obvious: Though you may wander in search of inner peace and experiment with all kinds of meditative practices, the peace and love and wisdom you seek are inevitably here all along, hidden within your own heart.

There's no place like home — and you've already arrived!

Throughout this chapter I've constructed the metaphor of the mountain, but now I'm going to knock it down with one sweep of my hand — like a wave washing away a castle in the sand. Yes, the journey of meditation requires steady effort and application like a climb up a mountain. (For more on effort and discipline, see Chapter 10.) But that metaphor hides some important paradoxes:

- **The summit doesn't exist in some faraway place outside you; it exists in the depths of your being — some traditions say in the heart — and awaits your discovery.** See the sidebar "Discovering the treasure in your own house" to see what I mean.

- **You can approach the summit in an instant; it doesn't necessarily take years of practice.** While meditating, for example, when your mind settles down and you experience a deep peace or tranquility, sense your interconnectedness with all beings, or feel an upsurge of peace or love, you're tasting the sweet water of *being* right from the source inside you. And these moments inform and nourish you in ways you can't possibly measure.

- **The mountain metaphor suggests a progressive, goal-oriented journey, whereas, in fact, the point of meditation is to set aside all goals and just *be*.** As the title of the bestseller by stress-reduction expert Jon Kabat-Zinn puts it, "Wherever you go, there you are." Or as Dorothy says in *The Wizard of Oz,* "There's no place like home." And the truth is, like Dorothy, you're always already there!

Of course, you're not going to give up all your doing and striving instantaneously and just be, even when you meditate. You have to slowly work up to letting it all go by practicing your meditation and gradually focusing and simplifying until you're doing less and less while you meditate — and *being* more and more. The following are a few of the stages you may pass through on the path to just *being:*

- Getting used to sitting still
- Developing the ability to turn your attention inward
- Struggling to focus your attention
- Being distracted again and again
- Becoming more focused
- Feeling more relaxed as you meditate
- Noticing fleeting moments when your mind settles down
- Experiencing brief glimpses of stillness and peace

Becoming aware of your awareness

Most of the time, you probably don't pay much attention to your awareness. Yet the truth is that it's crucial to everything you do. When you watch TV, study for an exam, cook a meal, drive your car, listen to music, or talk with a friend, you're being aware, or paying attention. Before you begin to meditate in a formal way, you may find it helpful to explore your own awareness.

First, notice what it's like to be aware. Are there times in your life when you're not aware of anything? Complete this thought: "I am aware of. . . ." Do this again and again and notice where your awareness takes you.

Do you tend to be more aware of internal or external sensations? Do you pay more attention to thoughts and fantasies than to your moment-to-moment sensory experiences? Notice whether a preoccupation with mental activity diminishes your awareness of what's happening right here and now.

Next, pay attention to whether your awareness tends to focus on a particular object or sensation or tends to be more expansive and inclusive. You may find that your awareness resembles a spotlight that flows from object to object. Notice how your awareness flows without trying to change it.

Does it shift quickly from one thing to another, or does it move more slowly, making contact with each object before moving on? Experiment with speeding up and slowing down the flow of awareness, and notice how that feels.

You may discover that your awareness is drawn again and again to certain kinds of objects and events, but not to others. Where does your awareness repeatedly wander? Which experience does it seem to selectively avoid?

Now experiment with gently directing your awareness from one focus to another. When you pay attention to sounds, you may notice that you momentarily forget about your hands or the discomfort in your back or knees. Try to focus on one object of attention for as long as you can. How long can you remain undistracted before your mind skips to the next thing?

And here's perhaps the greatest paradox of all: If you practice meditation diligently, you may eventually come to realize that you've never left home, even for an instant.

Developing and Directing Awareness: The Key to Meditation

If, as the old saying goes, a journey of a thousand miles begins with a single step, then the journey of meditation begins with the cultivation of *awareness,* or *attention.* In fact, awareness is the mental muscle that carries you along and sustains you on your journey, not only at the start but also every step of the way. No matter which path or technique you choose, the secret of meditation lies in developing, focusing, and directing your awareness. (Incidentally, attention is just slightly focused awareness, and I use the two terms more or less interchangeably throughout this book. See the sidebar "Becoming aware of your awareness.")

To get a better sense of how awareness operates, consider another natural metaphor: light. You may take light for granted, but unless you've developed the special skills and heightened sensitivity of the blind, you can barely function without it. (Have you ever tried to find something in a pitch-dark room?) The same is true for awareness: You may not be aware that you're aware, but you need awareness to perform even the simplest tasks.

You can use light in a number of ways. You can create ambient lighting that illuminates a room softly and diffusely. You can focus light into a flashlight beam to help you find things when the room is dark. Or you can take the very same light and concentrate it into a laser beam so powerful that it can cut through steel or send messages to the stars.

Likewise, in meditation, you can use awareness in different ways. You can increase your powers of awareness by developing **concentration** on a particular object. (For a brief list of meditation objects, see the section "Different paths up the same mountain" earlier in this chapter.)

Then, when you've stabilized your concentration, you can, through the practice of **receptive awareness,** expand your awareness — like ambient light — to illuminate the full range of your experience.

Next, you can concentrate even further in order to **cultivate** positive emotions and mind-states. Or you can use awareness to investigate your inner experience and **contemplate** the nature of existence itself.

These four practices — *concentration, receptive awareness, cultivation,* and *contemplation* — constitute the major uses of awareness throughout the world's great meditative traditions. I discuss them in the following sections.

Building concentration

To do just about anything well, you need to focus your awareness. The most creative and productive people in every profession — for example, great athletes, performers, businessmen, scientists, artists, and writers — have the ability to block out distractions and completely immerse themselves in their work. If you've ever watched Rafael Nadal hit a forehand shot or Meryl Streep transform herself into the character she's portraying, you've witnessed the fruits of total *concentration.*

Some people have an innate ability to concentrate, but most of us need practice to develop it. Buddhists like to compare the mind to a monkey — constantly chattering and hopping about from branch to branch, topic to topic. Did you ever notice that most of the time, you have scant control over the whims and vacillations of your monkey mind, which may space out one moment and obsess the next? When you meditate, you calm your monkey mind by making it *one-pointed* rather than scattered and distracted.

Many spiritual traditions teach their students concentration as the primary meditation practice. Just keep focusing your mind on the mantra or the symbol or the visualization, they advise, and eventually you will attain what is called *absorption,* or *samadhi.*

In absorption, the sense of being a separate "me" disappears, and only the object of your attention remains. Followed to its natural conclusion, the practice of concentration can lead to an experience of union with the object of your meditation. If you're a sports enthusiast, this object could be your tennis racket or your golf club; if you're an aspiring mystic, the object could be God or *being* or the absolute. (For more on the spiritual benefits of concentration, see Chapter 15. And if you want to use meditation to improve your performance at work or play, check out Chapter 18.)

Even though you may not yet know how to meditate, you've no doubt had moments of total absorption, when the sense of separation disappears: gazing at a sunset, listening to music, creating a work of art, looking into the eyes of your beloved. When you're so completely involved in an activity, whether work or play, that time stops and self-consciousness drops away, you enter into what psychologist Mihaly Csikszentmihalyi calls *flow.* In fact, Csikszentmihalyi claims that activities that promote flow epitomize what most people mean by *enjoyment.* Flow can be extraordinarily refreshing, enlivening, and even deeply meaningful — and it is the inevitable result of unbroken concentration.

Opening to receptive awareness

The great sages of China say that all things comprise the constant interplay of *yin* and *yang* — the feminine and masculine forces of the universe. Well, if concentration is the yang of meditation (focused, powerful, penetrating), then *receptive awareness* is the yin (open, expansive, welcoming).

Where concentration disciplines, stabilizes, and grounds the mind, receptive awareness loosens and extends the mind's boundaries and creates more interior space, enabling you to familiarize yourself with the mind's contents. Where concentration blocks extra stimuli as distractions to the focus at hand, receptive awareness embraces and assimilates every experience that presents itself.

Most meditations involve the interplay of concentration and receptive awareness, although some more-advanced techniques teach the practice of receptive awareness alone. Just be open and aware and welcome whatever arises, these techniques encourage, and ultimately you will be "taken by truth." Followed to its conclusion, receptive awareness guides you in shifting your identity from your thoughts, emotions, and the stories your mind tells you to your true identity, which is *being* itself. (For more on thoughts, emotions, and stories, see Chapter 5.)

Of course, if you don't know how to work with attention, these instructions are impossible to follow. That's why most traditions prescribe practicing concentration first. By quieting and grounding the mind just enough so it can open without being swept away by a deluge of irrelevant feelings and thoughts, concentration provides a solid foundation on which the practice of meditation can flourish.

Using contemplation for greater insight

Although concentration and receptive awareness provide enormous benefits, ultimately it's insight and understanding — of how the mind works, how you perpetuate your own suffering, how attached you are to the outcome of events, and how uncontrollable and fleeting these events are — that offer freedom from suffering. And in your everyday life, it's creative thinking — free from the usual limited, repetitive patterns of thought — that offers solutions to problems. So *contemplation* is the third key component that transforms meditation from a calming, relaxing exercise to a vehicle for freedom and creative expression.

After you've developed your concentration and expanded your awareness, you eventually find that you have access to a more penetrating insight into the nature of your experience. You can use this faculty to explore your inner terrain and gradually understand and undermine your mind's tendency to cause you suffering and stress (see Chapters 6 and 12). If you're a spiritual seeker, you can use this faculty to inquire into the nature of the self or to reflect on the mystery of God and creation. And if you're a person with more practical concerns, you may ponder the next step in your career or relationship or contemplate some seemingly irresolvable problem in your life. (For more on the uses of meditation in ordinary life situations, check out Chapter 17.)

Cultivating positive, healing states of mind

Some meditations aim to open the heart and develop certain life-affirming qualities like compassion, lovingkindness, equanimity, joy, or forgiveness (see Chapter 11). On a more practical level, you can use meditation to cultivate a proactive, healthy immune system or to develop poise and precision in a particular sport. For example, you can visualize killer T cells attacking your cancer or imagine yourself executing a dive without a single mistake (see Chapter 18). These are the kinds of meditations I've chosen to call *cultivation*.

Where contemplation aims to investigate, inquire, and ultimately see deeply into the nature of things, cultivation can help you transform your inner life by directing the concentration you develop to strengthen positive, healthy mind-states and withdraw energy from those that are more reactive and self-defeating.

Making Meditation Your Own

Developing and directing your awareness may be the foundation of effective meditation, but like any good foundation, it's only the beginning. The next step is to build your house brick by brick, meditation session by meditation session, discovering what works for you and what doesn't, until your practice is grounded and stable. Or, to conjure the journey metaphor, awareness is the muscle that propels you up the mountain. But you need to choose your route, find your pace, and navigate the obstacles that get in your way. In other words, you need to fashion and maintain your own practice and troubleshoot the difficulties that arise.

Designing your own practice

When you begin to develop and direct your awareness in meditation, you're faced with the challenge of putting all the pieces together into an integrated practice that's uniquely suited to your needs. (For more on designing your own practice, see Chapter 14.) For example, consider the following possibilities:

- ✔ You may find yourself drawn to forms of meditation that emphasize focused concentration and have only minimal interest in the more open, allowing quality of receptive awareness.

✔ You may cherish the peace and relaxation you experience when you simply sit quietly without any effort or focus, not even the effort to be aware.

✔ You may have a specific purpose for meditating, such as healing an illness or resolving a disturbing psychological issue, and feel drawn only to approaches that help you meet your goals.

The key is to experiment with different forms of meditation and trust your intuition to tell you which ones are best suited for you at this particular point on your journey up the mountain. Inevitably, yin and yang tend to balance each other out. That is, you may start out with intense concentration and end up with more relaxed, receptive awareness. Or you may begin in a more receptive mode and gradually discover the virtues of focus. The journey of meditation has its own lessons to teach, and no matter what your intentions may be, you'll generally end up encountering those lessons that you were destined to learn.

Of course, if you intend to maintain your practice from week to week and month to month, which is the only way to reap the benefits of meditation, you probably need to draw on some of those time-honored qualities that every sustained enterprise requires: motivation, discipline, and commitment (see Chapters 5 and 10). These qualities have earned a bad rap in Western culture, where people generally expect to have their needs met right now, if not sooner, but they actually aren't difficult to cultivate. In fact, they arise naturally when you're engaged in and — dare I say it — passionate about what you're doing.

Mindfulness: Meditation as a way of life

Although I provide a variety of different techniques for your enjoyment and exploration, this book offers as its primary approach what the Buddhists call *mindfulness* — ongoing attention to whatever arises moment to moment.

Based on my years of experience and training, I've found that mindfulness, which blends concentration and receptive awareness, is one of the simplest techniques for beginners to learn and also one of the most readily adaptable to the busy schedules most people face. After all, if you're like me, you're primarily concerned with living a more harmonious, loving, stress-free life, not lifting off into some disembodied spiritual realm divorced from the people and places you love.

In fact, the beauty, belonging, and love you seek are available right here and now — you only need to clear your mind and open your eyes, which is precisely what the practice of mindfulness is intended to teach! When you pay attention to your experience from moment to moment, you keep waking up from the daydreams and worries your mind fabricates and returning to the clarity, precision, and simplicity of the present, where life actually takes place.

The great thing about mindfulness is that you don't have to limit your practice to certain places and times — you can practice waking up and paying attention wherever you happen to be, at any time of the day or night.

Eating a piece of fruit

For this in-the-moment exercise, imagine that you've just arrived from another planet and have never encountered an orange before. Now take a few minutes to experience a piece of fruit in a fresh new way:

1. **Place an orange on a plate and close your eyes.**

2. **Set aside all thoughts and preconceptions, open your eyes, and see the fruit as though for the first time.**

   Notice the shape, the size, the color, and the texture.

3. **As you begin to peel the orange, notice how it feels in your fingers.**

   Notice the contrast between the flesh and the peel and observe the weight of the fruit in your hand.

4. **Slowly raise a piece of the orange to your lips and pause a moment before eating.**

   Notice how it smells before you begin.

5. **Open your mouth, bite down, and feel the texture of its soft flesh and the first rush of juice into your mouth.**

6. **Continue to bite and chew the orange, remaining aware of the play of sensations from moment to moment.**

   Imagining that this may be the first and last orange you will ever eat, let each moment be fresh and new and complete in itself. Notice how this experience of eating an orange differs from your usual way of eating a piece of fruit.

Troubleshooting the challenges

As your meditation practice deepens and evolves, you may find yourself encountering unexpected challenges that you don't quite know how to handle. Here again, the mountain metaphor comes in handy. Say you're half-way up the trail when you hit a patch of icy terrain, or boulders block your path, or a thunderstorm sends you scurrying for cover. What do you do? Do you pull out your special equipment and consult preestablished guidelines for dealing with the difficulties? Or do you just have to improvise as best you can?

The good news, as I mention earlier in this chapter, is that people have been climbing this mountain for thousands of years, and they've crafted tools and fashioned maps for traversing the terrain as smoothly and painlessly as possible. For example, if powerful emotions like anger, fear, sadness, or grief sweep through your meditation and make it difficult for you to stay present, you can draw on techniques for loosening their grip. (For guidelines on meditating with challenging emotions and habitual patterns, see Chapter 12.) Or if you encounter some of the common obstacles and roadside distractions on the path of meditation, such as sleepiness, restlessness, rapture, or doubt, you can count on time-honored methods for moving beyond them so you can continue on your way.

Whatever you experience on your journey, you're likely to find expert guidance in the pages of this book, drawn not only from my own experience as a practitioner and teacher but also from the accumulated wisdom of the world's meditative traditions. I cover all the basic approaches and potential issues and refer you to other resources for further investigation and study, if you're so inclined.

Chapter 2

Why Meditate?

*I*f you're like me, you want to know what you're going to get for your time and energy before you commit to an activity. I mean, why pump the StairMaster for an hour or puff and grunt through a spinning class if you can't expect to slim down, beef up, and increase your stamina? Or why put aside an evening each week to attend a gourmet cooking class if you're not going to end up making dynamite fettuccine or duck a l'orange?

The same is true for meditation. Why spend 10 or 15 or even 20 minutes of your hard-earned free time each day following your breath or repeating the same phrase again and again when you could be playing a game on your smartphone, spacing out in front of the tube, or browsing the Web? Because of the innumerable benefits, that's why!

But before delving into these benefits, this chapter explores some of the problems that meditation can help resolve. You know the old expression "If it ain't broke, don't fix it"? Well, the reality is that many of us find that our lives are "broke" in some pretty significant ways. After all, you bought this book for a reason or two. Now it's time to find out what some of those reasons may be.

How Life Drives You — to Meditate

Although you may be reluctant to admit it, at least publicly, life doesn't always live up to your expectations. As a result, you suffer — from stress, disappointment, fear, anger, outrage, hurt, or any of a number of other unpleasant emotions. Meditation teaches you how to relate to difficult circumstances and the tensions and emotions they evoke with balance, equanimity, and compassion. But before I describe the positive solutions that meditation has to offer — and rest assured, there are plenty — I'd like to take you on a whirlwind tour of the problems they're intended to solve.

The myth of the perfect life

In my years as a psychotherapist and meditation teacher, I've noticed that many people suffer because they compare their lives to some idealized image of how life is supposed to be. Cobbled together from childhood conditioning, media messages, and personal desires, this image lurks in the shadows and becomes the standard to which every success or failure, every circumstance or turn of events, is compared and judged. Take a moment to check out yours.

Perhaps you've spent your life struggling to build the American dream — two kids, house in the suburbs, brilliant career, what Zorba the Greek called the "full catastrophe." After all, that's what your parents had (or didn't have), and you decided that you owed it to them and to yourself to succeed. Only now you're juggling two jobs to save the money for a down payment, the marriage is falling apart, and you feel guilty because you don't have enough time to spend with the kids.

Or maybe you believe that ultimate happiness would come your way if you could only achieve the perfect figure (or physique). The problem is, diets don't work, you can't make yourself adhere to exercise regimens, and every time you look in the mirror, you feel like passing out. Or perhaps your idea of earthly nirvana is the perfect relationship. Unfortunately, you're watching the years pass by, you still haven't met Mr. or Ms. Right, and you scour the personals while secretly fearing that you must have some horrible social disease.

Whatever your version of the perfect life — perfect vacations, perfect sex, perfect health, even perfect peace of mind or total freedom from all tension and stress — you pay a high price for holding such high expectations. When life fails to live up to those expectations, as it inevitably does, you end up suffering and blaming yourself. (Take it from me — I've fallen into this trap again and again!) If only you had made more money, spent more time at home, been a better lover, gone back to school, lost those extra pounds . . . the list is endless. No matter how you slice it, you just don't measure up.

Or perhaps you're among the elite few who manage to get everything you want. The problem is, you eventually find yourself becoming bored and wanting more — or you spend every spare moment struggling to protect or control what you have.

The great meditative traditions have a more humane message to impart. They teach that the ideal earthly life is a myth. As an old Christian saying puts it, "Man proposes; God disposes." Or, in the words of a popular joke, "If you want to make God laugh, tell her your plans." These traditions remind us that far more powerful forces are at work in the universe than you and me. You can envision and intend and strive and attempt to control all you want — and ultimately even achieve some modicum of success. But the truth is, in the long run, you and I have only the most limited control over the circumstances of our lives. (For more on letting go, see Chapter 10.)

When things keep falling apart

Because it runs counter to everything you've ever been taught, you may have a difficult time accepting the basic spiritual truth that you and I have only limited control over the events in our lives. After all, isn't the point of life to go out and "just do it," as the old Nike ads urged? Well, yes, you need to follow your dreams and live your truth; that's a crucial part of the equation.

But when life turns around and slaps you in the face, as it sometimes does, how do you respond? (Look at the Olympic skiers who spend years in training only to have their hopes for a medal wiped out in an instant by bad weather or a patch of ice!) Or when it levels you completely and deprives you of everything you've gained, including your confidence and your hard-won self-esteem, where do you go for succor and support? How do you deal with the pain and confusion? What inner resources do you draw upon to guide you through this frightening and unknown terrain? Consider the following story.

One day a woman came to see the Buddha (the great spiritual teacher who lived several thousand years ago in India) with her dead child in her arms. Grief-stricken, she had wandered from place to place, asking people for medicine to restore him to life. As a last resort, she asked the Buddha if he could help her. "Yes," he said, "but you must first bring me some mustard seed from a house in which there has never been a death."

Filled with hope, the woman went from door to door inquiring, but no one could help her. Every house she entered had witnessed its share of deaths. By the time she reached the end of the village, she had awakened to the realization that sickness and death are inevitable. After burying her son, she returned to the Buddha for spiritual instruction. "Only one law in the universe never changes," he explained, "that all things change and all things are impermanent." Hearing this, the woman became a disciple and eventually, it is said, attained enlightenment.

Appreciating impermanence

In his book *Thoughts without a Thinker,* psychiatrist Mark Epstein recounts this teaching by the Thai meditation master Achaan Chah. "You see this goblet?" Achaan Chah asks. "For me this glass is already broken. I enjoy it; I drink out of it. It holds my water admirably, sometimes even reflecting the sun in beautiful patterns. If I should tap it, it has a lovely ring to it. But when I put this glass on the shelf, and the wind knocks it over or my elbow brushes it off the table and it falls to the ground and shatters, I say, 'Of course.' When I understand that this glass is already broken, every moment with it is precious."

Of course, life offers far more than sickness and death; it also presents us with moments of extraordinary love, beauty, wonder, and joy. But like the woman in the story, we in the West — and the United States especially — tend to deny the dark side of life. We relegate our old and dying to nursing homes, ignore our homeless, restrict our impoverished minorities to ghettoes, and confine our mentally ill and developmentally challenged to hospitals and asylums, while plastering our billboards and magazines with the smiling faces of youth and prosperity.

The fact is, life is a rich and perplexing interplay of light and dark, success and failure, youth and age, pleasure and pain — and, yes, life and death. Circumstances change constantly, apparently falling apart one moment, only to come together the next. As the contemporary Zen teacher Shunryu Suzuki puts it, everything is constantly "losing its balance against a background of perfect balance."

TIP

The key to your peace of mind lies not in your circumstances, but in how you respond to them. As the Buddhists say, suffering is wanting what you don't have and not wanting what you do have, while happiness is precisely the opposite: enjoying what you have and not hungering for what you don't have. This concept doesn't mean that you must give up your values, dreams, and aspirations — only that you need to balance them with the ability to accept things as they are.

Meditation gives you an opportunity to cultivate acceptance by teaching you to reserve judgment and to open to each experience without trying to change or get rid of it. Then, when the going gets rough, you can make use of this quality to ease your ruffled feathers and maintain your peace of mind. (If you want to find out how to accept things the way they are, turn to Chapters 7 and 12.)

Dealing with the postmodern predicament

Of course, it's news to no one that circumstances change constantly — certainly pundits and sages have purveyed this truth for ages. But at no time in history has change been as pervasive and relentless — or affected our lives so deeply — as during the past 10 or 15 years. Watching the evening news or reading a paper, we're flooded with statistics and images of violence, famine, natural disaster, global climate change, and economic instability, all depicting a world that seems to be coming increasingly unstitched.

On a more personal level, you may have lost your job because of corporate downsizing, ended a relationship because your lover was shipped off to another state, been a victim of a violent crime, or lost a bundle in a volatile market. Perhaps you spend your spare time figuring out how to stay one step ahead in a competitive work environment. Or you may simply lie awake each night worrying about when the tidal wave of change will finally reach you and sweep you away. Does any of this sound familiar?

Sociologists call this period the *postmodern era,* when constant change is becoming a way of life and time-honored values and truths are being rapidly dismantled. How do you navigate your way through life when you no longer know what's true and you're not even sure how to find out? Do you search for it on the Web or somehow glean it from the latest pronouncements of media soothsayers and corporate CEOs?

TRADITIONAL WISDOM

Accepting things the way they are

In the Zen tradition, they tell the story of a poor farmer who lost his only horse. His friends and neighbors bemoaned his plight, but he seemed unperturbed. "We'll see," he said with an enigmatic smile.

Several days later, his horse returned with a pack of five wild stallions that had joined it along the way. His neighbors rejoiced in his good fortune, but he did not appear to be excited. "We'll see," he said again.

The following week, while attempting to ride and tame one of the stallions, his beloved only son fell and broke his leg. The ever-solicitous neighbors were beside themselves with grief, but the farmer, though he comforted and cared for the boy, did not seem to be concerned about the future. "We'll see," he mused.

At the end of the month, the local warlord arrived in the farmer's village to conscript all the healthy young men to fight in the latest campaign. But the farmer's son . . . well, you can imagine the rest of the story.

In case you hadn't noticed, life's a roller-coaster ride, and you can't control the ups and downs. If you want to hold on to your lunch — and your sanity — you need to learn how to maintain your peace of mind.

Despite the unarguable advantages of all the electronic devices that have become indispensable since the 1990s, you may have noticed that the faster you communicate, the less you really connect with others in a rich and meaningful way. Sure, you're constantly being stimulated and distracted by Twitter posts, Facebook status updates, text messages, and emails — but do they really provide you with the intimacy and fulfillment you crave?

Such relentless change exacts a steep emotional and spiritual price, which we tend to deny in our collective attempt to accentuate the positive and deny the negative. Here are a few of the negative side effects of life in the postmodern age:

- **Anxiety and stress:** When the ground starts shifting beneath your feet, your first reaction as you attempt to regain your stability may be anxiety or fear. This gut-level response has been programmed into our genes by millions of years of living on the edge. These days, unfortunately, the tremors never stop, and small fears accumulate and congeal into ongoing tension and stress. Your body may feel perpetually braced against the next onslaught of difficulties and responsibilities — which makes it virtually impossible to relax and enjoy life fully. By relaxing your body and reducing stress, meditation can provide a much-needed antidote.

- **Fragmentation:** Most Americans once lived, shopped, worked, raised their kids, and spent their leisure time in the same community. They encountered the same faces every day, worked the same job for a lifetime, stayed married to the same person, and watched their children raise their own children just down the block. Now we often shuttle our kids off to school or daycare and commute long distances to work, while checking our messages on the cellphone. On the way home, we may stop by the mall, and we may spend our evenings aimlessly surfing the Web. We change jobs and partners more frequently than ever, and when our children grow up, they often move to another state — or another country! Although we may not be able to stay the tide of fragmentation, we can use meditation to connect us with a deeper wholeness that external circumstances can't disturb.

- **Alienation:** When our lives appear to be made up of disconnected puzzle pieces that don't fit together, no wonder we wind up feeling completely stressed out. With so much downsizing and outsourcing, many people are forced to work at marginal jobs that pay the bills but fail to connect them to a deeper sense of value or purpose. According to an article in *American Demographics* magazine, more people are flocking to small towns in an attempt to recapture a sense of community, and fewer and fewer are voting in each election, apparently because they believe that they have little power to change things. Never before, it seems, have human beings felt so alienated, not only from their work and their government but also from others, themselves, and their own essential being — and most of us don't have the skills or the know-how to reconnect! By bridging the chasm that separates us from ourselves, meditation can help to heal our alienation from others and the world at large.

✔ **Loneliness and isolation:** With people moving from place to place more frequently, and families fragmenting and scattering across the globe, you're less and less likely to have regular contact with the people you know and love — and even if you do, you may be too busy to relate in a mutually fulfilling way. Instead of sharing family dinners, mom, dad, and the kids call or text each other on the fly while hurrying from one activity or job to the next, rarely ending up in the same place at the same time. Of course, you may not be able to stem the forces that keep us apart. But you can use your meditation to turn every moment with your loved ones into "quality time."

✔ **Depression:** When people feel lonely, alienated, stressed out, and disconnected from a deeper source of meaning and purpose, it's no wonder that some end up feeling depressed. In a nation where Prozac is a household word, millions of people take mood-altering chemicals each day to keep from feeling the pain of postmodern life. Meditation can connect you with your own inner source of contentment and joy that naturally dispels the clouds of depression.

✔ **Stress-related illness:** From tension headaches and acid indigestion to heart disease and cancer, the steady rise in stress-related illness reflects our collective inability to cope with the instability and fragmentation of our times — and fuels a billion-dollar healthcare industry that at times only masks the deeper problems of fear, stress, and disorientation. As numerous scientific studies have shown, the regular practice of meditation can actually reverse the onslaught of many stress-related ailments. (See the section "How to Survive the 21st Century — with Meditation" later in this chapter.)

Four popular "solutions" that don't really work

Before I leave the litany of postmodern woes and suggest some solutions that actually work, I'd like to offer a quick look at a few popular approaches to handling stress and uncertainty that create more problems than they solve:

✔ **Addiction:** By distracting people from their pain, encouraging them to set aside their usual concerns and preoccupations, and altering brain chemistry, addictions mimic some of the benefits of meditation. Unfortunately, addictions also tend to fixate the mind on an addictive substance or activity — drugs, alcohol, sex, gambling, and so on —

making it even more difficult for people to be open to the wonders of the moment or to connect with a deeper dimension of *being*. Besides, most addictions involve a self-destructive lifestyle that ultimately intensifies the problems the addict was attempting to escape.

- ✔ **Fundamentalism:** By advocating simple, one-dimensional answers to complex problems, offering a sense of meaning and belonging, and repudiating many of the apparent evils of postmodern life, fundamentalism — be it religious or political — provides a refuge from ambiguity and alienation. Alas, fundamentalists divide the world into black and white, good and bad, us and them, which only fuels the fires of alienation, conflict, and stress in the world at large.

- ✔ **Entertainment:** When you feel lonely or alienated, just turn on the tube, download a movie to your computer or smartphone, or head to your local multiplex. That will calm your anxiety or soothe your pain — or will it? In addition to providing entertainment, the media seemingly create community by connecting us with other people and the events around us. But you can't have a heart-to-heart conversation with a TV celebrity or hug your favorite movie star. Besides, the media (intentionally or not) manipulate your emotions, fill your mind with the ideas and images of the popular culture, and focus your attention outside yourself — rather than give you the opportunity to find out what you really think, feel, and know.

- ✔ **Consumerism:** This bogus solution to life's ills teaches that wanting and having more is the answer — more food, more possessions, more vacations, more of every perk that plastic can buy. As you may have noticed, however, the thrill fades fast, and you're quickly planning your next purchase — or struggling to figure out how to pay the credit-card bill that arrives like clockwork at the end of the month. Need I say more?

How to Survive the 21st Century — with Meditation

Now for the good news! As I mention earlier in this chapter, meditation offers a time-honored antidote to fragmentation, alienation, isolation, stress — even stress-related illnesses and depression. Although it won't solve the external problems of your life, it does help you develop inner resilience, balance, and strength to roll with the punches and come up with creative solutions.

To get a sense of how meditation works, imagine for a moment that your body and mind are a complex computer. Instead of being programmed to experience inner peace, harmony, equanimity, and joy, you've been programmed to respond to life's inevitable ups and downs with stress, anxiety, and dissatisfaction. But you have the power to change your programming. By putting aside all other activities, sitting quietly, and attuning yourself to the present moment for a minimum of 10 or 15 minutes each day, you're developing a whole new set of habitual responses and programming yourself to experience more positive emotions and mind-states. (For more on the actual practice of meditation, see Chapters 7 and 11.)

Of course, if you find it distasteful to think of yourself as a computer, you can picture life as an ocean, with the constant ups and downs you experience as the waves that churn and roil on the water's surface. When you meditate, you dive beneath the surface to a quiet place where the water is calmer and more consistent.

Whatever your favorite metaphor, the point is that meditation provides a way of transforming stress and suffering into equanimity and ease. In this section, you get to see how meditators have been reaping the remarkable benefits of meditation for millennia — and how you can, too!

Advanced technology for the mind and heart

Traditionally, the Western world has emphasized external achievement, and the East has valued inner development. The great scientific and technological advances of the past 500 years originated in the West, while yogis and roshis in the monasteries and ashrams of Asia were cultivating the inner arts of meditation. (See Chapter 3 for more about the history of meditation.) Now the currents of East and West and North and South have joined and are intermingling to form an emerging global culture and economy. As a result, we can apply the inner "technology" perfected in the East to balance the excesses of the rapid technological innovations perfected in the West!

Like master computer programmers, the great meditation masters throughout history developed the capacity to program their bodies, minds, and hearts to experience highly refined states of being. While we in the West were charting the heavens and initiating the Industrial Revolution, they were chalking up some pretty remarkable accomplishments of their own:

- ✔ Penetrating insights into the nature of the mind and the process by which it creates and perpetuates suffering and stress

- ✔ Deep states of ecstatic absorption in which the meditator is completely immersed in union with the Divine

- ✔ The wisdom to discriminate between relative reality and the sacred dimension of *being*

- ✔ Unshakable inner peace that external circumstances can't disturb

✔ The cultivation of positive, beneficial, life-affirming mind-states, such as patience, love, kindness, equanimity, joy, and — especially — compassion for the suffering of others

✔ The ability to control bodily functions that are usually considered involuntary, such as heart rate, body temperature, and metabolism

✔ The capacity to mobilize and move vital energy through the different centers and channels of the body for the sake of healing and personal transformation

✔ Special psychic powers, such as *clairvoyance* (the ability to perceive matters beyond the range of ordinary perception) and *telekinesis* (the ability to move objects at a distance without touching them)

Of course, the great meditators of the past used these qualities to seek liberation from suffering, either by withdrawing from the world into a more exalted reality or by achieving penetrating insights into the nature of existence. Yet the meditation technology they developed — which has become widely available in the West in the past few decades — can be used by the rest of us in ordinary, everyday ways to yield some extraordinary benefits.

The mind-body benefits of meditation

Although the earliest scientific studies of meditation date back to the 1930s and 1940s, research into the psychophysiological effects of meditation took off in the 1970s, fueled by a burgeoning interest in Transcendental Meditation (TM), Zen, and other Eastern meditation techniques. Since then, thousands of studies have been published, with an exponential increase in research in the past 10 to 15 years as brain-imaging technology has become increasingly sophisticated. (For a detailed discussion of meditation research, see Chapter 4.) For now, here is a brief synopsis of the most significant benefits of meditation:

Physiological benefits:

✔ Decreased heart rate

✔ Lower blood pressure

✔ Quicker recovery from stress

✔ Decrease in *beta* (brainwaves associated with thinking) and increase in *alpha*, *delta*, and *gamma* (brainwaves associated with deep relaxation and higher mental activity)

✔ Enhanced *synchronization* (that is, simultaneous operation) of the right and left hemispheres of the brain (which positively correlates with creativity)

- Fewer heart attacks and strokes
- Increased longevity
- Reduced cholesterol levels
- Decreased consumption of energy and need for oxygen
- Deeper, slower breathing
- Muscle relaxation
- Reduction in the intensity of pain

Psychological benefits:

- More happiness and peace of mind
- Greater enjoyment of the present moment
- Less emotional reactivity; fewer intense negative emotions and dramatic mood swings
- More loving, harmonious relationships
- Increased empathy
- Enhanced creativity and self-actualization
- Heightened perceptual clarity and sensitivity
- Reductions in both acute and chronic anxiety
- Complement to psychotherapy and other approaches in the treatment of addiction

A Dozen More Great Reasons to Meditate

You don't have to join some cult or get baptized or bar mitzvahed to enjoy the benefits of meditation. And you don't have to check out of your everyday life and run off to a monastery in the Himalayas. You simply need to practice your meditation regularly without trying to get anywhere or achieve anything. Like interest in a money-market account, the benefits just accrue by themselves.

Awakening to the present moment

When you rush breathlessly from one moment to the next, anticipating another problem or hungering for another pleasure, you miss the beauty and immediacy of the present, which is constantly unfolding before your eyes.

Tuning in to your body

Like Mr. Duffy in James Joyce's novel *Ulysses,* most of us "live a short distance" from our bodies. The following meditation, which has counterparts in yoga and Buddhism, helps reestablish contact with the body by drawing attention gently from one part to another. Because it cultivates awareness and also relaxes the muscles and internal organs, it makes a great preamble to more formal meditation practice. Allow at least 20 minutes to complete. (For complete audio instructions, listen to Track 3 on the CD.)

1. **Lie on your back on a comfortable surface — but not too comfortable, unless you plan to fall asleep.**

2. **Take a few moments to feel your body as a whole, including the places where it contacts the surface of the bed or floor.**

3. **Bring your attention to your toes.**

   Allow yourself to feel any and all sensations in this area. If you don't feel anything, just feel "not feeling anything." As you breathe, imagine that you're breathing into and out of your toes. (If this feels weird or uncomfortable, just breathe in your usual way.)

4. **When you're done with your toes, move on to your soles, heels, the tops of your feet, and your ankles in turn, feeling each part in the same way that you felt your toes.**

Take your time. The point of this exercise is not to achieve anything, not even relaxation, but to be as fully present as possible wherever you are.

5. **Gradually move up your body, staying at least three or four breaths with each part.**

   Follow this approximate order: lower legs, knees, thighs, hips, pelvis, lower abdomen, lower back, solar plexus, upper back, chest, shoulders. Now focus on the fingers, hands, and arms on both sides; and then on the neck and throat, chin, jaws, face, back of the head, and top of the head.

   By the time you reach the top of your head, you may feel as though the boundaries between you and the rest of the world have become more fluid — or have melted away entirely. At the same time, you may feel silent and still — free of your usual restlessness or agitation.

6. **Rest there for a few moments; then gradually bring your attention back to your body as a whole.**

7. **Wiggle your toes, move your fingers, open your eyes, rock from side to side, and gently sit up.**

8. **Take a few moments to stretch and reacquaint yourself with the world around you before standing up and going about your day.**

Meditation teaches you to slow down and take each moment as it comes — the sounds of traffic, the smell of new clothes, the laughter of children, the worried look on an old woman's face, the coming and going of your breath. In fact, as the meditative traditions remind us, only the present moment exists anyway — the past is just a memory and the future a fantasy, projected on the movie screen of the mind right now.

Making friends with yourself

When you're constantly struggling to live up to images and expectations (your own or someone else's) or racing to reinvent yourself to survive in a competitive environment, you rarely have the opportunity or the motivation to get to know yourself just the way you are. Self-doubt and self-hatred may appear to fuel the fires of self-improvement, but they're painful — and besides, they contribute to other negative mind-states, such as fear, anger, depression, and alienation, and prevent you from living up to your full potential.

When you meditate, you learn to welcome every experience and facet of your being without judgment or denial. In the process, you begin to treat yourself as you would a close friend, accepting (and even loving) the whole package, the apparent weaknesses and shortcomings, as well as the positive qualities and strengths.

Connecting more deeply with others

As you awaken to the present moment and open your heart and mind to your own experience, you naturally extend this quality of awareness and presence to your relationships with family and friends. If you're like the rest of us, you tend to project your own desires and expectations onto the people close to you, which acts as a barrier to real communication. But when you start to accept others the way they are — a skill you can cultivate through the practice of meditation — you open up the channels for a deeper love and intimacy to flow between you.

Relaxing the body and calming the mind

As contemporary health researchers have discovered — and traditional texts agree — mind and body are inseparable, and an agitated mind inevitably produces a stressed-out body. As the mind settles, relaxes, and opens during meditation, so does the body — and the longer you meditate (measured both in minutes logged each day and in days and weeks of regular practice), the more this peace and relaxation ripples out to every area of your life, including your health.

Lightening up!

Perhaps you've noticed that nonstop thinking and worrying generate a kind of inner claustrophobia — fears feed on one another, problems get magnified exponentially, and the next thing you know, you're feeling overwhelmed and panicked. Meditation encourages an inner mental spaciousness in which difficulties and concerns no longer seem so threatening, and constructive solutions can naturally arise — as well as a certain detachment that allows for greater objectivity, perspective, and, yes, humor. That mysterious word *enlightenment* actually refers to the supreme "lightening up"!

Enjoying more happiness

Research reveals that the daily practice of meditation for just a few months actually makes people happier, as measured not only by their subjective reports but also by brain-mapping technology. (For more on meditation and happiness, see Chapter 16.) In fact, meditation is apparently one of the only things that can permanently change your *emotional set point* — your basic level of relative happiness that scientists say stays the same throughout your life, no matter what you experience.

If you want lasting happiness, leading-edge science and spiritual wisdom have the same advice to offer: Forget about winning the lottery or landing the perfect job — and begin meditating instead!

Experiencing focus and flow

When you're so fully involved in an activity that all sense of self-consciousness, separation, and distraction dissolves, you've entered what psychologist Mihaly Csikszentmihalyi calls a state of *flow* (see Chapter 1). For human beings, this total immersion constitutes the ultimate enjoyment — and provides the ultimate antidote to the fragmentation and alienation of postmodern life. No doubt you've experienced moments like these — creating a work of art, playing a sport, working in the garden, making love. Athletes call it "the zone." Through meditation, you can discover how to give the same focused attention to — and derive the same enjoyment from — every activity.

Feeling more centered, grounded, and balanced

To counter the escalating insecurity of life in rapidly changing times, meditation offers an inner groundedness and balance that external circumstances can't destroy. When you practice coming home again and again — to your body, your breath, your sensations, your feelings — you eventually grow to realize that you're always home, no matter where you go. And when you make friends with yourself — embracing the dark and the light, the weak and the strong — you get thrown off-center less and less frequently by the "slings and arrows" of life.

Getting into the habit

Take a habit that you wish you could break but can't. Maybe it's smoking, drinking coffee, or eating junk food. The next time you do it, instead of spacing out or daydreaming, turn it into a meditation. Pay close attention as you draw the smoke into your lungs, for example, or chew the French fries. Notice how your body feels. Whenever your mind drifts off, notice where it goes — you may have favorite fantasies that accompany this habit — and then gently bring it back to your experience.

Don't try to stop or change the habit; just do it as usual, except this time you're doing it with full awareness. The next time you indulge the habit, notice how you feel. Has your attitude changed in any way? What are you aware of this time that you weren't aware of before?

Enhancing your performance at work and at play

Studies have shown that basic meditation practice alone can enhance perceptual clarity, creativity, self-actualization, and many of the other factors that contribute to superior performance. In addition, specific meditations have been devised to enhance performance in a variety of activities, from sports to schoolwork (see Chapter 18).

Increasing appreciation, gratitude, and love

As you begin to open to your experience without judgment or aversion, your heart gradually opens as well — to yourself and others. You can practice specific meditations for cultivating appreciation, gratitude, and love (see Chapter 11). Or you may find, as so many meditators have before you have, that these qualities arise naturally when you can gaze at the world with fresh eyes, free from the usual projections and expectations.

Aligning with a deeper sense of purpose

When you practice making the shift from doing and thinking to *being* (see Chapter 1), you discover how to align yourself with a deeper current of meaning and belonging. You may get in touch with personal feelings and aspirations that have long remained hidden from your conscious awareness. Or you may connect with a more universal source of purpose and direction — what some people call the *higher self* or *inner guidance*.

Awakening to a spiritual dimension of being

As your meditation gradually opens you to the subtlety and richness of each fleeting but irreplaceable moment, you may naturally begin to see through the veil of appearances to the sacred reality at the heart of things — and you eventually may come to realize (and this one could take lifetimes!) that the very same sacred reality is actually who you are in your own heart of hearts. This deep insight — what the sages and masters call "waking up from the illusion of separation" — cuts through and ultimately eliminates loneliness and alienation and opens you to the beauty of the human condition.

Chapter 3

Zen and Now: Where Meditation Comes From

*W*hen you think of meditation, do you still envision an Asian monk or yogi sitting cross-legged in deep concentration? Well, meditation was definitely refined in the temples, caves, and monasteries of the East and Near East — but fortunately for you and me, it has made its way west over the past 100 years or so and become a mainstay of yoga studios, fitness centers, and mainstream magazines. Meditation also appears, though less conspicuously and in slightly different form, in the Judeo-Christian tradition. Did you know, for example, that many of the biblical prophets meditated? Or that Jesus engaged in some form of meditation when he retreated to the desert for 40 days?

Meditation dates back to our earliest ancestors, who gazed in wonder at the night sky, crouched in bushes for hours waiting for game, or sat in reverie beside communal fires. Because meditation involves a shift from thinking and doing to just *being* (see Chapter 1 for more about *being*), our forebears had a head start on you and me. After all, their lives were simpler, their thinking more rudimentary, and their connection to nature and the sacred far stronger.

Although you can certainly practice meditation without knowing where it comes from, tracing its development grounds it in a historical and spiritual context. So, join me for a brief overview of meditation's evolution as a *sacred practice* in various parts of the world.

Shamans: The first great meditators

Long before the time of the Buddha or the great Indian yogis, shamans in hunter-gatherer cultures throughout the world used meditative practices to enter altered states of consciousness, known as *trances.* Focusing their minds through drumming or rhythmic chanting; dancing in simple, repetitive steps; and sometimes using hallucinogenic plants, these men and women left their bodies and journeyed to the "world of the spirits." From there, they brought back sacred wisdom, healing abilities, magical powers, and spirit blessings for the sake of the tribe.

Cave paintings dating back at least 15,000 years depict figures lying on the ground in meditative absorption. Scholars have determined that these figures were shamans journeying in trance to ask the spirits for a successful hunt. Other cave paintings from a similar period show shamans who transformed into animals—a typical practice that continues to this day. (Depending on your belief system, you may be inclined to dismiss such experiences as figments of an overactive imagination. But the shamans and their followers have no doubt that such journeys and transformations actually occur.)

Though shamanism declined with the shift from hunting and gathering to farming, shamans still act as healers, guides for the dead, and intermediaries between humans and spirits in parts of Siberia, North America, Mexico, South America, Africa, Australia, Indonesia, and Asia. In recent years, through the writings of Carlos Castaneda, Michael Harner, and Joseph Campbell, more and more Westerners have taken an interest in shamanism — and some have even become accomplished shamans themselves.

Making the Indian Connection

You can find meditation's deepest roots in India, where *sadhus* (wandering holy men and women) and *yogis* have cultivated the practice in one form or another for more than 5,000 years. Attribute it to the climate, which slows the pace of life, or to the monsoon, which forces people to spend more time indoors, or just to the unbroken line of meditators over the ages. Whatever the reasons, India provided the fertile soil in which the meditative arts flourished and from which they spread both east and west.

The earliest Indian scriptures, the *Vedas,* don't even have a word for meditation, but the Vedic priests performed elaborate rites and chants to the gods that required tremendous concentration. Eventually, these practices evolved into a form of prayerful meditation that combined the use of breath control and devotional focus on the Divine. (See Chapter 1 for more on focus.) The deeper they delved, the more these priests realized that the worshipper and the object of worship, the individual being and the divine being itself, are one and the same — a profound insight that continued to inspire and instruct spiritual seekers through the ages.

From the garden of Vedic and post-Vedic spirituality sprouted three of India's best-known meditative traditions — yoga, Buddhism, and tantra — which I cover in the following sections.

Classical yoga: The path of blissful union

When you think of yoga, do you picture people twisting and stretching their bodies into challenging poses? Even if you practice hatha yoga yourself, what you may not know is that such "poses" are just one component of the traditional path of classical yoga, which includes breath control and meditation. (For a comprehensive introduction to yoga, check out *Yoga For Dummies* by Georg Feuerstein and Larry Payne, published by Wiley.)

The practitioner of classical yoga aims to withdraw from the material world, which is considered illusory, and merge with the formless but ultimate reality of consciousness. After preparing the body with *asanas* (the familiar hatha yoga poses), cultivating refined energy states through various breathing practices, and excluding all external distractions, the yogi focuses on an intermediate object, such as a *mantra* (repetition of a meaningful word or phrase) or a sacred symbol, and then on consciousness itself. Finally, the yogi arrives at a state known as *samadhi,* in which all traces of separation dissolve, and the yogi blissfully unites with consciousness.

Compiled and codified by Patanjali (a sage of the second century A.D.), the philosophy and practices of classical yoga gave rise to numerous and, at times, competing schools over the centuries. Most of the yogis and swamis who have taught in the West trace their lineage to classical yoga.

Early Buddhism: The roots of mindfulness meditation

The historical Buddha was a Hindu prince who, according to the traditional account, renounced his luxurious life to find answers to the mystery of suffering, old age, and death. After practicing asceticism and yoga for many years, he decided that rejecting the world and mortifying the flesh would not lead to the understanding he sought. Instead, he sat down under a tree and began looking deeply into his own mind. After seven days and nights of intensive meditation, he woke up to the nature of existence — hence the name *Buddha,* or "the awakened one."

The art of the mantra

As Herbert Benson, M.D., explains in his groundbreaking book *The Relaxation Response,* the meditative repetition of a mantra tends to calm the mind and relax the body. But the earliest practitioners of mantra had more spiritual intentions, such as invoking the power of a particular deity, cultivating and strengthening positive qualities, or achieving union with divine reality.

Though the term *mantra* (meaning "mind protection") derives from the Sanskrit, the practice appears in one form or another in virtually every religion. Sufis repeat the phrase *La ila'ha, il'alahu* ("There is nothing but God"), Christians say the "Our Father" or the prayer of the heart ("Lord Jesus Christ have mercy on me"), Buddhists intone sacred invocations like *om mani padme hum* or *namu amida butsu,* and Hindus repeat one of the many praises or names of God.

Essentially, mantras are sounds infused with numinous or spiritual power by a teacher or a tradition. When you repeat a mantra — aloud, under your breath, or mentally (actually considered the most potent method) — you resonate with a particular spiritual frequency and with the power and blessings the sound has accumulated over the years.

The practice of mantra focuses and stabilizes the mind and protects it from unwanted distractions. For this reason, mantra recitation often accompanies more formal meditation practices. To experiment with a mantra, just choose a word or phrase with deep personal or spiritual meaning for you. (Traditionally, you would receive a particular mantra directly from your teacher.) Then sit quietly and repeat it again and again, allowing your mind to rest on the sound and the feeling it evokes. When your mind wanders, just come back to your mantra.

The Buddha taught that we suffer because we cling to the false belief that (a) things are permanent and can be relied upon for happiness, and (b) we have an abiding *self* that exists independently of other beings and makes us who we are. Instead, he taught that everything changes constantly — our minds, our emotions, our sense of self, and the circumstances and objects in the external world.

To be free from suffering, he counseled, we must liberate ourselves from ignorance and eliminate fear, anger, greed, jealousy, and other negative mind-states. The approach he prescribed involves both practices for working with the mind and guidelines for living in the world in a virtuous and spiritual way. (For a comprehensive introduction to the teachings and practices of Buddhism, check out *Buddhism For Dummies* by Jonathan Landaw and Stephan Bodian, published by Wiley.)

Meditation lies at the heart of the historical Buddha's approach. The practice of meditation he taught, known as *mindfulness,* involves wakeful attention to our experience from moment to moment.

Here are the four traditional foundations of mindfulness:

- Awareness of the body
- Awareness of feelings
- Awareness of thoughts and mind-states
- Awareness of the laws of experience (the relationships between what we think and what we experience)

Departing from the other teachers of his day, who generally recommended withdrawing from the world to seek ecstatic union with the Divine, the Buddha taught the importance of gaining direct insight into the nature of existence and into how the mind creates suffering. He likened himself to a physician who offers medicine to heal wounds rather than a philosopher who provides abstract answers to metaphysical questions.

Indian tantra: Finding the sacred in the world of the senses

Many Westerners associate the word *tantra* with traditional sexual practices that have been adapted to appeal to a popular audience. However, *tantra* developed in the early centuries A.D. as a major form of Indian spiritual practice and thought. Believing that absolute reality and the relative world of the senses are inseparable, *tantrikas* (practitioners of tantra) use the senses — including the practice of ritual sex — as gateways to spiritual realization. Needless to say, such an approach has its pitfalls; whereas yoga and Buddhism can veer toward life-denial, tantra can be confused with sensual indulgence.

Tantric meditation frequently involves practices for awakening the *kundalini shakti,* believed to be a powerful energy associated with the divine feminine that resides at the base of the spine. When stimulated, the shakti rises through an energetic channel located in the spine and activates and opens each of the seven energy centers, or *chakras,* in its path. These centers, which vibrate at different frequencies and are associated with different physical and psychological functions, are located at the perineum, the genitals, the solar plexus, the heart, the throat, the forehead, and the crown of the head, respectively. (For more on chakras, turn to Chapter 12.) Ultimately, the shakti may erupt through the crown chakra in a burst of ecstasy. At this point, the practitioner realizes his or her identity with the Divine, while still fully contained in a physical body.

To the Roof of the World — and Beyond

Before it left India for good at the end of the first millennium A.D., Buddhism went through significant changes. The early teachings developed into what we now call *Theravada* — the dominant approach in Sri Lanka and Southeast Asia, emphasizing a progressive path to liberation largely limited to monks and nuns. At the same time, another major current emerged that preached the ideal of the *bodhisattva* — the person who dedicates his or her life to liberating others. Known as the *Mahayana* ("the great vehicle"), this second major branch of Buddhism was more egalitarian and offered the possibility of enlightenment to everyone, whether lay or monastic.

From India, wandering monks and scholars transported Mahayana Buddhism over the Himalayas (the "roof of the world") to China and Tibet. There it mingled with indigenous spiritual teachings, set down roots, and evolved into a number of different traditions and schools, most notably Ch'an (*Zen* in Japanese) and Vajrayana Buddhism, which took the practice of meditation to new heights. (For more on the different branches of Buddhism, see *Buddhism For Dummies*.)

Ch'an (Zen): The sound of one hand

You've no doubt read about the Zen masters who whacked their disciples with a stick or bellowed instructions at the tops of their lungs. But you may not realize that Zen is a unique blend of Mahayana Buddhism (which is egalitarian) and the native Chinese tradition known as Taoism (which emphasizes the seamless and undivided nature of life, known as the *Tao*). Although Indian monks began transporting Buddhism to China in the early centuries A.D., Zen did not emerge as a separate current until the seventh or eighth century. Zen departed radically from traditional Buddhism by emphasizing direct, wordless transmission of the enlightened state from master to disciple — sometimes through behavior that, by ordinary standards, would be considered eccentric or even bizarre.

Although the other traditions of Buddhism increasingly focused on scriptural study, Zen cut through the metaphysical underbrush and said, Just sit! Meditation became the primary means for dismantling a lifetime of attachment to the material world and realizing what the Zen masters call *Buddha nature,* the innate wisdom that exists within each of us.

Zen also introduced those seemingly unsolvable riddles known as *koans* — for example, "What is the sound of one hand?" or "What was your original face before your parents were born?" By totally immersing himself in the koan, the monk could ultimately see into the nature of existence — what the Zen masters called *satori.*

In Japan, Zen developed some of its notorious samurai intensity and gave rise to the austere, pristine aesthetic that has made rock gardens and brush paintings so typical of Japanese culture. From Japan, of course, Zen made its way to North America, encountered the Beat generation of the 1950s, and set the stage for the recent explosion of interest in meditation. (For more on Zen in North America, see the section "The Americanization of Meditation," later in this chapter.)

Vajrayana Buddhism: The way of transformation

Like China (where Buddhism encountered Taoism), Tibet had its indigenous religion, called *Bonpo*, which included magical practices designed to appease the local spirits and deities. When the great Indian master Padmasambhava brought Buddhism from India to Tibet in the seventh century A.D., he first had to conquer the hostile spirits that resisted his efforts. Ultimately, these spirits were incorporated into Tibetan Buddhism as protectors and allies in an elaborate pantheon that included various Buddhas and *dakinis* (awakened women).

Tibetan Buddhists believed that the historical Buddha taught simultaneously at different levels, depending on the needs and abilities of his disciples. The most advanced teachings, they said, were kept secret for centuries and ultimately conveyed to Tibet as the *Vajrayana* ("the diamond way"). In addition to traditional mindfulness meditation, this approach incorporated elements of Indian tantra and involved powerful practices for working with energy. Instead of eliminating negative emotions and mind-states like anger, greed, and fear as traditional Buddhism recommends, the Vajrayana teaches practitioners how to transform negativity directly into wisdom and compassion.

Meditation in Tibetan Buddhism also employs *visualization* — the active use of the imagination to invoke potent spiritual forces that fuel the process of spiritual realization.

From the Middle East to the Rest of the West

Although meditation in the Judeo-Christian and Islamic traditions had its own independent development, meditators in the Middle East may have been influenced by the practices of their counterparts in India and Southeast Asia (see the earlier sections of this chapter). Historians do have evidence that traders and pilgrims traveled between the two regions constantly, and Buddhist monks appeared in Rome in early Christian times! There's even the rumor, buoyed by some interesting historical coincidences, that Jesus may have learned how to meditate in India. While Indian meditators — following the ancient insight that *atman equals Brahman* ("I and the ground of *being* are one") — turned their attention progressively inward, seeking the sacred in the depths of their own being, Western thinkers and theologians pointed to a God that purportedly exists outside the individual. At the same time, mystics in the West wrestled with the paradox that God is both inside and outside, personal and transcendent.

Meditation in the Western religions usually takes the form of *prayer* — that is, direct communion with God. But the meditative prayer of the monks and mystics differs from ordinary prayer, which often includes complaints and requests. Instead, meditative prayer approaches God with humility and devotion, contemplates His divine qualities, and invites His presence into the heart of the meditator. Ultimately, the goal is to surrender the individual self completely in union with the Divine.

Christian meditation: Practicing contemplative prayer

The Christian equivalent of meditation, known as *contemplative prayer,* dates back to Jesus, who fasted and prayed in the desert for 40 days and nights. In contemplation, says Father Thomas Keating, whose *centering prayer* has helped revitalize interest in Christian meditation, you open your awareness and your heart to God, the ultimate mystery, who dwells in the depths of your being, beyond the reach of the mind. (See the "Centering prayer" sidebar for more about the practice taught by Father Keating.)

After the time of Jesus, the first great Christian meditators were the desert fathers of Egypt and Palestine in the third and fourth centuries, who lived largely in solitude and cultivated awareness of the Divine presence through constant repetition of a sacred phrase. Their direct descendants, the monks, nuns, and mystics of medieval Europe, developed the contemplative practice of repeating and ruminating over a scriptural passage (not to be confused with thinking about or analyzing it!) until its deeper significance revealed itself to the mind. Both of these practices, explains Father Keating, harken back to Jesus's admonition, "When you pray, go into your closet, your innermost being, and bolt the door."

In the Eastern Orthodox Church of Greece and Eastern Europe, monks have long engaged in a similar practice combining *prostrations* (full-body bows) with the repetition of the Jesus prayer ("Lord Jesus Christ have mercy on me, a sinner") until all practices drop away to reveal a deep interior silence filled with love and bliss.

MEDITATION

Centering prayer

Developed in the past few decades by Father Thomas Keating, a Catholic priest, and based on traditional Christian sources, *centering prayer* is a contemplative practice that opens the mind and heart to the Divine presence. Unlike a mantra, which is designed to clarify or calm the mind, centering prayer purifies the heart to become a vehicle for God's transformative grace. Instead of repeating it again and again like a mantra, you hold it in your awareness as an object of contemplation.

Here are the instructions for practicing centering prayer, as given by Father Keating (whose words appear in quotation marks):

1. **Choose a "sacred word as a symbol of your intention to consent to God's presence and action within."**

2. **Settle comfortably and silently introduce the sacred word.**

   When your attention wanders, gently bring it back.

3. **Stay with the same word during the period of contemplation.**

Some people may prefer to "turn inwardly toward God as if gazing upon him," without words. In any case, the same guidelines apply. When we open to God, says Father Keating, we find that God is "closer than breathing, closer than thinking, closer than choosing — closer than consciousness itself."

In recent years, many Christian ministers and monastics have been influenced by the Hindu and Buddhist teachers who have appeared in the West in increasing numbers. (See the section "The Americanization of Meditation," later in this chapter.) In response, some have adapted Eastern practices to the needs of Christian audiences. Others, like Father Keating, have delved into their own contemplative roots and resuscitated practices that had become dusty with disuse.

Meditation in Judaism: Drawing closer to God

According to Rami Shapiro, rabbi of Temple Beth Or in Miami, Florida, and author of *Wisdom of the Jewish Sages,* mystical interpreters of the Bible have found evidence of meditation dating back to Abraham, the founder of Judaism. The Old Testament prophets apparently entered into altered states of consciousness through fasting and ascetic practices, and mystics in the first few centuries A.D. meditated on a vision of the prophet Ezekiel.

Contemplating the stars

In his book *Jewish Meditation*, Rabbi Aryeh Kaplan describes a traditional technique based on the biblical verse "Lift your eyes on high and see who created these [stars], the One who brings out their host by number, He calls them all by name . . ." (Isaiah 40:26):

1. **On a clear night, lie or sit comfortably out of doors, gazing up at the stars.**

2. **While repeating a mantra, focus your attention on the stars as though you are probing them to reveal the mystery behind them.**

   You can use the traditional Jewish mantra *r'bono shel olam* ("master of the universe")

to help you deepen your concentration and your sense of the sacred. Or feel free to use a mantra of your own choosing.

As Rabbi Kaplan puts it, you are "calling to God in the depths of the heavens, seeking to find Him beyond the stars, beyond the very limits of time and space."

3. **Remain absorbed in your contemplation for as long as you want.**

According to Rabbi Kaplan, this meditation "can bring a person to an overwhelmingly deep spiritual experience."

But the first formal Jewish meditation, says Shapiro, centered on the Hebrew alphabet, which was considered the divine language through which God created the world. "If you could see into the alphabet," explains Shapiro, "you could see into the source of creation and thereby become one with the creator Himself."

Like practitioners in all the God-centered religions, Jewish meditators have traditionally used sacred phrases or verses from scripture as mantras to bring them closer to God. As one great Hasidic master used to say of the phrase *r'bono shel olam* ("master of the universe"), if you just repeat it continuously, you will achieve union with God. And it is precisely this union that Jewish meditation intends to induce.

Like Christianity, Judaism has been inspired by Eastern influences in recent years to revive its own meditative traditions. Rabbis like Shapiro (who practices Zen meditation) and David Cooper (who trained in Buddhist mindfulness meditation) are creating a Jewish meditative renaissance by forging a new synthesis of ancient techniques from East and West.

Meditation among the Sufis: Surrendering to the Divine with every breath

Since the time of the prophet Mohammed in the seventh century A.D., Sufis have worn the garments of Islam. But, according to the American-born Sufi teacher Shabda Kahn, their roots go back much farther, beyond Mohammed or Buddha or other famous teachers, to the first awakened person. Sufis claim to be a fellowship of mystical seekers whose sole purpose is to realize the Divine in their own hearts. The forms of Sufism have varied from century to century and teacher to teacher, and from one geographical location to another, but the basic teaching is the same: There is nothing but God.

Meditation in Sufism generally takes the form of chanting a sacred phrase, either silently or out loud, while breathing deeply and rhythmically — a practice known as *zikr,* "remembrance of the Divine." Kahn explains that Sufis retranslate the biblical beatitude "Blessed are the poor in spirit" to "Blessed are those who have a refined breath." When the Sufi has cultivated and refined the breath, he or she can use it as a method for surrendering to the divine presence in each moment — with every breath.

The Americanization of Meditation

If you harken back to the counterculture of the 1960s and 1970s to find the first seeds of meditation on American soil, you may be surprised to discover that the roots go far deeper. Some of the earliest settlers transplanted Eastern ideas when they fled to the colonies, seeking freedom for their particular brand of Christianity. And many of the framers of the Declaration of Independence and the U.S. Constitution — men like Thomas Jefferson and Benjamin Franklin — belonged to secret fraternities informed by the mystical teachings of Sufism and Judaism.

Toward the one

To prepare for more advanced meditative practices, Sufis often begin with a *darood* — the recitation of a sacred phrase coordinated with the breath. The American-born Sufi master Samuel Lewis, who died in 1971, taught the following exercise:

1. **Start to walk in a rhythmic fashion and synchronize your breathing with your pace — four steps for each inhalation and four steps for each exhalation.**

2. **As you walk, repeat the phrase "toward the one" — one syllable per step with a silent space on the fourth step.**

   Notice that the rhythm of your breath strengthens and develops as you walk.

3. **Continue for as long as you like, with wholehearted attention.**

"The Sufi practices living in the breath 24 hours a day," says Shabda Kahn, a Sufi teacher who studied with Lewis.

Transcendentalism and Theosophy (1840–1900)

The first major influx of Eastern teachings began in the 1840s and 1850s, when Transcendentalists like Ralph Waldo Emerson and Henry David Thoreau read Hindu scriptures in English translations of German adaptations from the Sanskrit! While Thoreau, whose ideas on civil disobedience were influenced by Eastern philosophy, withdrew to Walden Pond to meditate in nature, his good friend Emerson was blending German idealism, Yankee optimism, and Indian spirituality to formulate his version of the Transcendentalist credo. In the process, he transformed the Hindu *Brahman* (the divine ground of *being*) into a more universal concept that he called the *Oversoul*.

Later in the century, the *Theosophists* — members of a largely Western movement, led by the Russian-born Madame Blavatsky, who adapted and popularized Indian spiritual thought — made Hindu meditation texts available to the ordinary reader, and followers of the New Thought movement practiced guided visualizations and mantra meditations adapted from Eastern sources.

But the landmark meditation event of the 19th century turned out to be the World Parliament of Religions, an international gathering of religious leaders and teachers held in Chicago in 1893. For the first time, Asian masters presented their teachings directly to Westerners on American soil. Following the conference, several of the masters (including the Indian sage Swami Vivekananda and the Japanese Zen teacher Soyen Shaku) toured the United States lecturing to interested audiences.

Yoga and Zen prepare the soil (1900–1960)

In the decades following the World Parliament, the Zen monk Nyogen Senzaki continued Soyen Shaku's work of sowing the seeds of meditation in the New World, and Swami Paramananda, a disciple of Swami Vivekananda, established centers where curious Americans could practice meditation and hear sophisticated Indian spiritual teachings. (The Vedanta Society, which grew up around the work of swamis Vivekananda and Paramananda and their disciples, continues to flourish in the United States and Europe.) In the 1920s, the Indian yogi Paramahansa Yogananda settled in the United States, and his work gradually blossomed into the Self-Realization Fellowship, which today boasts followers throughout the Western world.

Perhaps the best-known spiritual teacher to arrive during this period was J. Krishnamurti, who settled in Southern California in the 1940s and attracted the English writers Aldous Huxley and Christopher Isherwood. Although Krishnamurti (who was groomed from childhood to be a world teacher by the Theosophists) shunned formal meditation and religious dogma in favor of dialogue and self-inquiry, Huxley and Isherwood helped to popularize the great Hindu scriptures.

By the 1950s, Zen began to significantly influence the American counterculture. While the poet Gary Snyder (who later won the Pulitzer Prize for his book *Turtle Island*) was off studying Zen in Japan, his friend and Beat colleague Jack Kerouac wrote novels that popularized Buddhist concepts such as *dharma, karma,* and *satori.* Also in the '50s, the great Japanese scholar D. T. Suzuki began teaching Zen at Columbia University in New York City, where his audiences included the young Thomas Merton, novelist J. D. Salinger, composer John Cage, and psychoanalysts Erich Fromm and Karen Horney. About the same time, the books of former Episcopalian priest and Zen aficionado Alan Watts — including *The Way of Zen* and *Psychotherapy East and West* — became popular sellers.

Meditation reaches Main Street (1960 to the present)

In the 1960s, a unique cluster of events set the stage for the mainstreaming of meditation. Many Baby Boomers, who were now reaching young adulthood, began experimenting with altered states of consciousness by using so-called mind-expanding drugs like marijuana and LSD. At the same time, the war in Vietnam prompted a national backlash among a sizable segment of the population and helped forge a counterculture opposed in many ways to the status quo. Popular music fueled the fires of discontent and touted the benefits of "tuning in, turning on, and dropping out" — words that in another time, place, and context might have referred to renouncing the world in favor of the monastic life. And political unrest in Asia (including shock waves from Vietnam and the Chinese takeover of Tibet) combined with the spirit of the times to bring a new wave of spiritual teachers to the New World.

From the standpoint of meditation, perhaps the landmark event of this era was the conversion of the Beatles to the practice of Transcendental Meditation (TM), which prompted thousands of their young fans to begin meditating, too. (Over the years, the TM movement has taught millions of Westerners how to meditate and has pioneered research revealing the mind-body benefits of meditation.) As psychedelics lost their luster, more and more people who had looked to drugs to provide meditative experiences like peace and insight turned to the real thing — and some even took refuge in the yoga communities and Zen centers constructed by their newfound teachers.

Native American meditation

When I describe the "Americanization" of meditation, I'm revealing my cultural bias. Clearly, Native Americans have been meditating here for tens of thousands of years. In addition to shamans, who play a special role in the life of the tribe (see the sidebar "Shamans: The first great meditators" earlier in this chapter), Native American boys and girls often mark the transition from childhood to adulthood by spending three or four days meditating alone in a sacred spot. By fasting, praying, focusing their minds, and opening their senses, they solicit dreams or visions that bring them special wisdom or power and help them contact their guardian spirits. As adults, Native Americans may also meditate alone in nature when they need spiritual sustenance or answers to important life questions. In addition, the practice of moment-to-moment mindfulness has always been an essential ingredient of traditional Native American life.

Since the 1970s, a new generation, with the savvy to translate the teachings for their brothers and sisters, has emerged in the West as sanctioned teachers of Eastern spiritual disciplines. As Alan Watts anticipated (in his book *Psychotherapy East and West*), the field of psychotherapy has been particularly open to Eastern influences — perhaps because psychotherapy, like meditation, purports to offer a solution for suffering. As a result, American spiritual teachers often couch their messages in language that appeals to proponents of "personal growth."

At the same time, scientific researchers like Herbert Benson, Jon Kabat-Zinn, and Dean Ornish have pioneered the mainstreaming of meditation. These days, books on meditation and related topics regularly appear on the *New York Times* best-seller list, and articles on the practice and benefits of meditation grace the pages of health and fitness magazines alongside articles touting the latest fitness craze or weight-loss routine. In one six-month period not long ago, *Time* magazine ran a cover story on the growing popularity of Buddhism, and *Newsweek* ran covers featuring the faces of Ornish and best-selling author and meditation expert Deepak Chopra. Without doubt, meditation has emerged as a mainstream American practice!

The Future of Meditation

Now that meditation has become so popular in the West, you may wonder how its influence will expand and evolve over the decades to come. Needless to say, no one really knows, but I'd be happy to offer some informed speculation, based on recent developments and cutting-edge research.

Some of the latest scientific studies use state-of-the-art technology to prove that regular meditation makes you happier, more empathic, and more resistant to disease (see Chapters 4 and 16). Coupled with earlier studies indicating a host of other health benefits, this growing body of research could lead to the mainstreaming of meditation in a number of important ways.

Take two meditations and call me in the morning

More and more doctors may prescribe regular sitting practice along with insulin, beta blockers, and blood-pressure medication for patients with serious illnesses like diabetes, heart disease, and hypertension. Indeed, many health-care practitioners already do! If the research into meditation's benefits continues to yield such convincing results, HMOs and other medical organizations may ultimately require physicians to include it as standard practice for certain ailments.

Talking back to Prozac

Mindfulness meditation has no harmful side effects and permanently lifts the mood of those who practice it for just three months (see Chapter 16). There's even a book devoted to using mindfulness-based cognitive therapy in the treatment of depression. Then why don't psychiatrists dispense mindfulness to their depressed or anxious patients, before potentially dangerous mind-altering drugs? Beats me! In a few years, though, more and more shrinks may be counseling their patients to follow their breathing as well as take their medication — and the book you hold in your hands may find its rightful place on psychiatrists' shelves, alongside the *Diagnostic and Statistical Manual of Mental Disorders!*

The more you sit, the less you pay

The work of Dean Ornish and other researchers has prompted some insurance companies to reimburse for stress-management programs and some hospitals to create their own. In the same way, the growing evidence for the health benefits of meditation may lead to a reduction in insurance premiums for those who meditate regularly — and to the offering of meditation classes in every hospital and clinic. Maybe you'll even get reimbursed for the occasional meditation retreat — after your co-pay, of course!

Playing with gravity

1. Sit in a chair and take a few moments to become aware of how gravity acts on your body.

2. Notice the weight of your legs and hips against the chair.

3. Stand up and notice how gravity pulls you toward the Earth.

4. Begin walking and, with each step, pay attention to the tug of gravity against your feet.

5. Look around and consider how all these objects are held in place by gravity — and how you move through a field of gravity like a fish swimming through water.

   This mysterious force is everywhere, even though you may not see or comprehend it.

6. Continue to be aware of this invisible but powerful field as you go about your day.

Spinning, stretching, and sitting

As the health benefits of meditation are more widely accepted and acknowledged, health clubs, spas, and resorts are increasingly including meditation classes and workshops alongside aerobics, spinning, weight-training, and hatha yoga. After all, meditation enhances your enjoyment of life at every level — and what better time to enjoy life than on a vacation!

Beyond these more obvious applications for meditation, I anticipate that meditation will become a more pervasive presence on the cultural landscape. Perhaps you'll be able to access meditation courses on TV, hear celebrity meditators eager to talk about their practice, and find regular references to meditation on sitcoms and talk shows. Some other, more visionary possibilities: meditation booths in public places, meditation classes in public schools, regular meditation breaks instead of coffee breaks in the workplace, meditation rooms next to board rooms in corporations — even meditation meetings beside prayer meetings in the halls of Congress! And why not? Because meditation reduces stress and improves health without ideological baggage, it's primed to infiltrate our lives in unprecedented — and unpredictable — new ways.

Chapter 4

Your Brain on Meditation and How It Impacts Your Life

In This Chapter

▶ Exploring meditation research through the decades

▶ Discovering how meditation changes and shapes your brain

*P*eople have been meditating for thousands of years, drawn by a desire for spiritual enlightenment, heightened states of mind and mood, the health and longevity that long-time practitioners often enjoy, and, for some intrepid adventurers, a fascination with exploring the unknown just because it's there! As far as we can tell, our ancestors never bothered to measure meditation's effects objectively; they were sufficiently motivated by the subjective reports of their teachers and the meditators who came before them. Besides, the point was never to quantify the practice, but to experience the effects directly from the inside.

As meditation has entered the mainstream in the West, however, it's piqued the interest of researchers eager to prove (or disprove) its numerous purported benefits. Many of these researchers learned to meditate before entering academia and brought with them a personal as well as professional curiosity to discover how meditation holds up under rigorous scientific scrutiny. Their results — cited in prestigious academic and professional journals and written up in magazines, newspapers, and blog sites — have been overwhelmingly positive, providing even more impetus to the growing popularity of meditation.

In this chapter, I take you on a guided tour of meditation research, from early forays in the first half of the 20th century to the ongoing brain studies of the past decade. As the methods have grown more accurate and sophisticated, the research has grown more fascinating and revealing. Did you know that you can reshape your brain through meditation? Read on for details!

Tracing the Origins of Meditation Research

Decades before meditation made significant inroads in the West, a few pioneering academics were seeking out Indian yogis and Zen meditators in their native habitats for impromptu studies of meditation's impact on vital bodily processes. With the advent of Transcendental Meditation (TM) in the 1960s, a new wave of research, prompted by the technique's growing notoriety — and by offshoots like Herbert Benson's relaxation response — led to convincing evidence of meditation's far-reaching health benefits. Before long, the scientific establishment was taking notice, prompting further investigation and ultimately ushering in a new era of government-funded research and groundbreaking studies. But first, those humble beginnings . . . .

Wiring up yogis and Zen monks

The first scientific study of meditation occurred in the 1930s, when an Indian graduate student at Yale received a fellowship to study the physiological effects of his own yogic breathing and found that his oxygen consumption decreased by as much as 25 percent. Soon, other researchers followed in his footsteps, traveling to India to study experienced yogic meditators and conducting the first experiments using rudimentary scientific instruments like electrocardiograms (EKGs) and blood pressure gauges. For these Westerners who were schooled in the scientific method, the Eastern adepts they studied — yogis who could stop their hearts and enter deep states of absorption — were like exotic animals: worthy of study, no doubt, but having little relevance to ordinary human beings.

In the 1960s, researchers at the University of Tokyo conducted a pioneering study of Zen teachers and their students, measuring brain waves using electroencephalographs (EEGs) and tracking pulse rates, respiration, galvanic skin response, and responses to sensory stimuli. They found that the meditators underwent an orderly progression in brain wave changes, beginning with a shift to more and larger alpha rhythms (brainwaves associated with relaxed attention) and culminating, as the meditation deepened, in an increase in theta (associated with deep relaxation, spiritual experience, and enhanced creativity). As it turns out, the predominance of alpha and, in more advanced meditators, theta, has proven in subsequent studies to be a consistent characteristic of meditation involving mindful attention.

Even more interesting, the researchers found that the Zen masters in their study didn't become habituated to a recurring sound the way ordinary controls did. Instead, they exhibited the same EEG patterns each time the sound occurred. In other words, they consistently maintained a calm, alert awareness to both internal and external sensations no matter how often they were stimulated.

Can meditation be accurately measured?

Throughout this book I speak in general terms about the benefits of meditation, which, as you may have noticed, are rather impressive. But in the interests of full disclosure, let me qualify these pronouncements with a few caveats:

✔ **Meditation techniques differ, sometimes significantly, and these differences translate into dissimilar research results.** For example, early researchers found that some techniques were excitatory and seemed to increase emotional arousal and, in some cases, even the symptoms of stress; whereas others were calming and stress reducing. (This book alone covers dozens of different techniques, but all the techniques I teach here fall into the second category.)

Likewise, Transcendental Meditation (TM) researchers claim their technique confers certain special benefits and induces a uniquely coherent brainwave pattern that other methods do not, while proponents of mindfulness insist that present moment awareness has powers to change the brain and heal the body that other approaches lack. For this reason, any attempt to generalize about meditation from studies of one technique alone should be taken with the proverbial grain of salt.

✔ **Even within a particular approach, meditators may have varying levels of expertise and** experience and employ subtle differences in technique. For instance, one study of mindfulness may use mindfulness-based stress reduction (MBSR), whereas another may use vipassana or mindfulness-based cognitive therapy (MBCT). Are they similar enough to compare and contrast? And how does a researcher determine who is an advanced meditator and who is an intermediate or a beginner?

✔ **Some experts insist that research on existing meditators fails to take into account the possibility that people who meditate already have certain health characteristics or brainwave patterns that draw them to meditate instead of achieving those characteristics or brainwaves through the practice itself.** The only way to get truly accurate and unbiased results, these critics claim, is to select a group of people at random, teach half to meditate, and leave the rest as non-meditating controls.

In the end, though, these caveats are just fine points and don't detract in any way from the basic implications of the extensive research, which are that meditation is good for you at every level — mind, body, and spirit — in a multitude of significant ways.

Studying TM and the relaxation response

By the 1970s, meditation had gained a small but devoted following in the West, and researchers didn't have to travel to India or Japan to study its effects anymore — they could turn their attention to the growing cadre of Western practitioners. In particular, Transcendental Meditation, introduced in the late '60s by Maharishi Mahesh Yogi and championed by the Beatles, funded an extensive study into the method's effectiveness and generated a flood of scientific papers, many of them written under the auspices of the organization's own Maharishi International University (now known as the Maharishi School of Management).

TM researchers claimed that the technique, which involves the repetition of a specially chosen mantra, induces a unique fourth state of consciousness distinct from the three familiar states of waking, dream sleep, and deep sleep. The primary characteristic of this fourth state, according to early TM researcher David Orme-Johnson, is the extraordinary brain coherence it elicits. *Coherence,* which can be measured by EEG, is the degree of correlation or synchrony between different parts of the brain. It's like the harmonious music created under a conductor's direction rather than the cacophonous noise generated when an orchestra tunes up. Orme-Johnson says, "All the benefits of TM can be explained by the increased EEG coherence it produces."

Based on his study of TM practitioners in the early '70s, Herbert Benson, MD, a cardiologist and professor at Harvard Medical School, identified what he called the *relaxation response,* a natural reflex mechanism that he found could be triggered by 20 minutes of daily meditation practice involving a quiet environment, repetition of a sound or phrase, a receptive attitude, and a comfortable sitting position. Essentially, he extracted what he considered the basic elements of TM from their spiritual context and promoted a generic alternative. Once initiated, this reflex apparently induces relaxation, reduces stress, and counteracts the fight-or-flight response. In subsequent studies, Benson found that the relaxation response had a beneficial effect on hypertension, headaches, heart disease, alcohol consumption, anxiety, and premenstrual syndrome. His 1975 bestseller, *The Relaxation Response,* was the first book to promote meditation to the mainstream on scientific grounds.

Measuring the health benefits of meditation

During the '70s and '80s, TM and relaxation-response research dominated the scientific study of meditation, and the results revealed meditation's exceptional benefits on a wide range of health measures, from blood pressure and cholesterol levels to longevity and frequency of doctor's visits. Here's a sampling of some of the research findings regarding meditation's effects on the body:

- ✔ **Heart rate:** Studies consistently show that the heart rate slows during meditation anywhere from 2 or 3 to 15 beats per minute, with greater declines for advanced meditators. At the same time (and possibly the reason for the decrease), cardiac output increases by as much as 15 percent.

- ✔ **Blood pressure:** One of the most frequently studied parameters, blood pressure consistently decreased in a score of studies by as much as 25 mmHg systolic (among normal and moderately hypertensive subjects).

- ✔ **Brainwaves:** As indicated earlier, meditators experience more alpha rhythms, both during and between practice sessions. Advanced meditators also have brief bouts of theta, during which they report feeling peaceful, spacious, and self-aware.

- ✔ **Dehabituation:** Whereas Zen meditators experience sounds freshly no matter how often they occur, yogic meditators (who are taught to withdraw their senses rather than heighten their awareness) habituate to sounds and gradually become less responsive.

- ✔ **Stress chemicals:** As one might expect from a practice renowned for reducing stress, meditation brings down the levels of *cortisol* (the primary stress hormone produced by the adrenals) by as much as 25 percent in advanced practitioners and *lactate* (a chemical released into the bloodstream during stress) by as much as 33 percent.

- ✔ **Cholesterol:** Regular practice of meditation reduces serum cholesterol levels as much as 30 mg/dL.

- ✔ **Metabolism:** Dozens of studies have found that meditation reduces oxygen consumption by as much as 55 percent, CO_2 elimination by up to 50 percent, and breathing rate from a norm of 14 to 16 breaths per minute to as few as 1 or 2.

- ✔ **Longevity:** Long-term studies of TM practitioners show they live on average nearly 8 years longer than their non-meditating counterparts, with 30 percent fewer cardiac fatalities and 50 percent fewer deaths from cancer.

- ✔ **Medical-care utilization:** An 11-year study of TM practitioners found they logged 74 percent fewer hospital days, 55 percent fewer outpatient visits, and 63 percent fewer total medical expenses than subjects in a non-meditating control group.

Assessing the limitations of the early research

As promising as early meditation research may have been, it did have some significant limitations. Consider the following:

- ✔ **Many of the early studies failed to use the randomly chosen, control-group methodology that's generally considered the gold standard by the scientific establishment.** Instead, some studies focused on only a handful of select subjects, and others didn't adequately compare meditating subjects to non-meditating controls.

✔ **Some of the research doesn't account for bias.** Just as many studies of new medications are contaminated by the fact that they're funded by big pharmaceutical companies, some of the early TM studies were called into question because they were funded and even conducted by the TM organization itself. This critique was compounded by the fact that TM charges a considerable fee to teach its technique rather than offering it for no or minimal charge, as most other meditative traditions do. (Many, though by no means all, of the TM research results have been replicated in subsequent studies.)

✔ **The early researchers, through no fault of their own, had no access to the more sophisticated technology that's emerged and evolved in recent decades.** As a consequence, most early meditation research focused on measurable behavioral, health, and lifestyle benefits rather than on more long-term neurological changes. Only in recent years have scientists been able to determine how profoundly and permanently meditation actually shapes the brain.

Mapping the Meditative Brain

Not long ago, scientists could get only a limited picture of brain functioning through EEG measures of the frequency and amplitude of the electromagnetic wave patterns generated by the brain. Now they have a growing understanding of which regions of the brain correspond to which neuropsychological functions and an increasingly refined ability to measure activation and even growth in particular areas. Hence, more and more research shows that meditation affects more than just outcomes. It shapes consciousness itself and influences how we experience life in a deep and lasting way.

As so often happens in science, many of these advances occurred as a result of growing technological sophistication. Rather than merely sticking electrodes on meditators' skulls and wiring them to basic EEG machines, scientists can now slide meditators into a functional MRI (fMRI) or a SPECT scanner and receive clear images of where and how the brain is being activated based on oxygen consumption (fMRI) or photon emission (SPECT). I wouldn't want to submit my brain to such intense scrutiny (or my body to one of those draconian devices), but hey, that's what volunteer test subjects are for, right? As a result of these technological advances, researchers can now pinpoint which areas of the brain a particular meditation practice activates. Then they can translate these findings into likely changes in behavior and mood.

The researchers' observations have significance not only for meditators and those who may like to use meditation to help reduce stress or alleviate illness, but they also reveal that the brain is far more malleable than scientists once thought. Indeed, this newly revealed *neuroplasticity* is inspiring efforts to use meditation and other techniques to keep the brain active and growing well into old age.

As the technology continues to evolve, the research will no doubt follow. And maybe one day in the not-too-distant future you will consult your doctor for depression or pain or cognitive decline and receive a prescription for meditation rather than painkillers, antidepressants, or Alzheimer's drugs.

In this section, I take you on a guided tour of the meditative brain, pointing out the regions that are most notably affected by regular meditation practice and explaining some of the changes that occur and how they can impact your life. I start off by looking at the growing importance of mindfulness in the field of meditation research.

Shifting mindfulness to center stage: Jon Kabat-Zinn and MBSR

In the 1980s and 1990s, the focus of meditation research began shifting from TM to mindfulness meditation, due largely to the groundbreaking work of Jon Kabat-Zinn. A long-time Zen meditator as well as a molecular biologist and professor of medicine, Kabat-Zinn founded the pioneering Stress Reduction Clinic at the University of Massachusetts Medical School in 1979 and began teaching a particular blend of present moment awareness and mindful hatha yoga he called mindfulness-based stress reduction, or MBSR.

Over the years, Kabat-Zinn and his colleagues at the clinic have taught thousands of people with a variety of health and stress-related problems. Subsequent studies have found that those who complete the eight-week MBSR program experience a significant reduction in stress, pain, and other symptoms and gain a boost in their immune system function. The clinic has trained more than 700 (and counting) MBSR facilitators, and hundreds of MBSR programs now exist worldwide.

From a research perspective, the good news about MBSR is that it quantifies and standardizes the teaching of mindfulness and strips it of its overtly spiritual components. As a result, scientists have a reliable reference point that allows them to compare and contrast their results. Mindfulness — which is freely available and commonly taught in a number of the world's spiritual traditions — gained additional recognition during this period through the study of the extraordinary meditative abilities of Tibetan monks and a series of dialogues between neuroscientists and the Dalai Lama.

Since the early 2000s, mindfulness research has grown exponentially, and today more studies of mindfulness are published each year than of every other method combined. There's even an online bulletin called *Mindfulness Research Monthly* that chronicles the latest developments.

Passing states or lasting traits?

When subjects are hooked up to devices like electroencephalographs (EEGs), electrocardiograms (EKGs), and blood pressure monitors while they're meditating, the results indicate only what happens to the body during the meditation process itself. In other words, the outcomes measure only states of mind or body that pass after the session has ended. But when subjects are studied over the course of time to determine whether, for example, their blood pressure remains lower between meditation sessions or they report being happier even after they give up meditation entirely, the results indicate the acquisition of traits that remain more or less constant throughout the meditator's life.

Early research focused primarily on states, but subsequent studies of the enduring health benefits of meditation emphasized the development of traits. For example, Transcendental Meditation (TM) studies showing that meditators have lower cortisol and cholesterol levels and generally live longer and use healthcare services less frequently suggest that meditation confers traits that persist between meditation sessions. Likewise, studies that show actual structural changes in the brain, like the growth of gray matter or increased inter-region connectivity, imply that the corresponding changes in cognition, emotion, and behavior last and become traits. Of course, given the extraordinary brain plasticity that researchers have documented, if you stop meditating for an extended period of time and focus your attention in significantly different ways, your brain could change back, and those hard-won traits could disappear!

Creating a working map of the brain

None of the advanced research into the impact of meditation on the brain would have been possible without sophisticated brain mapping and the growing appreciation of how different regions of the brain influence mind, mood, and behavior. Though multiple areas of the brain are generally involved, here are the main regions that seem to be activated by meditation (don't let the anatomical jargon throw you; I keep it simple):

- **Prefrontal cortex:** This is the area of the brain responsible for complex planning, personality expression, decision making, delayed gratification, the moderation of social behavior, and the regulation and inhibition of emotions. As its name implies, the prefrontal cortex lies at the front of the cortex.

- **Anterior cingulate cortex:** Situated around the corpus callosum (the structure that joins the left and right hemispheres of the brain), the anterior cingulate cortex enables you to pay attention — including attention to attention itself — and acts as a bridge or mediator between thoughts and emotions. As a result, it performs a significant function in regulating emotion and the empathic "social brain."

✔ **Amygdala:** A primary component of the limbic system, or emotional brain, this almond-shaped structure plays a major part in the processing and remembering of emotional reactions, particularly fear, and the learning of emotionally based behaviors. The amygdala is largely responsible for the fight-flight-or-freeze response, which meditation helps regulate.

✔ **Hippocampus:** This region plays an important role in the formation of new memories based on experienced events, in the consolidation of short-term memory into long-term memory, and in spatial navigation. Damage to the hippocampus is one of the early causes of Alzheimer's disease.

Pinpointing the location of positive emotions

One of the meditating academics I allude to earlier in this chapter, Richard Davidson, a distinguished professor of psychology and psychiatry at the University of Wisconsin, director of the Waisman Laboratory for Brain Imaging and Behavior, and director of the Laboratory for Affective Neuroscience and the Center for Investigating Healthy Minds, has focused his efforts on tracking positive emotion in the brain and on the ways in which meditation evokes it. In his early research, he discovered that the activation of the left prefrontal cortex (LPFC) closely correlates with the experience of positive emotion — the happier you are, the more your LPFC lights up — apparently because it helps dampen the negative emotions generated by the amygdala. By contrast, right prefrontal cortex (RPFC) activation correlates with negative emotions.

When he studied Tibetan Buddhist monks in the early 2000s, Davidson was amazed at how activated their LPFCs became, and he decided to extend his studies to see whether ordinary people could achieve similar results. His seminal research revealed that subjects who completed an eight-week MBSR program increased their left-sided activation both at rest and in response to emotional stimuli. At the same time, they reported significant reductions in anxiety and other negative emotions, and these reductions continued long after the program ended. The implications? If you want to be happier . . . learn to meditate! (For a detailed discussion of meditation and happiness, see Chapter 16.)

Seeing how meditation changes the brain

Armed with the latest information on how the brain works, researchers have been studying the correlations between meditation, the activation of different parts of the brain, and changes in behavior, cognition, and emotion. The results are far from conclusive — they're more like tantalizing glimpses of a vast new terrain of exploration — but they do point to meditation's enormous potential for furthering human psychological and neurological development by activating, integrating, and coordinating various brain regions. Important new studies appear every year, investigating meditation's impact on the brain. The following sections show just a few of the more fascinating recent developments.

No doubt this field of investigation will continue to grow in the next few decades as devices for measuring the brain become more sophisticated, and the correlation between brain regions and cognitive and behavioral functions grows more precise. If you're curious about the latest discoveries, do an online search for "brain meditation research."

Growing more gray matter and shrinking the amygdala

One of the most exciting things about fMRIs is that they enable scientists to watch the brain change and grow — and grow it does under the influence of meditation! Researchers at Massachusetts General Hospital found that study participants who took the MBSR course and practiced mindfulness meditation for about a half hour a day for only eight weeks actually grew more *gray matter* (the neurological material of the neocortex, or higher brain) in regions associated with attention and memory, stress management, empathy, and emotional integration. By contrast, the amygdala, the seat of stress and anxiety in the brain, shrank in size.

Now, rather than merely having the testimony of meditators who say they feel more loving, more focused, and less stressed out, scientists have measurable proof that the brain grows and changes in ways that correspond with meditators' subjective reports.

Reducing pain activation

Numerous studies have reported that meditators experience less pain than non-meditating controls. Recent fMRI research helps explain why. After just four days of mindfulness meditation training, participants in one study meditating in the presence of noxious stimulation reduced their pain unpleasantness by 57 percent and their pain intensity ratings by 40 percent. When researchers measured their brains, they found reduced activation in regions associated with pain as well as increased activation in the anterior cingulate cortex and other areas involved in regulating and reframing emotional intensity. Not only were the meditators' brains registering less pain, but they were also processing the sensory experience in ways that made it more bearable.

Enhancing brain connectivity and slowing age-related decline

Not only does meditation grow the gray matter in the brain, it strengthens and accelerates the connections between different regions throughout the brain and slows age-related brain atrophy. Using the latest brain-imaging technology, researchers at UCLA found that subjects who meditated had *white matter fibers* (those involved in brain connectivity) that were more numerous, more dense, and more insulated than those who didn't meditate. Researchers also found that these fibers declined far less as the meditating subjects aged. The differences were particularly pronounced in white matter connecting the front and back of the cerebrum as well as the frontal cortex (the area associated with decision making, delayed gratification, and emotional regulation) and the limbic system (the locus of emotion).

These findings provide further evidence that meditation assists in regulating and modulating emotion by helping to integrate the more self-reflective and emotional areas of the brain.

Minimizing the wandering, daydreaming mind

Although daydreaming is sometimes associated with increased creativity, recent studies show that people are significantly less happy when their minds wander than when they're engaged with the task at hand. Not surprisingly, brain research indicates that experienced meditators have decreased activation in an area of the brain called the *default mode network,* which is closely associated with the wandering mind. This decrease continues even when they're not meditating. Even more fascinating is the research finding that when the meditators' default mode is active, the brain regions that govern self-monitoring and cognitive control are active, too. In other words, meditators daydream less, but when they do, they're much more aware of it and come back more readily to present moment awareness and the relative happiness it provides.

Part II
Getting Started

The 5th Wave   By Rich Tennant

"The kids love it when Chuck meditates."

In this part . . .

You have an opportunity to explore for yourself what brings you to meditation — and what you hope to get out of it. Then I lead you (gently) step by step through the process of discovering how to meditate. First, you experiment with turning your mind inward and developing concentration. Then you explore the practice of *mindfulness,* which means paying attention to whatever you're experiencing. And you get to experiment with deliberately cultivating positive emotions like love and compassion. By the end of this part, you know all the little tricks that make meditation easy and fun, from how to sit still and follow your breath and where and when to meditate to what kind of gear you need and how to use it. If you follow the instructions, you'll be a savvy meditator in no time.

Chapter 5

Laying the Foundation: Motivation, Attitude, and Beginner's Mind

- -

- -

As an effective practice for reprogramming your mind and opening your heart, meditation has no parallel. But traditionally, meditation never stands alone. It's always accompanied by an emphasis on motivation and attitude (that is, on the qualities of mind that fuel the fires of meditation and keep you going when the going gets tough).

Some meditation teachers may urge you to take a vow to dedicate your meditation to the well-being of others, rather than hoarding all the goodies for yourself. Others may ask you to consider your deepest aspirations or intentions or attitudes — what one Zen master calls your "inmost request." Whatever the term used to describe it, you need to look deeply into your own mind and heart to clarify the reasons that motivate you to meditate. Then you can consult this motivation when the practice becomes boring and uneventful, which it inevitably does.

My teenage nephew aspires to become a professional baseball player. Despite the odds, he may just make it. He's a 6'5" left-hander with a mean fastball and the work ethic of a winner. Recently, he asked me to teach him how to meditate so he can pitch with more poise and composure. Then there's my thirtysomething cousin with a Harvard MBA, who works at a prestigious East Coast investment firm. When we talked by phone the other day, he wondered whether meditation could help relieve the unremitting stress that comes with his job. A close friend in her fifties who was just diagnosed with breast cancer wants to learn how to meditate in order to deal with her fear and facilitate her healing. And one of my therapy clients asked for meditation instruction to help quiet her mind so she can get a clearer picture of the recurring patterns of thinking and acting that disrupt her life and make her unhappy.

Your end is your beginning

It's one of the great mysteries of meditation that you inevitably end up where you began. Like Simon in the sidebar "Discovering the treasure in your own house" in Chapter 1, you ultimately find that the treasure was hidden under your own hearth all along, and that the path you follow only serves to lead you home again. As T. S. Eliot put it in his poem "Four Quartets," "The end of all our exploring/Will be to arrive where we started/And know the place for the first time."

To clarify this mystery, the Tibetans make a distinction between the *ground,* the *path,* and the *fruition.* The confused, busy, suffering mind, they say, has within it the peace, love, and happiness you seek — the ground, or basis, for awakening. But the clouds of negativity (doubt, judgment, fear, anger, attachment) that obscure this ground — which is who you really are in your heart of hearts — have become so thick and impenetrable that you need to embark on the path of meditation to clear away the clouds and bring you closer to the truth.

When you finally recognize your essential *being* — the moment of fruition — you realize that it has always been right here, where and who you already are, nearer than your own heart and more immediate than your breath. This essential *being* is identical to what the Zen folks call *beginner's mind.*

You may be driven to meditate by pain or suffering or desperation of some kind, or you may simply be dissatisfied with the quality of your life — the level of stress, the lack of enjoyment, the speed and intensity. Whatever your story, you need to be sufficiently motivated if you're ever going to take the trouble to change your routine, slow down, and turn your attention inward for at least 15 or 20 minutes each day. In this chapter, you have an opportunity to face your unique brand of dissatisfaction and cultivate the motivation that keeps you meditating week after week.

Beginning (and Ending) with Beginner's Mind

Ultimately, the great meditation teachers advise that the best attitude to take toward your meditation is an open mind, completely free from all preconceptions and expectations. One of my first meditation teachers, Zen master Shunryu Suzuki, calls this attitude *beginner's mind* and counsels that the goal of meditation is not to accumulate knowledge, learn something new, or achieve some special state of mind, but simply to maintain this fresh, uncluttered perspective.

"If your mind is empty, it is always ready for anything; it is open to everything," Suzuki writes in his book *Zen Mind, Beginner's Mind.* "In the beginner's mind, there are many possibilities; in the expert's mind, there are few." Suzuki teaches that beginner's mind and *Zen mind* — the awake, clear, unfettered mind of the enlightened Zen master — are essentially the same. Or, as another teacher puts it, "The seeker is the sought; the looker is what he or she is looking for!"

Needless to say, it's easier to talk about beginner's mind than it is to maintain or even recognize it. But that's precisely the point. The "don't-know mind" of the beginner can't conceptualize or identify beginner's mind (just as the eye can't see itself, even though it's the source of all seeing). No matter which meditation technique you choose, try to practice it with the innocent, open, "don't-know" spirit of beginner's mind. In a sense, beginner's mind is the *non-attitude* underlying all attitudes, the *non-technique* at the heart of all successful techniques.

Here are the characteristics of beginner's mind:

- **Openness to whatever arises:** When you welcome your experience in meditation without trying to change it, you align yourself with *being* itself, which includes everything — light and dark, good and bad, life and death — without preference.

- **Freedom from expectations:** When you practice beginner's mind, you encounter each moment with fresh eyes and ears. Instead of meditating to achieve some future goal, you sit with the confidence that the open, ready awareness you bring to it ultimately contains all the qualities you seek, such as love, peace, happiness, compassion, wisdom, and equanimity.

- **Spacious and spontaneous mind:** Some teachers liken beginner's mind to the sky: Though the clouds may come and go, the boundless expanse of sky is never damaged or reduced. As for spontaneity, Jesus summed it up when he said, "You must become as little children to enter the kingdom of heaven." Free from expectations and open to whatever arises, you naturally respond to situations in a spontaneous way.

- **Original, primordial awareness:** A famous Zen *koan* (provocative riddle) goes like this: "What was your original face before your parents were born?" This koan points to the ineffable, primordial quality of mind, which predates your personality and even your physical body. Perhaps beginner's mind should really be called *beginningless mind!*

Exploring What Motivates You to Meditate

Most of the time, folks don't talk much about motivation unless it's deficient or missing and needs to be amped up in some way. In your own life, you may be the kind of person who does what comes naturally, or you may do things because they're fun (or exciting or educational or merely interesting). Or perhaps you're the responsible sort who fills her life with obligations and spends her time meeting them.

Whatever your motivational style, you may find, on closer investigation, that the motivation or attitude you bring to an activity has a dramatic impact on your experience of the activity. Take sex, for example. If you do it out of lust or boredom or fear, your sexual pleasure will be permeated by the flavor of the feeling that motivated you. However, if you have sex as a heartfelt expression of love for your partner, you may move in the same way, touch the same places, use the same techniques, but have an exponentially different experience.

Well, meditation is like sex — what you bring to it is what you get! In fact, the meditative traditions suggest that your motivation determines the outcome of your practice as much as the technique you use or the time you spend. In other words, Christian meditators tend to experience God or Christ, Buddhist meditators tend to see emptiness or Buddha nature, and those who seek healing or peace of mind or peak performance tend to get what they came for.

Spiritual traditions often rank attitudes and motivations as higher or lower, and they generally agree that the motivation to help others before helping oneself is the highest. But you have to begin where you are, and being honest with yourself is more important than pretending to have some motivation you don't genuinely hold. The more you meditate, the more you open your heart and reveal your natural, inherent concern for the well-being of others.

The following sections cover the five basic motivational styles. Check them out to get a sense of where you stand. Note that the boundaries between these styles are fuzzy at best, and most people tend to be a blend of a few or even all five.

Empty your cup

Consider the old Zen story about a scholar who visited a famous Zen master to inquire into the meaning of Zen. The scholar asked question after question but was so full of his own ideas that he rarely gave the master an opportunity to answer.

After about an hour of this one-sided dialogue, the master asked the scholar if he wanted a cup of tea. When the scholar held out his cup, the master filled it but just kept on pouring.

"Enough," the scholar cried out. "The cup is full. It won't hold any more."

"Yes," replied the master, "and so is your mind. You can't learn Zen until you empty your cup."

MEDITATION

Reflecting on your life

The great spiritual teachers and meditation masters have always reminded their students of the brevity of life. The medieval Christian mystics kept a skull on their desks to remind them of their own mortality. And Buddhist monks and nuns in some Asian countries still meditate in cemeteries to deepen their awareness of impermanence. Whether it be tomorrow, next year, or many years from now, you and I will eventually die. Remembering this from time to time can help to clarify your life's priorities and remind you of your reasons for meditating.

Of course, if you find it too depressing to think about dying, by all means feel free to skip this exercise. But, if you try it, you may discover that your initial aversion fades as you open your heart to the preciousness of life. Take ten minutes or more to do this guided meditation (which is adapted from the book *A Path with Heart* by Jack Kornfield):

1. **Sit quietly, close your eyes, and take a few deep breaths, relaxing a little with each exhalation.**

2. **Imagine that you're at the end of your life and death is quickly approaching.**

   Be aware of the tentativeness of life — you could die at any moment.

3. **Reflect on your life as you watch it replay before your eyes like a video.**

4. **As you reflect, choose two things you've done that you feel good about now.**

   They may not be important or life-changing; in fact, they may be simple, seemingly insignificant events.

5. **Look deeply at what makes these moments memorable; look at the qualities of mind and heart you brought to them.**

6. **Notice how these memories affect you; examine the feelings and other memories they stir up.**

7. **In light of these memories, consider how you might live differently if you had your life to live again.**

   What activities would you give more time to than you do now? What qualities of *being* would you choose to emphasize? Which people would you give more (or less) of your attention to?

8. **As you end this exercise and go about your day, notice whether your attitude toward your life has changed in any way.**

Improving your life

Imagine for a moment that your life's a mess and you're struggling to get it together, so you take up the practice of meditation. You figure it will teach you the concentration and self-discipline you need to succeed. Or maybe you have a difficult time in relationships, and you want to calm your mind and even out the emotional rollercoaster so you're not constantly in conflict with others.

Looking deeply into your own heart

Sit quietly, take a few deep breaths, and set aside some time to inquire into your own heart and mind for responses to these questions:

✔ What brings me to practice meditation?

✔ What motivates me to meditate?

✔ What do I hope to achieve?

✔ What do I expect to learn?

Set aside the first thoughts that come to mind, look more deeply, and ask the question, "What is the dissatisfaction or suffering that drives me?"

✔ Do I want to reduce stress and calm my mind?

✔ Do I want to be happier and more accepting of myself?

✔ Do I seek answers to the deeper, existential questions like "Who am I?" or "What is the meaning of life?"

Perhaps you're even attuned to the suffering of others and aspire to help them before helping yourself. Or maybe you just want to improve your own life in some way. Whatever responses you get, just write them down without judgment, refer to them as needed to help keep you motivated, and allow them to change and deepen over time.

Perhaps you suffer from some chronic illness and hope that the regular practice of meditation will reduce your stress and improve your health in general. Or maybe you just want to enhance your performance at work or in sports; or learn how to take greater enjoyment from your family, friends, and leisure activities.

Whatever the scenario, your primary concern at this level is to fix or improve yourself and your external circumstances, which is a thoroughly noble intention.

Understanding and accepting yourself

At a certain point in your development, you may get tired of trying to fix yourself (or perhaps you've done such a good job that it's time to move on to the next phase). At this point, you realize that some patterns keep recurring and that struggling to change them just makes them more entrenched, so you decide to shift from "fixing" to self-awareness and self-acceptance. As NBA coach Phil Jackson puts it in his book *Sacred Hoops,* "If we can accept whatever hand we've been dealt, no matter how unwelcome, the way to proceed eventually becomes clear."

I like to compare change to one of those woven Chinese finger puzzles that were popular when I was a kid: The harder you pull, the more stuck you get. But if you move your fingers toward one another — the gesture of self-acceptance — you can free them quite easily. If you're tormented by self-blame, self-doubt, or self-judgment, you may be drawn to meditation as a way of learning to accept and even love yourself.

In my work as a psychotherapist, I've found that mean-spirited self-criticism can wreak havoc in the psyches of otherwise well-balanced people — and the antidote almost inevitably involves self-acceptance, or what the Buddhists call "making friends with yourself." When you practice accepting yourself fully, you soften and open your heart not only to yourself but ultimately to others as well. (For more on self-acceptance, see Chapters 8, 12, and 13.)

Realizing your true nature

Although you recognize the value of improving or making friends with yourself, you may be spurred to meditation by a desire to penetrate the veils that separate you from the true source of all meaning, peace, and love. Nothing less will satisfy you! Perhaps you're obsessed with one of the great spiritual questions, like "Who am I?" "What is God?" or "What is the meaning of life?" Great Zen masters say that such an intense yearning for truth is like a red-hot iron ball lodged in the pit of your stomach. You can't digest it, and you can't spit it out; you can only transform it through the power of your meditation.

Your quest may be motivated by personal suffering, but you're unwilling to stop at self-improvement or self-acceptance and feel compelled to reach the summit of the mountain I describe in Chapter 1 — the experience the great masters call *enlightenment* or *satori*. When you realize who you essentially are, the separate self drops away and reveals your identity with *being* itself. This realization, in turn, can have wide-reaching ramifications including, ironically, a happier and more harmonious life and complete self-love and self-acceptance.

Awakening others

The Tibetan Buddhists teach that all meditators must cultivate the most important motivation of all: to see others as no different from yourself and to put their liberation before your own. Known as *bodhichitta* ("awakened heart"), this selfless aspiration actually accelerates the meditative process by offering you an antidote to the natural human tendency to hoard accomplishments and insights and defend personal psychic and spiritual territory. Unless meditation is bolstered by bodhichitta, say the Tibetans, it can take you only so far along the path to self-realization.

Expressing your innate perfection

In the Zen tradition, the highest motivation for meditating is not to attain some special state of mind but to express your innately pure and undefiled "true nature" — what I refer to earlier as *beginner's mind,* or in Chapter 1 as *pure being.* With this motivation, you never leave your own hearth; instead, you sit with the confidence that you already are the peace and happiness you seek. This level of motivation requires tremendous spiritual maturity, but when you get a glimpse of who you really are, you may find yourself moved to meditate in order to actualize and deepen your understanding.

Living in Harmony with Your Meditation

After you determine what motivates you to meditate, you may benefit from a few guidelines for developing a mind-set and a lifestyle that support your practice. In other words, meditators over the centuries have discovered that how you act, what you think about, and which qualities you cultivate can have an immediate impact on the depth and stability of your meditation.

Every spiritual tradition emphasizes "right" conduct of some kind — and not necessarily on the basis of rigid notions of right and wrong. When your actions don't jibe with your reasons for meditating — for example, when you're meditating to reduce stress but your actions intensify conflict — your everyday life may be working at cross-purposes with the time you spend on your cushion. (The Hebrew word for *sin* originally meant "off the mark.") The more you meditate, the more sensitive you become to how some activities support or even enhance your meditation and others disturb or discourage it.

Of course, a never-ending feedback loop exists between formal meditation and everyday life: How you live affects how you meditate, and how you meditate affects how you live.

With these thoughts in mind, here are ten basic guidelines for living in harmony with the spirit of meditation:

> ✔ **Be mindful of cause and effect.** Notice how your actions — and the feelings and thoughts that accompany them — influence others and your own state of mind. When you flare up in anger or lash out in fear, observe how the ripples can be felt for hours or even days in the responses of others, in your own body, and in your meditation. Do the same with actions that express kindness or compassion. As the Bible says, "As you sow, so shall you reap."

✔ **Reflect on impermanence and the preciousness of life.** Death is real, say the Tibetans; it can come without warning, and this body, too, will one day be food for worms and other earthly creatures. By reflecting on how rare it is to be a human being at a time when physical comforts are relatively plentiful and the practice of meditation and other methods for reducing stress and relieving suffering are so readily available, you may feel more motivated to take advantage of the opportunities you have.

✔ **Realize the limitations of worldly success.** Check out the people you know who have achieved the worldly success you aspire to. Are they really any happier than you are? Do they have more love in their lives or more peace of mind? Through meditation, you can achieve a level of inner success that's based on joy and tranquility rather than material gain.

✔ **Practice nonattachment.** This classic Buddhist counsel may seem on first blush like an impossible task. But the point here is not to be indifferent or to disengage from the world, but to notice how attachment to the outcome of your actions affects your meditations and peace of mind. What would it be like to act wholeheartedly, with the best of intentions, and then let go of your struggle to get things to be a certain way?

✔ **Cultivate patience and perseverance.** If nothing else, the practice of meditation requires the willingness to keep on keeping on. Whatever you call it — discipline, diligence, perseverance, or just plain stick-to-itiveness — you'll reap the greatest benefits if you meditate regularly day after day. Besides, the qualities of patience and perseverance translate nicely to every area of life. (For more on effort and self-discipline, see Chapter 10.)

✔ **Simplify your life.** The busier and more complicated your life, the more agitated your mind is likely to be when you meditate — and the greater your stress level will be as well. Pay particular attention to all those extra activities you tack on to an already crammed schedule (perhaps to avoid taking a deep breath, hearing your heartbeat, facing your fears, and dealing with other unpleasant feelings like loneliness, emptiness, grief, or inadequacy). If you stop running and listen closely, you may hear the voice of your own inner wisdom.

✔ **Live with honesty and integrity:** When you lie, manipulate, and compromise your core values, you may be able to hide from yourself for a time — but only until you reach your meditation cushion. Then the proverbial you-know-what hits the fan, and every peccadillo comes back to haunt you. Meditation mirrors you back to you, and what you see may motivate you to actualize more of your positive potential.

✔ **Face situations with the courage of a warrior.** Unlike their battlefield counterparts, meditation "warriors" cultivate the courage to drop their aggression and defensiveness, face their fears, and open their hearts to themselves and others. Easier said than done, you may say, but meditation teaches you how — and then you need to be willing to follow through in real-life situations. Ultimately, every moment becomes an opportunity to practice. (For more on how to meditate in every moment of life, see Chapter 17.)

✔ **Trust the technology of meditation.** It helps to remember that people have been meditating successfully for thousands of years — far longer than they've been using, say, laptops or the Internet. Besides, I'm talking low-tech technology here, including things anyone can do, such as breathing and paying attention. Just trust the technology, follow the instructions, and let go of the results.

✔ **Dedicate your practice to the benefit of others.** As I mention earlier, the Tibetans call this dedication *bodhichitta* ("awakened heart") and regard it as essential for meditation that's life-changing rather than merely cosmetic. Studies of the impact of prayer on healing, cited in *Healing Words: The Power of Prayer and the Practice of Medicine* by Larry Dossey, M.D., have shown that prayers that request specific results aren't nearly as effective as those that ask for the best for all concerned. In other words, the love you take is equal to the love you make!

Looking for the last time

Imagine that you will never see your friends or your loved ones again and then follow these steps:

1. **Sit quietly, take a few deep breaths, and close your eyes.**

2. **Let the usual thoughts, feelings, and preoccupations that surround you disperse like fog on a sunny morning.**

3. **Look at the objects and people in your field of vision as though for the last time.**

How do they appear to you? How do you feel? What thoughts go through your mind?

4. **Consider the beauty and preciousness of this moment, which is the only one you have.**

5. **Reflect on the recognition that every moment is like this one.**

6. **As you finish this meditation, let whatever insights you've gained continue to suffuse your experience.**

Chapter 6

How Your Mind Stresses You Out and What You Can Do about It

....

In This Chapter

▶ Scuba-diving through your thoughts and feelings

▶ Checking out the many ways your mind causes stress

▶ Using mediation to ease your stress and suffering

....

*F*or thousands of years, pundits and sages in both the East and West have been saying that problems originate in the mind. So you won't be surprised if I join the chorus of voices and agree. Yes, they're right: Your mind by itself "can make a heaven of hell and a hell of heaven" (as English poet John Milton put it). But how, you may be wondering, can this cute little truism help you when you don't know what to do about it? "Sure, my mind's the problem," you may say, "but I can't exactly have it surgically removed."

You can begin by becoming familiar with how your mind works. As you may have noticed, it's a rather complex assortment of thoughts, ideas, stories, impulses, preferences, and emotions. Without a diagram, it can be as difficult to negotiate as the jumble of wires and hoses under the hood of your car.

When you have a working knowledge of how your mind is structured, you can begin to notice how those thoughts and feelings distort your experience and keep you from achieving the happiness, relaxation, effectiveness, or healing you seek. Then you can discover how meditation can teach you to change all that by focusing and calming your mind, and ultimately by delving more deeply and unraveling the habitual stories and patterns that keep causing you suffering and stress. Who knows? You may not need a lobotomy after all!

Is it higher or deeper?

Spiritual teachers and personal growth advocates have a dizzying fondness for up and down metaphors. Some talk about digging down into your inner experience like a miner, or having profound insights, or feeling or knowing things deeply. Others talk about higher consciousness or transcending the mundane or having a mind like the sky. (I make the best of both worlds by using the two directions more or less interchangeably.)

To some degree, the difference lies in the personal preferences of the particular writer or teacher. But it can also refer to an attitude toward inner experience: If you believe that the wellspring of *being* lies deep inside you, beneath the personal, then you talk about *down*. If you believe that it exists in the upper echelons of your being or comes down like grace or spirit from above, then you talk about *up*.

In my humble opinion, if you dive deep enough, you find yourself at the top of the mountain. And if you rise high enough, you find yourself at the bottom of the sea. In the end, it's the same place anyway. Ultimately, pure *being* has no location — it's everywhere in everyone all the time.

Taking a Tour of Your Inner Terrain

Because I'm an avid hiker and swimmer, I'm fond of using natural metaphors, which actually lend themselves quite nicely to describing meditation. In Chapter 1, I compare practicing meditation to climbing a mountain. Here I turn that metaphor on its head, so to speak, and have you imagine that the journey you're taking is down to the bottom of a lake. (If you want to picture yourself in a wetsuit and scuba gear, go right ahead.) In fact, the lake I'm referring to is *you* — you're journeying to the depths of your own *being*.

Sifting through the layers of inner experience

When you meditate, in addition to developing your concentration and calming your mind, you may find yourself delving deeper into your inner experience and uncovering layers you didn't even know existed. What do you suppose lies at the bottom? The great meditative traditions have different names for it: essence, pure being, true nature, spirit, soul, the pearl of great price, and the source of all wisdom and love. The Zen folks call it your original face before your parents were born. You may like to picture it as a spring that gushes forth the pure, refreshing, deeply satisfying water of *being* without reservation. (For more on this spring, see Chapter 1, where it awaits the climber at the top of the mountain of meditation.)

This wellspring of *being* is who you really are in your heart of hearts before you became conditioned to believe that you're somehow deficient or inadequate, as so many folks do. It's your wholeness and completeness before you began to feel separate or lonely or fragmented. It's the deep intuition of being inextricably connected with something larger than yourself and with every other being and thing. And it's ultimately the source of all peace, happiness, joy, and other positive, life-affirming feelings (even though you may think they're caused by outside circumstances). Of course, people experience this source differently, which explains why there are so many words to describe it.

Connecting in some way with this source or spring of pure being is actually the point of meditation, whether you're aspiring to become enlightened or just trying to reduce stress, enhance your performance, or improve your life. And meditation definitely takes you to this source, as I explain later in this chapter. But when you meditate, you also begin to encounter material that seems to come between you and the experience of being, just as you may encounter layers of sediment, algae, fish, and debris on your way to the bottom of a lake. These layers don't pose a problem unless the inner water is turbulent, in which case they can make it difficult to see clearly. (By *turbulence,* I mean a busy, agitated mind or a troubled, frightened, defended heart.)

In more or less the order in which you may encounter them in meditation, I cover these layers in the following sections.

Mind chatter

When you turn your attention inward, the first thing you're likely to encounter is the ceaseless chattering of your mind. The Buddhists like to compare the mind to a noisy monkey that swings uncontrollably from thought-branch to thought-branch without ever settling down.

Most of the time, you may be so caught up in this chatter that you're not even aware it's happening. It may take the form of reliving the past or rehearsing for the future or trying to solve some problem in the present. Whatever the content, your mind is constantly talking to itself, often spinning a story with you as the hero or the victim. (Research indicates that a very small percentage of people experience no inner dialogue at all, but have only images or feelings instead.)

Intense or recurring emotions

Just as an action film or a romantic comedy takes you on a rollercoaster ride of emotions, so the *dramas* your mind keeps spinning out evoke their own play of feelings. If you're trying to figure out how to make a killing in the stock market, for example, or ask out that attractive man or woman you just met at work, you may feel fear or anxiety, or possibly excitement or lust. If you're obsessing about the injustices or unkindnesses you suffered recently, you may experience sadness, grief, outrage, or resentment. Together with these emotions, of course, go a range of bodily sensations, including tension, arousal, contraction in the heart, or waves of energy in the belly or the back of the head.

Some of these feelings may be pleasurable; others are unpleasant or even painful. But emotions in themselves don't pose a problem. It's just that as long as you keep reacting to the dramas inside your head, you may be cutting yourself off from others and from deeper, more satisfying dimensions of your being. You may miss what's really going on around you as well. (For more on working with emotions in meditation, see Chapter 12.)

Grasping and pushing away

At a somewhat subtler level of experience than thoughts and emotions lurks a perpetual play of like and dislike, attachment and aversion. The Buddhists teach that the key to happiness and contentment lies in wanting what you have and not wanting what you don't have. (For more on happiness, see Chapter 16.) But often, we're somehow dissatisfied with what we have. We yearn for what we don't have and we struggle to get it. Or we may become deeply attached to what we have and then suffer when time and circumstances change it or take it away. Because change is unavoidable, this tendency to either hold on tight to experience or push it away can cause constant suffering.

Negative beliefs and life scripts

Here's another nature metaphor for you: Imagine that your thoughts and emotions and even the dramas that keep running through your brain form the leaves and branches of some inner, subterranean bush or tree. (Think wild and uncontrollable here, like blackberries or bamboo.) What do you suppose constitutes the root from which the leaves and branches relentlessly spring?

Well, you may be surprised to discover that the root is a cluster of beliefs and stories, many of them negative, that have formed as the result of what people — especially people who are significant in your life, like loved ones and friends — have done to you and told you over the years. These beliefs and stories have intertwined over your lifetime into a kind of life script that defines who you think you are and how you view the people and circumstances around you. (I say "surprised" because most people are clueless when it comes to life scripts. Although you may have noticed some resemblance between your life and, say, *Survivor, Days of our Lives,* or *The Simpsons.*)

The point is this: Your tendency to identify with your life script actually limits your range of possibilities and causes you suffering by acting as a *filter* through which you interpret your life in negative ways. To return to the bush metaphor, you can keep pruning back the branches, but you'll keep living out the same old story until you pull it up by the roots.

TIP

How to tell the difference between thoughts and feelings

In my work as a psychotherapist, I've found that many people have trouble distinguishing between thoughts and feelings. For example, if I ask "What are you feeling?" they may reply, "I feel like I shouldn't be so open with my partner anymore." Even though this insight begins with the right word, it's actually a judgment rather than a feeling.

Here are a few pointers for telling the difference:

✔ **Feelings occur as a set of recognizable sensations in your body.** When you're angry, for example, you may feel tension in your shoulders and jaw and experience a rush of energy in the back of your head. When you're sad, by contrast, you may feel a heaviness in your chest and heart and a congested feeling in your sinuses and throat. Through meditation, you can discover how to experience your feelings directly as sensations, separate from the thoughts and stories that perpetuate them. (For more on meditating with thoughts and feelings, see Chapter 12.)

✔ **Thoughts are the images, memories, beliefs, judgments, and reflections that float through your mind and often give rise to your feelings.** If you follow the word *feel* with the word *like*, you're probably voicing a thought or a belief, rather than a feeling. You can practice breaking strong feelings down into their component parts by asking: What are the thoughts and images in my mind that keep me feeling the way I do? And what am I actually experiencing in my body right now, aside from my thoughts?

Thoughts not only generate feelings but they also often masquerade as feelings (so you won't actually feel the ones you have), attempt to talk you out of your feelings, judge your feelings, or suppress them entirely. The more you can disentangle your thoughts and feelings, the more clearly and consciously you can relate with (and express) your inner experience.

The sense of separation

Even deeper than your stories — some would say the soil in which the stories grow — lies a feeling of being cut off or separate from life or being itself. Although the meditative traditions teach that separation is actually an illusion and that everyone is inextricably connected to one another, the sense of being separate runs deep. Often it dates back to early childhood experiences, such as when you were forced by circumstances to separate prematurely from your mother or some other nurturing figure. Sometimes it can be traced to the birth trauma itself, such as when you had to exchange your placental paradise for a colder, harsher reality. Or maybe, as some traditions contend, it comes packaged with the embryonic hardware.

Becoming aware of your inner dialogue

Begin this meditation by paying attention to your thoughts. After several minutes, notice what the voices inside your head are telling you. (If you're not aware of any voices, you may want to observe feelings or images instead.) Does one voice predominate, or do several voices vie for your attention? Do they criticize or encourage you? Shame or praise you? Or do they focus primarily on the other people in your life? Do any of the voices argue with one another?

What kind of emotional tone do these voices have? Are they loving and gentle or angry and impatient? Does one voice sound more like you than the others? Do any of them remind you of people in your life — past or present? How do these voices make you feel?

Allow ten minutes for this exercise initially. When you have the knack of it, you can stop from time to time during the day and pay attention to your inner dialogue. The important point is that you're not your thoughts — and you don't necessarily have to believe the messages they impart. (See the sidebar in this chapter, "You are not your thoughts and feelings.")

Whatever its origins, this feeling of separation may give rise to a kind of primordial fear: If I'm separate, then I must end at my skin, and everything out there must be *other*. Because these others are often bigger than I am, and I have only the most limited control over their actions, my survival must be at stake, so I need to protect myself at all costs.

Life scripts, which are discussed in the preceding section, evolve as strategies for surviving in a world of apparent separation, in which others are perceived as potentially unfriendly, withholding, demanding, or rejecting.

Discovering how turbulence clouds your mind and heart

Needless to say, when you're experiencing inner turbulence, you may find it difficult to connect with *being* when you sit down to meditate. Sometimes, of course, you may have moments when your mind just settles by itself and you can see all the way down to the bottom of the lake. (To use another nature metaphor, think of those overcast days when the cloud cover suddenly parts and the sun shines through with all its warmth and radiance.) These moments may be marked by feelings of inner peace and tranquility, upsurges of love and joy, or intimations of your oneness with life. But most of the time, you may feel like you're doing a breaststroke through muddy water.

The turbulence and confusion you encounter when you meditate doesn't suddenly materialize on cue. It's there all along, clouding your mind and heart and acting as a filter that obscures your clear seeing. You may experience it as an inner claustrophobia or density. In other words, you're so full of your own emotions and opinions that you have no room for the ideas and feelings of others or even for any new or unfamiliar ideas and feelings that may well up inside you. Or you may get so caught up in your drama that you're not even aware that you're filtering your experience.

For example, I have a friend, a computer programmer, who received plenty of love and support as a child. Now, as an adult, he thinks of himself as inherently competent and worthy, even though he's no Steve Jobs. As a result, he enjoys his career, experiences only minimal anxiety when he makes work-related decisions, sees others as inherently supportive, and exudes a palpable self-confidence that draws others to him and invites them to trust him.

By contrast, I have another friend, an independent entrepreneur, who has several advanced degrees and has taken countless work-related training courses, but who believes deep down that he's inherently unworthy. No matter how hard he works, he can't seem to get ahead. Besides, he doesn't really enjoy his work because he's constantly anxious that he may fail, and he imagines that others are conspiring to undermine or discredit him.

You are not your thoughts or feelings

Find a quiet spot where you can sit for the next ten minutes. When you're comfortably settled, do the following:

1. **Take a few slow, deep breaths.**

2. **Turn your attention to your thoughts. (If you tend to be an emotional person, you can do the same exercise with your emotions.)**

   Instead of getting caught up in your thoughts (or emotions) as you might usually do, watch them closely, the way an angler watches the tip of a rod or a tennis player watches a ball. If you find your attention wandering, come back to the task at hand.

   At first, your mind may seem like wall-to-wall thoughts or emotions, and you may have difficulty determining where one thought leaves off and the next one begins. You may also find that certain thoughts or emotions keep recurring like popular tunes (for example,

repetitive worries or favorite images or fantasies). If you're especially attentive, you may begin to notice that each thought or emotion has a beginning, a middle, and an end.

3. **At the end of the ten minutes, stop and reflect on your experience.**

   Did you experience some distance from your thoughts or emotions? Or did you keep losing yourself in the thinking or feeling process?

The point of this exercise is not to see how well you can track your thinking or feeling; instead, the point is to give you the experience of being the observer of your thoughts. Believe it or not, you're the thinker, *not* the thoughts themselves! As you begin to gain some perspective on your thoughts through the practice of meditation, you may find that your thoughts start losing the power they once had over you. You can have your thoughts, but they won't have you.

Thinking and feeling with a meditator's mind

In case you're worrying that meditation may stop you from thinking and feeling, in this sidebar I provide a few helpful distinctions I picked up from one of my teachers, Jean Klein, author of *Who Am I?* and *The Ease of Being.*

Jean likes to distinguish between ordinary thought and creative thought, functional thought and psychological memory, and emotivity and emotion. (Although he teaches a direct approach to spiritual truth through self-inquiry rather than meditation, I've taken the liberty of applying his insights because I believe they're also relevant to the practice of meditation.)

✔ **Ordinary thought versus creative thought:** When your mind keeps churning out an endless series of thoughts linked together like boxcars on a train, with no spaces between them, you're trapped by your own claustrophobic thinking process and don't have any room for fresh, original thinking or problem solving. But when your mind is completely open and *unfurnished,* as Jean likes to say — a state of mind you can cultivate in meditation — you have plenty of inner space for creative thoughts to bubble up from their source in pure being. Unlike

ordinary thoughts, these thoughts are completely appropriate to the situation at hand.

✔ **Psychological memory versus functional thinking:** The more you meditate, the more you free your mind of *psychological memory,* which is the turbulent, obsessive, self-centered kind of thinking that's generated by your stories and centers on the separate, fragmented person you imagine yourself to be. Instead, your thoughts become primarily functional, arising in response to circumstances and then stopping when they're no longer required.

✔ **Emotivity versus emotion:** The powerful, disturbing emotions that sometimes seem to run your life — which Jean Klein calls *emotivity* — are actually rooted in your stories, not in reality, and they have little in common with true emotion. Subtler than emotivity and rooted in love, *true emotion* arises naturally from *being* itself in response to situations where the illusory sense of separation has been diminished or dissolved through the practice of meditation (or some other spiritual practice like self-inquiry).

In each case, the way my friend views himself and interprets what's going on around him determines whether he's happy or stressed out.

As these examples indicate, it's the inner turbulence and confusion through which you filter and distort your experiences — not the experiences themselves — that cause most of your suffering and stress. The good news is that meditation can teach you how to calm the troubled waters of your mind and heart, turn some of your inner claustrophobia into inner spaciousness, and find your way past your filters (or avoid them altogether) so you can experience life more directly — and reduce your stress in the process.

The Bad News: How Your Mind Stresses You Out

Recently a friend of mine in her mid-30s decided to ask for a raise. Even though she'd worked with the company as a graphic designer for years and was long overdue for a pay increase, she was overcome with self-doubt. Every day as she drove to work, she agonized and obsessed as conflicting voices and feelings battled it out inside her.

In particular, she kept rehearsing her upcoming conversation with her boss and reviewing all the things she'd done to make her worthy of more money. She ran through all the projects she'd completed as well as the successful ads and brochures she'd designed. Sometimes she emerged from these imaginary conversations feeling triumphant; other times she emerged crestfallen and defeated. As she listened to all this mind chatter, her feelings fluctuated wildly, from excited and confident to afraid and uncertain.

At times, she heard a barely audible voice (sounding suspiciously like her father's) arguing that given her overall ineptitude, she didn't deserve a raise and that she was lucky to have a job at all. In response, she felt ashamed and hopeless. Next, an angry, vindictive voice stepped in, arguing that her boss was an ungrateful autocrat and that she should barge into his office and put him in his place. Then a confident, affirmative voice reminded her how much she contributed at work and what a fine person she was overall. Finally, a voice that sounded a lot like her mother's counseled her to stay calm and unruffled and be thankful for whatever crumbs life sent her way.

After nearly a week of intense inner struggle and stress, during which she had difficulty sleeping and could barely function at work, my friend finally made an appointment with her boss. Filled with conflicting emotions, she entered his office. She was immediately offered a raise even larger than the one she had planned to request! As it turned out, all the images, emotions, and ideas her mind and body had churned out over the days leading up to the meeting had no connection with what ultimately happened.

Does any of this sound familiar? Like my friend — indeed, like just about everyone I know, including me! — you may spend much of your time engrossed in the captivating but ultimately illusory scenarios fabricated in the original "fantasy factory" (the one that predates Disney and Pixar), the *neocortex*.

One moment you may be worrying about the future — how am I going to make enough money, orchestrate a great vacation, impress my lover, amuse my kids? — and subsequently lost in a reverie filled with hope and fear. The next moment, you may be obsessed with the past — why didn't I tell the truth, take that job, accept that proposal? — and you're overcome with regret and self-recrimination.

Hearts and minds

When I talk about how the "mind" causes suffering and stress, I use the term generically to include emotions as well as thoughts because the two are inseparable. Certain Eastern languages, such as Chinese and Sanskrit, even use the same word to refer to both mind and heart, and many Eastern sages teach that the mind actually resides in the heart center.

When you have a thought about potentially charged situations — such as relationships, work, financial problems, or life transitions — you almost invariably have an emotional response (subliminal though it may be). In fact, the field of mind-body medicine has corroborated the view that the mind and body can't really be separated. Thoughts give rise to chemical changes in the blood that affect metabolism and immunity, and alterations in blood chemistry, through drugs or environmental toxins or stressors, can change how you think and feel.

Similarly, the stories that run your life consist of complex layers of emotions, beliefs, and physical contraction that can't easily be teased apart. Through the practice of meditation, you can begin to peel back these layers, infuse them with awareness, and gain insight into the patterns that hold them together.

And like my friend, you may have noticed, much to your chagrin, that you have remarkably little control over the worrying, fantasizing, and obsessing your mind generates. Instead of having thoughts and feelings, it may often seem that the thoughts and feelings are having you!

The reason these thoughts and feelings seem uncontrollable is that they spring from a deeper story or life script that may be largely unconscious. For example, you may hold the subliminal notion that nothing you do is quite good enough, so you push yourself anxiously to make up for your shortcomings. Or, quite the contrary, you may believe that you deserve more than you're getting, so you're unhappy with what you have. Perhaps you believe that you're inherently unattractive, so no matter how much you compensate, you feel embarrassed and uncomfortable around the opposite sex. Or maybe you see intimate relationships as inherently threatening, so you do all you can to avoid being vulnerable.

Your inner story or drama has a powerful momentum that carries you along, whether you're aware of it or not. Sometimes it may seem like a tragedy, complete with villains and victims. At other times, it may seem more like a comedy, a romance, a fantasy, or a boring documentary. The point is, you're the center around which this drama revolves, and you're often so enthralled by the scenery that you can't really see what's going on outside in the real world around you.

As a result, you may be constantly acting and reacting excessively and inappropriately, based not on the actual circumstances but on the distorted pictures inside your brain. (If you're like me, you've no doubt had moments when you suddenly woke up, as though from a dream, and realized that you had no idea what the person you were interacting with really meant or felt.) Besides, you risk missing entirely the beauty and immediacy of the present moment as it unfolds.

As I mention earlier, it's this inner drama, not the experiences themselves, that causes most of your suffering and stress. Not that life doesn't serve up shares of difficult times and painful situations for everyone, including the homeless in American cities and the starving children in Africa. But the mind often adds an extra layer of unnecessary suffering to the undeniable hardships of life by interpreting experience in negative or limited ways. (See the sidebar in this chapter, "Distinguishing between suffering, pain, and stress.") The following sections highlight some of the major ways your mind stresses you out.

Preoccupation with past and future

Like most minds, yours may flit from past to future and back again, and it may only occasionally come to rest in the present. When you're preoccupied with what may happen next month or next year, you churn up a range of stressful emotions based on hope, fear, and anticipation that have nothing to do with what's happening right now. And when you're reliving the past — which after all has no existence except as thoughts and images inside your brain — you may bounce from regret to resentment to sadness and grief.

By contrast, when you meditate, you practice bringing your mind back again and again to the present moment, where, as the Persian poet Rumi says, "the only news is that there's no news at all." By returning to the simplicity of the here and now, you can take refuge from the stressful scenarios of your mind. (See the section "Returning to the present moment," later in this chapter.)

Resistance to the way things are

Most people struggle unhappily to get what they believe they need in order to be happy while at the same time ignoring or actively disliking what they already have. Now, don't get me wrong; I'm not suggesting that you just sit back passively and do nothing to improve your life. But as one of my teachers used to say, the secret to improving your life is first to accept things just the way they are, which is precisely what the practice of meditation can teach. In particular, resistance to the way things are usually comes in one of two flavors: resistance to change and resistance to pain.

Resistance to change

Like it or not, constant change is unavoidable. If you try to resist the current of change by holding on to some image of how things are supposed to be, you're going to suffer because you can't possibly get life to hold still and conform. As the Greek philosopher Heraclitus used to say, "You can't step into the same river twice."

Through meditation, you can discover how to flow with the current of change by developing an open, flexible, accepting mind. In fact, meditation provides the perfect laboratory for studying change because you get to sit quietly and notice the thoughts and feelings and sensations coming and going. Or you can stiffen up and resist and make the process more painful. Did you ever notice how some people become more crotchety and depressed as they age, while others age gracefully and with a joyful twinkle in their eyes? The difference lies in their ability to adapt to the challenging changes life brings their way.

Resistance to pain

Like change, pain is inevitable. So, too, is pleasure. In fact, you can't have one without the other, though most people would love to have it some other way. When you tighten your belly and hold your breath against the onslaught of pain, be it emotional or physical, you actually intensify the pain. And when you affix a story to the pain — for example, "This shouldn't be happening to me" or "I must have done something to deserve this" — you just Velcro an extra layer of suffering on top of the pain, which causes your body to tighten and resist even more and only serves to perpetuate the pain rather than relieve it.

Through meditation, you can learn to breathe deeply, soften your belly, cut through your story, and relax around your pain. (To discover how to soften your belly, see Chapter 11.) Often, the pain naturally lets go and releases — and even when it doesn't, it generally becomes much easier to bear.

A judging and comparing mind

The tendency of your mind to compare you to others (or to some impossible ideal) and to judge every little thing you do as imperfect or inadequate just keeps you anxious, frustrated, and upset. Generally, this tendency originates in your stories or life script, a deeply held cluster of often negative beliefs. (See the "Negative beliefs and life scripts" section earlier in this chapter.) After all, if you believe that you're lovable and inherently perfect just the way you are, your mind has nothing to compare you with.

When you practice meditation, you can develop the capacity to observe the judgments and comparisons of your mind without identifying with them or mistaking them for truth. (For more on this capacity, see the "Penetrating your experience with insight" section later in this chapter.)

Distinguishing suffering, pain, and stress

Suffering, pain, and stress? Yikes! Who wants to burden their brains with such unappetizing topics? However, the clearer you are about suffering, pain, and stress, the more easily you can minimize their impact on your life. Consider the following helpful (and admittedly unofficial) distinctions:

✔ *Pain* **consists of direct, visceral experiences with a minimum of conceptual overlays.** Your best friend says something mean to you, and you feel a painful constriction in your heart. You hit your thumb with a hammer, and it aches and throbs. You get the flu, and your head feels like someone's squeezing it in a vice. Pain hurts, pure and simple.

✔ *Suffering* **is what happens when your mind makes hay with your pain.** For example, you decide that because she hurt your feelings, your best friend must secretly hate you, which means something must be terribly wrong with you. And the next thing you know, you're feeling depressed as well as hurt. Or you turn your headache into a sure warning sign of some serious illness, which just heaps a big dose of fear and hopelessness onto an already difficult situation.

Suffering, in other words, results from seeing situations through the distorting lens of the story your mind tells you.

✔ **The *stress response* is a physiological mechanism for adapting to challenging physical or psychological circumstances.** Certain physical stressors, such as extraordinary heat or cold, an extremely loud noise, or a violent attack, are stressful no matter how your mind interprets them. But the stressful effect of most stressors depends on the spin your mind adds to the situation. For example, driving to work in heavy traffic, sitting at your desk for eight hours handling paperwork and phone calls, and then driving home may be only mildly stressful on a purely physical level. But when you're afraid of arriving late, have a conflicted relationship with your boss, feel angry at several of your clients or co-workers, and are still mulling over the argument you had with your spouse or best friend yesterday, it's no wonder you crawl home at the end of the day completely exhausted. Just as your mind can transform pain into suffering, so it can parlay ordinary stressors into extraordinary stress.

Learned helplessness and pessimism

As numerous psychological studies suggest, your ability to deal with stressful situations largely depends on whether you believe you have the resources necessary to cope. That's right. The *belief* that you have what it takes is perhaps your greatest resource. If your story keeps telling you that you're inadequate, it's just making stressful situations more stressful.

Meditation can teach you coping skills like focusing and calming your mind; returning to the present moment; and cultivating positive emotions and mindstates that help you avoid negative, distracting thoughts and empower you to deal with difficult circumstances and people. (See the section "The Good News: How Meditation Relieves Stress" later in this chapter.) Ultimately, you can discover how to see beyond your story and make direct contact with the true source of optimism and joy, the wellspring of pure *being* inside you.

Overwhelming emotions

Although you can't necessarily identify your story, you may be painfully aware of how powerful emotions like anger, fear, longing, grief, jealousy, and desire cloud your mind, torment your heart, and cause you to act in ways you later regret.

Initially, meditation doesn't eliminate these emotions, but it does teach you how to focus and calm your mind and prevent the emotions from distracting you. If you want, you can then use meditation to observe these emotions as they arise without avoiding or suppressing them. Over time, you can develop penetrating insight into the nature of these emotions and their connection to the underlying stories that keep generating them. Ultimately, you can investigate these stories and even dismantle them entirely. (For more on meditating with challenging emotions, see Chapter 12.)

Fixation of attention

The tendency of the thinking mind to obsess or fixate on certain thoughts and emotions causes the body to contract in response. Have you ever noticed how tense and anxious you can get when you mentally rehearse the same scenario again and again, even when it's an ostensibly positive one? By contrast, an alert, open, fluid mind — which you can develop through the regular practice of mindfulness meditation (see Chapter 7) — allows you to flow from experience to experience without getting fixated or stuck. Ultimately, you can practice *receptive awareness* (see Chapter 1), the spacious, skylike quality of mind that welcomes whatever arises.

Clinging to a separate self

The great meditative traditions teach that the root cause of suffering and stress, which gives rise to your stories, is the belief that you're inherently separate from others, from the rest of life, and from *being* itself. Because you feel separate and alone, you need to protect yourself and ensure your survival at all costs. But you have only limited power, and you're surrounded by forces beyond your control. As long as you keep struggling to defend your turf, you're going to keep suffering no matter how hard you try. Meditation offers you the opportunity to relax your guard, open your awareness, and ultimately catch a glimpse of who you really are, beyond your stories and the illusion of a separate, isolated self.

The Good News: How Meditation Relieves Suffering and Stress

Now for the good news! In case you found all the talk earlier in this chapter depressing, let me reassure you: Your story or drama may masquerade as who you really are, but it's not. Your essential being remains pure and unharmed, no matter how elaborate and compelling your story becomes. Besides, as stubborn and intractable as they may seem, your mind and heart are actually malleable. Through the regular practice of meditation, you can reduce your suffering and stress by stilling and ultimately dissipating the turbulence and confusion inside you. As one ancient Zen master put it, "If your mind isn't clouded by unnecessary things, this moment is the best moment of your life."

To begin with, you can develop the skill of *focusing and concentrating* your mind, which calms it and prevents it from becoming agitated. As your concentration deepens, thoughts and feelings that have been building up inside naturally bubble up and evaporate — a process I like to call *spontaneous release.*

When you've developed strong concentration, you can expand your awareness to include thoughts, feelings, and the deeper patterns and stories that underlie them. Then, through the power of *penetrating insight,* you can explore the various layers of inner experience, get to know how they function, and ultimately use this understanding to dismantle the patterns that keep causing you stress.

Developing focus and concentration

So your mind chatters constantly, swirling you up and stressing you out, and you're wondering what you can do to quiet it down. Well, you can begin by practicing a meditation technique that emphasizes concentration, such as following or counting your breaths (see Chapter 7) or reciting a mantra (see Chapter 3). When you get the knack, you can keep shifting from your inner dialogue to the present moment, wherever you happen to be. And if you're so inclined, you can develop positive qualities that counteract some of the negative tendencies of your mind and heart.

Stabilizing your concentration

If you've ever tried to quiet your mind by preventing it from thinking, you know how hopeless that can be. (See the sidebar in this chapter, "Stopping your mind.") But the more you invest your mental energy in a single focus during meditation, the more one-pointed your mind becomes, and the more the distractions recede to the background. Eventually, you can develop the ability to stabilize your concentration on a single focus for minutes at a time, gently returning when your mind wanders off.

With increased one-pointedness comes an experience of inner harmony and stillness, as the sediment in the turbulent lake of your mind gradually settles, leaving the water clean and clear. This experience is generally accompanied by feelings of calm and relaxation and occasionally by other pleasurable feelings like love, joy, happiness, and bliss (which incidentally originate at the bottom of the lake in pure *being*).

At deeper levels of concentration, you may experience total absorption in the object — a state known as *samadhi*. When this power of focused concentration is directed like a laser beam to everyday activities, you can enter what psychologist Mihaly Csikszentmihalyi calls *flow* — a state of supreme enjoyment in which time stops, self-consciousness drops away, and you become one with the activity itself.

Returning to the present moment

When you've begun to develop your concentration, you can use it to keep shifting in everyday life away from your inner drama and back to the present moment. You may not eliminate the turbulence, but you can keep seeing beyond it. It's kind of like taking off your sunglasses and looking at things directly or like opening your eyes wide when you start falling asleep. The more you look past the drama, the more you see the freshness of *being* itself reflected in what you see. Returning to the present moment again and again forges a trail that allows you to do an end run around your drama and strengthens your direct connection with life. (For more on returning to the present moment, see Chapters 7 and 16.)

Cultivating positive emotions and mind-states

You can use the concentration you develop in meditation to cultivate positive alternatives to agitation, fear, anger, depression, and the other powerful emotions that arise when you're involved in your story. (In fact, the practice of cultivation itself can develop your powers of concentration.) These positive mind-states include lovingkindness, compassion, equanimity, and joy. (For more on cultivating positive emotions, see Chapter 11.)

Allowing spontaneous release

When you meditate regularly, you start to notice that thoughts and feelings that have accumulated inside you naturally dissipate like mist rising from the surface of a lake. You don't have to do anything special to make this happen. It simply occurs naturally as your concentration deepens and your mind settles down. You may sit to meditate feeling weighted down by worries or concerns and then get up half an hour later feeling somehow lighter, more spacious, and more worry-free. Who knows how this mysterious process happens? You may say that meditating is like lifting the lid on a boiling pot of soup: You create space for the water to evaporate and relieve the pressure that has been building up inside.

To encourage this process of spontaneous release, you can practice meditation techniques that involve *receptive awareness* — open, spacious awareness that welcomes whatever arises. (You need to develop your concentration first.) When your mind is no longer fixated on a particular object — be it a thought, a memory, or an emotion — and is expansive and unattached like the sky, you're no longer investing energy in your drama. Instead, you're inviting whatever's churning inside you to unfold and let go.

Penetrating your experience with insight

In the previous sections, I highlight concentration and awareness techniques that show you how to circumvent your drama, develop alternatives to your drama, and still your mind so that your drama doesn't disturb you. The problem with these techniques is that they leave your inner stories more or less intact, and when your concentration weakens or your lovingkindness wanes, the same old distracting thoughts and troubling emotions come back to stress you out!

Through the practice of penetrating insight, however, you can get to know your drama, gain an understanding of how it causes suffering, see beyond it, and eventually free yourself from it entirely.

Becoming aware of your inner experience

When you sit quietly for 10 or 15 minutes and notice your thoughts and feelings, you're making a radical shift in your relationship to your inner experience. (For more on observing thoughts and feelings, see Chapter 12.) Instead of being swept away by the current, you become, for the moment, an observer on the shore, watching the river of your experience flow by. Though the difference may seem inconsequential and you may not feel that you're making any headway, you've actually begun to loosen your story's stranglehold on your life. Gradually, you begin to notice spaces in your mind's chatter, and what once seemed so serious and solid slowly becomes lighter and infused with fresh air. You may find yourself laughing at your tendency to worry and obsess, or perhaps you pause and notice what you're feeling before you react.

As you practice welcoming your experience just as it is, including your judgments and self-criticisms, you may also discover that your attitude toward yourself begins to change in subtle ways. Instead of impatience or contempt, you may begin to notice a certain self-acceptance creeping in as you become more familiar with the repetitive patterns of your mind. Hey, you may even develop a measure of compassion for yourself as you see how self-critical or distracted or frightened you can become.

Becoming aware of your story and how it confuses you

When you meditate regularly and observe your thoughts and feelings, you begin to notice recurring themes and story lines that keep playing in your mind. Perhaps you become aware of the tendency to obsess about all the times people misunderstood you or failed to give you the love you wanted. Maybe you see how you compare yourself to other people and judge yourself better or worse than them. Possibly you find yourself fantasizing about the ideal mate, even though you've been happily married for years. Or you may notice that you're constantly planning for the future while ignoring what's happening right here and now.

Whatever your particular patterns may be, you can observe how they keep arising to disturb you and pull you away from the reality at hand (which may be some simple task like following your breath or reciting your mantra). Gradually, you realize that your story is just that: a story your mind keeps spinning that separates you from others and causes you pain. As John Lennon put it, "Life is what's happening while you're busy making other plans." When you start seeing your story for what it is, you don't allow it to confuse you in the same way anymore.

Changing your story

As you may notice after you meditate for a while, just being aware of your story can begin changing it in subtle (or even not-so-subtle!) ways. When you develop a certain distance from your story — knowing at some level that it's just your story, not who you really *are* — you naturally become less reactive, people respond to you differently, and circumstances shift accordingly. Soon your life is just not the same old story anymore!

Of course, you may already be struggling to change your life by manipulating circumstances or reprogramming your mind with affirmations or positive thinking. But first you have to bring the power of penetrating insight to bear on your habitual patterns and stories; otherwise, healthier perspectives and patterns can't take root, and you just keep running in the same old grooves.

Seeing beyond your story to who you really are

Even though you may become aware of your story, gain some distance from it, and begin to alter it in certain fundamental ways, you may still identify with it until you can catch a glimpse of who you really are beyond your story.

Such glimpses can take a number of different forms. Perhaps you have unexpected moments of peace or tranquility, when your thoughts settle down — or even stop entirely — and a sweet silence permeates your mind. Or you may experience a flood of unconditional love that momentarily opens your heart wide and gives you a brief glimpse of the oneness beyond all apparent separation. Or maybe you have a sudden intuition of your inherent interconnectedness with all beings or a sense of being in the presence of something far vaster than yourself. Whatever the insight that lifts you beyond your story, it can irrevocably alter who you take yourself to be. Never again can you fully believe that you're merely the limited personality your mind insists you are.

I can still remember how fresh and clear everything appeared after my first meditation retreat — the colors so vivid, people's faces so radiant — even though I'd spent five days doing nothing but struggling to count my breaths from one to ten without losing my way. I felt as though a bandage had been ripped from my eyes, allowing me to see things clearly for the first time. Everything I encountered seemed to radiate *being,* and I knew as never before that I belonged on this Earth. Of course, the intensity faded after a few days, but I never forgot that first glimpse of *clear seeing,* free from the perceptual filters I'd been carrying around for a lifetime.

Freeing yourself from your story

When you've caught a glimpse of who you really are, beyond your mind (and even your body), you can keep reconnecting with this deeper level of *being* in your meditations as well as in your everyday life. To resurrect the metaphor of the lake I describe earlier in the chapter, you can dive down to the bottom again and again because you know what it looks like and how to find it. (Most approaches to meditation offer the possibility of such a glimpse. For more-specific instructions, see Chapter 14.)

Even though your story may continue to play on the video screen of your brain, you can develop the capacity to disengage from it or even disidentify from it entirely. As a friend of mine put it, you come to realize that the personality is a case of mistaken identity and that who you are is the vast expanse of *being* itself, in which your personal thoughts and feelings arise and pass away.

Such a profound realization may take years of meditation to achieve, yet it's always available to you no matter how long you've meditated — indeed, whether you've ever meditated at all! Many people report laughing uproariously when they finally see that their true nature was right there all along, as plain as the proverbial nose on their face.

Contrary to popular belief, people who learn to integrate this realization and live their understanding in a moment-to-moment way don't become more detached and disengaged from life. Rather, because their story and their sense of separation have lifted like a fog, they actually perceive situations and people with more immediacy and compassion, and they can act more appropriately according to the circumstances.

Stopping your mind

Many people believe that the point of meditation is to stop the mind. To get a visceral sense of the futility of such efforts, you can attempt to stop your mind and see what happens. Try the following exercise:

1. **Sit quietly and take a few slow, deep breaths.**

2. **For the next five minutes, try to stop thinking.**

   That's right. Do whatever you can to keep your mind from generating more thoughts. Try humming to yourself or concentrating on your big toe or recalling a beautiful day

in nature. Or just try being as still as you possibly can. Do whatever you think will work for you.

3. **At the end of five minutes, reflect on your experience.**

   How successful were you? Could you actually stop thinking for an extended period of time? Did you find that the struggle to stop thinking just generated more thoughts? In case you hadn't noticed, this exercise reveals how stubborn and tenacious your thinking mind can be.

Chapter 7

Mindfulness Meditation: Awareness of the Here and Now

In This Chapter

▶ Changing your thinking from outward to inward

▶ Discovering five quick ways to relax your body

▶ Tuning in, slowing down, and exploring your breath and other sensations

▶ Playing with the zoom lens of awareness

*I*f you're looking for simple, concise meditation instructions, you've come to the right chapter. You can muse forever about meditation's benefits or the nature of the mind, but there's nothing quite like attempting to practice to show you how stubborn and wild the mind can actually be.

As I mention in Chapter 6, the Buddhists like to compare the mind to a monkey that swings uncontrollably from branch to branch — from plan to memory, thought to emotion, sight to sound — without ever settling down in one place. Some contemporary teachers prefer the more domestic analogy of the wayward puppy that keeps wandering impulsively from one place to another, blithely peeing on the carpet wherever it goes. You know what it's like trying to train a puppy: You can't overpower it or subdue it or sit on it until it agrees to obey. Well, the same holds true for your mind. In fact, if you attempt to force your mind to calm down, you just swirl it up even more and end up going nowhere fast, like a puppy chasing its tail!

Instead, the practice of meditation involves gently returning your mind again and again to a simple focus of attention. In this chapter, you have an opportunity to find out how to meditate on your breath — one of the most popular forms of meditation throughout the world's spiritual traditions. You also discover mindfulness techniques for "training your puppy," balancing relaxation and alertness, and extending your meditation to include welcoming the full range of present-moment experience.

Paradoxically, the mundane, repetitive, seemingly inconsequential activity of attending to your breath can eventually lead to all the glamorous benefits meditation promises to provide, including reduced stress; enhanced performance; increased appreciation and enjoyment of life; deeper connection with your essential being; and even advanced meditative states, such as unconditional love or transformative insights into the nature of existence. But before you get carried away counting your cookies (or your puppy biscuits, as the case may be), you need to take the first step toward the cookie jar.

Turning Your Attention Inward

As the old saying goes, a journey of a thousand miles begins with a single step. In the case of meditation, this simple but essential step involves turning your mind away from its usual preoccupation with external events — or, just as often, with the story it tells you about external events — and toward your inner sensate experience.

If you're like most people, you're so caught up with what's happening around you — the look in other people's eyes, the voices of family and co-workers, the latest news on the radio, the messages appearing on your computer screen — that you forget to pay attention to what's happening in your own mind, body, and heart. In fact, popular culture has been designed to seduce you into searching outside yourself for happiness and satisfaction. In such a confusing and compelling world, even the most rudimentary gesture of self-awareness can seem like a challenge of monumental proportions.

Just take a few minutes right now to turn your mind around and pay attention to what you're sensing and feeling. Notice how much resistance you have to shifting your awareness from your external focus to your simple sensate experience. Notice how busily your mind flits from thought to thought and image to image, weaving a story with you as the central character.

Because these habitual patterns are so deeply rooted, doing something as seemingly innocuous as returning your attention again and again to a basic internal focus, like your breath, can take tremendous courage and patience. You may be afraid of what you'll discover if you venture into essentially unknown terrain or afraid of what you'll miss if you turn inward even for a few moments. But this shift from outer to inner is precisely the simple but radical gesture that meditation requires.

Although I talk about turning inward, the shift I'm suggesting actually has several related dimensions:

✔ **Content to process:** Instead of becoming engrossed in the meaning of what you're sensing, thinking, or feeling, you can shift your interest and attention to *how* experiencing occurs or to the mere fact of experience itself. For example, instead of getting lost in thinking or daydreaming, you can notice how your mind flits from thought to thought — or merely observe that you're thinking. Instead of becoming transfixed by your fear or what you imagine it means or is trying to tell you, you can notice how the waves of tension move through your belly — or simply note that you're feeling.

✔ **Outer to inner:** Initially, you need to balance your usual tendency to be so outer-directed by paying particular attention to inner experience. Eventually, you'll be able to bring the same quality of awareness to every experience, whether inner or outer.

✔ **Secondhand to direct:** Even more helpful than inner and outer is the distinction between secondhand experience and direct experience. *Secondhand experience* has been filtered and distorted by the mind and is often concerned with thoughts about the past or future, whereas *direct experience* is found only in the present and accessed through the senses. In addition to turning inward, meditation involves turning your attention away from the story your mind spins about your experience and toward the direct experience itself.

✔ **Doing to being:** You spend virtually all your waking hours rushing from one task, project, or activity to another. Do you remember what it's like to just *be*, the way you did when you were a baby or a little child, whiling away a summer afternoon just playing or lying in the grass? Meditation gives you the opportunity to make this crucial shift from doing to being.

Relaxing Your Body

As the field of mind-body medicine reminds us — and yogis and sages have been telling us for millennia — your body, your mind, and your heart form one seamless and inseparable whole. When your thoughts keep leaping like the proverbial monkey from worry to worry, your body responds by tightening and tensing, especially in certain key places like the throat, the heart, the solar plexus, and the belly. When the discomfort gets intense enough, you register it as an emotion — fear, perhaps, or anger or sadness.

Because meditation connects you with your direct experience — and ultimately with a realm of pure *being* beyond the mind — it naturally relaxes your body while it focuses your mind. As a beginner, though, you may not experience this natural relaxation for days or even weeks. So practicing one of the techniques in the following list *before* you meditate can be helpful, especially if you tend to be noticeably tense. Of course, relaxing your body has its own wonderful benefits, but your body won't stay relaxed until you're able to work with your mind.

Deep relaxation

Here's a meditation you can do any time you have 15 or 20 minutes to spare and want to shed some of the tension you've accumulated in your busy life. It's also a great way to prepare for the other meditations in this book because it leaves you feeling relaxed, refreshed, and in touch with yourself.

1. **Find a comfortable place to lie down. Take off your shoes, loosen your belt and other tight clothing, and stretch out on your back with your arms resting at your sides, legs slightly apart.**

2. **Sense your body as a whole, including the places where it contacts the surface of the bed or floor.**

3. **Close your eyes and bring your awareness to your feet. Wiggle your toes, flex your feet, and then let go of all tension as much as you can, allowing your feet to melt into the floor.**

4. **Shift your awareness to your lower legs, thighs, and hips. Imagine them becoming heavy and relaxed and melting into the floor.**

   If the image of melting doesn't appeal to you, you might try dissolving, sinking, or disappearing.

5. **Bring your awareness to your lower abdomen. Imagine all tension draining away, your breath deepening, and your belly opening and softening.**

6. **Bring your awareness to your upper abdomen, chest, neck, and throat, feeling the areas opening and softening.**

7. **Bring your awareness to your shoulders, upper arms, lower arms, and hands. Imagine them becoming heavy and relaxed and melting into the floor.**

8. **Bring your awareness to your head and face. Feel the tension melting away from your face across your head and into the floor.**

9. **Scan your body from head to toe, searching for any remaining areas of tension or discomfort.**

   If you find any, just imagine them relaxing completely.

10. **Experience your body as one field of relaxation, without parts or edges.**

11. **Continue to rest in this way for five or ten minutes more; then very slowly begin to wiggle your fingers and toes, stretch your arms and legs, open your eyes, and gradually come up to a sitting position.**

Check in with yourself and notice how you feel. Do you feel more relaxed? Does your body feel lighter or more expanded? Does the world appear different in any way? Now gently get up and go about your day.

If you've never deliberately relaxed your body before, start with the meditation in the "Deep relaxation" sidebar nearby. Because the meditation takes at least 15 minutes to complete, you probably won't do it each time you meditate, but it does show you how to relax your body part by part. When you've practiced this exercise a few times, your body will remember what being deeply relaxed feels like, and you can then advance to one of the five-minute relaxations listed here. (By the way, deep relaxation is a great antidote for insomnia; just practice it in bed and then drift off to sleep!)

So here are five brief relaxation techniques:

- **Shower of relaxation:** Imagine taking a warm shower. As the water cascades across your body and down your legs, it carries with it all discomfort and distress, leaving you refreshed and invigorated.

- **Honey treatment:** Imagine a mound of warm honey perched on the crown of your head. As it melts, it runs down your face and head and neck, covering your shoulders and chest and arms, and gradually enveloping your whole body down to your toes. Feel the sensuous wave of warm liquid draining away all tension and stress and leaving you thoroughly relaxed and renewed.

- **Peaceful place:** Imagine a safe, protected, peaceful place — perhaps a forest, a meadow, or a sandy beach. Experience the place fully with all your senses. Notice how calm and relaxed you feel here; now allow that feeling to permeate every cell of your body.

- **Body scan:** Beginning with the crown of your head, scan your body from top to bottom. When you come to an area of tension or discomfort, gently allow it to open and soften; then move on.

- **Relaxation response:** Choose a word or brief phrase that has deep spiritual or personal significance for you. Now close your eyes and repeat this sound softly, again and again. (For more detailed instructions on practicing the relaxation response, see Chapter 20.)

Developing Mindfulness

This chapter highlights an approach to meditation known as *mindfulness* — moment-to-moment awareness of your experience as it occurs. Mindfulness combines *concentration* (highly focused awareness) and a more receptive awareness that simply welcomes whatever arises. Because mindfulness grows like a house on a foundation of concentration, you need to strengthen and stabilize your concentration before you can proceed to the full practice of mindfulness. That's why the initial meditations provided here emphasize focusing on a particular object of concentration — your breath.

Ultimately, the goal of mindfulness meditation is to develop the capacity to be fully present for whatever is occurring right here and now. When you've stabilized your concentration by focusing on your breath, you can expand your awareness to include the full range of sensations, both inside and outside, and eventually just welcome whatever presents itself, including thoughts, memories, and emotions.

Though supremely simple, this advanced technique can take years of patient practice to master, but you may have glimpses of a more expanded awareness after only a few weeks of regular meditation.

TIP

Letting go of your expectations

When you invest in the stock market or work out at a gym, you expect results, and you keep checking the quotes or the scale to tell you how well you're doing. If you bring the same attitude to meditation, however, you're defeating the purpose, which is to let go of your thoughts altogether and just be present in the here and now. One of the great paradoxes of meditation is that you can't reap the benefits until you drop all your expectations and accept things the way they are. Then the benefits come back to you a thousandfold.

When you begin meditating, you're going to keep wondering whether you're doing it right. But don't worry; there's no wrong way to meditate — except perhaps sitting and trying to measure how well you're doing! One day you may feel like you're on top of the world. You're full of energy, your mind is clear, and you can follow your breath with relative ease. "Wow, now I'm getting the hang of it," you think. The next day you're so overwhelmed by thoughts or emotions that you sit for 20 minutes without even noticing your breath. Welcome to the practice of meditation! The point isn't to do it right, but just to do it — again and again.

One of my Zen teachers used to compare meditation to walking in the fog on a warm summer day: Though you may not pay attention to what's happening, pretty soon you're soaking wet.

Focusing on your breath

Compared to posting on Facebook or catching a movie on HBO, watching your breath may seem like a boring way to spend your spare time. The fact is, the media have conditioned us to be stimulation junkies by flooding our senses with computerized images and synthesized sounds that change at laserlike speed. Recently, I heard the head of an ad agency brag about how his latest TV spot bombarded the viewer with six images per second — far faster than the conscious mind can possibly register them.

By contrast, paying attention to the coming and going of your breath slows your mind to match the speed and rhythms of your body. Instead of six images per second, you breathe an average of 12 to 16 times per minute. And the sensations are far subtler than anything you'll see or hear on TV — more like the sights and sounds of nature, which is, after all, where you and your body came from.

Besides, the great thing about your breath as a focus of meditation is that it's always available, always changing, yet is always more or less the same. If your breath were totally different each time, it wouldn't provide the stability necessary for you to cultivate concentration; if it never changed in any way, you'd quickly fall asleep and never have an opportunity to develop the curiosity and alertness that are so essential to the practice of mindfulness.

As a preliminary to the practice of following your breath, you may want to spend a few weeks or months just counting your breaths. It's a great way to build concentration, and it provides a preestablished structure that constantly reminds you when you're wandering off. If you were a neophyte Zen student, you might spend years counting your breaths before you graduated to a more challenging practice. But if you're feeling adventurous or already have some confidence in your concentration, by all means start with following your breath. Trust your intuition to tell you which method is right for you.

Counting your breaths

Begin by finding a comfortable sitting position that you can hold for 10 or 15 minutes. (For a complete discussion of sitting posture in meditation, including diagrams, see Chapter 8.) Then take a few deep breaths and exhale slowly. Without trying to control your breath in any way, allow it to find its own natural depth and rhythm. Always breathe through your nose unless you can't for some reason.

Now begin counting each inhalation and exhalation until you reach ten; then return to one. In other words, when you inhale, count "one," when you exhale, count "two," when you inhale again, count "three," and so on up to ten. If you lose track, return to one and start again.

To help you concentrate, you may find it useful to extend the number in your mind for the full duration of the inhalation or exhalation, instead of thinking the number quickly once and then dropping it. For example, allow "o-o-o-n-n-n-e" to last as long as the inhalation, "t-w-o-o-o-o" to last as long as the exhalation, and so on. You may also find it helpful to subvocalize the numbers, especially at first, saying "one" ever so softly to yourself as you inhale, "two" as you exhale, and so on.

As ridiculously easy as this exercise may seem at first-read, you may be surprised to discover that you never manage to reach ten without losing count — or go on autopilot and suddenly find yourself on breath 29! You don't have to stop your mind chatter in any way. But if you get distracted by your thoughts and lose track of your breath, come back to one and start again.

The meaning of the breath

Traditional cultures identified the breath with the life force that animates all things. For example, the Latin word *spiritus* (the root of both *spirited* and *spiritual*), the Greek word *anima* (from which we derive the word *animated*), the Hebrew word *ruach,* and the Sanskrit word *brahman* may sound quite different, but they have one thing in common: They all mean both *breath* and *spirit* or *soul.* When you follow your breath with awareness, you're not only harmonizing your body and mind, which gives you a sense of inner harmony and wholeness but you're also exploring the living frontier where body, mind, and spirit meet — and attuning yourself to a spiritual dimension of being.

Getting to know your breathing

When you first begin paying deliberate attention to your breath, you may be surprised and somewhat frustrated to discover that your body tenses up and your breathing becomes stiff, labored, and unnatural. Suddenly, you can't remember how to breathe anymore, even though you've been doing it just fine ever since your first breath at birth.

Don't worry: You're not doing it wrong. You just need to develop a lighter, gentler touch with your awareness so you're following but not controlling your breath. Following your breathing is kind of like learning to ride a bicycle — you keep falling off until one day, miraculously, you just keep going. From then on, it's second nature.

You may find it helpful to begin by exploring your breathing, without necessarily trying to track it from breath to breath. Notice what happens when you breathe: how your rib cage rises and falls, how your belly moves, how the air passes in and out of your nostrils. You may find that some breaths are longer and deeper, while others are shorter and shallower. Some may go all the way down into your belly, while others barely reach the upper part of your lungs before exiting again. Some may be rough or strong; others smooth or weak.

Spend five or ten minutes exploring your breathing with the fresh curiosity of a child encountering a flower or a butterfly for the first time. What did you discover that you didn't know before? How does each new breath differ from the last? When you feel comfortable with your breath, you can begin the practice of counting or following your breaths.

When you get the knack of counting each in-breath and out-breath — say, after a month or two of regular practice — you can shift to counting only the exhalations. If your mind starts wandering on the inhalations, though, just go back to the first method until you feel ready to move on again. Eventually, you may want to simplify the practice even further by simply noting "in" on the inhalation and "out" on the exhalation.

Following your breaths

Begin by sitting and breathing exactly as you did for counting your breaths. (If you'd prefer to follow the audio instructions for this meditation, listen to Track 4.) When you feel settled, allow your attention to focus either on the sensation of your breath coming and going through your nostrils or on the rising and falling of your belly as you breathe. (Although you're welcome to alternate your focus from one session to the next, you're better off sticking with a single focus for the entire meditation— and eventually using the same focus each time you meditate.)

Give your full attention to the coming and going of your breath the way a mother tracks the movements of her young child: lovingly yet persistently, softly yet precisely, with relaxed yet focused awareness. When you realize that your mind has wandered off and you're engrossed in planning or thinking or daydreaming, gently but firmly bring it back to your breath.

At the end of your exhalation (and before you inhale again), there's often a gap or a pause when your breath is no longer perceptible. At this point, you can allow your attention to rest on a predetermined touchpoint, such as your navel or your hands, before returning to your breath when it resumes.

Thoughts and images will definitely continue to skitter and swirl through your mind as you meditate, but don't worry. Just patiently and persistently keep coming back to your breath. Gradually, you may even develop a fascination with all the little sensations of your belly and ribcage shifting and opening and changing shape as you breathe; or of your breath caressing the tip of your nose, tickling your nostrils, and cooling your nasal passages as it enters and leaves. You may also notice that your mind tends to quiet down or your thinking tends to change on either the exhalation or the inhalation. By attuning to a subtler level of experience while you meditate, you can open yourself to a subtler appreciation of each moment of life as it unfolds.

Expanding to sensations

As soon as you've developed a certain ease in following your breath, you can expand your awareness as you meditate to include the full range of sensations both inside and outside your body: feeling, smelling, hearing, seeing. Imagine that your awareness is like the zoom lens on a camera. Until now, you've been focused exclusively on your breath; now you can back away slightly to include the field of sensations that surrounds your breath.

Minding your body instead of your breath

Some people find it virtually impossible to count or follow their breaths. So instead, they focus on their body as a whole when they meditate. You can begin by drawing your awareness slowly down through your body from your head to your feet; then switch to holding your whole body in your awareness at once. When your mind wanders off, just come back to your body. Or you can use the Zen approach of focusing on a particular part of the body, like the lower back or lower abdomen. When you find a focus that works for you, however, stick with it. The point is to develop your mindfulness, not to meander through your body in search of a place to meditate.

Just sitting

As an alternative to mindfulness meditation, you may want to experiment with the Zen practice known as *just sitting,* which usually involves two phases or steps: just breathing and just sitting.

When you're adept at following your breath, you can practice *becoming your breath* — merging yourself completely with the flow of the inhalation and exhalation, until you, as a separate observer, disappear and only your breath remains. Now you're no longer breathing; instead, your breath is breathing you. Like welcoming whatever arises, this practice, known as *just breathing,* is supremely simple but requires a quality of awareness that's both focused and relaxed.

The next step, *just sitting,* involves expanding to include the whole realm of sensate experience. But instead of being aware or mindful of your experience, you "disappear," and only your experience remains — seeing, smelling, hearing, sensing, thinking. As a Zen friend of mine put it, "When you sit, the walls of the meditation hall come down, and the whole world enters." Ultimately, this practice takes you to the same place as mindfulness; it's simply the Zen alternative.

If you find it difficult to expand your awareness all at once, you can begin by exploring a sensation when it calls attention to itself. For example, you're following your breath when a pain in your back cries out for your attention. Instead of staying focused on your breath as you would have done before, you can turn your attention to the pain and explore it fully until it no longer predominates in your field of experience. Then come back to your breath until you're once again called away.

You can also experiment with expanding your awareness to include one particular kind of sensation, such as bodily feelings or sounds. For example, you can spend an entire meditation just listening to the sounds around you, without focusing on any sounds in particular. In this way, you're able to balance the highly concentrated awareness required to follow your breath with the more receptive, all-inclusive awareness necessary to welcome a broad range of sensations. This blend of focus and receptivity lies at the heart of the practice of mindfulness.

As you get the knack of including sensations in your meditations, you can experiment with expanding your awareness to include the full sensate field (that is, hearing, seeing, smelling, touching, and tasting). Begin by following your breathing and then just open your lens wide, allowing sensations to arise and pass away in your awareness.

The point of meditation isn't to discover some cool techniques to occupy your leisure hours; it's to make the simple but momentous shift from doing to being. Don't make the mistake of turning your meditation practice into another urgent item on your list of things to do. Use it, instead, as a welcome oasis from doing, an opportunity to *be,* without strategy or agenda. In other words, keep it simple. Play with a few of the techniques at first to decide which one feels right for you; then stick with the one you've chosen. Which method you use really doesn't matter; they all end up depositing you in the here and now.

Welcoming whatever arises

When you become accustomed to including sensations in your meditation practice, you can open your awareness wide and welcome any and every experience — even thoughts and emotions — without judgment or resistance. Just like sensations, thoughts and feelings come and go in your awareness like clouds in the sky without pulling you off center. If you do lose your balance, by all means just return to open, nonjudgmental, present-moment awareness.

Just as the sky is never disturbed or constricted no matter how many clouds pile up, so this spacious, open awareness is undisturbed by the experiences that pass through. At first, you may find your attention drawn here and there like a flashlight, exploring one object and then another. But just keep coming back to this open, skylike awareness. (For more on welcoming whatever arises, see Chapter 12.)

Training Your Puppy: Reining In Your Wandering Mind

Like a wayward puppy, your mind means well. It just has a will of its own and some pretty obnoxious habits to unlearn. Just as you wouldn't hit a puppy for peeing on the carpet but would keep carrying it patiently back to its little pile of papers, you need to keep leading your wandering mind patiently back to its focus of concentration, without anger or violence or judgment of any kind. After all, you want your "puppy mind" to like you and treat you as a friend, instead of cowering in your presence.

In fact, your mind deserves even more patience than a puppy because it's developed the tendency to fantasize, worry, and obsess through a lifetime of poor training. As you practice being kind and patient with your mind, you naturally soften and relax into the present moment, which is, after all, the point of meditation. On the other hand, if you force your mind to concentrate like a drill sergeant pushing his troops, you're just going to wind up tense and uncomfortable, and you probably won't be motivated to meditate again.

Coming back to your breath

Set your watch or clock to signal the beginning of every hour. When the alarm sounds, stop whatever you're doing and follow your breath with full attention for 60 seconds. If you're doing something that can't be stopped, like driving a car in traffic or talking to your boss, follow your breath as attentively as you can while engaging in the activity.

As I note in other chapters, discovering how to meditate is a lot like practicing a musical instrument. First, you need to assemble some basic techniques; then, you get to practice the same scales over and over. Like following your breath, playing scales can seem incredibly boring, but week by week, you become imperceptibly better, until one day you graduate to playing simple tunes. And the more you practice, the more subtleties you notice, and the more interesting even playing simple scales — or following your breath — becomes.

The historical Buddha compared meditating to tuning a stringed instrument. If you make the strings too tight, they break, and you can't play the instrument at all. If you make them too loose, you can't get the right sounds. Likewise, you need to listen to your instrument (your body and mind) when you meditate to determine what kind of tuning you need. If you're tense, you may want to begin with some deep relaxation; if you're sleepy or foggy, you may need to sit up straight, pay attention, and emphasize your concentration.

As you gently bring your puppy back again and again, you also get to notice the themes and stories that repeatedly draw your attention away. Perhaps your mind keeps returning to worries about job security, or arguments with your partner or spouse, or sexual fantasies, or popular songs. Whatever the favorite bones your puppy likes to chew, you gradually become familiar with them as you watch them distract you.

After weeks and months of regular practice, you develop a deeper understanding of how your mind works and how it causes suffering and stress. And like hit tunes you love at first but eventually get tired of hearing, the same old stories start to lose their power to disturb you, and you develop greater equanimity and peace of mind. (For more on working with your stories and habitual themes, see Chapter 12.)

Chapter 8

Preparing Your Body for Meditation

*P*erhaps you know a few meditation techniques, but you haven't really begun to practice them because you can't sit still for more than a few minutes, let alone 5, 10, or even 15.

Maybe your back or your knees start hurting, and you worry you may be doing yourself irreparable harm. Or your body starts itching in the oddest places, and you can't resist the urge to scratch. Or every sound reaches your ears magnified a thousandfold — in Dolby stereo, no less — and you start imagining burglars or leaky faucets behind every door.

Perhaps you had a teacher (or a mother or father!) who made you sit at your desk until you finished your schoolwork, and now even the thought of having to sit without moving makes you squirm uncomfortably.

Yes, the simple act of sitting still is guaranteed to flush out every ounce of restlessness you never knew you had. And, yes, meditation works best when you can keep your body relatively motionless and your back relatively straight. So what to do?

In this chapter, you explore the topography of meditation and find out what sitting still has to teach you. You discover some great techniques for straightening your spine without hurting your back. And you experiment with an assortment of sitting positions to find the one that works best for you. (For audio guidance in preparing your body for sitting meditation, listen to Track 5 on the CD.)

Putting a Snake into a Stick of Bamboo — or the Subtle Art of Sitting Still

When talking about the practice of sitting still, one of my first meditation teachers, the Zen master Shunryu Suzuki, used to say that the best way to show a snake its true nature is to put it into a hollow stick of bamboo. Take a moment and give this unusual metaphor some thought. What could he have possibly meant by it?

Well, imagine that you're a snake in bamboo. What does it feel like? Every time you try to slither, which is after all what snakes like to do, you bump against the walls of your straight-as-an-arrow home. If you pay attention, you start to notice how slippery you actually are.

In the same way, sitting in a certain posture and keeping your body relatively still provides a stick of bamboo that mirrors back to you every impulse and distraction. You get to see how fidgety your body can be — and how hyperactive your mind can be, which is actually the source of your body's restlessness. "Maybe I should scratch that itch or answer that phone or run that errand." For every plan or intention, there's a corresponding impulse in your muscles and skin. But you'll never notice all this activity unless you sit still.

The funny thing is, you can sit in the same position for hours without restlessness when you're happily engrossed in some favorite activity like watching a movie or surfing the Web or working on a hobby. But try to do something you find boring or unpleasant — especially an activity as strange and unfamiliar as turning your attention back on yourself and following your own breath, or paying attention to your own sensations — and suddenly every minute can seem like an hour, every ache can seem like an ailment of life-threatening proportions, and every item on your to-do list can take on irresistible urgency.

When you're constantly acting and reacting in response to thoughts and outside stimulation, you don't have a chance to get to know how your mind works. By sitting still like the snake in bamboo, you have a mirror that shows you just how slippery and elusive your mind can be.

Keeping still also gives you a tremendous edge when you're working on developing your concentration. Imagine a heart surgeon or a concert pianist who can't quiet her body while plying her craft. The fewer physical distractions you have, the easier it becomes to follow your breath, practice your mantra — or whatever your meditation happens to be.

Sitting still, doing nothing

When I was a young Zen meditator, I worked as an attendant in a nursing home that hosted a range of patients, from a young woman recovering from bone cancer to our local congressman's father, who was dying of emphysema.

Amidst this busy throng, I was fascinated by one person in particular — an old Italian fisherman who had lost both legs in a fishing accident. When his family members came to visit, he would hold court with great dignity, receiving their respect as the family patriarch. Where other patients might be content to lie in bed all day in their hospital gowns, he would dress and groom himself each day and sit with pride — and upright posture — in his wheelchair, silently observing the drama that unfolded around him.

One day, I was running back and forth, unsure of what I was supposed to be doing. Seeing this, he called out to me, with a mischievous gleam in his eye, "Hey! You got nothing to do?" "Yeah," I said," obviously flustered, "I don't know what I'm supposed to be doing." "You got nothing to do," he said, "then sit down!"

A word of caution, however: These sitting instructions aren't intended to turn your body into a stone, any more than the bamboo is meant to turn the snake into a stick. As long as you're alive, you're going to keep moving. The point is to set your intention to sit still and notice what happens. The Buddha liked to use the metaphor of a stringed instrument like a sitar or guitar — if the strings are too loose, you can't play it, and if they're too tight, they'll break. If you're too rigid with yourself, you'll just end up miserable — but if you keep shifting your body this way and that, you'll never get your mind concentrated and quiet enough to reap the benefits of meditation.

How to Sit Up Straight — and Live to Tell About It

If you examine the meditation poses depicted in the world's great spiritual traditions, you'll find that they all have one thing in common — the unshakable stability of a mountain or tree. Look at the kneeling pharaohs in the Egyptian pyramids, for example, or the cross-legged Buddhas in Indian caves or Japanese temples. They sit on a broad base that appears to be deeply rooted in the earth, and they have a grounded presence that says, "I can't be budged. I'm here to stay" (see Figure 8-1).

When you sit up straight like a mountain or a tree, your body acts as a link between heaven and earth — and, by analogy, connects your physical, embodied existence with the sacred or spiritual dimension of being. Many traditions talk about the importance of bridging the apparent chasm that separates us from God or the Absolute. Jewish and Sufi mystics teach that the soul is a spark of the heavenly fire that yearns to return to its source. Christians depict the soul as a dove ascending, and Indian tantric yogis (see Chapter 3) describe the ecstatic union of *Shakti,* the feminine energy of spiritual evolution that rises through the spine, with *Shiva,* the masculine principle of detached transcendence.

If you find all this spiritual stuff too esoteric or airy-fairy, you might consider that sitting up straight confers some practical benefits as well. By aligning the spine and opening the channels that run through the center of the body, upright sitting encourages an unimpeded circulation of energy, which, in turn, contributes to wakefulness on all levels — physical, mental, and spiritual. Besides, it's a lot easier to sit still for extended periods of time when your vertebrae are stacked like a pile of bricks, one on top of the other. Otherwise, over time, gravity has this irritating habit of pulling your body down toward the ground — and in the process, causing the aches and pains so typical of a body at war with the forces of nature. So the most comfortable way to sit in the long run is straight, which puts you in harmony with nature.

Figure 8-1: Sit like a mountain (here shown in full lotus) for grounding and stability.

Dealing with pain

If you sit in the same position for an extended period of time, you're going to experience some physical pain or discomfort, no matter how much stretching you do! An ache in your back here, some knee pain there, a twinge in your shoulder, pins and needles in your foot — the list of complaints is potentially endless. And the longer you sit, the more intense the discomfort may become — and the stronger the temptation to move or fidget to avoid it.

Instead of instantly shifting your position or struggling to ignore your discomfort, practice gently expanding your awareness to include your discomfort, while continuing to attend to your breath or other object of meditation. If the pain is strong, you can explore it directly with the same mindful, compassionate attention you bring to your breath.

Notice also how your mind responds to your discomfort. Does it fabricate some story about your discomfort: "I'm not sitting correctly. There must be something wrong with my back. Maybe I'm ruining my knees"? And does it

intensify your discomfort by judging it as bad or undesirable, causing you to tense up around it?

By opening your awareness to your pain and how your mind responds to it, you can actually begin to soften and relax in relation to the pain — and you may notice that it diminishes accordingly. Because physical and emotional pain are unavoidable, sitting meditation provides a wonderful laboratory for experimenting with new ways of relating to suffering and discomfort in every area of your life — and ultimately moving beyond them.

By the way, you also have the option of moving (with awareness) when the pain or discomfort becomes too intense. Just play at your own edge between opening and resisting. And remember that certain kinds of pain may merit your immediate attention — especially shooting pain, pain that begins as soon as you start sitting, and sharp (rather than dull) pain in your knees. In such cases, you're better off trying a different sitting position.

Of course, you can always lean against the wall — or so you may think. But your body tends to slouch when it leans, even subtly, in any direction; and the point of doing meditation is to rely on your direct experience, rather than to depend on some outside support to "back you up." When you sit like a mountain or a tree, you're making a statement: "I'm deeply rooted in the earth, yet open to the higher powers of the cosmos — independent, yet inextricably connected to all of life."

What to do from the waist down — and other fantasies

Just as a tree needs to set down deep roots so it won't fall over as it grows, you need to find a comfortable position for the lower half of your body that you can sustain for 5, 10, or 15 minutes — or longer, if you want to obtain the maximum benefits from meditation. After several millennia of experimentation, the great meditators have come up with a handful of traditional postures that seem to work especially well. Different though they may appear from the outside, these postures have one thing in common: The pelvis tilts slightly forward, accentuating the natural curvature of the lower back.

The following poses are arranged more or less in order, from the easiest to the hardest to do, though ease all depends on your particular body and degree of flexibility. For example, some people take to the classical *lotus* position (whose name derives from its resemblance to the flower) like a duck to . . . well, to a lotus pond. Besides, the lotus, though difficult, has some definite advantages (see the sidebar "Why the Buddha sat in lotus position," later in this chapter), and you can work up to it by stretching your hips using the yoga exercises described in the section "Preparing Your Body for Sitting," later in this chapter. Above all, don't worry about which looks the coolest; just experiment until you find the one that works best for you.

Sitting in a chair

Notice that I say sitting, not slouching (see Figure 8-2). The trick to meditating in a chair is positioning your buttocks somewhat higher than your knees, which tilts your pelvis forward and helps keep your back straight. Old-fashioned wooden kitchen chairs work better than the upholstered kind; experiment with a small cushion or foam wedge under your buttocks.

Figure 8-2:
If you meditate in a chair, you may have to update a few old habits.

Kneeling (with or without a bench)

This position is popular in ancient Egypt and in traditional Japan, where it's called *seiza* (pronounced *say-za*; see Figure 8-3). Kneeling can be hard on your knees unless you have proper support. Try placing a cushion under your buttocks and between your feet — or use a specially designed seiza bench, preferably one with a soft cushion between you and the wood. Otherwise, your bottom and other tender parts may fall asleep.

Figure 8-3: Use a cushion or a bench to make sure your tender parts don't fall asleep when you kneel.

Easy position

This position is not recommended for extended periods of sitting because it's not very stable and doesn't support a straight spine. Simply sit on your cushion with your legs crossed in front of you, tailor-fashion. (Believe it or not, tailors once sat this way!) Your knees don't have to touch the floor, but do keep your back as straight as you can.

You can stabilize the position by placing cushions under your knees; gradually decrease the height of the cushions as your hips become more flexible (which they naturally will over time). When your knees touch the ground, you may be ready for Burmese or lotus position (see the following sections for these positions).

This pose can be a short-term alternative for people who can't manage the other positions in this section, can't kneel because of knee problems, or don't want to sit on a chair for some reason.

Burmese position

Used throughout Southeast Asia, the Burmese position (see Figure 8-4) involves placing both calves and feet on the floor one in front of the other. Though less stable than the lotus series, it's much easier to negotiate, especially for beginners.

With all the cross-legged poses, first bend your leg at the knee, in line with your thigh, before rotating your thigh to the side. Otherwise, you risk injuring your knee, which is built to flex in only one direction, unlike the ball-and-socket joint of the hip, which can rotate through a full range of motion.

Quarter lotus

Exactly like half lotus (see the following section), except that your foot rests on the calf of your opposite leg, rather than on the thigh (see Figure 8-5).

Figure 8-4:
Burmese position is an easy, comfortable, cross-legged alternative that's popular in Southeast Asia.

Figure 8-5:
As its name implies, quarter lotus is a fraction as hard as its more ambitious counterpart, full lotus.

Half lotus

The half lotus is easier to execute than the famous full lotus (see the following section) and nearly as stable (see Figure 8-6). With your buttocks on a cushion, place one foot on the opposite thigh and the other foot on the floor beneath the opposite thigh. Be sure that both knees touch the floor and your spine doesn't tilt to one side. To distribute the pressure on your back and legs, remember to alternate legs from sitting to sitting, if you can — in other words, left leg on the thigh and right on the floor, then left on the floor and right on the thigh.

Full lotus

Considered the Everest of sitting positions (refer to Figure 8-1). With your buttocks on a cushion, cross your left foot over your right thigh and your right foot over your left thigh. As with its more asymmetrical sibling, half lotus, it's best to alternate legs in order to distribute the pressure evenly.

Full lotus has been practiced throughout the world for many thousands of years. The most stable of all the poses, don't attempt it unless you happen to be particularly flexible — and even then I suggest preparing by doing some of the stretches described later in this chapter, in the section "Preparing Your Body for Sitting."

Figure 8-6:
In half
lotus, try to
alternate
your legs
between
sittings as
much as
you can.

Why the Buddha sat in lotus position

Unfortunately, we didn't learn to sit cross-legged on the floor when we were kids, the way most Indians and many other traditional Asians did. As a result, you may find it difficult to sit cross-legged at first and you may feel inclined to retreat to the apparent ease and comfort of a chair. But I'd like to encourage you to give cross-legged sitting a try at some point, if your body and comfort level allow. It isn't necessarily as difficult or as painful as it appears — and besides, it has some unique advantages.

For one thing, crossing your legs creates a solid, stable foundation for the rest of your body and tends to tilt your pelvis forward naturally at just the right angle to support your spine.

Also, there's something about sitting the way the great meditators of the past used to sit that lends a

certain power and authority to your meditation — as though crossing your legs immerses you in a river of awareness that dates back thousands of years.

Finally, sitting with your buttocks on or close to the earth directly connects you with gravity and the other energies the earth emanates — and gives a palpable feeling of groundedness and strength to your meditation.

Ultimately, of course, whatever you do with the lower half of your body is fine, as long as you can sit comfortably and keep your back straight with relative ease. But you can work up to the groundedness of cross-legged sitting by gradually stretching your hips, until, one day, both knees touch the floor and — *voilà!* — you've arrived.

Meditating on your posture

As an alternative to following your breath, especially when you want to calm your mind before turning to the practice of mindfulness (see Chapter 7), you can experiment with the time-honored Zen technique of concentrating on a particular part of your body. Try placing your mind in the palm of your hand, if your hands are folded in Zen *mudra* (refer to Figure 8-1 and the "What to do with your eyes, mouth, and hands" sidebar in this chapter), or on your belly, at a point about 2 inches below your navel (known as the *hara* in Japanese). After you practice this approach for a period of time and your attention stabilizes, you can expand your focus to include your whole body, maintaining the same level of Zen-style concentration.

Straightening your spine without rigor mortis

When you're settled into a comfortable sitting position, with your pelvis tilted slightly forward, you can turn your attention to straightening your back. Of course, *straight* is a misnomer when used to refer to the spine because a healthy back actually has several distinct curves, one at the lumbar region or lower back, another at the thoracic area or midback, and a third at the neck or cervical spine.

Unfortunately, these natural curves are often exaggerated by the demands of computer workstations and other sedentary environments, and you gradually get into the habit of sitting hunched over, with your shoulders rounded, your upper back collapsed, and your neck and head craned forward like a turkey vulture — the way I'm sitting right now!

You may not be able to reverse sitting habits like these in a few sessions of meditation, but you can experiment with *extending* your spine — a more accurate term than straightening — and slowly but surely softening those curves back to their natural, graceful arch. You may find yourself carrying these new sitting habits into your other activities so that in time, you're gently correcting your posture while driving your car or sitting at your desk, for example.

What to do with your eyes, mouth, and hands

When I started meditating back in the '60s, I couldn't for the life of me figure out what to do with my eyes. They kept crossing and shifting uncontrollably from focused to unfocused, and I became obsessed with doing something right that had always been second nature for me. I mean, I'd never worried about what to do with my eyes before! Eventually, I just forgot about them, and they never bothered me again.

To save you similar confusion about your eyes and other salient body parts, I offer the following guidelines:

Eyes: Initially, you need to decide whether you want to sit with your eyes closed, wide open, or half open. Then you can just forget about your eyes and let them do what they do. Each alternative has its pros and cons.

Keeping your eyes closed draws your attention away from external distractions and helps you focus on your inner experience. Unfortunately, it also encourages daydreaming and thinking. Keeping your eyes wide open is actually the most difficult position because it expands your awareness to include the full range of outer as well as inner experiences. The good news is that this position makes it easier for you to rise from a sitting position and extend your meditation to your everyday, eyes-open activities. The bad news is that if you haven't developed enough concentration, you can easily be distracted by anything that crosses your field of vision.

I generally recommend that people sit with eyes half open, Zen style, gazing with soft focus at a spot on the floor about 4 or 5 feet in front of them — in other words, looking down at a 45-degree angle. If you're feeling restless or distracted, you can close your eyes a little more (or completely); if you're feeling sleepy or dull, you can open them wider. And if you find yourself staring, just relax your eyes and soften your focus.

Hands: You can put your hands pretty much anywhere they feel comfortable, as long as you keep them there for the entire sitting period. Seasoned meditators generally put their hands one of two places: in their laps or on their thighs.

✔ **In your lap:** Try simply clasping your hands. Or you can attempt the more formal Zen *mudra* (hand position) in which your left palm is placed on top of your right about 4 or 5 inches below your navel, with your thumbs lightly touching near your navel, thereby forming an oval with your fingers.

✔ **On your thighs:** Simply rest your hands there, palms down. Or turn them up and, if you want, touch your index finger to the thumb of each hand, forming an oval in a traditional yoga mudra. As with all the other options in this chapter, experiment until you find the one that works best for you.

Mouth: Keep it gently closed (but not clenched) as you breathe through your nose, with your tongue lightly touching the roof of your mouth so it doesn't wander all over the place as tongues are wont to do.

Try one or all three of the following images to help you discover what a straight or extended spine feels like. Don't bother to look in the mirror or compare yourself to some ideal you've picked up in books (even this one). The important thing is how your body feels from the inside. You want to feel centered, stable, grounded — and aligned with the force of gravity:

 ✔ **Suspending your head from a string:** Imagine that your entire body is suspended in the air from a string attached to the crown of your head. (The *crown* is the highest point on the top of your skull, toward the back.) As you feel the string pulling your head up into the air, notice how your spine naturally lengthens, your pelvis tilts forward, your chin tucks, and the back of your neck flattens slightly.

 ✔ **Stacking your vertebrae one on top of another:** Imagine your vertebrae as bricks that you're stacking one on top of the other, beginning with the first at the base of the spine. Feel your spine growing up toward the sky brick by brick, like a skyscraper.

 ✔ **Sitting like a mountain or tree:** Imagine your body as a mountain or tree with a broad base that extends deep into the earth and a trunk or peak that reaches toward the sky (see Figure 8-7). Notice how stable, grounded, and self-sufficient you feel.

Figure 8-7: Here's how you look from the side when you extend your spine.

TRADITIONAL WISDOM

Four tried-and-true meditation positions — plus a few more

If you can't sit comfortably in any of the usual sitting positions, you can take heart from the Buddhist tradition, which offers four equally acceptable alternatives for formal meditation:

- ✔ Sitting
- ✔ Standing
- ✔ Walking
- ✔ Lying down

Giant statues in India and Southeast Asia show the Buddha himself meditating while lying on his right side with his head cradled in his hand. Yogis and ascetics have long meditated while standing, sometimes on one leg. And walking meditation is still widely practiced throughout the world, from the Zen monasteries of Japan and the forest monasteries of Thailand to the Sufi communities of the Middle East and the Christian hermitages of Europe and North America.

Of course, the Sufis recognize a fifth traditional posture—the spinning dance of the dervishes—and the Taoists teach the martial art t'ai chi as a moving meditation. In the West, some of the followers of Swiss psychologist C. G. Jung have developed a meditative form known as *authentic movement,* and some Christians practice walking in contemplation around a spiral labyrinth. Ultimately, any activity can become a meditation if you do it mindfully, as I describe in Chapter 17.

At formal silent retreats, I've seen people meditating in wheelchairs, newcomers perched on high cushions surrounded by bolsters, and old-timers who do nothing but walk or lie down for ten days. And I've seen a photo of the great Indian yogi Swami Muktananda meditating while roosting like a bird in a tree. The point is, there's no one right way to do it—just discover what works for you.

When you know what it feels like to sit upright with your spine extended, you can rock your body from side to side like a pendulum, first broadly and then in gradually decreasing arcs until you come to rest in the center. Next, you can tilt your pelvis forward slightly, accentuating the natural curvature of your lower back, and then lean forward and backward from the waist (keeping your back straight) until you come to center. Finally, tuck your chin and draw your head back gently. Now you're ready to begin your meditation.

At first, you may need to use these techniques and images again and again to help you return to a comfortable, upright sitting position. But eventually, you'll find that sitting up straight becomes a far more intuitive and immediate affair — you'll just sit down, rock a little from side to side, gently extend your spine, and start meditating.

Zafus, benches, and other exotic paraphernalia

Depending on which meditation tradition you explore, you're likely to encounter a range of different sitting devices. Some yogis I know like to plop down a tiny rectangular bag filled with rice before they artfully settle onto it and cross their legs in full lotus. Many Zen folks and other Buddhists prefer the plump round cushions known as *zafus* (Japanese for "sitting cushions"), often combined with flat, square cushions filled with cotton batting for extra height, if needed (see Figure 8-8).

Figure 8-8:
Check out this sitting gear: zafu, support cushion, and padded bench.

Ten quick steps to prep your body for meditation

This handy list provides a user-friendly summary of the steps described in detail earlier in this chapter:

1. Arrange your legs.

2. Lengthen your spine.

3. Rock your body from side to side like a pendulum.

4. Rock your body from front to back.

5. Tilt your pelvis slightly forward and soften your belly.

6. Tuck your chin gently.

7. Rest your tongue on the roof of your mouth and breathe through your nose, if possible.

8. Rest your hands on your thighs or in your lap.

9. Relax your body from head to toe, letting go as much as possible of any tension or discomfort.

10. Begin your meditation.

Zafus have infiltrated the meditation halls of every spiritual lineage and denomination, from Sufis and Buddhists to Christian monastics (see Chapter 3 for more about Sufis). Zafus are traditionally stuffed with *kapok,* which are silky natural fibers that keep their shape despite repeated sittings. In recent years, zafus filled with buckwheat husks have gained in popularity, and I've come across rectangular sitting cushions filled with cotton batting or with firm polyurethane foam.

Before buying a zafu, be sure to try out a number of different shapes and sizes, checking them for relative comfort, stability, and height. You want to be able to sit so both knees touch the floor, if possible, and your pelvis tilts slightly forward.

If you're a kneeler, you can try sitting on a zafu or other convenient cushion placed on the floor between your legs, or you can use one of the meditation benches designed exclusively for the purpose. Again, experiment before buying. If you're a chair sitter, choose one with a firm cushion and a straight back — not one of those plush armchairs into which you can comfortably disappear and drift off. Just be sure your buttocks are somewhat higher than your knees.

Keeping good head and shoulders

In Zen, good posture refers to more than how you position your back and legs; it refers to an attitude toward life in general. Attentive yet relaxed, you face each moment and each situation directly, with a bearing that suggests: "I'm open to whatever arises. I'm present and ready to respond." One of my teachers, the Tibetan meditation master Chogyam Trungpa Rinpoche, used to call this "keeping good head and shoulders."

If you have an alarm watch, set it to beep every hour for the rest of the day. (If you don't, just do this exercise at random times.) When your watch beeps, take a moment to pay attention to your body. How am I standing or sitting right now? Am I slouching or slumping? And if so, how would it feel to gently extend my spine and align myself with gravity?

Notice how this subtle shift affects your mood and your outlook on life as you go about your day.

Chapter 9

Where to Sit, What to Wear, and Other Practical Stuff

*W*hen I began meditating in college, I took the bus and subway once a week from my West Side apartment to the little Zen center on Manhattan's Upper East Side. Each time I entered the front door, the smell of incense, the Japanese straw mats, the simple altar, and the dark robes of the members all reminded me that I had entered a special place — a place devoted to the practice of meditation. I could feel my breath deepening and my mind slowing down, and I was frustrated to find that I couldn't translate the quality of meditation I experienced there to the cramped little apartment I shared with three friends.

Over the years, I've learned that the physical environment surrounding your meditation — where, when, and how long you sit; what you wear; what kind of energy you invest — can have a powerful impact on the quality of your meditation. Trying to count your breaths in a busy airport or a noisy office can be an enjoyable challenge, of course, but you'll go deeper faster in a quiet place that's specifically devoted to meditation.

You may fantasize about going off to an ashram or some other spiritual community where everything is conveniently taken care of and all you have to do is meditate, eat, and sleep. Such places do exist, of course, and you may be lucky enough to find one. But if the circumstances of your life don't allow for time away, you may just have to carve the time and space for meditation out of the raw material of your busy life. That's why I include this chapter.

In these pages, you find out how to choose just the right spot for your meditation, get some guidelines for determining when and how long to sit, and pick up a few pointers for setting up an altar that will inspire your efforts. Creating and maintaining your own meditation niche is the next best thing to meditating in a monastery. (For more about meditating with others, turn to Chapter 17.)

What to Wear: Choosing Comfort over Fashion

This one may seem like a no-brainer, but you'd be surprised how many people show up for meditation wearing designer jeans or tight skirts that make it virtually impossible for them to breathe or cross their legs. The key to comfortable sitting is this: Keep clothing loose and roomy and avoid constricting your breathing or your circulation in any way. Sweat clothes generally make great sitting gear. If you're into meditation chic, you can buy a sleek but comfortable yoga outfit online in a variety of colors and materials.

Because body temperature and blood pressure tend to drop during meditation, you may get chillier than usual, so be sure to have a sweater or woolen blanket nearby as a wrap.

When to Meditate: Any Time's the Right Time

If you're incredibly busy, pencil in formal periods of meditation whenever you can find the time. But if you have the luxury of having a number of options, I fill you in on some of the best times to sit in the following sections.

Ultimately, every moment and every activity can provide an opportunity to be mindful. (For more on mindfulness in everyday life, see Chapter 17.)

First thing in the morning

Traditionally, the hour or two right after you wake up — preferably around sunrise — is considered the best time to meditate. Your mind and body are refreshed and energized by deep sleep, and you haven't yet started to obsess about your usual worries and concerns. As a result, you may find it easier to focus and stay present. By meditating first thing in the morning, you also set the tone for the rest of the day and can extend whatever peace of mind you generate to your other activities.

Before bed

Some people take an hour or two to wake up from the dreamy fog of sleep, and others have just enough time to roll out of bed, grab a cup of coffee, and rush out to join the morning commute. If you're groggy when you get up or have to switch to high gear the moment your feet hit the floor, try meditating in the evening before bed. It's a great way to prepare for sleep because it allows your mind to settle down and shift naturally and with ease from waking to slumber. In fact, meditators who sit at bedtime often report that their sleep is more restful and they need less of it.

Of course, the downside to meditating right before bed is that you may feel as though you're too tired, sleepy, or stressed out to meditate, so you may wind up taking a hot bath, watching TV, or going to bed early instead. But when you get into the habit, you'll find that evening meditations are an excellent option with some distinct advantages of their own.

Right after work

Though not as reliable as mornings or bedtimes because it's often usurped by errands, early dinners, or family emergencies, the transition between work and home can be a fitting moment to take a few deep breaths and let your body and mind settle — instead of reaching for the paper or flipping on the tube.

Lunch hours and coffee breaks

If you have an office of your own and a time set aside for lunch or coffee — a big *if* because more and more people eat on the fly these days — plan on bringing your food or scoring your java in advance and spending the rest of the time meditating. You may even set aside a special space in your office — including an altar, if you're so inclined.

Walking meditation

Between periods of formal sitting, meditators throughout the world have long practiced walking with mindful awareness. Besides breaking the monotony of uninterrupted sitting, it's a great meditation in its own right — and a wonderful way to practice extending the mindfulness you learn on your cushion or chair into the ordinary world of movement and activity.

In some Zen monasteries, walking meditation more closely resembles a kind of restrained, conscious running. In parts of Southeast Asia, the movement may be almost imperceptibly slow. Here's a more moderate approach you can practice not only between periods of sitting meditation but also anytime you want to slow down a little and pay attention as you walk. If the weather allows, by all means walk outside. Or you can just walk back and forth in your house. (For detailed audio instructions, listen to Track 6.)

1. **Begin by walking at your usual pace, following your in-breath and out-breath as you walk.**

2. **Coordinate your breathing with your steps.**

For example, you can take three steps for each inhalation and three steps for each exhalation — which, as you may notice, is considerably slower than most people walk. If you want to change the speed of your walking, just change the number of steps per breath. But maintain the same pace each time you walk. (If your inhalations and exhalations are different lengths, just adapt your walking accordingly.)

3. **In addition to your breathing, be aware of your feet and legs as you lift and move them.**

Notice the contact of your feet with the ground or floor. Gaze ahead of you, with your eyes lowered at a 45-degree angle. Resist the temptation to look around and "sightsee." Be relaxed, easy, and comfortable as you walk.

4. **Enjoy your steady, mindful walking for as long as you want.**

If your attention wanders or you start to hurry, gently bring your attention back to your walking.

While waiting for your kids and at other predictable downtimes

If you're like many parents, you may spend hours each week shuttling your kids from one activity or playdate to another — and sitting in the car or running errands while you wait for them to finish. Instead of picking up a magazine or listening to the news, try meditating. (You can take the same approach to waiting for your doctor or dentist.) Although you may not be in the best environment and your posture may not be ideal, look at it this way: It's a stretch of precious idle time. Use it wisely.

How Long to Meditate: From Quickies to the Long Haul

Meditation resembles sex in a number of ways, and this is one of them: You may prefer it short and quick or long and slow. But whatever your predilections, you'd probably agree that some sexual contact with your beloved is better than no sex at all.

Well, apply this dictum to meditation, and you'll get the drift. If you can't schedule a half-hour, then meditate for a few minutes. Sitting for five or ten minutes every day is much better than sitting for an hour once a week — though you may want to do both. As with all the guidelines in this book, experiment with the different options until you find the one that suits you best.

Digital alarm watches, smartphones, and tablets provide good ways to time your meditations without watching the clock, and some offer a variety of pleasant sounds to alert you. Or you may want to signal the beginning and end of your meditation with the sound of a small bell, as is done in many traditional cultures.

Whether you have five minutes or an hour to meditate, here I show you how to make the most of your time:

- ✔ **Five minutes:** If you're a beginner, a few minutes can seem like an eternity, so start off slowly and increase the length of your sittings as your interest and enjoyment dictate. You may find that by the time you settle your body and start to focus on your breath, your time is up. If the session seems too short, you can always sit a little longer next time. As your practice develops, you'll find that even five minutes can be immeasurably refreshing.

- ✔ **Ten to 15 minutes:** If you're like most people, you need several minutes at the start of meditation to get settled, a few more minutes to become engaged in the process, and several minutes at the end to reorient — which means that 10 or 15 minutes leaves you a little in the middle to deepen your concentration or expand your awareness.

  When you've made it this far, try leveling off at 15 minutes a day for several weeks, and watch how your powers of concentration build.

- ✔ **Twenty minutes to an hour:** The longer you sit, the more time you'll have between preliminaries and endings to settle into a focused and relaxed state of mind. If you have the motivation and can carve out the time, by all means devote 20 minutes, 40 minutes, or an hour to meditation each day. You'll notice the difference — and you'll understand why most meditation teachers recommend sitting this long at a stretch. Perhaps it's the human attention span — look at the proverbial 50-minute hour of psychotherapy or the optimal length for most TV shows.

Keeping your practice steady and regular is better than splurging one day and abstaining for the rest of the week.

What to Eat and Drink — and Avoid — before You Meditate

Big meals can make you drowsy, especially when they're high in carbohydrates, so eat lightly if at all before you sit. Or wait at least one hour after a major repast. You may even consider following the traditional Zen guideline to eat until you're two-thirds full, instead of bursting at the seams — it may not be bad for your waistline, either.

As for drinking (and smoking), here are a few suggestions: I do know seasoned meditators who like to down a cup of cappuccino before they sit, and at least one Zen master who made it a habit of meditating first thing in the morning after drinking too much sake the night before. But as a general rule, abstaining from mind-altering substances (for example, coffee, alcohol, tobacco, marijuana, and other recreational drugs) before meditating is best.

As your practice grows and you observe the benefits of being present and focused, rather than zoned out or drugged up, you may naturally diminish your intake. In fact, you may discover that meditation makes you more sensitive to your state of mind and provides a natural high that renders these substances unnecessary or obsolete. And if your primary motivation for meditating is to reduce stress or enhance your health, you may consider abstaining entirely from your substance of choice. Believe it or not, indulging only adds to the burden of stress you're already experiencing.

Where to Meditate: Creating Sacred Space

Perhaps you've seen those Chinese paintings where a bearded sage in a flowing robe sits in deep contemplation at the base of some majestic peak with a waterfall thundering beside him. Maybe you've even had moments when you wished you could become that sage, disappear into the mountains, and meditate in silence and simplicity for the rest of your days. Alas, life doesn't usually support us nowadays in actualizing such fantasies!

Meditating in nature

As you may have already noticed, the natural world has an unparalleled capacity to relax your body and calm your mind. When you're sitting by the ocean listening to the surf or hiking in the mountains among the rocks and trees, you don't have to practice some formal meditation technique — just open your senses and let nature work its magic. Without any effort on your part, you begin to feel your mind settle down, your worries dissipate, your breathing deepen and slow, your tension melt away, and your heart fill with gratitude and love.

As a species, we evolved in the natural world, and the plants and animals have been teaching us how to meditate for as long as we've had legs to cross. When you meditate in nature, you've arrived where you belong, and the ease and familiarity you feel there invites you to return home to yourself, to your innermost "nature." (How fascinating and appropriate that the words are the same!) Entering a natural setting can stop your mind in its tracks, causing you to sense the presence of something deeper and more meaningful.

Make it a point to meditate in nature as often as you can, and take note of the state of mind and heart that it evokes. Even if you live in the inner city, you can usually find some park or garden or small patch of woods or water. Then, when you meditate at home again, you can invoke the resonance of your moments in nature to help you deepen your practice.

Instead of shaving your head and heading for the hills, however, you can follow a few simple guidelines, which I outline in the following sections, for carving out a special place for the practice of meditation. You'll find that the space you set aside will enrich your life in ways you can't imagine.

Why it's best to stay put

Just as it helps to have a regular time to meditate, there are some definite advantages to sitting in the same location day after day, instead of moving from place to place. These include the following:

✔ **Fewer distractions:** As a beginner, you already have plenty of distractions to contend with, both inner and outer. Why add all the nuances of a constantly shifting external environment? After you get used to seeing those little stains on the carpet and those cracks in the paint, you can free up your attention for the matter at hand: meditation.

✔ **Good vibes:** The more often you sit there, the more you infuse your spot and its environs with the energy of your efforts — your good vibes, if you will. Whenever you return, your meditation is buoyed and supported by the energy you've invested, just as you feel especially comfortable and relaxed in your favorite chair.

✔ **Peaceful memories:** When you've picked your spot, you start associating it with meditation, especially if you keep your altar or your sitting gear there. Just passing it on your way to other activities reminds you to come back to meditate when you next have a chance. And if your meditation involves spiritual aspirations, your spot becomes a sacred site where your deepest insights and reflections take place.

How to pick the right spot

If you share a small apartment with a partner or friend, or your family has usurped every square foot of usable space at your house, by all means choose the only vacant corner and make it your own. If you have more leeway, here are a few guidelines for picking your spot. And remember, even a modest patch of floor that meets these criteria is better than a sumptuous suite that doesn't.

✔ **Off the beaten track:** You know the heavily trafficked highways in your house, so be sure to avoid them. And if you don't want someone inadvertently barging in on you just when you're starting to settle, tell your housemates you're going off to meditate — they'll understand. And if they don't . . . well, that's another issue you may eventually have to face.

✔ **Away from work:** If you work at home or have a desk devoted to personal business, keep it out of sight — and mind — when you're meditating. And if possible, remember to shut off your phone; nothing is quite as distracting as wondering who's trying to reach you! (If you forget to turn off the phone, simply welcome the ringing as part of your meditation and resist the urge to get up and answer.)

✔ **Relatively quiet:** Especially if you live in the city, you probably won't be able to eliminate the usual background noises — the drone of traffic, the shouts and laughter of kids on the street, the hum of the refrigerator. But you should, if at all possible, avoid audible conversations, especially among people you know; and the sounds of TV, radio, popular music, and other familiar distractions. These kinds of recognizable noises can pull your mind away from its appointed task, especially when you're just starting out. Of course, the guided meditations on the CD (or downloadable files, if you're reading a digital copy of this book) are a notable exception!

✔ **Not too dark or too light:** Sitting in a bright, sunny spot may be too energizing and distracting, just as sitting in the dark can put you to sleep. Be sure to modulate the lighting with your attention level in mind: If you're sleepy, open the blinds or turn on an extra light; if you're wired, tone down the illumination accordingly.

✔ **Fresh air:** Because we're talking about breathing here, it's great to have a supply of fresh air where you meditate. Avoid musty basements and windowless closets; besides being bad for your health, they tend to lower your energy (along with your oxygen level) and lull you to sleep.

✔ **Close to nature:** If you don't have a tree or a garden outside the window near where you meditate, you may want to have a plant or a vase full of flowers or a few stones nearby. Not that you'll be gazing at them while you sit, but natural objects radiate a certain special energy that lends support to your practice. Besides, you can pick up a few pointers by watching how rocks and trees meditate — they've been doing it a lot longer than you have. (See the sidebar "Meditating in nature" for more information.)

How to set up an altar — and why you may want to bother

For many people, the word *altar* is fraught with associations. Maybe you have memories of being an altar boy as a kid — or you recall altars you've seen on special occasions like weddings or funerals or memorial services.

For the purposes of this book, I use *altar* to refer to a collection of objects with special meaning and resonance for you that you assemble in one place and use to inspire your meditations. If you're a Christian, for example, your altar may include a crucifix or a picture of Jesus; if you're a Jew, you may have a holy book or a Star of David; or, if you're a Buddhist, you may choose a statue of Buddha or a photo of your teacher. And if you have no particular religious inclinations, you may be quite content with a few stones, a candle, and a potted plant.

Which direction should I face?

If you meditate with your eyes closed, it doesn't really matter which way your body is pointed. But if you keep your eyes open, you're better off avoiding busy, distracting views. For example, Zen monks (in certain traditions, anyway) usually sit facing a wall. Or you can gaze out on a relaxing, natural vista (if you have one) or just face your altar, with its attractive array of meaningful objects. Whatever you see when you meditate, make sure it's simple and contributes to your peace of mind.

Although an altar isn't essential to meditation, it can be a creative and constantly evolving expression of your inner life, a reflection of your deepest aspirations, values, and beliefs. Gazing at your altar before you sit can evoke your connection to a spiritual dimension of being — or it can merely remind you of why you're here: to develop concentration, relax, open your heart, heal your body. Here are some of the main ingredients that appear on many altars (see Figure 9-1); feel free to improvise and add or subtract as you see fit:

- ✔ Bells
- ✔ Candles
- ✔ Flowers
- ✔ Incense
- ✔ Natural objects
- ✔ Pictures (of nature or inspirational figures)
- ✔ Sacred texts
- ✔ Statues (of inspirational figures)

Figure 9-1:
Use an altar to inspire your meditation.

Finding the beauty

Even in the most chaotic and unappealing situations, you can attune yourself to a quality or dimension of beauty, if you try. Imagine that your mind is like a CD player, and you're trying to tune in to a particular track. Or consider one of those figure-ground puzzles. At first, you can't even perceive the shape in the background. But as soon as you've seen it, you merely need to shift your awareness to see it again.

So the next time you find yourself in an unpleasant place or circumstance — preferably not one with a strong emotional charge because that may make this exercise too difficult — do the following:

1. **Take a moment to look for the beauty.**

   You may notice a patch of green grass in the distance, or a bouquet of flowers on a table, or the laughter of a child, or an aesthetically pleasing piece of furniture. Or you may just notice a warm feeling in your belly or heart.

2. **Take a deep breath, set aside your stress and discomfort, and enjoy the beauty.**

   Allow yourself to resonate with it for a few moments as you would with a favorite piece of music or a walk in the woods.

3. **Shift your focus back to the situation at hand and notice whether your attitude has changed in any way.**

   Know that you can shift your awareness in this way whenever you feel inclined.

Some traditions recommend that altars appeal to all the senses — hence, the incense, bells, flowers, and candles, which are mainstays on many home altars. In particular, the fragrance of your favorite incense can quickly become hyperlinked in your brain with meditation, causing you to relax just a little whenever you smell it.

As with your meditation, it's best to keep your altar simple at first. Use a small, low table or cabinet (if you meditate on the floor) covered with a special piece of cloth. If you want, you can enrich and expand it over time, or you may prefer to keep a stash of objects and rotate them as the spirit moves you. For example, you can adapt your altar to the seasons, with flowers in spring, seashells in summer, dried leaves in autumn, pine boughs in winter, and so on.

One cautionary note about pictures: You may want to devote your altar to mentors, teachers, and other figures whose presence fills you with unadulterated inspiration — and consign to your desk or bureau pictures of those loved ones for whom your feelings may be more complex, like children, parents, spouses, and friends.

Chapter 10

Just Doing It: Discipline, Effort, and Letting Go

. . . .

In This Chapter

▶ Developing great meditation habits without getting uptight

▶ Discovering the secret to having more energy in meditation and in life

▶ Learning the three aspects of discipline and the five stages of letting go

. . . .

*A*s I mention in previous chapters, meditation has quite a bit in common with sports. First you have to learn the mechanics — how to sit up straight, position your legs, relax your body, and focus on your breath. Then you need to understand the rules of the game — how long it takes, where you should practice, what you should wear. But when you're clear on the details, you need to know how to apply yourself so you can get the most from what you've discovered.

Say that you want to run a marathon and you get some expert coaching on the fundamentals of running. Then you start jogging 3 or 4 miles every day. The next step is to figure out how to work with your mind and your body so you can go the distance without exhausting yourself completely. You have to master some intangible inner qualities like discipline, effort, and a certain ease or comfort in your execution. These qualities can't really be taught, only described and evoked.

Well, the same is true for meditation. Discipline grabs you by the collar and sits you down day after day, even when the going gets tough. Effort keeps focusing your mind and bringing it back again and again to your breath or your mantra (or some other object of meditation). And letting go allows you to relax and open up to whatever you're experiencing, no matter how challenging or difficult. Discovering how to apply these three ingredients to the practice of meditation is just what this chapter is all about.

Discipline Just Means "Again and Again"

If you're like most folks, the word *discipline* may be a bit of a turnoff. Perhaps it reminds you of some bossy teacher who made you stay after school or childhood punishments that were intended to "set you straight." Or maybe you associate discipline with soldiers marching single-file or with prisoners forced to obey their keepers. But the discipline I'm talking about here is quite different.

When I say *discipline,* I mean the kind of self-discipline that prompts top athletes like Kobe Bryant and Serena Williams to get up every morning and run several miles and then practice their shot or their stroke over and over, long after they've gotten it right. It's the kind of self-discipline that motivates great writers to sit at their computers each day, no matter how they feel, and pound out their copy.

The truth is, you already have self-discipline, though you may not be aware of it. You need self-discipline to get to your job on time or to orchestrate a schedule filled with business commitments, personal interests, and family responsibilities. You need self-discipline to pay your bills or keep up a garden or take care of your kids. You merely need to apply the same self-discipline to the practice of meditation.

Again, self-discipline is nothing more than the capacity to do something again and again. But I find it helpful to break self-discipline down a little further into three parts: commitment, consistency, and self-restraint. I explain each in the following sections.

Making a commitment to yourself — and keeping it

When you commit to marriage or some other monogamous relationship, you make an agreement with yourself and your partner to stay together through thick and thin, no matter what life brings. Without this commitment, you may be tempted to leave when your partner becomes angry or does something you can't stand or when you find yourself withdrawing or "falling out of love." Of course, you can always decide to end the relationship, but as long as you're committed, you're going to do all you can to maintain it.

The same holds true for meditation. *Commitment* is the foundation for your meditation practice. Without commitment, you won't keep meditating when you're tired, have a headache, don't feel like it, would rather do something else, or run up against some of the roadblocks I cover in Chapter 13.

And what prompts you to make the commitment to meditate in the first place? You have to be motivated (see Chapter 5), which means you have to know how you can benefit from what meditation has to offer (see Chapter 2), and you must have strong personal reasons for continuing. These reasons may include a desire to alleviate personal suffering or stress, an aspiration to achieve greater focus and clarity, and a concern for the welfare of others.

The commitment process usually involves the following five distinct steps:

- ✔ **Becoming motivated:** Ouch, life hurts! I need to find out how to deal with my pain.

- ✔ **Setting your intention:** I know what will help! I'll meditate for 30 minutes every day!

- ✔ **Making an agreement with yourself:** From now until the end of the month, I agree to get up at 7 a.m. and count my breaths before I go to work.

- ✔ **Following through:** Whew! I didn't realize how hard it would be to sit still for so long, but I refuse to break my agreement with myself!

- ✔ **Gaining momentum:** Wow! The more I meditate, the easier it gets. I'm really beginning to enjoy it.

Of course, these steps may occur in a somewhat different order, and you may find yourself repeating some of them again and again. In fact, the commitment deepens through constant repetition.

Being consistent, day after day

Take sports again. If you train for a day and then slack off for a week, you won't make much progress. In fact, you may end up straining a muscle or hurting your back because you haven't conditioned your body gradually, as most fitness gurus recommend.

Likewise, when you practice meditation, you're developing certain mental and emotional muscles like concentration, *mindfulness* (ongoing attention to whatever is arising, moment to moment), and receptive awareness. (See Chapter 1 for more about these mental and emotional "muscles.") Here, too, consistency is the key. You need to keep it up and keep it regular, no matter how you're feeling day to day. In fact, your feelings provide the fodder for your meditation practice as you expand your awareness from your breath to include the full range of your experience. You don't have to be any special way — just show up and be yourself!

If you don't dig sports, try gardening

Although meditating has a lot in common with practicing and playing a sport, for some folks, meditating may be more akin to gardening. After you plant the seeds, you don't try to force the seedlings out of the ground, do you? You just water and fertilize, thin, and then water some more. Eventually the little shoots appear on their own, coaxed into the light by some complex and mysterious mixture of chemistry, genetics, phototropism, and who knows what else.

The point is, you don't have to know — you just have to do your part, and then get out of the way! If you get carried away and overwater or disturb the ground prematurely, you only interfere with the process.

In the same way, you need to exert just the right amount of consistent effort in your meditation. Don't overwater or keep scratching the ground searching for signs of progress, but don't go away for a week and leave your plot unattended, either. Do what you need to do without fixating on the results, and your garden will blossom quite naturally, all by itself.

As one old Chinese Zen master used to say, "Sun-faced Buddha, moon-faced Buddha" — by which he meant, happy or sad, energetic or tired, just sit as the being you happen to be.

Be especially wary of two extremes: laziness or *self-indulgence* ("I'd rather be sleeping, resting, watching TV") and *perfectionism* ("I'm not ready to meditate. I'm not smart or good or focused enough.") Remember, I'm talking about meditation for beginners here — and besides, the best way to become "good enough" to meditate is to just do it!

Restraining yourself, both on and off the cushion

Broadly speaking, *self-restraint* is the quality of mind that keeps you from acting on every impulse or desire that flits through your brain. It helps you discriminate between behavior that's useful and supportive and behavior that's unsupportive or even harmful. If you're an athlete, you need self-restraint to prevent you from eating junk food or staying out late when you're training for a big competition. If you're a meditator, self-restraint can function on several different levels:

✔ **Before meditation:** You may choose to eat well and in moderation or to avoid mind-altering substances, such as tobacco or caffeine, because you want to keep your mind clear and fresh for your meditation.

✔ **During meditation:** You can use self-restraint to keep pulling your mind back from its habitual fantasies and preoccupations to the object of your meditation, be it your breath or a mantra or some other focus. Be careful, however, not to confuse self-restraint with repression, avoidance, or judgment. You don't need to criticize yourself for wandering off, nor do you want to push certain "undesirable" thoughts or feelings out of your mind. Instead, just welcome whatever arises, while gently returning your focus to the object of your meditation.

✔ **After meditation:** As your practice deepens and strengthens, you build a certain power or energy of mind. In the East, they call this power *samadhi*. (For more on energy, see the later section "The Right Kind of Effort: Not Too Tight or Too Loose.") You can blow off this energy by daydreaming or planning or obsessing, or you can use self-restraint to channel your energy back into your practice of being mindful from moment to moment.

Like self-discipline, self-restraint has a bad rap in today's culture. After all, aren't you supposed to say what you think and do what feels right? But what feels right in the moment may not be the same as what feels right in the long run. Self-restraint is the faculty that helps you distinguish between the two. For example, you may be tempted to charge those plane tickets to Hawaii because it feels right, but you may have different feelings altogether when you get your credit card statement. In the same way, it may feel great to spend your meditation indulging in fantasy. But it's only fun until you start wondering in a month or two why you still can't count your breaths from one to ten. Above all, though, remember to be gentle with yourself!

Doing what you love

Choose an activity you especially enjoy. Maybe it's dancing, cooking, painting, making love, or simply playing with your kids. The next time you engage in that activity, give yourself to it wholeheartedly. Don't hold back or conserve your energy in any way. Experiment with losing yourself completely in the activity the way children do. Don't keep looking at your watch or wondering how you're doing; just do it without reservation until you and the activity seem to merge and become one.

How do you know when to stop the activity? Do you suddenly find yourself disengaging? Or do you reach a natural stopping point when you intuitively know it's time? And how do you feel when you're done? Do you feel drained and tired? Or do you feel energized and excited? Think of this exercise the next time you sit down to meditate.

Digging your way to freedom

One of the great meditative traditions tells the story of a prisoner who is sentenced to life for a crime he did not commit. At first, he bemoans his fate and indulges in fantasies of revenge and regret. Then he bestirs himself and decides to get free no matter what happens. So he starts digging a hole in the wall of his cell with a spoon — kind of like Tim Robbins in *The Shawshank Redemption.*

Day after day, week after week, year after year the prisoner digs, making slow but steady progress. Then one day, worn out from his labors, he leans against the back door of his cell, which gives beneath his weight! In an instant, he realizes that all these years, while he was slaving away at his attempts to get free, the door to freedom was open all along. But he might never have realized it had he not worked so hard to escape.

The point of this story is clear: If you practice your meditation with steady and consistent effort, you'll eventually experience moments when all effort drops away, the door opens wide, and you're simply present, aware, peaceful, and relaxed.

Although these moments may seem quite ordinary when they occur, they can have a powerful, healing effect on your body and mind because they offer you a brief glimpse of your essential wholeness and completeness, free from the overlays of conditioning and striving.

Yet the paradox is that the door is always open and the glimpses of being are always available — in a loving glance, a child's laughter, or the silence of the trees — but you may have to exert effort and practice for years before you stumble upon them. And then again, you may not!

The Right Kind of Effort: Not Too Tight or Too Loose

If discipline is the capacity to keep doing something again and again, *effort* is the quality of energy and exertion you bring to the activity itself. Although it may take discipline to show up at the gym every day, it takes effort to do those aerobics, lift those weights, or shoot those hoops. I'm sure you know what I'm talking about! As with self-discipline, you may find it helpful to break effort into three convenient parts: *energy, earnestness,* and *effortless effort.*

Giving your energy 100 percent

A secret "law of energy" applies just as well to meditation as it does to sports (and to life in general). This law states that the more you expend, the more you get back in return. You can be stingy about your energy, parceling it out from one activity to the next as though you have just so much to give and no more. But if you love something and give yourself to it wholeheartedly, you may notice that the energy just feeds on itself and keeps growing and growing.

In a legendary game in the NBA finals one year, Michael Jordan was suffering from an intestinal flu so severe that he needed fluid IVs and could barely stand. Yet, carried aloft by his own dedication (what he called "heart") and fueled by an energy that seemed drawn from a source far vaster than his own exhausted body, he suited up for his team and scored 38 points. Jordan embodied the quality of wholeheartedness.

In meditation, too, the more wholeheartedly you practice, the more you tap into a seemingly limitless energy source. It's as though the flame inside your heart begins channeling the fusion energy that runs the sun. But don't confuse wholeheartedness with struggle; when you meditate, remember to relax and open while you focus your mind. It's this unique balance of active and receptive, yang and yin, that characterizes the practice of meditation. (For more on this balance, see the section, "Making an effortless effort.")

Applying yourself earnestly

Where self-restraint keeps you from doing what may be harmful or unhealthy and wholeheartedness supplies the spark that ignites your meditation, earnestness keeps bringing your mind back to your focus. No matter what thoughts or feelings arise to seduce you away, you just keep plugging along following your breaths, chanting your mantra, or paying mindful attention in everyday life. Just as it takes consistency to return to your sitting day after day, it takes earnest application to return to the focus of your meditation moment after moment, without struggling or giving up. Earnestness isn't sexy or exciting — it's just essential! (Perhaps this is what Oscar Wilde meant by *The Importance of Being Earnest.*)

Making an effortless effort

When I was a neophyte meditator, one of my teachers, the Zen master Shunryu Suzuki, used to say, somewhat mysteriously, "Follow the wave, drive the wave." But I never really knew what he meant until I started to surf. Now I understand!

When I'm out there on the ocean floating on my board, alone with the wind and the sky, I'm excruciatingly aware of how small and insignificant I am in comparison to the awesome power of the water. It would be presumptuous of me to say that I surf the waves — in fact, the waves surf me!

I know that I can't possibly attempt to control the water in any way. Yet I do need to exert a certain effort: I need to concentrate on the swell, paddle at just the right time, and position my body in just the right way to catch the wave at its apex so that it can carry me to the shore. And I need to stay focused as I shift my weight ever so subtly from side to side in order to ride the wave as fully as I possibly can.

Well, meditation is like surfing. If you push too hard and try to control your mind, you'll just end up feeling rigid and tight, and you'll keep wiping out as the result of your effort. But if you hang back and exert no effort at all, you won't have the focus or concentration necessary to hold your position as the waves of thought and emotion wash over you.

Like surfing — or any other sport, for that matter — meditation requires a constantly shifting balance of yang and yin, driving and following, effort and effortlessness. As I mention in Chapter 1, concentration is the yang of meditation (focused, powerful, penetrating) and receptive awareness is the yin (open, expansive, welcoming). Although you may have to exert considerable effort at first just to develop your concentration, try not to become tense or obsessive about it. Let your effort be effortless, like a seasoned surfer's.

Eventually, your concentration will arise quite naturally and take only minimal effort to maintain, and you'll be able to relax and open your awareness to whatever arises. Even the notions of yin and yang (awareness and concentration) will ultimately drop away, and you can just *be,* with effortless effort, which is the real point of meditation.

In addition to effortless effort, meditation poses a number of other paradoxes that the mind can't quite comprehend but that the body and heart find easy to grasp. To practice meditation, it helps to be

- **Serious yet lighthearted:** Meditation is about lightening up, but if you're not serious enough, you won't make any progress.

- **Alert yet relaxed:** Learn to balance these two qualities in your meditation. If you become too relaxed, you risk falling asleep, but if you're too alert (that is, wired), you could become tense.

- **Spontaneous yet restrained:** You can be totally in the moment and open to whatever arises in your awareness without becoming impulsive or indulging every fantasy or whim.

- **Engaged yet dispassionate:** While being focused and attentive, you can avoid getting caught up in the compelling and emotionally charged stories your mind spins out.

Knowing How to Let Go and What to Let Go Of

In certain parts of Asia, the story goes, the locals have an ingenious method for catching monkeys alive. The hunter cuts a hole in a coconut just big enough for a monkey to reach in with its hand, but not big enough for it to remove its closed fist. Then the hunter puts a ripe banana inside, attaches the coconut to a string, and waits. Upon grabbing the banana, the monkey becomes so attached to keeping the fruit that it refuses to let go, and the hunter can reel the animal in like a fish on a hook.

As I mention in Chapter 7, your mind is like a monkey in more ways than one. Not only does it leap about from thought to thought like a monkey in a tree, but it also has the annoying tendency of holding tightly to certain ideas, opinions, thoughts, memories, and emotions — as though its life (and yours) depends on it — and pushing away others with equal force.

This constant shifting between attachment and aversion causes you stress because you're constantly struggling to control what can't be controlled. Thoughts and feelings come and go whether you like them or not, and the stock market falls and relationships end despite your preferences to the contrary. (For more on how the mind causes suffering and stress, see Chapter 6.)

Accepting and letting go

Holding on tightly and pushing away hard, lusting and hating, defending and attacking — traditionally known as *attachment* and *aversion* — are the primary causes of suffering and stress. Along with indifference, they form the proverbial three poisons of meditation lore.

Fortunately, you can cultivate the antidotes to these poisons by practicing the two most important gestures or functions of meditation: accepting and letting go. They're inextricably entwined: Until you accept, you can't let go; until you let go, you have no room to accept again. As one Zen master put it, "Let go of it, and it fills your hand." Here's a little exercise that gives you an opportunity to practice both accepting and letting go:

1. **Begin by sitting comfortably and taking a few deep breaths. Now place your attention on the coming and going of your breath.**

2. **After a few minutes, shift your awareness to your thoughts and feelings.**

   Take the attitude that you're going to welcome whatever arises in your experience without judging or rejecting it.

3. **As thoughts and feelings come and go, notice the movement to avoid or push away or not see what you find unpleasant or unacceptable.**

   Accept this movement as you continue to welcome your experience, whatever it may happen to be.

4. **After five or ten minutes, when you have a feel for accepting, shift your attention to the process of letting go.**

   Take the attitude that you're going to let go of whatever arises, no matter how urgent or attractive.

   Notice the movement to hold on or indulge or get involved with thoughts and feelings you find pleasant or compelling. Gently restrain yourself and continue to loosen your grip and let go.

When you have a feel for both accepting and letting go, you can combine them in the same meditation. Whatever arises, welcome and let go, welcome and let go. This is the twofold rhythm of mindfulness meditation.

In Alcoholics Anonymous and other 12-step programs, people recite the following prayer: "Grant me the serenity to accept what I cannot change, the courage to change what I can, and the wisdom to know the difference." In meditation, you develop the power to control or change what you can — not the events or circumstances of your life, but how you relate to them — and the peace of mind to accept what you can't.

Meditation teaches you how to loosen your monkey-grip on your experience and create a kind of inner spaciousness and relaxation by letting go of control and allowing things to be the way they are. This process has several dimensions or stages, which often (though not always) occur in the order of the following sections.

Suspending judgment

If you're like most people, you're constantly judging your experience as good, bad, or indifferent and reacting accordingly:

- ✔ "Ooh, I like that. I'm going to try to get more of it."
- ✔ "I hate that. I'm going to avoid it at all costs."
- ✔ "That doesn't do anything for me. I'm not going to pay any attention to it."

When you meditate, you begin to notice the steady stream of judgments and how they dominate your mind and distort your experience. Instead of indulging this habitual pattern, you can practice witnessing your experience impartially, without judgment. When judgments arise, which they undoubtedly will, you can just be aware of them, while avoiding the temptation to judge them. Gradually, the habit of judging will loosen its grip on your mind.

Accepting

The flip side of suspending judgment involves learning to accept things just the way they are. You don't necessarily have to like what you see, and you're welcome to change it, but first you need to experience it fully and clearly, without the overlays of judgment and denial. For example, you may have lots of anger bubbling up, but you may believe that this particular emotion is bad or even evil, so you refuse to acknowledge it.

In meditation, you have an opportunity to observe the anger just as it is — recurrent angry thoughts, waves of anger in the belly — without trying to change or get rid of it. (For more on meditating with challenging emotions and mind-states, see Chapter 12.) The more you welcome the full range of your experiences in this way, the more space you create inside yourself to contain them — and the more you defuse those old familiar conflicts between different parts of yourself.

Letting go

Participants in 12-step programs sometimes talk about "letting go and letting God." The first stage involves letting go of the illusion that you have unlimited control over your life. In mindfulness meditation, you can practice letting go by dropping all struggles to control your mind (as well as all ideas you may have about how your meditation is supposed to look) and by relaxing into the present moment as it unfolds, both inside and outside. Believe it or not, you already know how to let go; you do it every night when you drift off to sleep.

Unmasking

Letting go also has a deeper dimension: The more you loosen the stranglehold of your likes and dislikes, preferences and prejudices, memories and stories, the more you open to the experience of just being, beyond any limited identities or interpretations. These identities are like the layers of an onion or like clouds that hide the radiance of the sun. As your meditation deepens, you can learn to accept and then let go of these clouds, without mistaking them for the light they obscure. By disidentifying more and more with what you are not — the masks that hide your true nature — you gradually begin to identify with what you are: pure *being*. (For more on pure *being*, see Chapter 1.)

Surrendering

As your meditation opens you to an experience of pure *being*, you may begin to recognize the value of the second stage of the 12-step dictum: "letting God." The truth is, the power or force that's actually controlling your life (and which you essentially are) is far bigger than your small self, and it's eminently trustworthy — some would even say it's sacred or divine.

When you begin to loosen your vice-grip on the steering wheel of your life, you don't plunge headlong into the chaotic abyss, as you may fear; instead, you relinquish your apparent control to the one who has always been in control — call it God or Self or pure *being*. In your meditation, you may actually experience this surrender as a deeper and deeper relaxation into the sacred silence or stillness that surrounds, suffuses, and sustains you.

Breathing with your belly

Healthy breathing involves opening and expanding both your belly and your chest. As a culture, we tend to value big chests and small bellies. As a result, most of us learn early how to "suck it in" and not let our bellies (or our feelings) show. (Believe it or not, in some cultures, a relaxed, expanded belly is considered attractive!)

The problem is, we don't allow ourselves to breathe with our bellies. This habit just limits the amount of life-enhancing oxygen we receive and accentuates the stress pattern of tightening our abdominal muscles and *diaphragm* (the big internal muscle that covers the bottom of the rib cage) and holding our breath.

To counteract this pattern and help relax, try the following exercise, drawn from hatha yoga:

1. **Notice how you're breathing right now.**

   Which parts of your body expand when you breathe, and which parts do not? How deeply and quickly (or slowly) are you breathing? Where does your breathing feel tight or constricted? How do your belly muscles and diaphragm feel?

2. **Make a conscious effort to expand your belly when you breathe.**

   I use the word "effort" advisedly because your abdominal muscles and diaphragm may be quite tight at first.

3. **Breathe deeply and slowly into your belly.**

   Notice your body's resistance to changing your habitual breathing patterns.

4. **Continue breathing in this way for five minutes and then breathe naturally.**

   Do you notice any differences? Do your abdominal muscles feel more relaxed? Are you breathing more deeply than before? Do you feel more energized or calm?

Practice this exercise regularly — at least once a day. It can be especially useful when you're stressed out or anxious and your belly starts to tighten and your breathing constricts. Just shift to belly breathing and notice what happens.

Chapter 11

Opening Your Heart with Love and Compassion

*P*erhaps you're wondering why I devote a chapter of this book to the heart. After all, isn't it true that meditation involves sitting quietly and focusing the mind, whereas affairs of the heart are best reserved for romantic encounters and intimate family discussions?

Well, the great meditative traditions teach that you can cultivate the energy of the heart in meditation the same way you cultivate awareness (for more on awareness, see Chapter 1). Whether it takes the form of love, joy, peace, compassion, or devotion, you can consciously and deliberately generate and expand this energy to create a field that benefits not only yourself, but also the people around you.

Like sunlight, the radiance of an open heart warms and nourishes everyone it touches. But the heart, like the sun, is often closed in and obscured by clouds, in the form of difficult emotions and mind-states like fear, anger, judgment, and doubt. When you practice meditation, you gradually dispel some of these clouds by quieting and calming your agitated mind (see Chapter 6). You can also work directly with unraveling the negative stories your mind tells you and dealing with challenging emotions, as I explain in Chapter 12. Then again, you can take the approach I describe in this chapter: You can burn the clouds away by amplifying the natural warmth of your heart through practices designed to cultivate love and compassion.

Before I show you how to do this, however, I'd like to take you on a guided tour of the territory. Yes, I know you know where your heart is. But have you ever explored it with focused attention? Do you know what causes it to close — and what keeps it closed? And have you ever considered all the ways you can benefit from opening it? Here are some answers.

How Your Heart Closes — and How You Can Open It Again

Needless to say, you weren't born with your heart closed. As anyone who's ever spent any time with a newborn knows, babies have hearts that radiate love like the sun in the tropics. But as you grow up, the bumps and bruises and hardships of life gradually force you to protect your tenderness and other softer emotions with a layer of toughness and defensiveness — the clouds I talked about earlier. This layer surrounds and encloses the heart, protecting your vulnerability — but also keeping your own love locked inside and the love of other people from entering.

Perhaps you're one of those rare individuals whose heart remains open most of the time. If so, congratulations! Or maybe you wrap yourself in a cloud cover — or something even denser, like armor — when you head out the door each morning, but lay it aside when you spend time with friends or family members. Perhaps your heart naturally opens and closes in an ebb and flow like the weather. Or you may be among the millions of people who have difficulty letting love in or extending it to others.

Don't lose heart! You can definitely discover how to open your heart again, as I discuss later in this section. But first I'd like to describe the factors that keep closing your heart when it opens — or keep it closed entirely — and the benefits that come with an open heart, in case you haven't already figured them out.

Some factors that keep closing your heart

Like most human beings, you close your heart, whether automatically or deliberately, because you feel angry, hurt, or threatened by others. Perhaps you're afraid they'll take advantage of your kindness or crush your tender feelings with their insensitivity or restimulate painful memories. Or maybe you're just ticked off about all the times you've been mistreated, and you don't want to let it happen again. We all have our own unique reasons for closing our hearts. Whatever yours happen to be, they may be preventing you from getting the love you really want.

Here are some of the most common factors that close the heart:

- **Fear:** When you're afraid, for whatever reason — of being attacked, criticized, manipulated, overwhelmed — you close your heart in self-defense.

- **Resentment:** When you hold on to old hurts and let bitterness and resentment build up, you shut your heart, not only to the people who hurt you but also to life itself.

- **Unresolved grief:** This natural human emotion can get stuck if you continue to mull over your losses and refuse to let go of the past. When grief fills your heart, you're reluctant to open it because you don't want to feel the pain inside.

- **Jealousy:** Actually a brand of resentment, jealousy can close your heart to the person who has what you wish you had — and to yourself as well for being somehow "inferior."

- **Pain:** Also known as hurt, this feeling, if allowed to build to intolerable levels, may cause you to board up your heart completely and post a sign saying, "Keep out! No trespassing!"

- **Grasping and attachment:** As long as you're emotionally attached to having life go a certain way, you're going to close your heart as soon as other people interfere. In fact, emotions like grief, pain, and even resentment are ultimately rooted in attachment — and the fear of losing what you're attached to.

- **Self-clinging:** If you believe that you're an isolated individual cut off from other people and from your own essential being, you're going to hold on to your own little piece of turf — your own possessions, your own accomplishments, your own happiness — and close your heart, if necessary, to defend it. Also known as *ego* in many of the meditative traditions, self-clinging perpetuates separation and gives rise to the other factors in this list.

Ultimately, of course, only the most enlightened, selfless people can keep their hearts open all the time. I mean, we're talking Jesus or the Dalai Lama here! As for the rest of us, we're going to keep closing our hearts again and again. Only when we've dissolved the barriers that separate us from others — which is what enlightenment is all about — can we keep our hearts open even in the most difficult circumstances.

But, enlightened or not, you can definitely develop the ability to open your heart when you choose to do so. In fact, the regular practice of meditation gradually erodes the experience of separation that causes the heart to stay closed in the first place. (For more on separation, see Chapter 6.) Who knows? One day you may open your heart and never close it again!

Kindness is key

The cultivation of an open heart definitely deserves a chapter of its own; however, traditionally it's regarded not as a separate technique or approach, but as the foundation on which meditation practice rests.

In Southeast Asia, for example, meditators are taught how to develop generosity, patience, and loving kindness before they learn how to meditate. And Tibetan practitioners dedicate the benefit of every meditation to the peace and harmony of all beings, not just themselves. As the Dalai Lama, recipient of the Nobel Peace Prize, says, "My religion is kindness."

You can follow every technique to the *T,* but if your heart's not in it, you won't reap all the wonderful benefits of meditation.

To be open to the present moment, for example, as mindfulness meditation teaches (for more on mindfulness, see Chapter 7), you need to be open with every dimension of your being: body, mind, spirit, and heart. So be sure to bring a measure of love and caring to your meditation — especially toward yourself!

Some good reasons for keeping it open

Imagine that an extraterrestrial lands on Earth and tries to make sense of us human beings from our pop music. It would probably conclude that we regard love (whatever that might be!) as infinitely more precious than everything else combined. But after the ET figures out how to measure love, it might be surprised to discover how little of the invaluable substance actually flows between us much of the time.

For creatures who want to be loved, appreciated, even adored, we certainly go about fulfilling our desire in a curiously unfulfilling way. Instead of manufacturing it ourselves in the little love machine inside our chests, we complain about not getting enough of it, search frantically for someone else to give it to us, and try to make ourselves more lovable by improving our looks or earning more money. But the truth is, the Beatles song has it right: The love you take is equal to the love you make. In other words, the most effective way to get love is to generate it yourself.

By cultivating caring, loving feelings, you can actually provide yourself with the nourishment you seek. At the same time, by radiating those feelings outward to others, you can touch their tender hearts and naturally elicit the same feelings in them, creating a flow of love that keeps circulating and building on itself.

If you've never experienced this kind of flow with someone yourself, you've perhaps met people who live this way. Their eyes sparkle with positive regard, their words speak well of everyone, and they elicit love wherever they go. Through the practices described here, you, too, can begin to generate a flow of loving feelings. It all depends on you.

Here are a few of the innumerable benefits of learning how to love:

✔ **Energy and expansiveness:** If you've ever been in love (maybe you are right now!), you know how vital and alive you can feel when your heart is wide open. Instead of the usual sense of limitation you ordinarily experience, you feel like you have no boundaries, as though you can't really tell where you leave off and the outside world (or your beloved) begins.

✔ **Peace and well-being:** When your heart is filled with love, you feel happy and peaceful for no external reason. In fact, *love, happiness, joy, peace,* and *well-being* are just different versions of the same basic energy, the loving, life-giving energy of the heart. (For more on happiness, see Chapter 16.)

✔ **Good health:** Yes, love is life-giving and life-enhancing. For one thing, it brings people together to create babies, and, in general, love contributes to optimal health by providing an immeasurable vital spark that not only nourishes the internal organs but also provides the body (and the person) with a reason to live. Dean Ornish, M.D., author of *Dr. Dean Ornish's Program for Reversing Heart Disease,* found that love is more important than any other factor in the healing process, including diet and exercise. To heal your heart, he discovered, you need to open your heart.

✔ **Belonging and interconnectedness:** As another old song puts it, love makes the world go round — and it certainly draws people together and keeps them connected. When you open your heart to others, you naturally feel joined with them in a meaningful way. In the deepest sense, love is the source of all meaning and belonging.

✔ **Spiritual awakening:** As they gradually erode your sense of separation from others, loving feelings can eventually reveal the essential nature of life, which is, paradoxically, also love. Ultimately, the Sufis teach, we are simply love searching for itself.

Discovering your "soft spot"

One of my teachers, the Tibetan meditation master Sogyal Rinpoche, used to refer to the place inside where you feel tender, loving emotions as your *soft spot.* The soft spot can be found in your heart, beneath all the toughness and defensiveness. To reach it, you have to risk encountering feelings you might otherwise wish to avoid, such as fear, grief, anger, and the others talked about earlier in this chapter. You'll know the soft spot when you get there because it has a tender sweetness to it that's often tinged with a certain sadness or melancholy about the human condition. (In fact, you may find it slightly painful to open your heart at first, simply because of this sadness, which is actually one of the seeds of compassion.)

The warrior of the heart

For all you tough guys (and gals) who believe that opening the heart is best reserved for sissies and fools, here's some wise counsel from the Tibetan meditation master Chogyam Trungpa. (No stranger to toughness, Trungpa, like the Dalai Lama and thousands of other Tibetans, escaped from his homeland when the Chinese invaded and walked across the Himalayas over a series of precipitous mountain passes to India.)

In his book *Shambhala: The Sacred Path of the Warrior,* he explains that facing your fear and negativity and being willing to keep your heart open, even in the most challenging circumstances, takes tremendous courage. Although you probably think of warriors as impenetrable, unfeeling, and heavily defended, Trungpa takes the opposite view. The sacred warrior who practices meditation, he suggests, is not afraid to feel tender — or to communicate this tenderness to others.

The point is, you can take care of yourself, even defend yourself from harm, when necessary, without closing your heart. An open heart doesn't make you powerless or ineffectual. Quite the contrary, it allows you to respond to situations wisely and skillfully because you feel others' suffering as well as your own.

Because you'll need to be familiar with your soft spot in order to practice the meditations provided in the remainder of this chapter, you may want to experiment with the following exercise:

1. **Begin by closing your eyes, taking a few deep breaths, and relaxing your body a little on each exhalation.**

   Remember to be kind to yourself.

2. **Imagine the face of someone who loved you very much as a child and whose love moved you deeply.**

   In the East, they recommend using your mother, but some Westerners tend to have more problematic relationships with their parents, so you may prefer to use your grandmother or grandfather or some other unconditionally loving figure. (If you never received love like this as a child, you can think of some famous person that you consider to be unconditionally loving, such as Jesus or Buddha or the Divine Mother.)

3. **Remember a particular instance in which this person showed his or her love for you and you really received it and allowed it to nurture you.**

4. **Notice the tender, loving feelings this memory evokes in your heart.**

   The place where you feel them is your soft spot.

5. **Notice if any other feelings accompany the tenderness and gratitude you feel.**

6. **If you find it difficult to re-experience the love, pay attention to what gets in your way.**

   What are some of the feelings standing guard over your soft spot?

7. **Begin to explore the area around your soft spot.**

   What is the state of your heart right now? What are some of the other feelings you find stirring inside, in addition to (or instead of) love? Do you notice any tension or bracing around your heart that keeps it from opening to love?

8. **Be aware of what you find, without judgment or self-criticism.**

Love begins with you

You may find it difficult to feel love and extend it to others because you didn't get much of it yourself as a child. Even though you never really learned how to give and receive love freely, people are constantly asking you for what you believe you don't have. You're like a person living in the desert with a dry well; you can't share any water with others because you don't have any yourself. Or you may find that your well has water but constantly runs dry just when you need it most.

The meditations provided in this chapter dig a well deep into your soft spot, where the waters of love never run dry. (In fact, the love I'm talking about doesn't belong to anyone; it just bubbles up from a mysterious and inexhaustible source.) You may need to prime the pump, though. That's why the traditional instructions counsel you to begin each meditation on love and compassion by focusing on yourself. When you've filled your own well to the brim, you can begin to extend the overflow to include others as well.

Just as you can't really heal others until you've healed yourself to a certain degree, you can't love others until you feel deeply loved yourself. Besides, you deserve love at least as much as anyone else. In the West, we often practice self-denial, while equating self-love with selfishness. Yet, the reverse generally holds true: People who love themselves give love more freely and generously than those who don't.

As a remedy for the widespread Western disease of self-criticism and self-denial, the meditative traditions offer the practice of self-love. In particular, as you work with opening your heart, you can remember to keep your heart open to yourself even, paradoxically, when your heart is closed.

MEDITATION

Appreciating your own goodness

If you have difficulty extending loving feelings to yourself, you may want to take five or ten minutes to reflect on your good qualities or the good things you've done in your life. Go ahead, it won't hurt you!

In the West, we have a cultural taboo against praising ourselves. Instead, we often focus on our shortcomings, which only ends up making us feel contracted and afraid. "Pride goes before a fall," chides the old slogan, suggesting that you'd better watch out because any satisfaction you take in yourself or your

accomplishments could destroy you. "Who do you think you are?" intones the childhood voice of an exasperated mother or father, unwittingly teaching shame and self-doubt.

Despite what your parents (or other influential people) may have implied or told you, it's okay to be happy and to feel good about yourself. By focusing on your goodness, you actually generate positive, expansive feelings that nourish you and everyone around you. "Joy," said the Buddha, "is the gateway to nirvana."

Feeling out the four dimensions of love

Like water, love comes in many shapes and sizes. Just as a crystal-clear mountain lake, a still forest pool, a trickling creek, and a roaring river are all composed of water, so tender emotions like kindness, compassion, joy, gratitude, forgiveness, devotion, generosity, and peace or equanimity arise in the heart and ultimately consist of love. ***Remember:*** These aren't abstractions — they're natural human qualities that you can learn how to cultivate and communicate to others.

REMEMBER

Among all these tender emotions, the Buddhists emphasize the following four as the cornerstones of a happy and fulfilling life (for more on love and happiness, see Chapter 16):

- ✔ **Lovingkindness:** Arises spontaneously in response to the kindness of others and consists of warm, loving, caring feelings that can be deliberately increased and extended. In its fully realized form, lovingkindness is a feeling of goodwill toward all beings without exception.

- ✔ **Compassion:** Takes love a step further. In addition to caring about others, you feel their suffering and naturally feel motivated to help relieve it. (The word *compassion* means "to suffer with.")

- ✔ **Sympathetic joy:** Is the flip side of compassion. It consists of happy feelings that arise in response to the happiness and good fortune of others.

- ✔ **Equanimity:** Can be cultivated through the basic meditation practices taught in this book; also known as steadiness of heart. No matter what happens, you expand to include it without allowing it to upset or disturb you.

In the following sections, I focus on love and compassion and techniques for cultivating them.

Generating Love for Yourself and Others

As I mentioned earlier, you have a love factory right here in your chest. Now you're going to discover how to use it! As a child, you probably received plenty of advice on how to use your mind. Your teachers taught you how to solve math problems and memorize facts; your parents may have helped you with your homework; perhaps you even read some books on speed-reading or improving your study habits. But did anyone ever sit you down and explain how to love? Sure, you had role models — but did they teach you how to do what they did? In this section, you're going to pick up some skills you never studied at home or in school.

Opening the gates

The following steps are a meditation for connecting with your soft spot and initiating the flow of unconditional love, also known as *lovingkindness*. (To distinguish this kind of love from conditional love, imagine the love of a good mother for her baby. She gives her love freely and unconditionally, without expecting anything in return except her baby's happiness and well-being.) As with all the meditations presented in this chapter, you may want to begin with five or ten minutes of a mindfulness practice like counting or following your breaths (see Chapter 7, or listen to the mindfulness track on the CD) in order to deepen and stabilize your concentration. After you get the knack, though, the cultivation of lovingkindness itself can be an excellent way to develop concentration. (For detailed audio instructions in lovingkindness meditation, check out Track 7 on the CD.)

1. **Begin by closing your eyes, taking a few deep breaths, and relaxing your body a little with each exhalation.**

2. **Imagine the face of someone who loved you very much as a child and whose love moved you deeply.**

   If no one comes to mind readily, imagine an all-loving spiritual figure like the Buddha or Mother Mary.

3. **Remember a time when this person showed his or her love for you and you really took it in.**

4. **Notice the gratitude and love this memory evokes in your heart. Allow these feelings to well up and fill your heart.**

5. **Gently extend these feelings to this loved one.**

   You may even experience a circulation of love between the two of you as you give and receive love freely.

6. **Allow these loving feelings to overflow and gradually suffuse your whole being.**

   Allow yourself to be filled with love.

Directing the flow

When you've initiated the flow of love, you can channel it, first to yourself and then to the other people in your life. After practicing the preceding meditation for five minutes or longer, continue in the following way:

1. **As you allow lovingkindness to fill your being, you may want to express the wishes and intentions that underlie this love.**

   For example, you might say to yourself, as the Buddhists do, "May I be happy. May I be peaceful. May I be free from suffering." Or you may want to choose something from the Western religious tradition, such as "May I be filled with the grace and love of God." Feel free to use whatever words feel right for you. Just be sure to keep them general, simple, and emotionally evocative. As the recipient, be sure to take in the love as well as extend it.

2. **When you feel complete with yourself for now, imagine someone for whom you feel gratitude and respect. Take some time (at least a few minutes) to direct the flow of love to this person, using similar words to express your intentions.**

   Don't hurry; allow yourself to feel the love as much as you can, rather than merely imagine it.

3. **Take some time to direct this lovingkindness to a loved one or dear friend in a similar way.**

4. **Direct this flow of love to someone for whom you feel neutral — perhaps someone you see from time to time but toward whom you have neither positive nor negative feelings.**

5. **Now, for the hardest part of this exercise: Direct your lovingkindness to someone toward whom you feel mildly negative feelings like irritation or hurt.**

   By extending love to this person, even just a little at first, you begin to develop the capacity to keep your heart open even in challenging circumstances. Eventually, you can extend love to people toward whom you experience stronger emotions like anger, fear, or pain.

Allowing life to keep opening your heart

As you go through your day, you no doubt encounter moments when you feel a spontaneous rush of love or compassion. Maybe you glimpse a homeless old woman pushing a shopping cart or hear a dog howling unhappily or see the face of a starving child or a grieving mother in some faraway place on the evening news, and your heart goes out in compassion. Or perhaps someone does something unexpectedly kind for you or a good friend reminds you that she loves you or you gaze into the eyes of someone you care about deeply, and you feel love and gratitude welling up in your heart.

Instead of rushing on to the next moment or pushing the feeling away uncomfortably, you can take some time to close your eyes, meditate on it, and allow it to deepen. Life has the capacity, all by itself, to keep opening your heart, if you let it. Your job is merely to gently extend those moments until they gradually begin to fill your life.

Like the other meditations in this book, lovingkindness can benefit from extended practice. Instead of a few minutes for each phase, try spending five or even ten. The more time and attention you give it, the more you'll begin to notice subtle (or not-so-subtle!) changes in the way you feel from moment to moment.

You may find that your heart continues to radiate a wish for the well-being of others (and yourself) long after you've ended your formal meditation. And you may discover that situations that once provoked you to harsh words or frightened withdrawal now elicit softer feelings like sympathy or compassion. Even if you feel nothing at first, just repeating your wishes and intentions can have a noticeable effect.

In her book *Lovingkindness,* the American Buddhist teacher Sharon Salzberg tells the story of a retreat in which she did nothing but extend lovingkindness to herself from morning to night for seven days. She reports that she felt absolutely nothing and found the whole endeavor excruciatingly boring. The day she left, she dropped a jar, which shattered all over the floor. Instead of a stream of self-recriminations, her immediate response was quite simple: "You're really a klutz, but I love you." "Wow," she thought, "something did happen after all."

Transforming Suffering with Compassion

When you've become proficient in opening your heart and extending love to yourself and others, you may want to experiment with *compassion,* which is simply another form of love. (Or you could just start here and leave lovingkindness till later.) When you're moved by the suffering of others and feel a spontaneous desire to help relieve their pain in some way, you're experiencing the emotion known as *compassion*. Unlike pity, compassion doesn't separate you from others or make you feel superior. Quite the contrary: In the moment of compassion, the walls that ordinarily keep you separate come tumbling down, and you feel others' pain as though it were your own.

You may be reluctant to cultivate compassion because you're afraid of being overwhelmed by the enormous suffering that surrounds you. After all, the world is plagued by violence, poverty, and disease, you might argue, and there's only so much you can do about it. But the truth is, the more you allow yourself to experience compassion, the less overwhelmed you actually feel!

If you just want to learn basic meditation for your own benefit, you don't have to bother reading this section. But if you want to extend the benefits of your meditation to others — and become a more compassionate human being in the process — then I couldn't recommend a more helpful set of practices. Begin by cultivating compassion. Then, if you want, you can experiment with using it to transform the suffering of others in your own heart. Though these practices may be simple, they're extremely effective for dissolving the clouds that hide the heart.

Some preliminary exercises for generating compassion

Here are some brief meditations for cultivating compassion. They have been adapted from *The Tibetan Book of Living and Dying* by Sogyal Rinpoche, a Tibetan meditation teacher, who writes, "The power of compassion knows no bounds."

Realizing that others are the same as you

When you're having difficulty with a loved one or friend, look beyond your conflict and the role this person plays in your life, and spend some time reflecting on the fact that this person is a human being just like you. She has the same desire for happiness and well-being, the same fear of suffering, the same need for love. Notice how this meditation changes your feelings for her and affects your difficulties.

Putting yourself in another's place

When you encounter someone who's suffering and you don't know how to help, take some time to imagine yourself in this person's position. What would it be like for you if you were experiencing the same problems? How would you feel? What would you need? How would you like others to respond? Notice if you have a clearer sense now of how to help this person.

REMEMBER

What if you can't open your heart — or difficult emotions arise when you do?

If you don't feel much of anything in your heart as you do the exercises in this chapter, don't worry. Just as you may need to pump for a while before you get water from an underground well, you may find that you need to repeat your wishes and intentions for the well-being of others again and again before you get any noticeable results — and that your feelings fluctuate from day to day. Just keep going, with the confidence that you'll eventually feel love arising in your heart. And if you don't, that's okay, too. Opening the heart and keeping it open poses a challenge even to the most loving among us, and no matter what you feel, your good wishes will have immeasurable benefit for everyone, including yourself.

Some people find that these heart-opening practices flush to the surface challenging negative emotions like grief, disappointment, fear, resentment, or rage. Based on losses and wrongs we experienced in the past, these strong feelings may form a crust over the heart that impedes the flow of love and compassion. To soften this crust and open the flow, you can practice meditations designed to cultivate forgiveness and gratitude (see Chapter 16).

The most important thing is that you're bringing to awareness the unresolved and unintegrated emotions that have kept your heart closed. Just extend lovingkindness to yourself and to the emotions themselves, welcoming them into your heart as much as you can. Just as Beauty's love turned the Beast into a prince, you can eventually transform your ugliest parts through the power of lovingkindness. (For more on working with challenging emotions, see Chapter 12.)

Imagining a loved one in place of another

Instead of putting yourself in the place of someone who's suffering, you may find it even easier to generate compassion if you imagine that someone you love deeply is experiencing the same difficulties. How would you feel? What would you do to help them? Now transfer these feelings to the person who's actually suffering, and notice how it changes your appreciation of the situation. (Not only will this meditation cause no harm to your loved one, assures Sogyal Rinpoche, they may actually benefit from having compassion directed their way.)

Dedicating the merits

When you know what compassion feels like, you can practice dedicating the value of all your positive actions to the well-being of others. In particular, you may want to follow the traditional practice of dedicating whatever virtue or merit may accrue from your meditations to all beings everywhere. You can do this simply by expressing the intention in words of your own choosing, accompanied by a heartfelt wish that all beings be happy and free of suffering.

Softening your belly

Stephen Levine, an American meditation teacher who has written extensively on healing and dying, counsels that the state of your belly reflects the state of your heart. By consciously softening your belly again and again, you can let go and open to the tender feelings in your heart. (The following meditation is inspired by his book *Guided Meditations, Explorations and Healings*.)

1. **Begin by sitting comfortably and taking a few deep breaths.**

2. **Allow your awareness to gradually settle into your body.**

   Become aware of the sensations in your head and slowly allow your awareness to descend through your neck and shoulders until you reach your torso and arms.

3. **When you reach your belly, gently soften this area of your body.**

   Consciously let go of any tension or holding.

4. **Allow your breath to enter and leave your belly.**

   When you inhale, your belly rises. When you exhale, your belly falls.

5. **With each breath, continue to soften your belly.**

   Let go of any anger, fear, pain, or unresolved grief you may be holding in your belly. You may want to help the process along by silently repeating a word or phrase like "soften" or "let go."

6. **As you continue to soften your belly, notice how your heart responds.**

7. **After five minutes or longer of this soft-belly meditation, open your eyes and go about your day.**

   Every now and then, check in with your belly. If you notice that you're tensing it again, gently breathe and soften.

Transforming suffering with the power of the heart

As you may discover when you do the following practice, the heart is a powerful organ indeed. Of course, I'm not referring to the physical heart, but to an *energetic center* located in the middle of the chest, right near the anatomical heart. Yet the two have an intimate connection, as Dr. Dean Ornish's work confirms: To heal your heart, you need to open your heart. (For more on energy centers, see Chapter 13.)

By doing this meditation regularly, you can actually develop the capacity to transform your own suffering and the suffering of others into peace, joy, and love. The amazing thing is, the process doesn't weaken or overwhelm you, as you might fear. Quite the contrary, it helps you develop confidence in the strength and resilience of your own heart and in your ability to touch the lives of others.

If you don't believe me, give this meditation a try. As soon as you get the knack, practice it regularly for several weeks, and notice what happens. Whether or not the people in your life suffer less (and they may), I can guarantee that you'll eventually end up feeling more peaceful and loving yourself. (For detailed audio instructions, check out Track 8 on your CD.)

1. **Begin by sitting in a comfortable position, taking a few deep breaths, and meditating in your usual way for a few minutes.**

   For complete meditation instructions, see Chapter 7.

2. **Close your eyes and imagine the most loving and compassionate individuals you've ever known or heard about gathered together above your head.**

   If appropriate, include religious or spiritual figures like Jesus, Mohammed, Mother Mary, the Dalai Lama, or your favorite saint or sage.

3. **Imagine that they all merge into one being, who glows and radiates the warmth and light of love and compassion.**

4. **Imagine that this being descends into your heart, where it takes the form of a sphere of infinitely radiant, infinitely compassionate light that merges with your own soft spot.**

In the following phases, you practice taking in negativity, transforming it in the sphere inside your heart, and sending out positive energy to yourself and others:

Phase 1: Transforming the atmosphere

1. **Take a moment to notice the state of your mind right now.**

2. **On an inhalation, breathe in any negativity, agitation, darkness, or depression you find there and take it into the sphere of light in your heart, where you imagine it being transformed into clarity, calm, peace, and joy.**

3. **On the exhalation, breathe these positive qualities into your mind and feel them filling and purifying it.**

4. **Continue to breathe in the dark and breathe out the light for several minutes.**

   If it helps, you might imagine the negative as a hot, dark smoke and the positive as a cool, white light.

Phase 2: Transforming yourself

1. **Imagine yourself in front of you and become aware of your own stress, suffering, and dissatisfaction.**

   You may find, for example, that you're angry with your boss or afraid of an upcoming challenge or still hurt or bitter about some mistreatment you received as a child.

2. **Allow yourself to feel compassion for yourself and your own suffering.**

3. **As you inhale, breathe in to the sphere of light in your heart whatever suffering you find and breathe out a soothing, caring, compassionate energy that envelops and fills the "you" in front of you.**

   If you find it helpful to use a particular image for this energy, such as fresh flowers or a cool breeze, go right ahead. Or you can use the image of white light suggested in the previous phase.

4. **Continue taking in and giving forth in this way for five minutes or longer.**

Phase 3: Transforming situations

1. **Recall a recent situation in which you acted badly or inappropriately.**

   Perhaps you blame yourself or feel guilty or remorseful, or maybe you've been resisting these feelings. Recollect the situation as vividly as possible.

2. **Notice how your actions affected the other people involved.**

3. **Take full responsibility for your actions.**

   Notice that I said *responsibility,* not blame. You blew it, and you whole-heartedly acknowledge that you blew it, without beating yourself up about it, but also without denying or justifying what you did.

4. **Breathe in the responsibility as well as any blame, pain, or other negative emotions involved and breathe out forgiveness, understanding, reconciliation, and harmony.**

5. **Continue in this way for several minutes.**

   If another situation comes to mind, set it aside and do this practice with it at another time.

Phase 4: Transforming others

1. **Imagine a friend or loved one who happens to be suffering right now.**

2. **Breathe in the person's pain and suffering with compassion and breathe out love, peace, joy, and healing.**

3. **After several minutes, begin to widen the circle of your compassion to include first other people you care about, then those toward whom you feel neutral, and then those you dislike or find difficult.**

   (For more on the order of this progression, see the section "How to Generate Love for Yourself and Others" earlier in this chapter.) Breathe in their suffering and pain, and breathe out peace, love, and joy, using any images you find helpful.

4. **Extend your compassion in this way, first to all the people in the world and then to all beings everywhere.**

   Though you won't be able to visualize them, you can sense their presence as you breathe in and breathe out.

5. **End the meditation by dedicating any virtue you may have accumulated through this practice to the benefit of all beings.**

You can do these phases out of order or separately, if you choose, but it's important to begin the practice each time with yourself.

Part III

Troubleshooting and Fine-Tuning Your Practice

The 5th Wave   By Rich Tennant

"Your meditation technique is fine. It's your turban that's too big."

In this part . . .

Learning how to meditate is like learning to drive a car. You can tool around the parking lot to your heart's content, but just wait 'til you hit rush hour.

In this part, I give you expert guidance in negotiating the twists and turns of meditating in heavy internal traffic — like when intense emotions or repetitive thinking threaten to box you in. Or when detours and distractions seem to throw you off course and you keep falling asleep at the wheel. And you have a chance to piece together all your newfound skills into a routine you can follow day after day.

Chapter 12

Meditating with Challenging Emotions and Habitual Patterns

*M*editation tends to make you calmer, more spacious, and more relaxed — at least most of the time. When you follow your breath, repeat a mantra, or practice some other basic technique every day, your mind begins to settle down naturally while thoughts and feelings spontaneously bubble up and release like the fizz in a bottle of soda. The process is so relaxing that the folks in Transcendental Meditation call it *unstressing*.

When you meditate regularly for a period of time, however, you may find that certain emotions or states of mind keep coming back to distract or disturb you. Instead of dispersing, the same sexual fantasies, sad or fearful thoughts, or painful memories may keep playing in your awareness like a CD stuck in the same groove. Or you may be meditating on lovingkindness (see Chapter 11) but keep coming up against unresolved resentment or rage. Instead of watching the mist rising from the lake, you've begun your descent into the muddy and sometimes turbulent waters of your inner experience. (Refer to Chapter 6 for a more detailed exploration of these waters.)

At first, you may be surprised, dismayed, or even frightened by what you encounter, and you may conclude that you're doing something wrong. But have no fear! The truth is, your meditation has actually begun to deepen, and you're ready to expand your range of meditation techniques to help you navigate this new terrain.

At this point, you may find it helpful to extend your practice of mindfulness (see Chapter 7) from your breathing and your bodily sensations to your thoughts and emotions. As you gently focus the light of your awareness on this dimension of your experience, you can begin to sort out what's actually going on inside you. In the process, you can get to know yourself better — even make friends with yourself. If you keep it up, you can eventually start to penetrate and even unravel some old habitual patterns of thinking, feeling, and behaving — patterns that have been causing you suffering and stress and keeping you stuck for a long, long time. (For more on how the mind causes suffering and stress, see Chapter 6.)

Making Friends with Your Experience

If you're like most of the people I know (including me!), you tend to be exceptionally hard on yourself. In fact, you probably treat yourself in ways you wouldn't consider treating any of your loved ones or friends. When you make a mistake, you may call yourself names or heap harsh judgments and criticisms on yourself, including a laundry list of all the other mistakes you've made over the years. When you feel some tender or vulnerable emotion, you may dismiss it as weak or wimpy and attempt to push past it rather than give yourself time to feel it fully.

Just the other day, for example, when I couldn't find my keys, I was startled to hear this irritable, impatient voice inside my head chiding me for being so stupid and forgetful! Sound familiar? Most of us hold some image of how we're supposed to act, think, and feel, and we're constantly struggling to get our experience and behavior to conform to it — and we blame ourselves when they don't.

In meditation, you have an opportunity to reverse this trend and explore your experience just the way it is without trying to judge it or change it. (For more on reserving judgment and accepting what is, see Chapter 10.) To replace the stress, conflict, and turbulence inside you with peace and harmony, you need to make friends with yourself, which means treating yourself with the same kindness, care, and curiosity that you would give to a close friend. You can begin by bringing a gentle, nonjudgmental awareness to your thoughts and feelings.

Embracing your thoughts and feelings

When you're familiar with following your breath and expanding your awareness to include sensations (see Chapter 6), you can expand your awareness even further to include thoughts, images, memories, and feelings. As with sensations, begin by following your breath and then allow yourself to explore a thought or feeling when it becomes so strong that it draws your attention to it. When it no longer predominates in your field of awareness, gently return to your breath.

Of course, if you've been meditating for a while, you may have noticed that you're constantly being carried away by the torrent of thoughts and feelings that flood through your mind. One moment you're counting or following your breaths or practicing your mantra, the next moment you're mulling over a conversation you had yesterday or planning tomorrow's dinner. It's as though you had inadvertently boarded a boat and suddenly found yourself several miles downstream. When this happens, you simply need to notice that you've wandered and immediately return to where you began.

Now, however, instead of viewing this dimension of your experience as a distraction, include it in your meditation with mindful awareness. When you find your attention wandering off into a thought or feeling, be aware of what you're experiencing until it loses its intensity; then gently return to your primary focus.

Naming your experience

As you expand your meditation to include thoughts and feelings, you may find it helpful to practice *naming,* or noting, your experience. Begin with mindful awareness of your breath, and then start silently naming the in-breath and out-breath. When you get really quiet and focused, you may even want to include subtleties such as "long breath," "short breath," "deep breath," "shallow breath," and so on.

Keep the naming simple and subdued, like a gentle, nonjudgmental voice in the back of your mind. As Buddhist meditation teacher Jack Kornfield says in his book *A Path with Heart,* give "ninety-five percent of your energy to sensing each experience, and five percent to a soft name in the background."

When you become adept at naming your breath, you can extend the practice to any strong sensations, thoughts, or feelings that draw your attention away from your breath. For example, as you follow and name your breath, you may find your focus interrupted by a prominent emotion. Name this experience softly and repeatedly for as long as it persists — "sadness, sadness, sadness" or "anger, anger, anger" — then gently return your attention to your breath. Take the same approach with thoughts, images, and mind-states: "planning, planning," "worrying, worrying," or "seeing, seeing."

Use the simplest words you can find, and focus on one thing at a time. This practice helps you gain a little perspective or distance from your constantly changing inner experience, instead of becoming lost in the torrent.

By naming particular thoughts and emotions, you're also acknowledging that they exist. As I mention earlier, people often attempt to suppress or deny experiences they deem undesirable or unacceptable, such as anger, fear, judgment, or hurt. But the more you try to hide from your experience, the more it can end up governing your behavior, as Freud so wisely pointed out more than a century ago.

Naming allows you to shine the penetrating light of awareness into the recesses of your heart and mind and invite your thoughts and feelings to emerge from their hiding place into the light of day. You may not like what you encounter at first, but you can name your self-judgments and self-criticisms as well. Ultimately, you may notice that you're not surprised anymore by what you discover about yourself. And the more you make friends with your own apparent shortcomings and frailties, the more you can open your heart to the imperfections of others as well.

Constant naming has disadvantages, however, because it separates you from your direct experience by placing words and concepts between your awareness and reality. So if you use this technique, do so lightly and judiciously as a first step in becoming acquainted with your inner life and making friends with yourself. Then gradually let go of the habit as you become more comfortable with being present for your experience just as it is.

Welcoming whatever arises

When you become accustomed to including sensations, thoughts, and feelings in your meditation, you can open your awareness gates wide and welcome whatever arises without judgment or resistance. Imagine that your mind is like the sky and that inner and outer experiences come and go like clouds.

At first, you may find your attention drawn here and there, exploring one object and then another. You don't have to control your attention in any way; just allow it to wander where it will, from thoughts to sensations to feelings and back again.

Eventually, you may have periods in your meditation when your mind feels spacious and expanded and doesn't seem to be disturbed by thoughts, feelings, or outside distractions. Whatever you experience, just keep opening your awareness and welcoming whatever comes. (For more on the different levels of experience you may encounter, see Chapter 6.)

A note of caution, however: This practice, though supremely simple, is actually quite advanced and requires well-developed powers of concentration to sustain. It's also difficult to teach; — rather like riding a bicycle. First, you have to *discover* what it feels like to hold your balance, and then you just keep returning to the balance point whenever you start to fall off.

Meditating with Challenging Emotions

As a psychotherapist, meditator, and meditation teacher, I've discovered a thing or two over the years about how people relate to the mysterious and sometimes formidable world of human emotions. For one thing, many people believe they have a Pandora's box of ugly, disgusting emotions like rage, jealousy, hatred, and terror hidden inside them, and they're afraid that if they open it up, these demonic energies will overwhelm them and those they love. For another thing, they tend to think that these "negative" feelings are bottomless and irresolvable and that they're better off avoiding them no matter how painful it may be to hold them in.

Unfortunately, you pay a steep price indeed if you spend your life resisting and denying your feelings. Unacknowledged negative feelings can impede the flow of more positive feelings like love and joy. As a result, you may end up feeling lonely and unhappy because you lack close emotional contact with others, and you may be unable to give and receive love when you have an opportunity to do so.

In addition, negative feelings that build up inside you tend to cause stress and depression, suppress the immune system, and contribute to stress-related ailments like ulcers, cancer, and heart disease. They also hold valuable life energy that you may otherwise channel in constructive or creative ways. Besides, emotions that are persistently suppressed and denied have an annoying habit of bursting forth inappropriately when you least expect them, prompting you to do and say things you may later regret.

Of course, some people go to another extreme and seem to be so completely awash in powerful emotional reactions that they can't make simple decisions or carry on a rational conversation. But these people aren't really experiencing their emotions, they're indulging them and allowing them to run their lives.

Meditation offers you an alternative way of relating with your emotions. Instead of suppressing, indulging, or exploding, you can directly experience your emotions as they are — as an interplay of thoughts, images, and sensations. When you've become skillful at following your breath and expanding your awareness to include the flow of thoughts and feelings — which may take months or even years — you can focus your attention on particular emotions that you find challenging or problematic and develop *penetrating insight* into the nature of the experience.

Instead of being bottomless or endless, as some people fear, you may find that even the most powerful emotions come in waves that have a limited duration when you experience them fully. As one of my teachers used to say, "What you resist persists." — and what you welcome has a tendency to let go and release. (See the sidebar "Facing your demons" later in this chapter.)

In the following sections, I provide some guidelines for exploring a few of the most common emotions. Although feelings come in many shapes and sizes, I've found that they're all more or less variants or combinations of a few basic ones: anger, fear, sadness, joy, excitement, and desire. (In my view, love is deeper than emotion; it's a fundamental expression of *being* itself.) Just as an artist's rich palette of colors can ultimately be broken down into blue, red and yellow, the difficult or challenging emotions like jealousy, guilt, boredom, and depression are combinations (or reactions) to four basic feelings: anger, fear, sadness, and desire. (If you find a certain feeling problematic, work on it as you would one of these four. For more on desire, see Chapter 13.)

Anger

After practicing meditation regularly for several years in my 20s, I prided myself on being consistently calm and even-tempered and never getting angry. Then one day, my girlfriend at the time confessed that she'd had an affair with another man! Without hesitating, I picked up a cup from the table and threw it against the wall. I remember being startled by the sudden intensity of my emotions. One moment I seemed perfectly peaceful, and the next moment I was flying into a rage. My anger may have been appropriate to the circumstances, but I certainly hadn't expressed it skillfully. Humbled, I headed back to the meditation cushion for some deeper investigation — after breaking up with my girlfriend, of course.

Many people, especially women, have a taboo against getting angry because they weren't allowed to express their anger, even as children. So they expend enormous amounts of energy trying to skirt around the feeling. Other people seem as though they're perpetually seething with current anger and old resentments, although they may not realize it themselves.

When you meditate with your anger, you may begin by noticing where and how you experience it in your body. Where do you find yourself tensing and contracting? What happens to your breathing? Where do you notice a buildup of energy? How does it affect softer emotions? As you continue to be aware of your anger, do you notice it shifting or changing in any way? How long does it last? Does it have a beginning and an end?

Next, you can turn your attention to your mind. What kinds of thoughts and images accompany the angry feelings? Do you find yourself blaming other people and defending yourself? If you investigate further and peel back the initial layer of anger, what do you find underneath? In my experience, anger generally arises in response to one of two deeper emotions: hurt or fear. When you're hurt, as I was by my girlfriend's betrayal, you may lash out in anger against the one you believe hurt you. And when you're afraid, you may protect yourself with the sword and armor of anger rather than acknowledge your fear, even to yourself. Beneath the hurt and fear, anger generally masks an even deeper layer of attachment to having things be a certain way. When circumstances change or don't go according to plan, you feel hurt or afraid and then angry in response.

With anger, as with all emotions, set aside any judgment or resistance you may have and face the anger directly. You may find that it becomes more intense before it releases, but stay with it. Beneath the anger may lie deep wellsprings of power, which you may eventually discover how to evoke without getting angry.

TRADITIONAL WISDOM

Facing your demons

The Tibetans tell a wonderful story about the great meditation master Milarepa, who lived about 900 years ago. Milarepa sought out remote caves high in the Himalayas where he practiced meditation. Once, he found himself in a cave inhabited by a company of demons that distracted him from his practice. (Demons apparently frequented caves in those days — looking for some action, no doubt!)

First, he tried to subdue them, but they wouldn't budge. Then he decided to honor them and extend friendliness and compassion to them, and half of them left. The rest he welcomed wholeheartedly and invited to return whenever

they wished. At this invitation, all but one particularly ferocious demon vanished like a rainbow. With no concern for his own body and with utmost love and compassion, Milarepa went up to the demon and placed his head in its mouth as an offering. The demon disappeared without a trace and never returned.

Consider the story of Milarepa the next time you're struggling with your own inner demons — emotions and states of mind you find challenging or unpleasant. Imagine what might happen if you welcomed them instead of trying to drive them away!

Fear and anxiety

Many people are reluctant to admit they're afraid, even to themselves. Somehow, they believe that if they acknowledge their fear, they give it power to run their lives. In other words, deep down, they're afraid of their fear! Men, especially, often go to great lengths to hide their fears or anxieties behind a facade of confidence or anger or rationality. At the other extreme, of course, some people seem to be frightened of just about everything.

The truth is, if you're human — and not bionic or extraterrestrial — you're going to be afraid or anxious at least occasionally. In addition to the raw rush of adrenaline you feel when your physical survival seems to be at stake, you experience the fear that inevitably arises when you face the unknown or the uncertain in life, which can be quite often these days. Ultimately, you're afraid because you believe that you're a separate, isolated entity surrounded by forces beyond your control. The more the walls that separate you from others crumble through the practice of meditation, the more your fear and anxiety naturally diminish. (For more on separation and isolation, see Chapter 6.)

As with anger, you can use your meditation to explore and ultimately make friends with your fear. After all, it's just an emotion like other emotions, composed of physical sensations, thoughts, and beliefs. When working with fear, it's especially important to be kind and gentle with yourself.

Begin by asking the same questions you asked about anger: Where and how do you experience it in your body? Where do you find yourself tensing and contracting? What happens to your breathing? Or to your heart? Next, notice the thoughts and images that accompany the fear. Often fear arises from anticipating the future and imagining that you'll somehow be unable to cope. When you see these catastrophic expectations for what they are and return to the present moment — the sensations in your body, the coming and going of your breath — you may find that the fear shifts and begins to disperse. Then when it returns, you can simply call its name — "fear, fear, fear" — like an old, familiar friend.

You may also want to amplify the sensations a little and allow yourself to shake or tremble, if you feel so inclined. You can even imagine the fear overwhelming you and doing its worst (knowing, of course, that you will survive). This approach is especially helpful if you're afraid of your fear, as so many people are. Facing your fear directly without trying to get rid of it or escape from it requires tremendous courage; yet these practices also have the capacity to bring you into the present moment and open your heart to your own vulnerability.

Sadness, grief, and depression

Most people find sadness easier to feel and express than anger or fear. Unfortunately, they don't give it the time and attention it deserves because they were told as children to stop crying before they were ready. Life inevitably presents you with a series of disappointments and losses; unexpressed sadness and grief can build up inside and ultimately lead to depression. (Many of the people I see in therapy suffer from mild depression, which may also result from repressed anger or "learned helplessness." For more on learned helplessness, see Chapter 6.)

To make friends with your sadness, you need to hold it gently and lovingly and give it plenty of space to express itself. As with anger and fear, begin by exploring the sensations. Perhaps you notice a heaviness in your heart or a constriction in your diaphragm or a clogged sensation in your eyes and forehead, as though you're about to cry but can't. You may want to amplify these sensations and see what happens.

Then pay attention to the thoughts, images, and memories that fuel the sadness. Perhaps you keep reliving the loss of a loved one or the moment when a close friend said something unkind to you. If you're depressed, you may keep recycling the same negative, self-defeating beliefs and judgments, such as "I'm not good enough" or "I don't have what it takes to succeed."

As you open your awareness to include the full range of experiences associated with the sadness, you may shed some heartfelt tears. In the process, you may also feel yourself lightening up and your sadness lifting a little. (To find out how to work with core beliefs, consult the following two sections of this chapter.) Ultimately, as long as you're open to your own suffering and the suffering of others, you will experience a certain amount of tender sadness in your heart.

Unraveling Habitual Patterns with Awareness

As you explore your emotions (as described in the previous section), you may gradually discover that they're not as overpowering or as endless as you feared. With mindful awareness, most emotions flow through your body and gradually release. For example, as you gently investigate your anger or fear, it may intensify at first, then break and disperse like a wave on the beach.

But certain persistent emotions and physical contractions, along with the thoughts and images that accompany and fuel them, seem to keep returning no matter how many times you notice and name them. These are the *stories* and habitual patterns that run deep in the body-mind like the roots from which recurring thoughts and feelings spring. (For more on these stories, see Chapter 6.)

In your meditations, you may keep replaying a story from your past (including all the accompanying emotions and mind-states) in which you suffer some abuse or injustice. Perhaps you see yourself as a failure and fantasize obsessively about an imaginary future in which you're somehow happier and more successful. Or you may worry repeatedly about your job or relationship because you believe you can't trust people or because the world's not a safe place.

In his book *A Path with Heart,* Buddhist meditation teacher Jack Kornfield calls these habitual patterns *insistent visitors* and suggests that they keep returning in your meditation (and your life!) because they're stuck or unfinished in some way. When you give them the loving attention and deeper investigation they require (applying the penetrating insight I discuss at length in Chapter 6), you may at first discover that they're more complex and deeply rooted than you had imagined. But with persistent exploration, they gradually unravel and reveal the hidden energy and wisdom they contain. In fact, the more you undo your patterns, the more you release the physical and energetic contractions that lie at their heart, and the freer, more spacious, more expansive — and, yes, healthier! — you become.

Here's a brief synopsis of the primary techniques for unraveling habitual patterns. Experiment with them on your own, and if you find them helpful, feel free to incorporate them into your meditation. If you get stuck or would like to delve deeper but don't know how, you may want to find yourself a meditation teacher or psychotherapist familiar with this approach. (For more on finding a therapist, see the section "Knowing How [and When] to Seek Help with Your Patterns" later in this chapter. For more on finding a teacher, see Chapter 15. And for a more detailed treatment of many of these techniques, check out *A Path with Heart* by Jack Kornfield.)

Naming your "tunes"

As a rather humorous way to start, advises Kornfield, you can name and number your "top ten tunes." (You can stop at five, if you prefer.) Then when a particular tune (habitual pattern) recurs, you can simply notice and name it without getting embroiled once again in the same painful pattern. This approach, another version of naming your experience (which I describe earlier), can be helpful but only takes you so far.

Expanding your awareness

The part of the pattern that reveals itself to you in your meditation may be just the tip of the proverbial iceberg. Perhaps you keep feeling tense in your lower belly, and you don't know why. If you expand your awareness, you may discover that beneath the surface lies fear about the future, and under the fear lies a layer of hurt. When you include thoughts and ideas as well, you may find that, deep down, you believe you're inadequate. So you're afraid you can't cope, and you feel hurt when people criticize you because it just corroborates your own negative self-image. By welcoming the full range of thoughts, images, and feelings, you create an inner spaciousness in which the pattern can gradually unfold and release. (Trust me, this approach actually works, though you won't get results instantaneously!)

Feeling your feelings

Patterns often persist until the underlying feelings are thoroughly felt. That's right, I said *felt*, not merely acknowledged or named! Many people keep their feelings at arm's length or confuse them with thoughts or ideas. I could always talk in the abstract about grief or fear, but it took years of meditation (and some skillful therapy; see the section "Knowing How [and When] to Seek Help with Your Patterns") before I knew how they actually felt in my body. Other people (as I mention in the earlier section "Meditating with Challenging Emotions") get completely entangled in their feelings. As you expand your awareness, ask yourself, "What feelings haven't I felt yet?"

PLAY THIS!

Replacing negative patterns with positive energy

Many meditative traditions suggest invoking outside help in the lifelong process of purifying and eliminating habitual patterns. No, I'm not talking about psychotherapy or Prozac here. I'm referring to spiritual beings or energies that purportedly exist for the sole purpose of inspiring and encouraging your spiritual evolution. Western religions have their angels and saints; Hinduism and Buddhism have their deities and protectors; and shamanism has its spirit helpers and animal powers.

Now, you may not buy all this spiritual stuff, but I'd suggest giving this exercise a try just the same. In place of spiritual allies, you may want to imagine people who have given you unconditional support in the past. Or you could just stick to the image of a luminous sphere. The point is, this exercise by itself can be a powerful ally in the process of dealing with painful or difficult emotions or experiences. As with all meditations, the more you practice it, the more effective it becomes. (For detailed audio instructions, check out Track 9.)

1. **Begin by sitting down and meditating in your usual way for several minutes.**

   If you don't have a usual way, you can find one in Chapter 6. Or just sit quietly and wait for further instructions.

2. **Imagine a luminous sphere of white light suspended about a foot above your head and slightly in front of you.**

   Like a sun, this sphere embodies and radiates all the positive, healing, harmonious qualities you most want to manifest in your life right now. You may want to be specific at first, recognizing qualities like strength,

clarity, peace, love. Eventually you can just flash on the light.

3. **Imagine yourself soaking up all these qualities with the healing light as though you were sunbathing.**

4. **Imagine this light radiating in all directions to the farthest corners of the universe and drawing the energy of all the benevolent forces that support your growth and evolution back into the sphere.**

5. **Visualize this positive, healing energy shining from the sphere like the light of a thousand suns streaming down through your body and mind, eliminating all negativity and tension, darkness and depression, worry and anxiety, and replacing them with radiance, vitality, peace, and all the other positive qualities you seek.**

6. **Continue to imagine this powerful, healing light flooding every cell and molecule of your being, dissolving any contractions and stuck places you may be aware of and leaving you clean, clear, and calm.**

7. **Visualize this luminous sphere gradually descending into your heart, where it continues to radiate this powerful light.**

8. **Imagine yourself as a luminous being with a sphere of light in your heart that constantly radiates clarity, harmony, and purity — first to every cell and particle of your own being and then, through you, to every other being in every direction.**

You can carry the feelings and images this exercise evokes throughout the rest of your day.

Feeling your feelings doesn't make them bigger or worse, at least not in the long run. It actually allows them to move through and release!

Noticing your resistance and attachment

As I mention earlier, what you resist persists — to which I add that what you're attached to persists as well. If a particular story or challenging emotion keeps replaying in your mind, explore your relationship to it. For example, ask: How do I feel about this particular pattern or story? Do I have a vested interest in holding on to it? If so, what do I get out of it? What am I afraid might happen if I let it go? Am I judging it as undesirable and struggling to get rid of it? If so, what don't I like about it? When you can relax and gently open to accept the pattern with awareness (as described in the previous sections), you may find that the pattern, which felt so tight and entrenched, relaxes as well.

Finding the wisdom

Sometimes recurring stories or patterns have wisdom to impart, and they won't stop nagging until you listen. If I keep having the same uncomfortable or difficult feeling during meditation and it doesn't shift or change with awareness, I may "give it a voice" and ask it to speak to me as though it were a close friend. "What are you trying to tell me?" I may ask. "What do I need to hear?" Sometimes I discover that a tender, vulnerable part of myself needs caring, nurturing attention. At other times, I hear the voice of responsibility reminding me to tend to some important commitment. (For a helpful way of listening to these voices and parts, see the sidebar "Focusing: Western meditation for getting unstuck" in this chapter.)

Getting to the heart of the matter

Like the great Tibetan meditator Milarepa (see the sidebar "Facing your demons" earlier in this chapter), sometimes you need to stick your head into the demon's mouth before it disappears for good. In other words, you may need to explore the *energetic contraction* that lies at the heart of your pattern.

When I use the term *energetic* here, I'm referring to the model of the human organism as a system of energetic pathways and centers that can get blocked or contracted. These blockages give rise to painful emotions and mind-states and may ultimately cause disease. (For more on energy pathways and centers, see Chapter 13.)

To explore the energetic contraction at the heart of your pattern, you can gently direct your awareness into the very center of the contraction and describe in detail what you find there. When you unearth the memory, feeling, or belief that holds the pattern together, you may find that the contraction releases, your awareness expands, and your meditation begins to flow more smoothly. (***Note:*** When you're dealing with exceptionally painful, deep-seated contractions, you may want to consult a qualified professional. See the section in this chapter "Knowing How [and When] to Seek Help with Your Patterns.")

Infusing the stuck place with being

After you've meditated for a while and received some glimpses of your own inherent wholeness and completeness (which I call *being* in Chapter 1), you may want to try the following shortcut. Set aside the thoughts and ideas that accompany your pattern and simply be aware of the physical and energetic contraction. Now shift your attention to your wholeness and completeness, which you may experience as a calm, relaxed energy in your body; a deeply loving feeling in your heart; a sense of expansiveness or space; some other feeling unique to you. Imagine your wholeness and completeness gradually spreading, penetrating, and infusing the contraction with pure being. Continue this exercise as the contraction releases and dissolves into being. (For an even more powerful version of this technique, refer to the sidebar "Replacing negative patterns with positive energy.")

Working with patterns before you get stuck

When you get the knack of observing your reactive patterns and repetitive stories and concerns and unraveling them in meditation, you can begin to work with them as they arise in everyday life. For example, you may notice in your meditation that you tend to rehearse a drama in which other people are constantly depriving you of what you rightfully deserve and you end up feeling hurt and resentful. When you notice this story and the beliefs that accompany it (for example, "I never get what I want" or "Nobody cares about me") showing up in your relationships or at work, you can use the skills you've acquired to step back a little and resist the temptation to get sucked in as usual.

The more consistently you unravel your patterns in meditation, the more quickly you can catch them as they arise — and the freer and less reactive you gradually become. Eventually, you can even begin to shift your identity from the patterns to the spacious awareness in which the patterns arise and pass away.

Working with habitual patterns: A case in point

Here's an example of how to work with habitual patterns, based on my own experience. Not long ago, I noticed a particular tightness in my lower abdomen, not only when I meditated but also between sessions. When the tightness persisted for several days, I decided to investigate it further. Gently, I directed my awareness and my breath to the area.

As I expanded my awareness, I noticed that I also felt tight in my throat and jaw. When I inquired into the feeling, I gradually became aware that I was afraid of something, though I wasn't sure at first of what. Not only that, I was resisting the feeling by tightening my jaw. Somehow I didn't like the feeling and wanted to get rid of it.

Without trying to change the feeling in any way, I meditated and breathed with it for a while. Soon, it began to loosen a little, but not to unravel completely. Then I gently asked for more information, and I realized that I was afraid of an upcoming presentation. Several memories of being made to feel inadequate as a child came vividly to mind, and I experienced waves of sadness and some tears, followed by compassion for myself.

As I directed my awareness to the center of the contraction in my belly, it quickly released, and feelings of ease and well-being filled the area instead. Feeling more relaxed and expanded, I returned to my usual meditation. Several days later, when I made the presentation, I noticed that I felt more relaxed and self-confident than usual.

Setting Patterns Aside — for Now

If you find that your habitual patterns are too deeply entrenched to unravel (at least for now!), you can still get some temporary relief by applying one or more of the techniques I discuss in the following sections.

You don't necessarily have to wrestle a pattern to the mat for the count of ten; sometimes you just have to get it to shift or budge a little so you can get on with your meditation.

Letting go (or letting be)

Believe it or not, you may be able to drop the pattern and move on. Be careful, though. If you push the pattern away indefnitely, it may come back to haunt you. Instead of struggle and aversion, this approach requires a willingness to accept things the way they are. (For more on the stages of letting go, see Chapter 10.)

Sometimes you can just stop, be aware of the contraction, and gradually relax your body until the contraction releases. (For detailed instructions on how to relax deeply, see Chapter 7.) Or you can shift your awareness to *being* itself (however you may happen to experience *being*), and just let the pattern be without trying to change it.

Shifting attention

As the Bible says, "There's a time for every purpose under heaven," including working with your habitual patterns. If you're preoccupied with more-pressing concerns, you may need to be able to set your patterns aside and shine your attention where you need it most. You can come back to your difficulties later, when you have the time and energy.

Moving the energy

Sometimes you may find it helpful to direct the energy bound up in a particular pattern into another activity. Go for a run or dance to loud music or wash the dishes. You may not be unraveling the pattern, but you're stealing its thunder, so to speak. (To continue the metaphor, you can even use the rain to water your crops.)

Perhaps you've seen one of those westerns where the hero goes out and chops some wood instead of picking up his gun and shooting his neighbors. Well, he's "moving the energy," whether he knows it or not. You can also move the energy internally (for example, by turning your fear about an upcoming event into excitement and curiosity).

Acting it out in imagination

When an emotion or impulse seems too intense to shift or move, you can act it out in your meditation by imagining yourself exaggerating it and then allowing it to unfold completely with mindful attention. This approach differs from mere fantasy, which tends to have an obsessive, unconscious quality. Instead, by paying attention as you give this emotion or pattern free rein, you get to realize that it's not as overpowering as you may have believed.

At the same time, you have an opportunity to observe its limitations and the damage or pain it could inflict. For example, you could imagine yourself enacting your rage or your desire mindfully and notice what happens. Does it completely overwhelm you? How does it affect the other people involved? Does it really bring you the fulfillment you seek?

Acting it out in real life — mindfully

When a pattern just seems too powerful to resist, you can act it out in life, as you usually do, but this time with mindfulness. Notice how you feel in your body as you follow the enactment through to completion. For example, you may be bravely trying to resist your desire for a hot fudge sundae but rapidly losing your willpower. Instead, you may go for it while noticing every bite and every sensation, both during and after. In fact, you can even try eating as much as you want. If you do it with awareness, you may find that you deriive so much enjoyment from the eating that you feel satisfied sooner and eat less. In the process, you may even transform your relationship to food. (For more on mindfulness in everyday life, see Chapter 17.) Be careful, however, not to act out patterns that are potentially dangerous to yourself or others.

Focusing: Western meditation for getting unstuck

Here's a meditation technique called *focusing* developed by Eugene Gendlin, a psychology professor at the University of Chicago, to help folks like you and me figure out where we're stuck and effect the necessary changes, both inner and outer. (Although this technique uses the same term, it differs from the focused attention described elsewhere in this book.)

By focusing on your felt sense about a problem — the place in your body where you hold it and know it — you can discover valuable information about who you are and what you really want and need. (For more-detailed instructions, I recommend Gendlin's book *Focusing*.)

1. **Begin by taking a few moments to settle comfortably and relax.**

2. **Check in with that place inside where you feel things and ask, "How am I doing? What doesn't feel quite right? What do I need to pay attention to right now?"**

   You're not looking for an intense emotion but something subtler and more elusive: a *felt sense.* (For example, a felt sense is the place inside that you consult when someone asks you, "What is your sense of that person or situation?" It's not a feeling, exactly, and definitely not a thought, but more like a bodily knowing.)

3. **Take whatever you get, set it aside, and ask the same questions again until you** have a list of three or four things you can focus on right now.

4. **Choose one, but don't go inside it. Instead, allow some space around it.**

   Set aside any thoughts and analyses you may have and just be with your felt sense of this one thing, in its entirety.

5. **Ask yourself, "What is the crux of this problem?"**

   Don't jump to any conclusions or try to understand it. Just allow this crux to emerge in the silence. You may find that what you get is different from what your mind expected. You'll know it in your body.

6. **Sit with the crux of this felt sense for a minute or more and allow a word, image, or feeling to emerge from it.**

   Don't try to understand it. Just be aware of the crux with gentle curiosity, waiting for a deeper knowing to reveal itself.

7. **Compare this word, image, or feeling with the felt sense in your body, asking "Is this right? Does this really fit?"**

   If it is, you'll notice a felt shift: a deep breath, sigh of relief, or slight relaxing inside. If not, ask the felt sense, "Then what does feel right?" and wait for an answer. *Remember:* You're asking your body, not your mind, for information.

8. When you receive an answer that feels right, sit with it in silence for a few moments and allow your body to respond.

The felt shift may continue to unfold, or you may experience a release of energy or some other noticeable reverberation in your body.

Here's an example of focusing. Say that you've been obsessing about a conversation you had yesterday with a friend, playing it over and over again in your mind without resolution. So you decide to set your thoughts aside and pay attention to your inner felt sense of the conversation. When you turn inward, you find that the felt sense is localized in your heart and the crux of it turns out to be something about your friend's tone of voice.

As you sit with the felt sense, you realize that the crux of the problem is not her tone of voice exactly, but it's something that was triggered in you. What is it? Well, it's a feeling of jealousy . . . no, that's not quite right; it's a sense of not quite measuring up, of not being as good as she is — or even more accurately, of not doing what you really love, the way she does. That's it. You're aware that you're not doing what you really want to do with your life, and your friend's words triggered that sense inside you.

With this realization, you notice a felt shift or release inside, possibly accompanied by tears of recognition and sadness. You've just completed a round of focusing. You can use the same technique for any other problem or felt sense.

Choosing a Therapist To Help with Your Patterns

Perhaps you're so full of negative thoughts and feelings that you find it virtually impossible to concentrate, even in meditation. The voices (or images) in your head keep spewing forth worries, regrets, judgments, and criticism with such volume and velocity that you can barely hear yourself think. Or maybe you can focus on your breath or recite your mantra with some success, but when a particularly compelling story or pattern gets triggered, you're swept away by the intensity.

My first suggestion is to keep meditating regularly and see what happens. How do you feel after a few weeks or months of steady practice? Are you making any headway? Do you feel more calm and peaceful? Does your concentration deepen?

If certain patterns persist, however — especially if they interfere with your capacity to do your work or maintain loving, satisfying relationships — you might consider psychotherapy. I know that some people still feel a little embarrassed or ashamed if they admit they need help with their problems. But look at it this way: People have been consulting medicine men and women, shamans, rabbis, priests, and local elders for as long as human beings have had problems.

The thing is, psychotherapy (our modern, secular version of wise counsel) comes in many shapes and sizes — as many, in fact, as the professionals who practice it. Without devaluing any particular brand of psychotherapy (after all, I'm talking about my own profession here), in the following sections, I offer a few guidelines for choosing a therapist who can help free you from the limitations of your habitual patterns. Admittedly, I base these recommendations on my own particular interests and preferences — and on more than 30 years as a therapist and 40 years as a meditator and meditation teacher.

Talk is important, but you need to do more

Even classical Freudian therapy, which consists entirely of talk, aims for the moment when the insights touch a deeper place and trigger an inner-felt shift or emotional release. (Remember the crucial point in the movie *Good Will Hunting* when Robin Williams tells Matt Damon, "It wasn't your fault"?) The problem is, talk-only therapy gets there more slowly — and sometimes not at all.

Unless you happen to have a Robin Williams nearby, find a therapist who combines talk with one or more techniques that take you deeper faster, such as hypnotherapy, guided imagery, active imagination, sand play, body-centered therapy, breathwork, focusing, or eye movement desensitization and reprocessing (EMDR).

Shop around

If you want the names of appropriate therapists, turn first to friends, family members, or others who share similar interests or values. Don't be shy you may be surprised to discover how many people you know who have seen a shrink in recent years. Call these therapists and spend some time talking with them over the phone. Remember, you have a right to ask them anything you want to know. You may even schedule a session or two with each one before making your decision. After all, you're better off spending a couple of hundred bucks now on trial runs than discovering in six months or a year that you made a mistake.

Choose the person, not the credentials

Even if a therapist comes highly recommended and the office wall is covered with degrees and certificates, be sure to check this person out first. Does the therapist listen to you carefully and hear what you say? Does she seem emotionally attuned as well as insightful? Do you feel comfortable in her presence? Do you trust this person with your most tender places and difficult issues? In the final analysis, you need to trust your feelings and your intuition on this one.

Decide whether spirituality matters to you

If you have a particular spiritual orientation — or are in the process of developing one — you may want to search out a therapist who comes similarly equipped. If you don't have a large enough selection to choose from, at least find a shrink who honors spirituality rather than debunks it. Not only will he be more open to talking with you about meditation and *transpersonal* (that is, beyond the personal) experiences, he also may be able to help you combine meditation with therapy to work on your issues more effectively.

For information on the counseling that I offer by phone and Skype to people throughout the world, check out my website at `www.stephanbodian.org`.

Checking in with your inner child

When you're feeling agitated or upset, you may want to check in with the little child inside you, the part of you that feels things deeply. Here's a meditation to help reassure and nurture your inner child.

1. **Begin by noticing what you're feeling and where you're feeling it.**

2. **Take some time to breathe and relax into the feelings.**

3. **Imagine that there's a little boy or girl inside you having these feelings.**

   This child is the young, undeveloped part of you. You may have an image or just a gut sense or inner knowing.

4. **Ask yourself these questions: "How old is this child? What is this child's name? What kind of attention does this child want from me right now?"**

The child may want to be reassured or held, or he or she may just want to play.

5. **If possible, imagine giving the child what he or she wants.**

6. **Continue to commune with this child for as long as you like, giving and receiving words or physical contact as appropriate.**

7. **When you're done, notice how you feel.**

   You may be more relaxed or confident or at least less upset or afraid.

8. **Be sure to give your inner child a hug (if the child feels comfortable receiving one), tell the child that you love him or her, and reassure the child that you'll check in with him or her again from time to time — and please do!**

Chapter 13

Troubleshooting Common Roadblocks and Side Effects

. . . .

In This Chapter

▶ Using sleepiness, fear, self-judgment, and other obstacles to meditation as grist for your mill

▶ Dealing with altered states and unusual experiences like rapture and bliss without getting distracted

▶ Exploring your seven energy centers and what they have to teach you

. . . .

L ike any journey, meditation can have its share of breathtaking vistas and roadside attractions that inspire you and pique your curiosity. But it can also present obstacles, detours, and breakdowns that keep you from moving forward. As I mention in Chapter 1, I like to think of this book as a detailed travel guide. This chapter provides a troubleshooting manual to use when you encounter engine trouble, a flat tire, or an unexpected delay.

Of course, you may just breeze along and get where you're headed with nary a glitch in your itinerary. If you're doing just fine in your meditation, you're welcome to skip this chapter for now. But if you want a preview of the obstacles you may face — or some suggestions for the obstacles you've already started to face — then read on. In this chapter, you can pick up some helpful tips for dealing with the most common roadblocks when they get in your way, and you can find descriptions of scenic way stations that could turn into detours if you get confused and don't know how to negotiate them carefully.

Navigating the Roadblocks on Your Meditative Journey

Although meditation can be as complex as you want it to be, the basic practice (as I mention in Chapter 1) is actually quite simple: Just sit down, be quiet, turn your attention inward, and focus your attention. Nobody ever said it would be easy, however — not all the time, anyway!

In addition to the difficult emotions and habitual patterns I describe in Chapter 12, every persistent meditator inevitably encounters at least a few of the many classical roadblocks or obstacles. (Don't be put off by the word *obstacle*. These challenges may slow you down, but they don't need to stop you.) You're not doing something wrong when you get sleepy or restless or bored or keep putting off your meditation or wonder whether it's worth the effort. In fact, you're merely confronting more of the habitual patterns that cause you problems in every area of your life. Meditation offers a laboratory in which to investigate these patterns with mindful attention so you can apply your results in your work, your friendships, or your family life. The "obstacles," in other words, provide grist for the mill of self-awareness and behavioral change.

As I encourage throughout this book, be sure to treat yourself and the roadblocks that arise on your journey with the same kindness, care, and curiosity that you would give to a close friend. The point is not to push through roadblocks to some loftier place of clarity and repose. Rather, the obstacles themselves provide exceptional raw material for your lab work as you discover how to open to whatever arises in your experience with gentle, nonjudgmental awareness. Instead of obstacles, you may prefer to think of them as messengers bearing the gifts of increased energy, wisdom, and self-acceptance. As I describe in Chapter 12, it can be helpful to begin by naming your experience before proceeding to further exploration.

The following sections offer guidance for dealing with the most common roadblocks that occur during meditation.

Sleepiness

Most people sleepwalk through much of their lives, paying only minimal attention to what's happening around them. Have you ever driven home and wondered, when you arrived, how you got there? Because the point of meditation is to wake up and be mindful, it's no wonder that all meditators contend with dullness and dreaminess at least occasionally.

Probably the most common roadblock, sleepiness comes in a number of shapes and sizes. Begin by exploring your experience: Where do you feel the sleepiness in your body? What happens to your mind? Are you physically tired or just mentally dull? You may be yawning because you haven't slept well in days. If that's the case, stop meditating and take a nap.

More often, though, your mind becomes foggy when you're resisting feeling some unpleasant or undesirable emotion like fear or sadness. You may ask yourself, "What am I avoiding right now? What lies just beneath the surface of this sleepiness?" (You could even extend this inquiry to the other moments of your life when you dull out or glaze over.)

 After you've been meditating for a while, you may find that you get sleepy when your mind settles down and no longer has lots of stimulation to keep it occupied. At this point, you may need to rouse your energy by opening your eyes wide and sitting up straight. If your sleepiness persists, you can get up and walk around or splash cold water on your face to help you stay awake.

Restlessness

When you have difficulty paying attention in your meditation because your mind is agitated, worried, or anxious, and you're eager to get on with other activities, you can begin by naming the restlessness (see Chapter 12 for details on naming feelings) and noticing how you experience it in your body. Perhaps you're tensing in your belly or head or have an uneasy feeling in your arms and legs. Maybe you notice that you're perched uncomfortably on the edge of your cushion as though you're ready to jump off at any moment and grab a bite to eat or make a phone call.

 Notice also what your mind is doing. Does it skip uncontrollably from topic to topic or worry obsessively about some upcoming event or responsibility? As much as possible, observe your restlessness without getting caught by the agitation — or seduced by the impulse to get up and go. You may also want to practice counting your breaths or try some other concentration technique to help quiet your mind until you can resume your regular practice (or perhaps that is your regular practice). Like sleepiness, restlessness can also be a response to painful or unpleasant feelings you don't want to experience.

Boredom

Like most people, you may believe you get bored because the object of your attention lacks value or interest. But you may want to examine your boredom more closely. The truth is that boredom arises because you're not paying close enough attention or because you have some judgment or preference that keeps you from showing up wholeheartedly for the present moment. In fact, most people have become accustomed to constant stimulation and have difficulty sitting still when focusing on something simple like . . . well, like following their breath.

Boredom, like restlessness, can prevent you from experiencing the subtler beauties of life — and meditation can provide a wonderful opportunity to explore your boredom. Begin by naming it "boredom, boredom" (see Chapter 12 for more on naming your feelings). How do you experience it in your body? What stories does your mind spin? Instead of reacting to your boredom, just let yourself be mindfully bored. You may become so fascinated by your own boredom that you're no longer bored!

Fear

Sometimes you sit down to meditate and notice that your mind is filled with fearful thoughts and feelings that weren't apparent before. Where did they come from? You may have been anxious or afraid about something but didn't realize it until you began to meditate. Or your mindful attention may have flushed old fears to the surface to be explored and released. Perhaps you're afraid of meditation itself. You may be afraid that you won't be able to do it right or deal with your stress, or you may be afraid of what challenging memories or feelings may come up while you meditate.

TRADITIONAL WISDOM

When fear is no longer an obstacle

In her book *When Things Fall Apart*, the American-born Buddhist teacher Pema Chodron tells the story of a young Westerner who went to India in the 1960s. He desperately wanted to overcome his negative emotions, especially fear, which he believed to be an obstacle to his progress.

The teacher he met there kept telling him to stop struggling, but the young man took this instruction as just another technique for getting rid of his fear.

Finally, his teacher sent him to a hut in the foothills to meditate. Late one night, while he was sitting, he heard a noise and turned to see a huge snake with hood lifted, swaying in the corner. The young man was terrified. He sat facing the snake, unable to move or fall asleep. He couldn't use any meditation techniques to avoid his feelings — he could only sit with his breath and his fear and the snake in the corner.

Toward morning, as the last candle flickered out, the young man experienced a flood of tenderness and compassion for all the animals and people in the world. He could feel their suffering and their longing, and he could see that he had been using his meditation to separate not only from others but also from himself.

In the darkness, he began to cry. Yes, he was angry and proud and frightened, but he was also unique and wise and immeasurably precious. With deep gratitude, he got up, walked toward the snake, and bowed. Then he fell asleep on the floor. When he woke up, the snake had disappeared — and so had his desperate need to struggle with his fear.

If so, you're not alone! Fear is one of the most pervasive and basic of human emotions. No wonder it rears its head in meditation. You can use your practice as an excellent opportunity to work with your fear by following the instructions offered in Chapter 12.

Doubt

This roadblock can be an especially challenging one because it calls the whole journey into question. "Do I have what it takes to meditate? My mind never settles down — maybe I should try yoga or t'ai chi. What's the point of following my breath? How can this practice possibly bring relaxation and peace of mind?" Of course, asking questions and getting satisfactory answers is important, but when you've decided to give meditation a try, you need to treat your doubts as grist for your mill, instead of constantly taking them seriously.

Doubt can also result from pushing yourself too hard and holding high expectations; in meditation you need to set your expectations aside (as I mention in Chapter 7) and just do it, with the faith that the benefits will naturally accrue over time. To develop such faith, you may want to read other books like this one that extol the virtues of meditation.

Doubt stirs up your mind and makes concentration difficult. Begin by naming your doubt (refer to Chapter 12) and noticing the sensations it evokes and the stories it spins. With mindful awareness, doubt gradually settles down and recedes to the background. Eventually, all your little doubts may even coalesce into a great doubt that motivates you to inquire deeply into the nature of existence and come up with some answers for yourself.

Procrastination

Like doubt, procrastination can bring your meditation to a screeching halt. After all, if you keep putting it off, you won't be able to reap the benefits. If you tend to procrastinate in other areas of your life, you now have an opportunity to look beyond your usual excuses to the deeper feelings and concerns that fuel this pattern. Take some time to ask yourself honestly — but also gently and without judgment — what gets in the way of your following through on your intentions.

As described in the previous sections, you may be afraid or bored or have doubts about the value of meditation. Perhaps a self-sabotaging part of you doesn't want you to make the positive changes that meditation offers, so it keeps undermining your efforts. Or you may be too restless and distracted to find the time for the very activity that could help you deal with your restlessness and distractibility. When you get your meditation back on track, you can explore these patterns further. (You may also want to refresh your motivation or develop self-discipline. If so, turn to Chapter 5 or Chapter 10.)

Hypervigilance

The next time you see a loving new mother, notice how she attends to her baby. Does she constantly monitor his face for signs of illness or discomfort? Of course not. If she has a healthy relationship with her child, she gently gazes into his eyes with warm and caring attention, but without anxiety or concern.

You may find it helpful to bring the same gentle, mindful attention to your meditation. If you tend to get obsessive or perfectionistic or laserlike in your focus, you may just end up getting more stressed out than when you began. Instead, relax your attention like a loving mother, noticing your experience without becoming concerned or tense. You may also want to inquire into the deeper fear that may be motivating your hypervigilance.

Hypervigilance may also take the form of constantly monitoring your progress, constantly asking "How am I doing now?" The problem is that true progress in meditation involves simply being present without extra concerns like wondering how you're doing. Again, you can relax your awareness and just let yourself do what you do.

Self-judgment

Like fear, self-judgment is a nearly universal human experience. You may focus your judgment on your meditation (you're not doing it right, or you don't know how to concentrate) or on your being as a whole (you're inadequate, unlovable, or not quite good enough). The judging mind may even disguise itself as an objective observer or a spiritual coach, constantly comparing your progress to some internalized ideal. "If you were like the Buddha, you would be totally calm and undisturbed," your mind may say. Or, "If you were a good Christian (or Muslim or Jew), you would experience no anger or fear." Unfortunately, as one of my teachers used to say, "comparison kills," meaning that it tends to dampen the unique vitality and expression that belong to you alone and can't be compared with anything else.

By naming or noticing your self-judgments (refer to Chapter 12), you can gain some distance from them rather than take their word as gospel, as so many folks do. What does your voice of judgment sound like? What stories does it foist upon you as truth? Does it remind you of someone — say, a parent or boss? Are you trying to push away parts of your experience because they're undesirable in some way? Notice how judgment feels in your body. When you get caught up in judgment, you may find yourself tightening and tensing in response.

As you become familiar with your judgments, you can begin to welcome them as old friends, not only in meditation but in everyday life as well — and without buying into their story.

Attachment and desire

Just as fear and judgment attempt to avoid or resist certain experiences, attachment holds on tight to what you have while desire keeps trying to find something better. When you're attached — to your career or your relationship or your material possessions, for example — you may resist letting go when circumstances change. Who wouldn't? But attachment can be a setup for pain because life has this curious tendency to do what it pleases, despite your preferences to the contrary. With desire, the dissatisfaction of not having what you want and having what you don't want runs like a painful undercurrent just beneath the surface of conscious awareness.

I'm not recommending complete nonattachment and desirelessness here. After all, only the Buddha could pull that one off! Nor am I equating desire with pleasure. In fact, the experience of desire can be extremely unpleasant, like a tormenting itch that never goes away, no matter how much you scratch; true pleasure, by contrast, fulfills a deep and natural human need. But I'm suggesting that you can discover how to create some space around your desires and attachments so that you're not overwhelmed by the unpredictable ups and downs of life. (For more on attachment, see Chapter 6.)

Attachment and desire can show up in your meditation in a number of forms. Perhaps you covet the moments of relative calm and become upset when your mind gets agitated or preoccupied. Or you may have a particular fondness for certain thoughts — fantasies of financial success, for example, or images of last month's vacation — and find that you're reluctant to let go of them and return to your breath or your mantra. Maybe you're constantly lusting and longing for some imagined fulfillment that's just out of reach.

As with the other roadblocks, you can explore your attachment and desire by first gently naming them as they arise (see Chapter 12) and then by noticing the thoughts and sensations that comprise them.

Pride

Here's a classic meditation scenario. You've been sitting regularly for a few weeks, and one day your mind calms down like the surface of a still forest pool. The next thing you know you're having the following thoughts: "Wow, I'm hardly thinking at all, and I've been following my breath now for at least five minutes without interruption. Cool! I'm really getting the hang of this meditation stuff. Pretty soon I'll be an expert. Maybe I'll even become enlightened. . . ."

In this scenario, not only have you been bitten by the bug of pride, which latches on to your accomplishments and uses them to bolster your self-image, but you've also gotten sidetracked in your meditation. Pride can also take the form of bragging to your family and friends about how often you meditate or merely feeling special and superior to others.

As I explain in the section "Attachment and desire," you may want to investigate the thoughts and feelings that make up your pride. Underneath it, you may find some fear or insecurity or a desire to be loved and appreciated. Or you can remind yourself that meditation has nothing to do with achievement and everything to do with being present in the moment for whatever is arising. As soon as you get puffed up about how well you're meditating, you're gone, so gently bring yourself back to your breath.

Avoidance

If you're trying to avoid confronting certain problems or challenges in your life, you may turn to meditation as a convenient escape and end up logging hours on your cushion that may be better spent paying your bills or preparing for a career change or sharing your feelings with your partner. The *New Yorker* magazine ran a cartoon a few years back that speaks to this issue: A Zen monk sits peacefully on his cushion, while behind a screen in the background lurks a huge, chaotic pile of stuff.

Meditation can help you calm your mind, open your heart, and face the fears and other feelings that may stand in your way, but ultimately you need to take down the screen and apply what you've learned to the real world. (In other words, meditation, like work, sex, and watching TV, can become addictive if you abuse it.) You're not becoming addicted if you spend a half hour or an hour each day meditating — or even if you head off for a retreat every now and then. But if you find yourself avoiding the challenges of life, pay attention. The themes that keep recurring in your meditation may not be distractions at all, but pressing concerns that require your response.

Bypassing

Just as you can hide out from life's problems, you can also use meditation as a convenient way to avoid facing deeper psychological and emotional issues. Particularly if you develop strong concentration, you can focus on your breath or some other object of meditation while actively suppressing unpleasant or "unspiritual" feelings. I know people who, after many years of meditation in monasteries or ashrams, finally discover that they're literally sitting on a lifetime of unresolved grief, resentment, or pain. If you follow the guidelines provided in Chapter 12 for working with your emotions, you may not have to contend with this particular roadblock.

Enjoying the Side Effects of Meditation without Getting Sidetracked

In addition to the roadblocks that arise in meditation, you may also encounter a number of unusual and compelling experiences on your journey — what I like to call the side effects or roadside attractions. Earlier in this chapter and in Chapter 12, I describe ordinary emotions, patterns, and mind-states that may prove challenging as your meditation deepens. In this section, I discuss what consciousness researchers call *altered states,* which are nonordinary experiences of body, mind, and heart that, though essentially harmless, may be startling, confusing, or frightening for the neophyte meditator.

Some people meditate for years and never experience anything out of the ordinary. As a Zen monk, for example, I kept hoping for some dramatic breakthrough but got only the occasional insight to punctuate thousands of hours of meditation. Others sit down and within a few sessions begin having glimpses of what researchers call the *transpersonal dimension* of experience. A friend of mind has always seen angels and other transcendent beings, both on and off her meditation cushion.

Meditation traditions differ too in how they regard such extraordinary experiences. Some teach that the point is simply to be here now and that anything else that occurs is merely a potential distraction. Another *New Yorker* cartoon puts it succinctly: A grizzled old monk sitting in meditation turns to his young companion and says, apparently in response to a question, "Nothing happens next. This is it." If a moment of true awakening occurs, according to these traditions, it merely takes the form of a shift in perspective without fireworks or flashy signs. By contrast, other traditions view extraordinary experiences as meaningful or possibly even necessary landmarks on the path to freedom and awakening. (For more on spiritual experiences, see Chapter 15.)

In mindfulness meditation, the method I describe in this book (see Chapter 7), you simply approach the extraordinary in the same way you greet the ordinary: with gentle, mindful attention. The point is to welcome whatever arises — and in the process to awaken to who you already are — so any experiences you encounter along the way are just roadside attractions. Enjoy them and keep going. If they become distracting or painful, you may want to seek a qualified teacher.

To help you deal with these experiences without getting sidetracked or overwhelmed, Buddhist teacher Jack Kornfield, in his book *A Path with Heart*, suggests that you keep in mind the following three guidelines:

✔ **Side effects are just that.** Don't get attached to them or take them as an indication of either spiritual accomplishment or spiritual failure. Just keep going.

✔ **Apply the brakes if you must.** If the side effects get too intense, stop meditating for a while and engage in more "grounding" activities that connect you with your body and the earth, such as working in the garden, getting a massage, or walking in nature. (To help you ground, try the meditation in the sidebar "What to do when you're feeling ungrounded.")

✔ **Appreciate altered states as part of the larger dance of meditation.** Don't get caught resisting or struggling with them. Just try to welcome them as you do every experience.

The following sections highlight a few of the extraordinary experiences you may encounter in your meditation. (For more-detailed descriptions of these experiences, I highly recommend *A Path with Heart.*)

Rapture and bliss

When your concentration deepens (but sometimes before), you may begin having nonordinary physical experiences known as *rapture*. Perhaps the most common form of rapture involves the pleasurable movement of subtle (or not-so-subtle) energy through the body. As it moves, this energy encounters areas of tightness and contraction that open and release in response. The energetic releases can take the form of vibrations, trembling, or sudden or repetitive spontaneous movements known in the yoga tradition as *kriyas*. For example, you may feel spasms going up your spine or involuntary movements of your arms or head.

Although the energy of rapture is generally experienced as pleasurable, you may be understandably surprised and a bit disturbed to find your body moving in ways you can't seem to control. Jack Kornfield, for example, reports that his arms began to flap like a bird's while he was meditating intensively in a monastery in Thailand. He followed his teacher's advice to observe the movements without trying to stop or control them, and they gradually subsided on their own.

Rapture refers to more than just energy; it comes in other forms and flavors too. For example, you may have chills or hot flashes for no apparent reason. Or you may experience your body as extraordinarily heavy and dense or as transparent and filled with light. Or you may have prickling or tingling sensations followed by waves of pleasure and delight. Rapture can take as many forms as the people who experience it.

You're not going insane or doing something wrong if you experience rapture; in fact, rapture generally signifies a deepening of concentration. As much as possible, keep meditating as you bring mindful awareness to your experience and allow the energy to do its healing work of releasing your stuck places. If the energy gets too intense, just stop meditating and do something ordinary and physical.

As for *bliss,* it's the powerful rapture that accompanies a spiritual insight or unitive experience. Mystics from the Judeo-Christian tradition, for instance, often report experiencing bliss when they achieve the pinnacle of their journey: oneness with God.

Visions and other sensory experiences

If you don't experience rapture, don't be disappointed — you may get your altered states in the visual channel. My friend who sees angels also has visions of traveling to other realms in her meditation where she meets enlightened beings that teach and empower her. These experiences don't disturb her; quite the contrary, she enjoys and even invites them.

Though you may not have such elaborate visions, you still may see colored lights or images of what appear to be past lives or vivid memories or glimpses of other realities. Again, don't be disturbed by these experiences. Simply take them as evidence of deepening concentration, and don't let them distract you from the focus of your meditation. Of course, if you find them meaningful, by all means appreciate what they have to offer. But the point of meditation, as I teach it in this book, is to cultivate awareness of the present moment, not to spend your meditation time exploring the endless world of altered states.

In addition to visual phenomena, you may also have auditory or olfactory experiences, including inner voices; music; powerful, resonant sounds; or unusual smells. Or you may find that your meditation heightens your perceptual sensitivity so that you see, hear, smell, feel, or taste things more acutely. (Depending on your particular tastes and what you happen to be sensing, you may find this increased sensitivity pleasant or unpleasant.)

Waves of emotion

As your mind settles down and you welcome your experience, you create inner space for unfelt (and possibly unconscious) emotions to bubble up and release. (For more on the process of spontaneous release, see Chapter 12.) One of my early Zen friends spent her first few years of meditation crying quietly on her cushion. She reported that her feelings generally didn't have much content or story line; rather, they just occurred as waves of energy in her body. Other people I know meditate regularly for years with little emotion, and then suddenly, like an airplane, they hit a patch of turbulence and experience days or even weeks of anger or grief.

If you find the emotions difficult to handle, you can consult the guidelines I provide in Chapter 12. Or you may want to seek the advice of a qualified meditation teacher. (For information on the meditation guidance I offer by phone, check out my website at www.stephanbodian.org. For advice on finding a teacher, see Chapter 15.) Otherwise, you can continue to sit with mindful awareness as you allow the emotions to ripple through your body, mind, and heart. Sometimes these feelings — which, incidentally, can include ecstasy and joy as well as sadness and pain — come from deep unconscious layers that hark back to early childhood or infancy. At other times, the feelings may seem like they have nothing to do with you at all. Whatever your experience, you can practice welcoming it with mindful awareness without trying to change it or push it away.

Energetic openings

When you meditate regularly for weeks or months, you generate energy that begins to accumulate in your body. Eventually, this energy may take the relatively subtle form of rapture (as described in the earlier section on the topic), or it may express itself as *kundalini,* the powerful life force that (according to the Indian tantric tradition) animates all things and lies coiled at the base of the spine like a serpent. (For more on Indian tantra, see Chapter 3.)

Meditation can awaken kundalini and send it up the central energetic channel (which is aligned with but distinct from the spine) — and so can certain other activities and events like childbirth, sex, prayer, powerful emotions, and physical trauma. As the kundalini rises — which may occur slowly and gradually or suddenly and unexpectedly — it encounters the seven major energy centers (also known as *chakras*) that lie situated along the central channel from the base of the spine to the crown of the head.

For a detailed map of the chakras, see Figure 13-1. The chakras in the figure are shown in order from the bottom up, with the first chakra located at the base of the spine and the seventh at the top of the head.

Figure 13-1:
A map of
the chakras
(energy
centers),
with the
traditional
symbols for
each one.

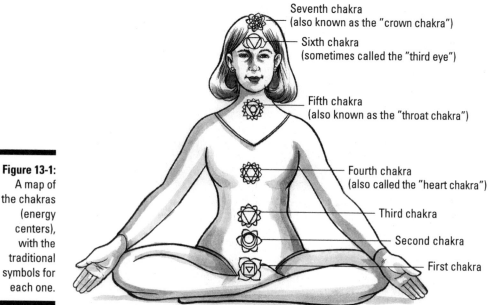

Seventh chakra
(also known as the "crown chakra")

Sixth chakra
(sometimes called the "third eye")

Fifth chakra
(also known as the "throat chakra")

Fourth chakra
(also called the "heart chakra")

Third chakra

Second chakra

First chakra

Described by those who can see them as spinning wheels or vortexes of energy, the chakras transform energy from one frequency to another (for example, from spiritual to emotional) and act as intermediaries between an individual's inner life and the external world. Apparently, they work best when they're open and relatively balanced. When they're closed or imbalanced — a common occurrence — you may experience certain problems, ailments, or issues that correspond with particular chakras.

In particular, people who meditate frequently may have a tendency to open their upper chakras (from the heart to the crown) relatively easily, while keeping their lower chakras relatively closed. For example, many people find it easier to have spiritual experiences or feel unconditional love for all beings than to deal with core personal issues like trust, safety, intimacy, and self-assertion. As a result, these lower centers may require special attention and tender, gentle investigation before they open.

Certain meditation techniques aim to awaken the kundalini and guide it through the chakras until it reaches the crown of the head, where it ultimately bursts forth in a moment of powerful illumination. Other techniques work on opening and energizing particular chakras. (See Chapter 11 for meditations that open the heart, for example.) The primary technique I propose in this book, known as mindfulness meditation, doesn't focus on the chakras at all. But people who practice mindfulness may experience the opening of particular energy centers as a side effect of their meditative journey. (Incidentally, Indian tantra, which has branches in both Hinduism and Buddhism, isn't the only tradition to talk about chakras. Jewish kabbalists, Sufi dervishes, and Taoist sages all have their own unique energy systems and centers.)

To help you recognize these openings if they occur, I describe each of the chakras in some detail in the following list. In addition to the experiences described, you may feel tightness or constriction in the area when a chakra is relatively closed and a noticeable increase of energy when it opens. Use the positive expressions to help relax and open each chakra, if you feel inclined.

- **First chakra:** Located at the base of the spine and connected with issues of survival and safety. When this chakra is relatively closed, you may feel insecure and ungrounded, possibly even terrified and mistrustful of your capacity to survive. As it opens, you may feel energy flowing down through your body into the earth, accompanied by images and feelings associated with safety and survival as well as an overall sense of stability and trust. *Positive expression:* "I'm safe and at home in the world and in my body."

- **Second chakra:** Located in the lower abdomen about 2 inches below the navel and connected with issues of sexuality, creativity, and emotional attachment. When it's relatively closed, you may feel ashamed of your body, sexually inhibited, and emotionally disconnected from others. As it opens, you may experience a rush of sexual feelings or imagery, including possible images of past abuse or dysfunction as well as a sense of potency, playfulness, and flow with others. *Positive expression:* "I'm a creative, sexual, emotional being."

- **Third chakra:** Located at the solar plexus just below the diaphragm and connected with issues of interpersonal power and authenticity. When this chakra is relatively closed, you may find it difficult to trust (either yourself or others), to set interpersonal boundaries, or to express or even acknowledge your own anger or vulnerability. As it opens, you may experience a release of anger or shame and a deepening and expansion of your breath, accompanied by feelings of personal power and vitality. *Positive expression:* "I trust myself and others."

✔ **Fourth chakra (often called the "heart chakra"):** Located in the center of the chest near the heart and connected with issues of love and self-esteem. When this chakra is closed, you may feel self-hatred, resentment, and alienation from others, and you may find it difficult to give and receive love freely. As it opens, you may experience a release of old grief or pain, accompanied by love or joy or poignancy and a sense of boundless expansiveness. (For more on opening the heart chakra, see Chapter 11.) *Positive expression:* "I'm loving and worthy of being loved."

✔ **Fifth chakra (also known as the "throat chakra"):** Located in the center of the throat and connected with issues of honest, direct, and responsible self-expression. When it's relatively closed, you may find it difficult to share your feelings, thoughts, or concerns without diluting or distorting them to make them more acceptable to others. As this chakra opens, you may experience a sudden upsurge of things you've always wanted to say, accompanied by increased confidence in your own voice and creativity. *Positive expression:* "I have a right to express my truth."

✔ **Sixth chakra (sometimes called the "third eye"):** Located between and slightly above the eyebrows and connected with intellectual clarity, intuition, and personal vision. When this chakra is relatively closed, you may have difficulty thinking clearly or planning for the future, and you may have strong personal opinions, prejudices, or negative beliefs about yourself. As this chakra opens, you may have sudden insights or intuitions that expand your intellectual or spiritual horizons, possibly accompanied by inner visions or even psychic abilities. *Positive expression:* "I see things clearly."

✔ **Seventh chakra (also known as the "crown chakra"):** Located at the very top of the head and connected with issues of freedom and spiritual transcendence. When this chakra is relatively closed (as it is in most people), you may feel cut off from the sacred or spiritual dimension of life. As it opens, you may feel a subtle pressure or pain at first, followed by a release of energy through the crown of the head and an influx of what people have described as grace, peace, blessing, or illumination. At the same time, you may feel your identity dissolving and merging with the vast expanse of being itself. Needless to say, the opening of this chakra is a precious event much sought after in certain spiritual traditions. *Positive expression:* "I am."

PLAY THIS!

What to do when you're feeling ungrounded

Sometimes people who meditate find that their upper chakras (that is, the energy centers from the heart to the crown) open more quickly than their lower chakras, bringing a rush of energy and insight to their head and shoulders while the lower half of their body remains relatively stagnant or numb. In particular, those who get sidetracked by some of the flashy side effects of meditation may start to feel ungrounded and lose touch with their basic needs for food, sleep, and physical exercise.

Track 10 is a simple exercise that can help you ground down into the earth when you start feeling like you're going to lift out of your body into some more ethereal realm:

1. **Begin by sitting quietly, closing your eyes, and taking a few slow, deep breaths.**

    If possible, sit on the ground with your back relatively straight (see Chapter 8 for more on sitting positions).

2. **Focus your awareness on your lower abdomen, at a point about 2 inches below your navel and 1½ inches inside your body.**

    Martial artists call this area the *t'an t'ien* and believe it's a focal point for life energy, or *chi*. Explore this area with mindful attention, noticing how it feels.

3. **Direct your breath into this area, expanding it when you inhale and contracting it when you exhale.**

Consciously and deliberately breathe into your t'an t'ien for five minutes or more, allowing your awareness and energy to concentrate there. Notice how your center of gravity shifts from the upper part of your body to your t'an t'ien.

4. **Continuing to breathe with your t'an t'ien, imagine that you're a tree with roots that go deep into the earth.**

    Both feel and visualize these roots originating in the t'an t'ien and growing down through the base of your spine into the ground, spreading through the soil as far down as you can imagine.

5. **Feel and visualize these roots drawing energy from the earth into your t'an t'ien on the inhalation, and feel the energy spreading down through the roots on the exhalation.**

    Continue to feel and visualize this circulation of energy — up on the inhale, down on the exhale — for five or ten minutes.

6. **When your t'an t'ien feels charged and strong, you can get up and go about your day.**

    Every now and then, stop for a moment or two and imagine your roots once again.

MEDITATION

Preparing for sleep

Most people go to bed at night filled with the worries, concerns, and excitements accumulated during the day. Instead, try preparing for sleep using one of the following exercises:

✔ **As you undress, imagine removing all your cares and responsibilities, one by one.** Imagine feeling yourself growing lighter, more relaxed, and more spacious, until your mind is completely empty and filled with a pleasant, rosy glow. Imagine this glow descending to your heart, and rest your awareness in the center of your heart as you drift off to sleep.

✔ **Before going to sleep, review your day in some detail.** Take some time to appreciate your positive accomplishments and experiences. When you come to something you regret, consider the lesson you learned. As you drift off to sleep, feel gratitude in your heart to all the people who contributed to your life today in various ways.

✔ **Lie on your back and feel the contact of your body against the bed.** Beginning with your feet and working slowly up through your legs, hips, torso, arms, neck, and head, gradually relax your body from bottom to top. When you're done, feel your body as one luminous sphere of relaxation as you drift off to sleep.

Chapter 14

Developing a Practice That Works for You

. . . .

In This Chapter

▶ Finding techniques that match your motivation

▶ Rounding out your practice with meditations for mind, heart, and body

▶ Discovering the benefits of regular meditation

▶ Fitting the pieces together into a practice that works for you

▶ Meditating with others in groups, workshops, and retreats

. . . .

As you may have noticed as you were flipping through some of the other chapters, I filled this book with meditation techniques drawn from a variety of different spiritual and secular sources. Maybe I'm just enthusiastic, but I wanted to make sure I covered all the bases and offered meditations that would appeal to just about everyone.

Needless to say, you can't practice all these techniques — nor would you want to. So in this chapter, I show you how to choose the ones that are appropriate for your purposes so you can cobble together a meditation practice that's well suited for your particular needs. You can also pick up a few tips on how to find other people to meditate with and how to design your own little monastic retreat for a day.

Fitting the Puzzle Pieces Together

In centuries past, ordinary folks didn't have the opportunity to thumb through a copy of *Meditation For Dummies,* pick and choose their favorite meditation techniques, and then sample them like connoisseurs at a wine tasting. Instead, they considered themselves extremely fortunate if they happened upon a teacher willing to impart some secret method. Then they took that method home and practiced it single-mindedly for the rest of their lives.

But times have changed, and you and I live in a veritable meditation superstore, with a different technique down every aisle. So what's a guy or gal to do with all the choices? Well, you need to know yourself, what you like or don't like, and what you're hoping to get out of your meditation. Next, you need to take a sip here and there, trust your taste buds, and eventually settle on a particular approach. Then you can use this approach as the centerpiece around which you construct a regular practice — just as, say, a wonderful meal can be constructed around an especially fine wine. But so much for epicurean metaphors!

Here are the principal pieces of a complete meditation practice as they're presented in this book. As you can see, I include both meditations themselves and related practices:

- Mindfulness meditation (Chapter 7)
- Mantra meditation (Chapters 3 and 15)
- Body scan and relaxation (Chapter 7)
- Walking meditation (Chapter 17)
- Lovingkindness meditation (Chapter 11)
- Compassion meditation (Chapter 11)
- Working with your emotions and habitual patterns (Chapter 12)
- Devotional meditation (Chapter 15)
- Insight practices like self-inquiry (Chapter 15)
- Healing meditation (Chapter 18)
- Mindfulness in action (Chapter 17)
- Using a meditation altar (Chapter 9)
- Chanting and/or bowing (Chapter 15)
- Dedicating your practice (Chapter 15)

How do you know which practices to include in your own custom-tailored routine? To begin with, you're better off starting out simple: Choose one technique and stick with it for a few months or even years. Then, when you feel confident in your ability to concentrate reasonably well, you may want to consider how traditional meditators combine different practices.

In the Buddhist tradition, for example, people generally mix meditations designed to cultivate wisdom with those that have the power to elicit compassion or love. Then they season the basic ingredients as needed with others like self-inquiry or healing meditations. Next, they throw in some walking meditation (to act as a bridge between sitting meditation and everyday life). Finally, they frame the whole routine by first reminding themselves why they're meditating and then, when they're done, by dedicating the virtue or power of the meditation to the benefit of others. Of course, this mixture of ingredients is no casual hodge-podge, but has evolved over several thousand years.

Maybe you're not as methodical as all that and would rather just use your intuition and do what feels right. If so, go for it! Ultimately, the process of choosing a set of meditation techniques may be as personal and mysterious as the process of choosing a mate. But before you make your choices, read the following sections, which provide a few pointers for checking your motivation, balancing your practice, and trusting your intuition.

Know your motivation

Just as you wouldn't take a hacksaw to a stick of butter or use your toothbrush to scrub your floor, you don't need to meditate three hours a day if you're just looking for a little stress-reduction. And you wouldn't want to limit yourself to ten minutes if you're determined to get enlightened by the end of next week. In Chapter 5, I describe five principal motivations for meditation:

- ✔ Improving your life
- ✔ Understanding and accepting yourself
- ✔ Realizing your true nature
- ✔ Awakening others
- ✔ Expressing your innate perfection

Knowing which of these best describes you can help you determine both how and how much you meditate. (Most people fall into the first three categories; the other two are generally reserved for seasoned meditators.) Mindfulness meditation (explained in detail in Chapter 7) makes a great foundational practice no matter what your motivation, and it can be extended to every moment of your life (see Chapter 17). But the rest is up to you.

For example, if you want to help heal a chronic ailment, you can add one or more of the healing meditations from Chapter 18. If you want to get to know yourself better or deal with difficult emotions or behaviors, you may want to pursue some of the techniques offered in Chapter 12. And if you're headed straight for the top of the meditation mountain (as described in Chapter 1), you can experiment with meditations from Chapter 15 for getting closer to God or gaining direct insight into your essential being.

Just remember that this book is merely an introduction; if you want to go deeper in any direction, you need other books and ultimately, perhaps, a teacher. For a listing of books you may want to read after this one, see the appendix. If you're hunting for a teacher, read the guidelines for finding one in Chapter 15.

Play to your strengths and fill in the gaps

In addition to motivation, you may want to know a little more about your general tendencies and personality traits and how they influence your meditation choices. For example, some people tend to be more cerebral and become attracted to meditation because they seek greater clarity or understanding. Others identify more with their feelings and may be drawn to meditation out of a deep desire to feel God's love or express their devotion or compassion or work closely with a particular teacher. Still others focus more on their bodies and turn to meditation for physical healing or energy or power. These three types — people who are oriented toward their heads, their hearts, and their bodies — are described in a number of the great meditative traditions and in the Western scientific tradition as well. Take a few moments to check out your predominant orientation.

The *head types* immediately gravitate to the insight practices, the *heart types* to the devotion and compassion practices, and the *body types* to the relaxation exercises and healing meditations. But the truth is that you have a heart, a mind, and a body, and you need to develop and cultivate all three in your meditation practice if you're going to evolve into a complete, well-rounded human being.

So notice your tendencies, and indulge them as much as you like. After all, you need to do what feels right — and often what feels right are the practices that fit your type. But you may also want to consider filling in the gaps by including meditations or other practices that stretch you in directions you don't ordinarily go. For example, do insight practices, but preface them with some devotional chanting or bowing (or, even better, do them with an attitude of kindness and compassion). Focus on compassion practices or working with your emotions, but also relax your body or be mindful of your sensate experience. Ultimately, any of the basic meditations help develop the different parts of you — heart, mind, and body — but be aware of your tendency to favor one over the others or to even sidestep one entirely.

The downside of being a dilettante

In every area of interest, from baseball to investing, you can amass a wealth of information to impress your family and friends without getting your hands dirty actually *doing* what you know so much about. (For example, you can memorize the stats for every player in the Major Leagues without ever learning how to throw a baseball.) The same holds true for meditation. As they say in Zen, "Painted cakes won't satisfy your hunger." And reading all the best meditation books in the world won't reduce your stress or calm your busy mind one iota. (You'll just end up becoming what one Buddhist teacher called a "spiritual materialist.") You need to roll up your sleeves and apply what you've read.

In the same way, you won't make any progress by dabbling in different techniques. ("Mmm, it's Tuesday; it must be time for mindfulness.") You need to choose one or two techniques and stick with them. Remember the old adage, "Jack of all trades and master of none"? Well, your goal is to master the art of meditation, not amass a few new tricks to add to your collection.

When you encounter restlessness or boredom (or any of the other "obstacles" described in Chapter 13), don't immediately conclude you've made a mistake. Instead, use your resistance and other difficult emotions and mind-states as grist for the mill of your meditation. (For instructions on how to do that, see Chapters 12 and 13.)

Also, life has an uncanny tendency to reveal your Achilles heel and show you precisely what qualities you need to develop, so pay attention. If you keep drawing "overly emotional" people into your life or if your partner's "intellectualizing" drives you crazy, perhaps you're being shown the very qualities you most need to add to your own repertoire.

Experiment, trust your intuition, and then settle down

You can't really tell how a particular meditation will affect you until you practice it regularly for a period of time. Just reading about it in a book like this one or listening to it on a CD won't tell you much. Similarly, practicing it once or twice may give you a taste and show you whether it's worth pursuing, but you won't get the impact the meditation was designed to evoke.

So begin by shopping around and sampling the meditations that catch your eye. Notice how you feel when you try them out. Then trust your intuitive sense of what's right and appropriate for you, and commit yourself to actually doing the practice regularly for a period of time. I'm talking months or even years here. That's right. I said "commit" — the dreaded C word. Simply put, you have to do the same meditation again and again if you want to reap the benefits. I know this advice runs counter to the quick-fix orientation of Western culture, but you won't find any shortcuts or get-enlightened-quick schemes in the world of meditation. As the old Nike ad puts it, "Just do it." Preferably you'll do it with kindness, gentleness, patience, and compassion, but ultimately you just have to do it again and again! (For more on discipline, effort, and commitment, see Chapter 10.)

Create a regular practice

After you have a few guidelines for putting the various pieces together, you can fashion a practice that you can do day after day. Remember to keep it simple. After all, the point of meditation is to relax your body and ease your busy mind, not make your life more complicated. Here are the basic stages for creating a regular practice that works for you:

- ✔ **Choose a core technique.** If you do nothing else, you've still created a viable meditation practice that will serve you quite well. I recommend mindfulness meditation because it teaches skills you can translate to every activity and moment of your life, but some people prefer mantra meditation or concentration on a visual object.

- ✔ **Round out your practice.** As I suggest in the earlier section "Play to your strengths and fill in the gaps," you may want to add another practice or two that cultivates different qualities of mind, body, or heart. But if you have only a snippet of time each day, stick with your core technique, instead of getting too complex.

- ✔ **Decide how much and how often.** Depending on your motivation and your reasons for meditating, you're going to sit longer or shorter periods more or less frequently. Your interest in meditation may also wax and wane somewhat with the cycles of your life. For example, you may have times when you focus more on outward achievement or family life, and times when you pay more attention to inner unfolding. For guidelines on scheduling your meditation, see Chapter 9.

- ✔ **Keep it regular.** I can't say this too often: Whatever else you do (and whatever the cycles of your life), stand by your core technique as you would your loved one or your kids. Stand by it through thick and thin, ups and downs, feast and famine, and any other clichés you can muster.

- ✔ **Add practices as needed, but stick with them.** For example, if you get sick, by all means add a healing meditation. If you want to open your heart some more, add a lovingkindness meditation. But don't sacrifice your core technique, and stick with your new one as well.

Respecting the cycles of practice

I generally don't like to talk about progress in meditation. I'd rather remind you that you've always been where you're headed, which is right here and now. If anything, meditation involves stripping away the veils that keep you from seeing what's been true all along.

It's especially important to realize that meditation doesn't entail linear development or improvement. Every day is a new day, and every meditation differs from the last. One day your mind may seem extraordinarily clear and still, like the proverbial forest pool, leading you to conclude that you finally have this meditation stuff down cold. The next day, without warning, your mind may seem as turbulent as the ocean during a hurricane. So much for linear improvement!

Instead of a line, I like to use the image of a spiral that keeps circling around and around but gradually rises. You may go through times when challenging life circumstances like career changes, losses, or separations stir up difficult emotions and patterns that pervade your meditation. Then you may go through more tranquil periods when your concentration deepens and your mind settles down. If you keep meditating patiently, without becoming overly discouraged or elated, you'll find that you gradually expand to include more and more of who you are — the ups and downs, the highs and lows, the rough spots and the smooth. In the process, you become more joyful and peaceful, but not in the measurable, linear way you may have expected.

✔ **Know when to go deeper.** If you find yourself hungering for more time on your meditation cushion, by all means pencil it in. The more you meditate, the deeper you'll go. Just remember that it's better to wait until you want to do more rather than pushing yourself because you think you "should." (For suggestions on doing a meditation retreat, see the section "Whenever Two or More of You: Meditating with Others.")

✔ **Seek help when you need it.** You can venture only so far into unknown terrain alone. If you start encountering problems in your meditation or experiences that confuse or scare you (or you just want to make sure you're doing it right), you may want to look for a teacher. (For an overview of meditation problems and pitfalls, check out Chapter 13. For a teacher, visit my website at www.stephanbodian.org or check out the guidelines in Chapter 15.)

Whenever Two or More of You: Meditating with Others

All the great meditative traditions agree: Meditating with others confers extraordinary benefits that enhance your individual practice and accelerate your personal and spiritual unfolding. Buddhists regard the community of practitioners as one of the three jewels or treasures of practice, along with the awakened teacher and the truth itself. Jews believe that God really listens when ten of His faithful convene together in prayer. And Jesus himself put it quite elegantly: "Whenever two or more of you are gathered in my name, there is love."

Besides, researchers like Dean Ornish have found that a sense of belonging or connectedness with others not only improves the quality of life but also increases longevity. In one study, people who answered yes to the questions "Do you draw strength from your religious faith?" and "Are you a member of any organization that meets regularly?" were seven times more likely to survive open-heart surgery than those who answered no. In another study, women being given the same conventional treatments for metastatic breast cancer were divided into two groups: one that met together once a week for mutual support and one that didn't. After five years, the women who met had lived twice as long as the ones who didn't.

On a more practical level, you may simply find encouragement from other meditators to persist at what may sometimes seem like a tedious pursuit. And you can discuss your practice and get useful suggestions based on others' experiences. They may already have solved the problems or traversed the terrain that you're just encountering.

You have several options for finding others to meditate with: You can seek out a group or class that's already meeting, form a group yourself, or attend a weekend workshop or group retreat. I discuss each in turn in the following sections.

Joining or forming a meditation group

Now that meditation has become a more mainstream pursuit, it's relatively easy to find classes at readily accessible venues like local meditation centers, churches or synagogues, adult-education programs, community colleges, fitness centers, and yoga studios. The problem is, you may not be drawn to the technique they're teaching, or you may already know how to meditate and simply want the support of other warm bodies.

If you can't find a suitable class, you can ask friends who meditate or check local bulletin boards or the classifieds for ads announcing the formation of leaderless groups. Or you could take the initiative and form such a group yourself! Participants don't have to practice the same technique or hold the same spiritual or religious beliefs. They just have to be willing to sit quietly in the same room together doing whatever they do. You could begin with a reading from the world's spiritual literature, if everyone seems amenable, and you might end with discussion or a Quaker-style silence in which people offer whatever the spirit moves them to share. Or you can just convene, sit quietly, smile at one another, and leave. The form is up to you.

Attending your first workshop or retreat

If you feel adventurous or simply want more in-depth instruction and guidance, you can sign up for an extended period of group meditation. Many of the organizations listed in the appendix of this book have regional centers that offer individual instruction and workshops, groups, and/or retreats. Or you can head for the main monastery, community, or ashram itself and get a taste of what it's like to live with a group of people whose primary focus is the practice of meditation.

Be sure you know in advance what you'll be doing on your retreat, and be wary of the tendency among some groups to proselytize for their own particular faith or ideology — unless, of course, you happen to be interested in those beliefs.

No matter how relaxed the atmosphere or gentle the approach of the retreat, you may feel a little scared at first because extended periods of silent meditation don't provide any of the usual diversions, such as cellphones or computers, that keep you from facing yourself. So don't be surprised if you sign up and then conjure all kinds of great reasons for canceling at the last minute, from sick kids to business emergencies. My suggestion: Stick with your original intention and go anyway. You'll be glad you did.

Here are a few other reasons you may come up with for putting off your first workshop or retreat along with some rejoinders:

- ✔ **"I'm not good enough yet."** Understandably, you may shudder at the prospect of sitting quietly for three or four hours (or more!) each day when you've had difficulty mustering the patience for even 15 minutes. But don't let your reservations stop you. You'll be surprised and pleased by how deep your concentration can go and how long you can sustain it when you have the support of a teacher and a group of like-minded people.

- ✔ **"I have back or knee problems."** If you have serious physical limitations, you may need to take special precautions and even follow a modified schedule, but don't be daunted or deterred. Just be sure to let the retreat leaders know beforehand so they can help you get comfortable. If you merely suffer from the usual aches and pains that accompany sitting, however, you may be pleased to discover that they actually improve or become less distracting during the course of your retreat. Many teachers also offer instructions for working with discomfort during retreat.

✔ **"I don't have the time."** What do you mean, exactly? Are you suggesting that every spare moment between now and next Christmas is booked in advance? Or do you really mean that you'd rather do other things with your time? Well, no problem. But if you decide you'd like to attend a retreat, I can guarantee that the time will materialize like magic. And who knows? You may find that the insight and peace of mind you bring back buys you more time than you spent.

Monk for a day: Creating your own solitary retreat

If you've been meditating regularly for a few weeks or months (or years) and feel inspired to practice for an extended period of time but would rather do it on your own (or don't have easy access to a group), you can design and follow your own retreat schedule. You'll need the time (even a half day will do at first), the place (a quiet room without cell phones, computers, or other distractions), and an extra dose of motivation and self-discipline.

Be sure to block out periods for both sitting and walking meditation (so you can rest your tired knees and back); leave some open, unstructured gaps in the program for just being or walking in nature or listening to the birds; and use the schedule as a guideline rather than as a rigid form that squeezes the life out of your practice. If you need to adapt it as inspiration or physical limitations dictate, please do. And be sure to maintain the spirit of meditation and the practice of mindfulness throughout your day, whether you're meditating, napping, or going to the bathroom. You may find it helpful to bring this book and CD along with you for guidance as needed.

Here's a suggested schedule for a one-day retreat that a beginner should be able to manage without strain. Again, feel free to adapt it to your own particular limitations, needs, and inclinations (and use the bathroom during walking meditation or breaks, as nature requires):

8:00 to 8:45 a.m.	Breakfast (eating meditation)
8:45 to 9:00 a.m.	Contemplation (of your deeper intention or motivation for doing this retreat)
9:00 to 9:30 a.m.	Sitting meditation
9:30 to 9:45 a.m.	Walking meditation
9:45 to 10:15 a.m.	Sitting meditation
10:15 to 10:30 a.m.	Stretch break
10:30 to 11:00 a.m.	Sitting meditation
11:00 a.m. to 12:30 p.m.	Reading or listening to an inspirational book or talk
12:30 to 1:30 p.m.	Lunch (eating meditation)
1:30 to 3:30 p.m.	Siesta, walk, yoga, or more inspirational reading
3:30 to 4:00 p.m.	Sitting meditation
4:00 to 4:15 p.m.	Walking meditation
4:15 to 4:45 p.m.	Sitting meditation
4:45 to 5:00 p.m.	Walking meditation (or stretch break)
5:00 to 5:30 p.m.	Sitting meditation
5:30 to 5:45 p.m.	Dedication (of the value of this retreat to the benefit of all)
5:45 to 7:00 p.m.	Dinner (eating meditation)

Evening Optional

7:00 to 7:30 p.m.	Sitting meditation
7:30 to 7:45 p.m.	Walking meditation
7:45 to 8:15 p.m.	Sitting meditation (or inspirational reading or listening)
8:15 to 8:30 p.m.	Walking meditation
8:30 to 9:00 p.m.	Sitting meditation
9:00 to 9:15 p.m.	Dedication

Who knows? After spending a day at your very own solitary retreat, you may never go back to seeing things in the old way again.

Seeing with the eyes of joy

Most of the time, people see the world through the filter of their wants, needs, expectations, and whatever mood happens to cast its long shadow across their minds. Here's an exercise for setting aside your filters and seeing things through the eyes of joy:

1. **Sit quietly, close your eyes, and take a few slow, deep breaths, relaxing a little with each exhalation.**

2. **Setting aside your thoughts, worries, and concerns, find a place inside where you feel happy or joyful.**

   Even though you may feel generally sad or angry or tired or anxious, you can still find at least some area inside where you experience happiness or joy — maybe a hidden place inside your heart or a quiet spot at the back of your head.

3. **Merge with this feeling and let it permeate your whole being.**

   If you're not sure how to do this, you may notice whether the feeling has a color or a temperature or a texture (or all three), and imagine this quality suffusing and completely filling your body.

4. **Open your eyes and face your surroundings and the people in your life with this joyful feeling.**

   If you find old, habitual patterns of seeing creeping back in, set them aside and continue to see things with the light of your own joy.

5. **Continue this exercise as long as you can.**

Part IV
Meditation in Action

The 5th Wave
By Rich Tennant

"I know it's not as exciting as bungee jumping, but this might be the time to take up meditating as a past-time."

In this part . . .

You discover how to extend your meditation into every area of your life. After all, what's the point of sitting calmly for half an hour, then stressing out for the rest of the day? When you can stay present and mindful and keep your heart open — even when you're arguing with your partner or driving in rush-hour traffic or dealing with a screaming child or an angry boss — you've discovered how to meditate no matter where you are.

In this part, you also explore the rich and deeply rewarding application of meditation for spiritual pursuits, and you pick up some great techniques for using the power of meditation to facilitate healing and enhance performance.

Chapter 15

Cultivating Spirituality

*T*hroughout this book, I refer repeatedly to *spirituality,* though I often disguise it in metaphors or abstractions. After all, how else could I express the inexpressible? In Chapter 1, I talk about climbing the mountain of meditation and briefly describe what you might encounter if you ever get to the top. Elsewhere, I use words like *pure being* or *true nature* or *innate perfection.* Well, if these rather puzzling allusions to a *spiritual dimension of being* piqued your interest, here's where you find out how to use meditation to explore spirituality to your heart's content.

No, I won't be giving you detailed instructions on how to get enlightened or meet God directly — you might have to check out other books and teachers for that. But I do offer a brief glimpse of what the spiritual path has to offer so that you know which direction to take on your journey.

If you've ever wandered through the spirituality or religion section of your local bookstore, you know how many books have been written purporting to show you the right way to go. But you may still be wondering what all this spirituality stuff means, anyway. Or you may want a little guidance in sorting out one approach from another. Here's where you find a few answers — based on my admittedly limited understanding, of course.

Note: The chapter you're about to read is filled with spiritual terminology that may prove offensive to the secular reader. If you find yourself squirming in your seat when you hear words like *spirit* or *grace* or *higher reality,* you may prefer to skip this chapter altogether. Then again, you *could* open yourself to a whole new dimension of experience. Oops, there's one of those words again!

What Does Spirituality Mean, Anyway?

If you meditate regularly, you're going to have spiritual experiences — guaranteed. By following your breath or reciting a mantra or merely sitting quietly and listening with full attention to the sound of the wind through the trees, you're cutting through your usual preoccupations and attuning yourself to the present moment. That's where glimpses of the spiritual dimension of being generally occur — in the present. (In fact, being present with awareness is an inherently spiritual activity. See the sidebar "Where the vertical meets the horizontal" later in this chapter.) To paraphrase an old saying, spiritual experiences are accidents — but you make yourself accident-prone when you meditate.

Here are a few of the experiences you may encounter:

- ✔ An insight into your interconnectedness with other beings and things

- ✔ An upsurge of boundless, unconditional love that spreads throughout your body

- ✔ A pleasurable stream of grace or blessings or illumination from above

- ✔ A direct perception of the empty, insubstantial, or impermanent nature of everything

- ✔ A current of energy up the spine through the energy centers that leaves you feeling more expanded or in touch with spirit (for more on the energy centers, see Chapter 13)

- ✔ An experience of subtle inner sounds, colors, or shapes that have spiritual significance

- ✔ An experience of your body dissolving into light or expanding its boundaries and dissolving into space

- ✔ A shift in identity from being the body-mind to being the space or awareness in which the body-mind exists

- ✔ A deep and certain knowing (beyond the mind) of a sacred presence that exists both within and beyond the world of space and time

- ✔ Visions of angels or other spiritual beings

- ✔ A direct awareness of the presence of the Divine

- ✔ The inner experience of being loved by (or even one with) God

How do you know you've had a spiritual experience? Or, to put it another way, what makes an experience spiritual? Well, you might get up from your meditation and actually say, "Wow, that was a spiritual experience." Or the experience may somehow fit with your spiritual beliefs and provide further proof or amplification of what you already know. Or perhaps you simply feel inspired or expanded or more loving or open to yourself and others as a result. (As I mention in Chapter 7, the word *spiritual* comes from the Latin for "breath" or "life force." Related words include *spirited, inspiring,* and *respiration.*)

The definitions of *spirituality* and *spiritual experience* really depend on the person you ask. Some people view spirituality as the vital spark that animates and enlivens their religious involvement. Others take their spirituality straight, without religious dogma or ritual. But whatever their orientation, all the definitions point to a glimpse of something deeper or higher or more real or more meaningful than our ordinary, workaday lives.

In his classic book *The Varieties of Religious Experience,* written at the turn of the 20th century, the American scholar William James notes that spiritual experiences generally have four characteristics:

- ✔ **Ineffability:** They can't be adequately expressed in words but must be experienced directly.

- ✔ **Insight:** They generally involve the discovery of deep, important truths that can't be understood by the rational mind.

- ✔ **Impermanence:** They last for a limited period of time but may recur, and their meaning may continue to reveal itself, even though the experiences themselves have faded into memory.

- ✔ **Passivity:** You can prepare for spiritual experiences, but once they occur, you receive them passively, and they unfold in your awareness with a power of their own.

Where does the "spiritual dimension" exist? Some people experience it inside themselves, as the heart or center or deepest part of their being, beneath the body or the personality. Others experience it outside, above, or all around them, through spiritual beings on other planes of reality (like angels or spirits or bodhisattvas) or simply as the current or spirit that infuses all life. You may get your spiritual experiences when you watch a sunset or walk along the beach, for example, or when you play with your kids or spend solitary time communing with yourself. Ultimately, it seems, the spiritual dimension exists both inside and outside of us, in our deepest heart of hearts and in every being and thing, beyond the ordinary limitations of space and time.

The "perennial philosophy": Where all religions converge

Just so you don't think this spirituality stuff belongs to one particular tradition or another, I'd like to point out that certain philosophers have surveyed the world's great religions, from Christianity to Zoroastrianism, and discovered that a common spiritual river runs through them all. This river is called the *perennial philosophy,* and it consists of three interconnected currents or principles. (I know this discussion is getting a little serious, but bear with me — I'll lighten it up as much as I can.)

- ✔ **A greater reality exists that underlies the ordinary world of things and lives and minds.** Whether they claim that it transcends or infuses or is essentially identical with the ordinary world, the great traditions agree that this divine or spiritual reality exists. Some call it *God* or the *Holy Spirit,* the one (or ones) who created the universe and continues to orchestrate your life from above. Others call it the *ground of being,* the impersonal essence that supports and sustains you. Still others call it *emptiness, essential nature, Self,* or *Tao.* Whatever they name it, this spiritual dimension is a sacred mystery that gives meaning, purpose, and truth to human life.

- ✔ **In each person there exists something similar to, or even identical with, this greater reality.** Here again, the traditions may disagree on the form this something may take. Christians call it *soul,* Jews refer to the *divine spark within,* Hindus call it *atman,* and Buddhists use words like *Buddha nature* or *true self.* But all agree that this something connects us with the greater (or higher or deeper) reality that underlies ordinary life.

- ✔ **The ultimate goal of human life is to realize this greater reality.** The Sufi mystic may seek to unite with it, the Buddhist monk may strive to awaken to it, the Christian contemplative may yearn to have glimpses of it — and the rest of us may be quite content to feel connected with it (or merely pay homage to it at church, temple, or synagogue every now and then). However you approach it, the great spiritual traditions agree that every human being harbors a deep longing (however buried or disguised) to realize this greater reality.

As I mention in Chapter 1, you can take many paths up the mountain of *being.* But all the paths agree that the mountain exists, that you're somehow called to climb it (perhaps just because "it's there," as George Mallory said of Everest), and that what you discover at the top exists (in some form, at least) inside you all along.

SPIRITUAL STUFF

Where the vertical meets the horizontal

Here's a helpful framework for understanding the relationship between the ordinary and the spiritual — and how meditation brings them together.

Your everyday life occurs on the horizontal plane of space and time, cause and effect. (Some traditions call this plane the *relative* level of reality.) You're constantly moving from here to there, past to future, planning for tomorrow and evaluating yesterday, doing and achieving and hurrying — and maybe occasionally stopping to relax or watch TV. The horizontal plane is where you evolve outwardly: You grow up, learn life's lessons, create relationships and family, pursue your career, and achieve some measure of maturity and wisdom — all extremely important accomplishments.

At the same time, a vertical plane exists that has nothing to do with space and time. (In contrast to the relative, this plane is called the *absolute* level.) It's the timeless or eternal realm that all the great religious traditions describe — the top of the mountain that I mention in Chapter 1.

They call it *vertical* because it intersects and pervades the horizontal in every moment. And if you know how to attune yourself to it, you can allow it to inform and inspire you; and suffuse your being with grace, spirit, wisdom, compassion — the words depend on the nature of your experience and the tradition you follow (if any).

Meditation brings you out of your time-bound planning and thinking into the present moment, precisely where the spiritual dimension meets your ordinary life. You know those bumper stickers that say: Grace happens? Well, it's more likely to happen when you're open to it.

As you sit and coordinate your body, breath, and mind through the practice of following your breath or reciting a mantra, you create an inner harmony or alignment that invites the influx of the vertical plane. (In fact, the vertical and horizontal planes are always intersecting — you just don't notice.) And when you keep coming back to the present moment in your ordinary life between meditations, you're more likely to see the spirit in every being and thing you encounter.

From faith to fruition: The levels of spiritual involvement

You can relate to all this spiritual stuff in a variety of ways. You can ignore it entirely — but I doubt that you would have gotten this far into the chapter if you had no interest in the subject at all. You can believe in it in one form or another. (Perhaps you have faith in the existence of angels; adhere to the doctrine of a particular religion; or read books about shamans, saints, or sages and believe in the reality they describe.) Or you can aspire to experience the spiritual dimension for yourself.

For convenience, I like to break spiritual involvement down into six levels. They aren't mutually exclusive — you can engage in one or two or all of them, if you like. They're not hierarchical; in other words, one isn't necessarily better or higher or more advanced than another. And they're certainly not hard and fast; they're just my way of making sense of something that's ultimately unfathomable. Here are the six levels:

- **Believing in spirit:** I use the word *spirit* here to refer to the greater reality I talked about earlier that underlies the ordinary world of people and things. Believing in spirit is an important first step because it opens you to the possibility of getting closer to it in some way.

- **Awakening to spirit:** When you have a glimpse of the spiritual dimension (one of the spiritual experiences listed earlier in this chapter), you no longer merely believe — now you know. But such experiences may fade and become little more than memories unless they're sustained or rekindled through regular spiritual practice.

- **Being in touch with spirit:** Sometimes the awakening leaves you substantially transformed. When you look at people and things, you no longer see them in the same old way. Instead, they're permeated with new meaning and depth, and you're in touch with the spiritual dimension wherever you go and whatever you do.

- **Being infused with spirit:** Not only do you sense the presence of spirit in every being and thing, now you know with certainty that spirit infuses every fiber of your own being as well — or, in other words, that you and spirit are essentially the same. You clearly experience spirit as the greater reality or substance of your life that connects you with everything.

- **Being one with spirit:** When separation falls away and you merge with the greater reality, you achieve the state of *oneness* that mystics and Zen masters describe. But until you thoroughly integrate this realization into every aspect of your life, you will still enter and leave the oneness without being fully established or rooted in it.

- **No separation between spirit and ordinary life:** Now you know without doubt that ordinary, everyday reality, the sacred spiritual dimension, and your own essential nature are one and the same. No matter where you go or what you do, you meet the divine in everyone and everything, without the slightest trace of separation.

Dissolving or expanding the self: The point of spiritual practice

The great spiritual traditions also agree that the primary reason we suffer — and the primary problem we need to resolve — is the experience of being a separate, isolated individual, cut off from God or source or our own essential nature. When you meditate, you're bridging the apparent chasm that separates you and connecting with your breath, with your body and senses, with your heart, with the present moment, and ultimately with a greater reality. (It's this connection that promotes healing, as Dr. Dean Ornish and other researchers have found. For more on Ornish's groundbreaking work on reversing heart disease, see Chapter 2.)

As I mention in the previous section, you can believe in spirit, awaken to it, stay in touch with it, and become infused by it — all very important and invaluable stages on the spiritual journey. (In fact, just about everyone I know, including me, lies somewhere along this continuum.) But the ultimate aim of spiritual practice is to help you overcome all apparent separation and become one with spirit completely.

Dissolving the self

What keeps you separate? Well, some traditions call it *ego* or *self*; others call it *personality, pride, self-image,* or *self-clinging.* Essentially, it's the beliefs and stories I describe in Chapter 5: the inner turbulence and self-centered preoccupations and patterns that keep you from seeing things clearly. Of course, these preoccupations and patterns run deep and can take a lifetime (or lifetimes!) of dedicated practice to undo, but you can begin to unravel them using some of the meditative practices described in Chapter 12. (At a deeper level of understanding, you're actually never separate from spirit even for an instant — you just think you are. But therein lies the riddle we all need to solve. As the great Indian sage Ramana Maharshi used to say, "The only thing that separates you from the Self is the belief that you're separate.")

As you unravel these patterns, you gradually dissolve the limited self you thought yourself to be and realize your identity with the greater reality. Again, this journey can take a long, long time (even lifetimes, if you believe in reincarnation), and it may be fraught with difficulties, fears, and uncertainties, as you'll discover if you read the biography of any great saint or sage. In addition, you need to develop a healthy measure of self-love and self-acceptance to navigate the journey at all. (You also need the guidance of an experienced teacher. For more on teachers, see the section "How to Find a Teacher — and Why You May Want to Bother" at the end of this chapter. For more on self-love, see Chapter 11.)

Expanding the self

In addition to dissolving the self, you can also understand the spiritual journey as an expansion of identity from the narrow to the vast, until you're finally identified with the *luminous, eternal vastness* itself (also known as spirit or God). The ancient Indian sages used the model of the five bodies, which are subtler and subtler levels of identification beginning with the physical body and moving to identification with the ground of being or greater reality itself.

Here's a similar model (based on the five bodies and loosely adapted from the writings of philosopher Ken Wilber) that you may find helpful in understanding your own spiritual experiences and unfolding. (Apologies, Ken, for turning some of your thinking on its head!) Remember that each time you expand your identity to a new level, you incorporate the level that came before instead of leaving it behind.

- **Physical body:** Some people seem to think of nothing else but eating, drinking, working, sleeping, and sexing — they're largely identified with their physical needs and instincts. Children, too, identify mostly with this level, though they also have one foot in the spiritual realm, especially during the first three or four years.

- **Persona:** As you grow up and interact more with others, you develop a personality — a set of habits and tendencies and preferences — along with a self-image based largely on how others see you. Gradually, you begin to expand your identity to include this social persona, and you may become preoccupied with how you look or come across or the other accouterments of a self-image, such as material possessions.

- **Mature ego:** If you spend enough time exploring your inner life and sorting through your deeper feelings, values, and visions, you may eventually develop a mature ego — a healthy, well-rounded sense of who you are, what you want, and how you can contribute to others. People who identify themselves with their mature egos seem grounded and self-confident and tend to be self-actualizers — that is, those who express their full potential as human beings in their relationships and career. According to traditional Western psychology, the mature ego represents the culmination of human development.

- **Energy body:** The spiritual traditions pick up where secular Western psychology leaves off. Beyond the body-mind lies the *energy body* (the aura that surrounds the physical body), which expands and contracts depending on your mood, your energy level, and countless other factors. (Whether you notice it or not, you're constantly reacting to the energy bodies of the people you meet.)

  The classic exercise for experiencing your energy body goes as follows: Rub your palms and fingers together vigorously for a few minutes, then hold them an inch or two apart and notice the energy field between them. Bring them closer together and farther apart, feeling the energy get denser and thinner and pulsate as your hands move. To explore this dimension further, check out the sidebar "Playing with your energy body" later in this chapter.

  People who expand their identities to include their energy body realize that they're more than just their body-mind, which opens them to a spiritual dimension of being.

- ✔ **Transpersonal dimension:** This broad category encompasses the full range of nonordinary experiences, from clairvoyance and other forms of extrasensory perception (ESP); to rapture and bliss; to visions of angels, gods and goddesses, and other otherworldly beings; to direct communion with your higher self — or even with a personal manifestation of God. (For more on rapture and bliss, see Chapter 13.) When you expand your identity to include these subtler levels of being, you know without doubt that who you are is far vaster than you once believed, and you begin to access a deeper source of wisdom and compassion as well. (Near-death experiences often fit this category, as do the experiences described in bestsellers like *Conversations with God* and *The Celestine Prophecy.*)

- ✔ **Glimpses of being:** When you experience *being* directly in all its innate perfection and completeness, you realize that you've never been separate from who you really are even for an instant. The Zen masters call such a direct experience of being *kensho* — literally, seeing your true nature — but you may need a number of kenshos before you know who you are without doubt and stop shifting back to a more limited identification.

- ✔ **Ground of being:** Only the great mystics and sages get this far. Now you're one with spirit or the ground of being without separation — in the words of the Indian scriptures, "You are That." Sure, you continue to eat, drink, sleep, and blow your nose, but you never forget even for an instant who you really are — and your being radiates wisdom and compassion to others.

Now that I've covered the territory, you can close your book and prepare for a quiz. No, seriously — people actually do have experiences like the ones I describe, and I thought you might like to know what you're getting yourself into if you decide to use your meditation for spiritual purposes. (Again, I strongly urge you to find a teacher if you do.) The approach of dissolving the self and the approach of expanding the self ultimately take you to the same place: the deep inner knowing that you and God or the ground of being are identical — "not two," as some teachers put it. Although most spiritual traditions tend to emphasize one approach over the other, they generally offer both as alternatives, depending on your inclinations.

In the same way, the world's spiritual traditions differ in the paths they emphasize. The Judeo-Christian tradition, for example, tends to focus on the *path of devotion,* whereas Buddhism for the most part stresses the *path of insight.* But those who practice devotion often have profound insights into the nature of existence, and those who pursue insight may also use devotional practices to assist them in their quest. Besides, some traditions, like Hinduism and Sufism, emphasize both. (The third principal path, *selfless service,* which involves dedicating every action to spiritual rather than personal ends, can be used to deepen the experience of either devotion or insight. For example, Mother Teresa served the poorest of the poor as an expression of her devotion to Jesus, while the bodhisattvas of the Buddhist tradition serve others to help free them from the limitations of ignorance.)

TRADITIONAL WISDOM

Playing with your energy body

Did you ever have the sense that you were bigger than your physical body? Or that the space you occupy expands and contracts depending on circumstances? (No, I'm not talking about dieting here.) Did you ever have the feeling that you had no boundaries and you went on forever? Well, you're experiencing the expansion and contraction of your energy body, the aura of energy that surrounds your physical body.

Here's a little exercise for playing with your energy body:

1. **Begin by sitting quietly; closing your eyes; and taking a few slow, deep breaths, relaxing a little on each exhalation.**

2. **Spend a few minutes imagining going for a walk in nature or spending time with someone you love.**

   Notice how big you feel.

   Then notice how your size (but not your waistline) changes when you imagine getting stuck in traffic or paying your bills or getting into an argument.

3. **Next, check out your energy body without imagining anything.**

   How far do you think it extends beyond your physical body? Six inches? Several feet?

Does it extend farther in front than behind? Farther above your body than below into the ground? Is it thicker than the air or thinner? Thicker in some places than in others?

4. **Pick a room where you feel comfortable, stand or sit near the center, and check out the boundaries of the room in every direction.**

5. **Fill the room with your energy — fill it with you!**

   Imagine it, sense it, visualize it, sing it — whatever helps you fill the space as much as you can.

6. **Draw your energy back in until it forms a sphere around you, about 2 or 3 feet away.**

   Notice how the energy becomes denser.

7. **Play with expanding and contracting your energy in this way several times; then relax and notice how you feel.**

By regularly experimenting with your energy body, you can acquire a direct understanding of the spiritual truth that you're more than your physical body. (This exercise is adapted from a series of exercises in the book *The Lover Within* by Julie Henderson.)

The Path of Devotion: In Search of Union

If you believe in the existence of a personal God or have had experiences of a presence greater than yourself that inspired feelings of awe and reverence, you may be drawn to the path of devotion. It's the primary spiritual path in the Judeo-Christian tradition and Islam, and forms one of the main currents of Hinduism.

Although devotees may feel deeply connected to God and believe that a spark of divinity shines in their hearts, they often experience themselves to be painfully separate from God. As the anonymous author of the mystical Christian text *The Cloud of Unknowing* puts it, "The person who has a deep experience of himself existing far apart from God feels the most acute sorrow. Any other grief seems trivial in comparison." Through contemplation, mantra recitation (see the section "Mantra: Invoking the Divine in every moment" later in this chapter), chanting, selfless service, and other devotional practices, devotees seek to get closer to God by focusing all of their love and attention on God — and ultimately, if they're mystically inclined, to merge with God completely in a state of ecstatic union.

As a bridge between the self and the Divine (especially when the Divine doesn't have a personal face, as in certain schools of Hinduism and Buddhism), devotion may also be directed to the spiritual guide. In the West, for example, the great Sufi poet Rumi spoke in rapturous terms of his love and reverence for Shams of Tabriz, his "friend" and teacher; and certain Christian mystics wrote love letters in which they directed the same devotion to one another as they directed to God. In the East, some Hindu teachers require the devotion of their students as an essential step toward spiritual maturity, and Tibetan Buddhists practice guru yoga, in which they revere the teacher as the embodiment of their own essential nature. (See the section "Guru yoga: Tibetan devotional practice" later in this chapter.)

Although the path of devotion follows the general guidelines for spirituality discussed earlier in this chapter, it also has its own unique aspects or phases of development. (Again, this stuff may seem pretty lofty — but if you're a budding mystic, you definitely want to have an overview of the path.) These phases include the following:

> ✔ **Developing virtue:** In all the great devotional traditions, devotees are required to prepare themselves for union with God by living a life of purity and restraint.

- **Cultivating a higher octave of love:** The devotee may begin by feeling personal love for God or teacher, but eventually this love evolves into an unconditional, transpersonal love that knows no bounds and does not depend on the love object to evoke. (For more on unconditional love, see Chapter 11.)

- **Overcoming duality:** Beginning with a painful sense of separation, the devotee gradually gets closer and closer and ultimately merges with God, until no trace of separation remains. As the Hindu sage Swami Vivekananda put it, "Love, the lover, and the beloved are one."

- **Transcending the personal God:** Ultimately, the devotee must transcend even God, if God is experienced as having a particular name or form. At this stage, the lover and the beloved dissolve into God as the absolute ground of being, the nameless, formless greater reality whose essence is love.

- **Everything is God:** The distinctions get pretty subtle at these higher levels, but here goes: When the devotee no longer needs to contemplate or meditate in order to experience oneness with God but sees God everywhere in every moment — waking or sleeping — he or she has reached the pinnacle of the devotional path. Now that the separate self and all self-centered striving have fallen away, every activity reflects a complete alignment with the divine purpose: "Not my will but Thy will be done."

To give you a flavor of the devotional path, here are three practices you might like to try. The first two have their counterparts in all the world's great spiritual traditions, and the third provides an example of devotional practice in the Buddhist tradition.

Mantra: Invoking the Divine in every moment

Throughout history, meditators and mystics in the great devotional traditions have recommended the constant recitation of a *mantra* (a sacred word or phrase usually transmitted directly from a teacher) to bring the devotee closer to the Divine. (For more on mantra, see Chapter 3, or listen to Track 2 on the CD.) At first, you can practice repeating it aloud; then, when you become proficient, you can repeat it silently to yourself; and ultimately you can graduate to purely mental recitation (which is considered the most powerful).

Some practitioners of mantra also manipulate a rosary (or *mala* in Sanskrit) to help them keep track, ticking off one bead for each recitation. (You can buy a basic mala in any meditation supply store or metaphysical bookstore.) Or you can coordinate the sound with the coming and going of your breath.

Although you might begin by limiting your mantra recitation to a few minutes or hours of meditation each day, the traditional goal is constant practice. That is, you want to get to the point where you're repeating the sound or phrase nonstop in order to keep your attention focused on the Divine and away from habitual patterns of thought. Ultimately, your mind will become one-pointed, and you'll think always and only of God — which is the first step on the path to union. (If you watched the movie *Gandhi,* you may remember that he died with the mantra "Ram" [one of the Hindu names for God] on his lips.)

Needless to say, you'll be lucky if you can remember your mantra for a few minutes at first. But if you've received a mantra from a teacher (or know a mantra you find particularly meaningful or resonant) and you feel strong devotion, who can say how far you can go in your practice? (For inspiration on your path, you might like to read the spiritual classic *The Way of a Pilgrim,* the anonymous story of a devout Russian Orthodox peasant who chants the Jesus prayer day and night.)

The practice of the presence of God

Here's a time-honored practice that has counterparts in all the world's great spiritual traditions. When you catch a glimpse of the sacred, you can practice seeing it everywhere you look, in everyone and everything. One ancient Zen master used to say "Buddha! Buddha!" to every being he encountered. When the contemporary Tibetan teacher Kalu Rinpoche visited an aquarium in San Francisco, he went around tapping the glass to get the fishes' attention so he could bless them and wish them happiness and well-being.

The *practice* is just that simple: Remember to see the sacred or divine in every being and thing. Brother Lawrence of the Resurrection, a 17th-century Catholic brother, called it the "practice of the presence of God." You may believe that everything is God, or infused by God, or created by God, or has the spark of divinity inside. Whatever your belief, the practice reminds you to look not at the surface or at what you like, don't like, want, or need, but at the sacred, spiritual dimension that is perpetually present. For those who do this practice, God, like beauty, is in the eyes of the beholder. (For example, instead of responding to the stressed-out expression on people's faces, you may want to look beyond to the love in their hearts or the gleam in their eyes or the purity of their essential nature, however hidden.)

Of course, the practice may be simple, but it's certainly not easy. You might begin by doing it for ten minutes and see how it goes. If you enjoy it, you can naturally extend it as you feel inspired. (To help you remember, you may want to repeat a phrase like "This, too, is divine," not constantly like a mantra, but intermittently, as a reminder.)

Guru yoga: Tibetan devotional practice

For the Tibetan Buddhist practitioner, the root teacher, or *guru,* embodies the wisdom and compassion of all the enlightened beings throughout space and time. By invoking the guru and "fervently praying with uncontrived devotion," in the words of the great contemporary master Dudjom Rinpoche (quoted in *The Tibetan Book of Living and Dying* by Sogyal Rinpoche), "after a while the direct blessing of the wisdom mind of the master will be transmitted, empowering you with a unique realization, beyond words, born deep within your mind."

The point of guru yoga, in other words, is to become one with the greater reality (call it God, spirit, or Buddha nature) by first merging with the mind and heart of an enlightened master. (In the Tibetan tradition, the wisdom mind of the guru, which is said to resemble the vastness of the sky, is ultimately identical with *being* itself.)

Fortunately, you don't have to be a Tibetan Buddhist to benefit from this practice. Here's a brief version that anyone can do (adapted from Sogyal Rinpoche's *The Tibetan Book of Living and Dying*):

1. **Sit quietly, close your eyes, and take a few slow, deep breaths, relaxing a little with each exhalation.**

   If you already know how to meditate, you can do so in your usual way for a few minutes.

2. **Imagine in front of you and above your head an enlightened being or saint for whom you feel particular love or reverence — perhaps Jesus, Buddha, Moses, or Mother Teresa.**

   If you don't gravitate toward saints and sages, just imagine a being of infinite wisdom and compassion. And if you don't find it easy to visualize, just sense this being alive in your heart.

3. **Intensify the experience by deepening your feelings of inspiration and devotion.**

   This being actually exists right here and now, and it embodies the blessings of all the enlightened saints and sages.

4. **Relax your body, feel the presence of this being in your heart, and call on it to help you realize your own essential nature.**

5. **Allow your mind and heart to merge with the mind and heart of this enlightened being as you ask to be filled with clarity and compassion.**

6. **Continue to merge your mind and heart with those of the enlightened being as you recite a devotional mantra, if you have one.**

(See the section "Mantra: Invoking the Divine in every moment" earlier in this chapter.) If you don't have one, just sit with reverence and devotion.

7. **Gradually feel your mind and heart becoming one with the guru's — that is, vast, clear, and luminous like the sky.**

8. **Imagine that thousands of rays of pure white light stream from the guru and penetrate every cell of your body, healing, purifying, and empowering you completely with the skylike mind of enlightenment.**

9. **Allow the guru to dissolve into light and become one with you so that you and the guru are inseparable.**

10. **Rest for several minutes in the vast, luminous, skylike nature of mind.**

Know without doubt that your mind and the mind of the guru are one.

REMEMBER

Chanting and bowing

Besides meditation and contemplation, the devotional path usually involves active practices like chanting, singing, and bowing. As you may have noticed if you've ever sung along with a gospel choir or chanted Indian devotional hymns, you can lift your spirits, open your heart, and intensify your devotion by raising your voice in praise of the Divine.

If you're devotionally inclined (or devotionally impaired!), try mixing your meditation with a little chanting or singing every now and then. Choose songs that have resonance or meaning for you. (For example, I know plenty of Hindus and Buddhists who love to sing "Amazing Grace.")

Traditional wisdom suggests that chanting sacred words and phrases also has the power to open, stimulate, and harmonize your energy centers. (For more on energy centers, see Chapter 13.) In this way, chanting helps "tune up" your body and prepare it for meditation and other spiritual practices.

As for bowing: What better way to practice surrendering your self-centered preoccupations and habitual patterns than by falling down on your knees on a regular basis? One famous Zen master wore a perpetual callus on his forehead from bowing repeatedly to soften his stubbornness. My first Zen teacher used to say, "Buddhism is a religion of bowing."

Of course, bowing figures prominently in the Judeo-Christian tradition and Islam as well; like meditation, it's a universally recognized practice for overcoming separation and approaching the spiritual dimension of being.

But bowing doesn't mean giving up your autonomy to some outside power or force. When you bow — to God, Jesus, Buddha, or the picture of a teacher or saint — you're ultimately bowing to your own essential nature.

In fact, I like to think of bowing as an expression of the essential oneness of inside and outside, the one bowed to and the one bowing. Or, as they say in India, "The divine in me bows to the divine in you."

The Path of Insight: Discovering Who You Are

If you find yourself seeking answers to core spiritual questions like "Who am I?" or "What is reality?" but don't have a particular interest in God or devotion, you may be drawn to the path of insight. Every religious tradition has its version or counterpart — Christianity has the *via negativa* (negative way) of the desert fathers, Judaism includes the mystical practices of Kabbalah, Hinduism has its nondual teachings (like Advaita Vedanta), and Buddhism focuses primarily on the cultivation of insight.

Unlike devotion, which concentrates the mind on a representation of the Divine, the path of insight uses direct investigation and awareness of present experience to see beyond surface appearances to the deeper reality that underlies them. When you keep questioning and looking deeply into what is apparently real, you inevitably happen upon the ultimately real — the formless, indestructible essence of all appearances. (It's kind of like peeling the layers of an onion.)

Now, the point of this approach is not to deny the relative reality of ordinary people and things (including you and me). Rather, the path of insight generally teaches that reality has two levels: the *relative* and the *absolute*. (See also the sidebar "Where the vertical meets the horizontal" earlier in this chapter.)

On the relative level, it's important to make a living, pay the bills, spend time with family or friends — if you pretend that the *relative* isn't real, you're going to have some problems. (Traffic court and bankruptcy spring immediately to mind!) As the Sufis say, "Trust in God, but make sure to tie your camel to the post."

At the same time, though, there's an absolute level — a Divine presence or sacred dimension that underlies this world and gives it meaning. When you encounter this level, you see the deeper reality of things, just as the mystic sees God everywhere she looks. Whether directly or more gradually, the path of insight in its various incarnations leads you to an experience or knowing of this absolute level of reality. (In the East, they call this knowing *enlightenment* or *liberation*. In the West, they call it *gnosis* — the Latin word from which "knowing" derives.)

Most of the core practices highlighted in this book show you how to investigate your present experience so that you can eventually develop insight. To give you a glimpse of the absolute level, here are three exercises designed to cut through your usual way of perceiving things to reveal a deeper reality. Generally, they work best after you've been practicing some basic meditation technique like following your breath or reciting a mantra.

Expanding your boundaries

Picking up where the energy body meditation leaves off (see the sidebar "Playing with your energy body" earlier in this chapter), this technique shows you that you don't end with your skin — or with the farthest edges of the Milky Way, for that matter.

1. **Begin by sitting quietly, closing your eyes, and taking a few slow, deep breaths, relaxing a little on each exhalation.**

2. **Sense the solidity and density of your body as you usually perceive it.**

3. **As you inhale, imagine that your head is filling with a soft, clear mist; and as you exhale, imagine that all solidity and density drain from your head, leaving it pleasantly empty, spacious, and open to sensation and life-energy.**

   Don't worry; you won't disappear!

4. **Breathe the mist into your neck and throat, and breathe out any tension or density, leaving the area spacious and open.**

5. **Continue to apply this meditation to your chest, lungs, and heart; your arms and hands; your abdomen and internal organs; your pelvis, buttocks, and genitals; and your thighs, lower legs, and feet.**

6. **Feel your whole body completely empty, spacious, and open to the current of life energy.**

   Rest in this feeling for a few moments without thought or analysis. Enjoy the buzz!

7. **If certain areas still feel dense or solid, breathe into them until they're empty and open.**

   You may notice that the boundaries of your body are now diffuse — you're not sure where you leave off and the outside world begins.

8. **Expand the boundaries of your body and your awareness until you include the whole room and everything it contains.**

9. **Expand to include the whole building, then the whole block, the whole town or city, and the state.**

   Take a few minutes with each expansion.

10. **Expand even further to encompass the Earth, then the solar system, the Milky Way, the universe, and beyond the farthest boundaries of the known universe.**

    Again, spend a few minutes at each level. You're vast beyond measure — you contain everything. Allow any thoughts, feelings, or sensations to arise within this vast expanse.

11. **After spending several minutes in the vastness, you can begin to pay attention to how you feel.**

    If you find it difficult to locate any feelings, that's fine — just enjoy the expansion for a few more minutes! Then check in with your body: Are you feeling more calm and relaxed than when you began? Has your breathing changed in any way?

12. **Gradually come back to your body before getting up and going about your day.**

    Notice whether your self-image or your experience of people and things has changed in any way.

You can practice the first part of this exercise (emptying and opening) by itself, if you like; it has the power to calm your mind and relax and harmonize your body. With regular practice, you'll be able to create a spacious, open, radiant feeling in your body with one sweep of your awareness.

Looking into the nature of mind

In Zen, they tell the story of the first Chinese patriarch Bodhidharma, who supposedly sat for nine years in meditation facing a wall without moving. The Zen folks credit this legendary character with all kinds of superhuman feats. For example, he reportedly cut off his eyelids so he could meditate without sleeping, and the first tea plants sprang up where his eyelids landed. (After all, tea is a kinder, gentler way to stay awake.)

Anyway, an earnest monk named Hui-ko came to Bodhidharma and humbly asked the patriarch to help pacify his troubled mind for him. After refusing to talk to Hui-ko for several days, Bodhidharma finally told him to find his mind and bring it to Bodhidharma to pacify. For months, the monk searched for his mind in meditation. Finally he returned to Bodhidharma and reported that he couldn't find his mind anywhere. "Ah, then I've pacified it for you," Bodhidharma replied — and Hui-ko was immediately enlightened. (You know how these Zen stories go!)

As this anecdote suggests, the Buddhists have devised some powerful techniques for exploring the mind and realizing its essential nature (which happens to be the greater reality I mention earlier in this chapter). And you don't have to study with a Zen master to get a taste of this essential nature for yourself. Here's an exercise I've adapted from the Tibetan tradition:

1. **Begin by sitting quietly; closing your eyes; and taking a few slow, deep breaths, relaxing a little with each exhalation.**

2. **Meditate in your usual way for a few minutes to relax and focus your mind; then allow it to rest in its "natural state," as the Tibetans put it, without doing anything special.**

   If you can follow this exercise with your eyes open and gazing straight ahead at the space in front of you, great — that's how the Tibetans do it. But if you get distracted, you can close your eyes.

3. **Begin by noticing a particular thought as it arises and endures in your mind.**

   For example, you can take a memory, a plan, or a fantasy. Then ask yourself the following questions:

   - Does this thought have a particular shape or form? How big is it?

   - Does it have a particular color or colors?

   - Does it have a beginning, a middle, and an end?

   - Where is the thought located? Is it inside or outside your body?

   - From where did this thought arise? Where does it go when you're no longer thinking it? How long does it last when you continue to think it?

   - Does the thought have substance or is it just empty, open, and filled with space? Does it leave a trace in your mind, like footprints on the beach, or does it leave no trace, like writing on water?

4. **Turn your attention to your mind itself and ask the following questions.**

   Don't think about or analyze your mind or become preoccupied with its contents, such as thoughts or feelings. Instead, just look at your mind the way you would look at a bird or a tree. (Remember, I'm talking about the mind here, not the brain.) Take a few moments to respond to each question:

   - Does your mind itself have a shape or form? How big is it? Does it have a color or colors?

   - Is your mind identical with your thoughts, or does it abide as the ground or space in which your thoughts arise and pass away?

   - Where is your mind located? Is it inside or outside your body? Does it have a beginning or an end?

   - Does your mind have substance like the earth or is it empty and spacious like the sky? Is it blank and dark, or is it bright and clear?

5. **Allow your mind to rest for a few minutes in its "natural state."**

Notice how the inquiry has affected you. Has your relationship to thoughts changed? Has your sense of identity shifted in some way? Do you feel calmer or more spacious? Take note of the changes; then gradually get up and go about your day.

Asking "Who am I?"

For as long as they've had the capacity to reflect on their experience, human beings have asked, "Who am I?" Zen masters, Sufi sheikhs, Indian sages, Jewish rabbis, and teachers of virtually every other spiritual persuasion have used this question to help their disciples see beyond their accustomed identities to a deeper realization of their essential nature.

When you first ask this question, you may come up with the usual answers: "I'm a woman," "I'm a father," "I'm an attorney," "I'm a runner." As you probe further, you may get more-spiritual answers, such as "I'm love incarnate" or "I'm a child of God." But if you just set these aside and continue to inquire, you'll eventually have a direct intuition of a more fundamental identity that has nothing to do with who you think you are.

Practice the following exercise with a partner, if possible. (One person begins by questioning; the other by answering.) If you don't have a partner handy, you can do it alone facing a mirror:

1. **Sit comfortably facing your partner, gazing at one another in a relaxed and natural way.**

2. **Allow the questioner to begin by asking, "Who are you?" Then the other person responds by saying whatever comes to mind.**

3. **After a pause, the questioner asks again, "Who are you?" and the other person again responds.**

   Of course, if you're doing it alone, you get to play both roles.

4. **Continue in this way for 15 minutes; then switch places for an equal amount of time.**

   If you're the questioner, don't critique or judge the answers in any way. Just listen, pause, and ask again.

   If you're the respondent, gently look for an answer; then respond. If you can't find one and have nothing to say for a moment or two, just sit with the silence and the not-knowing. You may become flustered or confused, start to laugh or cry, or have moments of deep stillness.

   Accept whatever arises, relax into the process, and keep going. Even a brief glimpse of who you really are can completely transform your life.

5. **When you're done, sit for a few minutes with your experience before getting up and going about your day.**

How to Find a Teacher — and Why You May Want to Bother

If you'd like to play tennis but don't know how, what do you do? You can watch other people play, maybe buy a book or two, and then head out to the court yourself and start practicing. But after you've mastered the basics, you may want to take a class or get some personal instruction to help you refine your stroke or eliminate the mistakes you've picked up along the way. Sure, self-taught prodigies do occasionally make it to the pros — but most good tennis players who want to improve their game eventually find a teacher.

The same holds true for meditation. You can practice the exercises provided in this book for weeks, months, or even years and reap the benefits without additional instruction. But at a certain point, you may encounter difficulties you don't know how to handle by yourself (see Chapters 12 and 13). Or you may start having spiritual experiences that give you glimpses of a greater reality and whet your appetite for further exploration. To continue moving forward and refining your meditation practice, you need to find yourself a teacher.

Choosing the right kind of teacher

Before you can find a teacher, however, you need to know what kind of teacher you want. Most meditation teachers have a particular spiritual affiliation — they're yogis or Zen Buddhists or Christian contemplatives, for example — and the instruction they offer comes packaged with a particular orientation toward the spiritual journey as well as particular teachings and terminology. No problem if that's what you're looking for — but if you want your instruction straight, without any spirituality, you may have a more difficult time finding a teacher.

Some hatha yoga teachers offer basic meditation instructions with a minimum of Sanskrit words, and they may even know the territory well enough to help you if you get stuck. More and more adult-education programs, community colleges, and local churches are offering generic meditation or stress-reduction classes, but you may want to look over the teacher's credentials first — he or she may be no further along in practice than you are. (For direct, nonsectarian instruction in the practice of meditation, you might want to check out my website, www.stephanbodian.org, for the individual sessions I offer. Or buy my smartphone app *Mindfulness Meditation*, available at www.mentalworkout.com, which offers complete instructions and guided meditations of various lengths.)

If you practice the mindfulness meditations provided in this book (see Chapter 7 or listen to Track 4 on the CD), you might check out the Vipassana tradition of Buddhism, also known as *insight meditation.* Jon Kabat-Zinn (author of the bestseller *Wherever You Go, There You Are,* long-time teacher of insight meditation, and founder of the mindfulness-based Stress Reduction Clinic at the University of Massachusetts Medical Center) has developed a program called Mindfulness-Based Stress Reduction that offers rigorous training in basic mindfulness practices. Or you could just take a class in Vipassana, use what you find meaningful and helpful, and leave the rest. Many teachers go light on the Buddhism, especially in introductory courses.

If you're drawn to a particular spiritual tradition or path, you should have less trouble finding a teacher. But you still may want to consider beforehand what kind of teacher you need. Here are four major categories of teachers, based on the content of their teachings and their relationships with their students. (The terms I use here won't necessarily show up on a teacher's résumé or brochure; they're just my way of making sense of the different roles teachers play. Some teachers may be a combination of several or all four.)

- ✔ **Instructor:** Teaches you techniques, offers good advice on how to implement them, and helps you troubleshoot or fine-tune. May be a friend or peer.

- ✔ **Mentor:** Gives you personal encouragement and support in your practice, offers guidance for getting unstuck, and provides a role model of someone who's been there before you. Usually teaches techniques as well.

- ✔ **Pandit:** Transmits knowledge by articulating and explaining spiritual teachings and texts. May be a scholar as well as a meditator.

- ✔ **Master:** Embodies the essence of the spiritual teachings. Helps you break through your stuck places and facilitates the process of expanding or dissolving the self. May (or may not) have an intense or challenging relationship with students.

Why you may need a teacher

As I mentioned earlier, a meditation instructor can help you refine your practice and deal with basic questions that arise along the way. But if you want to deepen your practice and use it as a means to spiritual ends (as described earlier in this chapter), you'll definitely want to find a spiritual mentor or master.

First of all, you may encounter difficulties and challenges like the ones described in Chapters 12 and 13. For example, you may have trouble dealing with intense recurring emotions like anger or fear. Or you may come up against roadblocks like doubt or procrastination and not know how to move forward on your own. Or perhaps you start having powerful currents of energy running up and down your spine and don't know how to make them stop. Suddenly you're in need of a teacher — pronto!

As you continue on your journey, you may encounter genuine spiritual insights and experiences that you don't know how to revisit or sustain. In fact, the process of spiritual unfolding more often resembles a confusing, trackless outback than a "path," as it is euphemistically called. The truth is, you never know what you're going to encounter when you practice intensively. As you experiment with expanding or dissolving yourself in your meditation, for example, you may meet with powerful opposition from the forces of your psyche that don't want you to change. After all, we're talking radical transformation here — and most of us resist even the most minor changes in our lives.

Your spiritual teacher may coach and support you through the transformational process and even accelerate it by confronting the ways in which you resist or hold back. Some teachers act more like *spiritual friends,* treating you with the camaraderie and equality you expect from a peer, while also sharing their wealth of understanding. Others act more like *traditional gurus,* transmitting their understanding directly to you while actively pushing against your stuck places. (Of course, many teachers lie somewhere between these two extremes and combine a little of both styles.)

Whatever their approach, however, all good teachers help create and sustain, through their relationship with you, a sacred vessel or space in which the difficult, wondrous, and ultimately liberating process of spiritual transformation can take place inside you.

What to look for in a teacher

Before I suggest what to look for in a teacher, I'd like to encourage you to examine your expectations and preconceptions. When you think of a spiritual teacher, what images or ideas come to mind? Perhaps you envision a cloistered monastic dressed in earth-colored robes who gives you spiritual counsel in hushed tones and then returns to his cell to continue his practice. Or maybe you think of a joyful, expansive being who lives in the world and radiates love and light wherever she goes.

Some people idealize the teacher and expect him to be perfect — and become disillusioned when it turns out he's not. Others go to the other extreme and have difficulty treating anyone with reverence or letting go long enough of their staunchly held opinions to allow the wisdom of others to enter. In the West, we tend to distrust authority and believe, like our pioneer and cowboy predecessors, that we can't rely on others and need to do it all ourselves. Besides, look at all those preachers, priests, and self-styled gurus, you may say, who get caught with their pants down. Although a healthy dose of skepticism can do wonders, too much can make you shy away from teachers (and hence from spiritual practice) entirely.

Whatever your expectations and preconceptions, you may need to set them aside when you look for a teacher because he or she may appear in a guise you don't anticipate. At the same time, you may want to compare your prospective teacher against the following checklist of qualities that the best teachers embody — in my humble estimation, at least. (I've based this list on my own observation over more than 40 years of spiritual practice and teaching.) Not all teachers will have every one of these characteristics, of course, but the more, the better:

✔ **They're humble, ordinary, down-to-earth, not arrogant or inflated.** In Zen monasteries, the head monk cleans the toilets.

✔ **They're honest, straightforward, and clear, not evasive or defensive.** As people gain spiritual maturity, they become increasingly free of psychological baggage.

✔ **They encourage independent thinking and open inquiry in their students, rather than blind obedience to a particular dogma or ideology.**

✔ **They're primarily concerned with the spiritual development of their students, not with fame, power, influence, or the size of their organization.**

✔ **They practice what they preach, rather than considering themselves exempt from the moral and ethical guidelines that others must follow.**

✔ **They embody the highest spiritual qualities, such as kindness, patience, equanimity, joy, peace, love, and compassion.**

How to find a teacher

The process of finding a teacher can be as mysterious as the spiritual journey itself. For some people, it's a lot like finding a lover or a mate — it involves a complex mixture of luck, availability, and chemistry. For others, it's simply a matter of following the counsel of a friend or showing up at the right place at the right time. I met my first teacher after looking up *Zen* in the local phone book. Other people I know met their teachers in dreams before encountering them in the flesh. In the words of a popular Indian expression, "When the student is ready, the teacher appears."

PLAY THIS!

Consulting the guru inside you

Before you go searching for a spiritual teacher, you may want to check out your own inner source of guidance and wisdom. Ultimately, it's the only thing you can really trust, and a good teacher will help you locate it. Yes, that's right; even *you* have a guru inside you. As Jesus said, "Seek and you shall find; knock and the door will open to you." Well, here's an exercise for seeking and finding:

1. **Begin by sitting quietly; closing your eyes; and taking a few slow, deep breaths, relaxing a little with each exhalation.**

2. **Take a few minutes to imagine yourself in a safe, comfortable, relaxing, peaceful place, using all your senses to make the experience as vivid as possible.**

3. **As you explore this peaceful place, you may begin to sense the presence of a wise and compassionate being.**

   Know that this being represents your higher self or deepest truth. (Feel free to use whatever words you prefer to name this being.) You may sense this presence somewhere in your body or you may just intuit that it's there. If you don't immediately sense this presence, continue to enjoy your peaceful place as you invite this presence to appear to you.

4. **Imagine yourself settling down in a particular spot and gazing out in front of you, relaxed and open.**

5. **Gradually, this wise and compassionate being materializes in the space in front of you.**

   Notice how it appears to you. It may take the form of a wise old man or woman or a Zen master or Christian contemplative, or it may appear as a rose or a tree or (if you're not visually inclined) merely a feeling in your belly or heart. Or it may just be an older, wiser version of you.

6. **Take whatever form appears to you and treat it with the respect and reverence you would reserve for a spiritual teacher.**

   Note: If this being seems critical or punitive in any way, it's not the one you're looking for, so ask it to step aside and invite the real one to appear.

7. **Spend a few minutes of silence in the presence of this wise and compassionate being.**

   You might imagine it radiating light and love in all directions as you silently receive what it has to offer.

8. **Take a few minutes or longer to ask any questions you have and receive answers.**

   Don't worry if this exchange seems strange or awkward at first; with practice, you'll find that this being develops a voice of its own.

9. **Before you say good-bye, you might ask this being to give you a gift that represents exactly the qualities you need right now.**

10. **When you feel complete, thank this being for spending time with you today.**

    Tell it that you would like to meet again in the future and say good-bye for now.

11. **Gradually shift your awareness to your sensate experience and open your eyes.**

12. **Take some time to reflect on your experience and the answers and gifts you received.**

Ultimately, you need to trust your intuition, your own inner knowing, when choosing a teacher — it's the only reliable equipment you have for navigating in this flawed phenomenal universe of ours. The best advice I ever received from a teacher came from a Tibetan lama, who touched my chest near my heart and said, "The true guru is inside you." (For instructions on how to meet your inner teacher, see the sidebar "Consulting the guru inside you," or listen to Track 11 on the CD.)

I've found myself drawn to teachers intuitively because of the qualities of being they seem to radiate. On the other hand, I've also stumbled on teachers unexpectedly through a serendipitous sequence of events. Be open but not gullible, skeptical but not cynical. Feel free to ask questions, expect good answers, and take your time. According to the Dalai Lama, Tibetan students may spend years checking out teachers to make sure they embody the teachings they espouse. Just as you wouldn't rush into a marriage, you shouldn't rush into anything as intimate and deep as a relationship with a spiritual teacher.

Discovering the sky of mind

Here's a brief meditation that you can do anytime you're outdoors to give you a taste of the vastness of your essential nature, which the Zen folks call, appropriately enough, "big mind."

1. **Preferably on a clear day, sit or lie down and look up at the sky.**

    Set aside your analytical mind for now and all you think you know about the sky.

2. **Take a few minutes to contemplate the vastness of the sky, which appears to stretch endlessly in every direction.**

3. **Gradually allow your awareness to expand to fill the sky — up and down, north and south, east and west.**

Let go of all sense of personal boundaries as you fill the sky with your awareness.

4. **Become the sky completely and rest in the experience for a few minutes.**

5. **Gradually return to your ordinary sense of yourself.**

    How do you feel? Has your awareness changed in any way?

After you get the knack of this exercise, you can do it for brief moments at any time of the day — for example, while walking your dog in the morning or gazing out your window on a break at work — to remind yourself who you are.

Chapter 16

Don't Worry, Be Happy — with Meditation

· ·

*H*ave you ever had the experience of thinking about something constantly because you believed it would make you happy — say, a better car, a fancy dress, a tropical vacation, or a new computer? You wanted it so badly that you could burst with anticipation, and then when you finally got it, you found that the object of your desires wasn't what you expected or that your happiness lasted for a few fleeting moments before you quickly reverted to your usual state of mind?

If so, you're not alone. Researchers have found that most people hover around an *emotional set point,* an accustomed level of happiness or unhappiness that's largely determined by their genetic endowment. Life circumstances may raise or lower your mood temporarily, but you quickly return to your emotional baseline. Even people who win the lottery or become paraplegics end up being just as happy or unhappy as they were before.

The ups and downs of gain and loss can't raise this baseline or lift you to a new level of well-being, but certain activities do have this unique power. Meditators have been cultivating positive mind-states like contentment, joy, and equanimity for thousands of years; and recently the emerging field of positive psychology has identified behaviors and lifestyle changes that can boost your mood permanently and optimize your enjoyment of life. At a time when more and more people identify themselves as anxious and depressed, these findings offer a healthier, more sustainable, and more deeply fulfilling alternative to mood-altering drugs.

In this chapter, I explore the characteristics of happy people and then catalogue the benefits of happiness, outline the recent developments in happiness research, and offer you a range of meditations and exercises for cultivating a happier, more joyful, more worry-free life.

Checking Out the Hallmarks of Genuine Happiness

Just about everyone would agree that happiness is an ultimate value, a state that all human beings desire and aspire to. Indeed, the vast majority of people — in countries as diverse as Slovenia and South Korea, Argentina and Bahrain, Greece and the United States — cite happiness when asked what they want most in life. But do you really know what happiness is — and can you recognize it when you're experiencing it?

Sure, when life circumstances fall into place and give you exactly what you want, you may spontaneously say, "I'm so happy." But much of the time you may find it easier to tell when you're unhappy or depressed than when you're genuinely happy. And after you've gained that elusive moment of undeniable happiness, you may not have a clue how to maintain or regain it.

Philosophers, psychologists, meditators, and spiritual teachers have been wrestling with the question of happiness for millennia, and they've come up with a variety of remarkably similar definitions. Most important, they largely agree on the key components that you can reliably cultivate and practice to infuse your life with happiness day after day. In this section, I explore some of the definitions of happiness and describe the key components of a happy life.

Recognizing happiness as your inherent condition

According to the great meditation masters and teachers, happiness is an "inside job" — that is, it's the end result of cultivating positive emotions like inner peace, love, compassion, joy, and equanimity. In fact, the highest teachings suggest that happiness is your natural state, your inherent condition, which is gradually obscured as negative thoughts and emotions and limiting beliefs and stories build up over a lifetime. Watch a young child at play (preferably one who hasn't been overly affected by mainstream media) and you can see the inherent joy, wonder, and delight that all human beings share deep down inside.

Life experiences lead people to take a more jaundiced view of life; to lose their innate appreciation and enjoyment; and to spend more and more time in frustration, anxiety, worry, guilt, and regret. The path to happiness, from this point of view, is to reconnect with the bright sun of your true nature, which is eternally positive and upbeat, while gradually peeling away the clouds of negativity that conceal it. Happiness, in other words, is your birthright — you merely need to reclaim it.

The Dalai Lama on the Art of Happiness

With his perpetual smile and joyful demeanor, the spiritual and temporal leader of the Tibetan people has become the embodiment of happiness for people of every religious and spiritual persuasion. The Dalai Lama, a lifelong meditator, believes that people can generate happiness by cultivating positive emotions and a peaceful mind. Consider this excerpt from his book *The Art of Happiness,* which provides tips for living a happy life:

> "As long as there is a lack of the inner discipline that brings calmness of mind, external facilities or conditions will never give you the feeling of joy and happiness that you are seeking," he cautions. "On the other hand, if you possess this inner quality, a calmness of mind, a degree of stability within, then even if you lack various external facilities that you would normally consider necessary for happiness, it is still possible to live a happy and joyful life."

Needless to say, the Dalai Lama recommends meditation — in particular, mindfulness and lovingkindness — for developing this quality of calm and stability. In addition, he emphasizes cultivating positive emotions, which he has found are conducive to happiness. (For complete instructions in mindfulness meditation, see Chapter 7. To read about lovingkindness, see Chapter 11.)

Ultimately, the Dalai Lama counsels readers that happiness doesn't happen overnight:

> "Achieving genuine happiness may require bringing about a transformation in your outlook, your way of thinking, and this is not a simple matter. [In] taking care of your physical body, you need a variety of vitamins and nutrients, not just one or two. In the same way, in order to achieve happiness, you need a variety of approaches and methods to deal with and overcome the varied and complex negative mental states. . . . It is not possible to accomplish that simply by adopting a particular thought or practicing a technique once or twice. Change takes time."

Experiencing a predominance of positive emotions

From a traditional spiritual perspective, the path to happiness lies in enhancing positive emotions like peace, love, joy, and equanimity while minimizing the negative ones like anger, sadness, fear, and impatience. Whether it's the seven virtues of Christianity or the four "heavenly abodes" of Buddhism, the predominance of these mind-states is believed to contribute to a happy life. And the good news is that the great meditation masters and sages have evolved time-honored techniques for accentuating and cultivating the positive.

Not surprisingly, the emerging field of positive psychology agrees that the happy life is one in which positive emotions predominate. Studies show that happy people have more positive mind-states than their less-happy counterparts, not just occasionally, but moment after moment and day after day. Sudden, short-lived bursts of extraordinary joy or excitement don't add much to a person's happiness quotient; it's the little pleasures, successes, and satisfactions that form the building blocks of lasting happiness. In fact, the happy moments apparently reinforce one another, fueling an upward spiral of positive feelings and life-affirming activities. For example, the joy of connecting with a friend may make you more attentive to your children or partner, which strengthens your family life, which increases your gratitude, which makes you more optimistic, which leads to a more fulfilling outcome at work, and so on.

Accepting what life brings

Life circumstances (together with a person's emotional set point, which I mention earlier) do contribute to happiness, but only by a measly 10 percent! Studies show, for example, that multimillionaires are only ever-so-slightly happier than the office workers and housekeepers they employ. And married people — often considered the paragons of happiness — are actually only a few percentage points happier than their unmarried counterparts.

If getting what you want doesn't give you the lasting happiness you crave, then what does? As it turns out, appreciating what you have really makes the difference. Research into the lives of genuinely happy people reveals that, even in the midst of trying times, these folks

- ✔ Feel and express gratitude for the good things in life
- ✔ Savor the pleasures life offers
- ✔ Dwell as much as possible in the present moment
- ✔ Don't let the inevitable ups and downs disturb their equanimity

By deeply embracing whatever life serves up, happy people find the resilience and strength to roll with the challenges while maintaining their peace of mind.

Of course, such deep acceptance is more easily valued than achieved, primarily because early conditioning and subsequent life experiences have programmed you to compare what you have with what you think you should have (or what others have), to argue with what life offers, and to struggle to impose your personal agenda. Besides actively cultivating gratitude and appreciation, the key is to practice working with the mind and letting go of the strong (mostly negative) beliefs that perpetuate your suffering. (For more on working with the mind, see Chapter 7.)

How happy are you?

Because happiness is such a subjective condition, it's notoriously difficult to measure. In the end, the best gauge is often a self-assessment or a test in which you answer questions designed to determine how happy you feel. Sonja Lyubomirsky, a psychology professor at the University of California and the author of *The How of Happiness: A New Approach to Getting the Life You Want,* has devised a simple four-item measure of overall happiness called the Subjective Happiness Scale, which she and other researchers have administered to a variety of people.

Take a few minutes to answer these questions to get a sense of where you stand on the happiness spectrum. (Of course, if you feel happy enough and don't care about scores, feel free to bypass this exercise entirely.) For each of the following statements or questions, select the number from the scale that you think is most appropriate in describing you.

1. In general, I consider myself:

   Not happy 1 2 3 4 5 6 7 Very happy

2. Compared to most of my peers, I consider myself:

   Less happy 1 2 3 4 5 6 7 More happy

3. Some people are generally very happy. They enjoy life regardless of what is going on, getting the most out of everything. To what extent does this characterization describe you?

   Not at all 1 2 3 4 5 6 7 A great deal

4. Some people are generally not very happy. Although they are not depressed, they never seem as happy as they might be. To what extent does this characterization describe you?

   Not at all 1 2 3 4 5 6 7 A great deal

Average the four numbers you selected; this is your score. The maximum score is 7. The average happiness score runs from about 4.5 to 5.5. College students tend to score lower (averaging a bit below 5) than working adults and older, retired people (who average 5.6).

Being in the flow of life

Have you ever had times when you got lost in what you were doing and suddenly looked up to discover that several hours had passed in what seemed like an instant? Even though you didn't remember exactly what you did, you knew that the experience felt exhilarating and unusually fulfilling. Psychologist Mihaly Csikszentmihalyi coined the term *flow* to describe such moments of complete immersion, in which time stops and self-consciousness drops away. Researchers have found that flow isn't only inherently enjoyable and refreshing but that the more time you spend in flow, the happier you are.

Flow can be found in any activity, whether work or play (or anything in between). However, you're more likely to experience flow if you choose a task that's neither too difficult nor too easy, and that challenges you and engages your concentration but doesn't frustrate or confound you. Learning a new language, playing a sport, solving a crossword puzzle, making a piece of furniture, talking with a friend, resolving a problem at work — each of these (and more!) can be conducive to flow if you allow yourself to be completely engaged.

As you may have noticed, flow entails the same quality of wholehearted attention that's cultivated in meditation. Practicing mindfulness meditation (as described in Chapter 7) on a regular basis helps you minimize distractions and develop present-moment awareness, making it easier to slip into flow as you engage in everyday activities.

Meaning and belonging

The great philosophers have long understood that being happy involves more than just feeling good. In order to be happy, you also need to feel that your life has meaning and purpose and that you're intimately connected with others and belong to a larger social or spiritual matrix. Studies show that the two factors that correlate most strongly with a person's happiness level are a strong network of loving family and friends and a robust religious or spiritual life.

According to positive psychology pioneer Martin Seligman, one of the most powerful ways to add both meaning and belonging to your life and boost your happiness in the process is to make what he calls a "gratitude visit." You write a letter expressing your gratitude to someone — a relative, teacher, coach, or friend — and then you visit the person and read the letter aloud. This exercise works on multiple levels simultaneously: It brings you into close and intimate contact with someone you value, it enhances your feelings of self-worth as you do something kind and appreciative for another, and it enriches your sense of connection to a wider social and spiritual milieu.

But you don't need to do make such a dramatic gesture (unless, of course, you're moved to). Simply participating in family gatherings, getting together with friends on a regular basis, going to church or synagogue or your local meditation group, or volunteering at a soup kitchen can afford your life some of the meaning and connectedness that contribute to happiness. In particular, being kind and generous to others, even when it may be inconvenient or uncomfortable (and you get nothing back in return) provides a major dose of happiness. In one study, participants who practiced five acts of kindness a week for six weeks reported being significantly happier than those who didn't.

Understanding an integrated definition of happiness

In the earlier sections of this chapter, I explore the hallmarks of happiness. In this section, though, I offer an integrated definition of happiness that ventures to include them all, with the understanding that, ultimately, happiness is a completely subjective experience or state and that only you can know what really makes you happy and whether you're actually happy.

According to happiness experts of every persuasion, happy people tend to spend much of their time in positive emotions and mind-states like peace, joy, contentment, satisfaction, gratitude, and love; and when they experience negativity, it's generally short-lived and doesn't disrupt their life in a significant way. They tend to move through life with a feeling of ease and flow, accepting what life brings while acting to benefit themselves and others. They connect regularly with a loving community of family and friends, participate in life in a meaningful and fulfilling way, and tend to have a relationship with a (higher or deeper) spiritual dimension of reality.

Of course, no one can meet this definition in every particular situation. But the more your life resembles this one, the more likely you are to be genuinely happy.

Studying Up on the Art and Science of Happiness

After you've boned up on the primary characteristics of a happy life and considered a more comprehensive definition of happiness (see the earlier section "Checking Out the Hallmarks of Genuine Happiness"), you may enjoy exploring how researchers in both the scientific and spiritual domains have been studying this elusive condition. Meditators have long plumbed the depths of happiness through the introspective lens of contemplation, while scientists have more recently been applying the external methods of the clinical trial.

For thousands of years, Buddhists have made happiness, and more specifically the relief of suffering, the primary focus of their meditative tradition. In the past few decades, scientists and psychologists have departed from their customary preoccupation with illness and dysfunction to investigate the realm of positive emotions and optimal mental and emotional health. Their findings are not only illuminating and instructive, but they also point to practical exercises for raising your happiness quotient. In the following sections, I show you the benefits of being happy as well as the findings from Buddhist meditators, scientists, and psychologists.

Why bother being happy?

Aside from the obvious answer to the question of why you should strive to be happy — because it feels good — sustained happiness has a number of measurable benefits that positive psychologists and other researchers have recently begun to calibrate and catalog. The following list, which is adapted from Sonja Lyubomirsky's *The How of Happiness: The New Approach to Getting the Life You Want,* shows a few of the most important benefits:

- ✔ Happier people are more energetic, generous, and cooperative and are better liked than their less-happy counterparts.
- ✔ They have more self-confidence and greater self-esteem.
- ✔ They're more likely to have more fulfilling relationships and richer social networks.
- ✔ Happier people are more effective at work, at least in part because they're more flexible and creative in their thinking.
- ✔ They have stronger immune systems, maintain better health, and live longer.
- ✔ On the whole, happier people provide more benefit to others around them.

As you can see, being happy contributes to your life in a number of significant ways. You could say that happiness is like yeast in bread. Just as yeast is a key ingredient that can enable a blend of flour and water to rise up and fulfill its potential as the staff of life, happiness is a key quality that can empower you to rise to every occasion and respond in the most effective and compassionate way possible.

The Buddhist understanding of happiness

From the Buddhist perspective, happiness begins and ends in the heart, and derives not from external things and circumstances but from the cultivation of certain heart-centered qualities, in particular the four "heavenly abodes" or forms of love: lovingkindness, compassion, equanimity, and joy in the well-being of others. Certain Buddhists emphasize the generation of *bodhichitta,* the compassionate intention to bring benefit to all beings and to relieve their suffering, which is considered the most direct way to ensure your own happiness.

Though these qualities may seem lofty and unattainable, they can be deliberately cultivated through the practice of meditation and compassionate action.

Buddhists also emphasize innate goodness and purity and teach that happiness doesn't need to be manufactured or achieved, but is instead your true nature (or natural state) before it's distorted by the negative conditioning imposed on you throughout your life. From the Buddhist perspective, your inherently happy condition is like a diamond in the rough that you can unearth and reclaim through the practice of meditation — in particular, meditations for working with the negative thoughts and emotions that obscure it. (For meditations on working with negativity, see Chapter 13.) The more clearly you recognize your naturally bright and joyful inner nature and the more time you spend abiding there, the happier you become.

Ultimately, Buddhists believe that you can only achieve permanent happiness by liberating yourself from the illusion that you're a solid, separate somebody isolated and apart from the totality of life. Accomplished through the practice of meditation and the cultivation of wisdom, liberation brings a deep and abiding recognition of the inherent perfection of things and an end to any struggle with the way things are. The profound happiness and peace that ensue are completely unshakable and can't be disturbed in any way by the vicissitudes of life.

The science of meditation and happiness

The scientific study of meditation and happiness has been fueled by the extraordinary levels of subjective well-being that researchers have discovered in Tibetan Buddhist monks. Much to the surprise of scientists, these life-long meditators turned out to be literally off the conventional charts in measures of happiness and empathy. In response to these findings, the Dalai Lama, spiritual leader of the Tibetan people, has met frequently with neuroscientists in an ongoing collaboration to study the relationship between meditation and optimal psychological health and well-being.

Some of the most important studies on meditation and happiness have been carried out by Dr. Richard Davidson, director of the Waisman Laboratory for Brain Imaging and Behavior at the University of Wisconsin as well as director of the Laboratory for Affective Neuroscience and the Center for Investigating Healthy Minds at the same university. As I describe in Chapter 4, Davidson pioneered research that maps the relationships between certain regions of the brain and their impact on mood and mental state.

In his early studies of Tibetan monks practicing compassion meditation, Davidson found that monks who had logged more than 10,000 hours in meditation showed an unparalleled and previously undocumented increase in brain waves in the area of the brain associated with positive emotion. In other words, they were the happiest people on record!

In subsequent experiments, Davidson has shown that even the simple practice of mindfulness meditation can be a significant mood booster. (For instructions in mindfulness meditation, see Chapter 7.) Perhaps his most famous study involved employees at a biotech firm who took an eight-week course in mindfulness involving three hours of training each week and 20 minutes a day of individual practice. After the training, not only had their brainwave activity increased in the area of positive emotions but these ordinary men and women, with just a few months of meditation experience, also reported feeling happier, less anxious, and more engaged in their work. In other words, you don't have to be a monk to reap the mood-altering benefits of meditation.

The insights of positive psychology

For most of its history, the field of psychotherapy has focused almost exclusively on relieving dysfunction and distress and, in particular, on curing or at least alleviating mental illness. According to the founder of psychoanalysis, Sigmund Freud, the point of spending hours on the couch or chair is to help exchange your neurotic misery for ordinary human unhappiness — which isn't a particularly sanguine prognosis!

In the 1960s and '70s, humanistic and transpersonal psychologists like Carl Rogers and Abraham Maslow broke with their psychoanalytic forebears by exploring optimal human functioning, peak experiences, and altered states and promoting the possibility that real happiness is actually attainable through psychological change.

The past few decades have witnessed the emergence of *positive psychology,* a growing field that builds on the insights of its predecessors and uses the latest research techniques to determine the hallmarks of happiness and provide evidence of how certain activities and practices actually help cultivate and enhance it. According to positive psychologists like Sonja Lyubomirsky, happiness — also known as *subjective well-being* — is characterized by "experiences of joy, contentment, or positive well-being, combined with a sense that one's life is good, meaningful, and worthwhile."

Some of the findings of positive psychology merely corroborate the perennial wisdom of the meditative traditions — for example, that gratitude, forgiveness, appreciation, connectedness, and living in the present moment contribute to lasting well-being. But other findings expand the traditional understanding — for example, by suggesting that an ongoing sense of meaning and purpose and an active participation in life also add to a person's happiness quotient.

According to researchers, 50 percent of your happiness is hardwired at birth and comes to you courtesy of your genetic endowment. For example, identical twins separated at birth and raised in drastically different circumstances have remarkably similar happiness measures. Another 10 percent derives from your life circumstances, including your health, wealth, material comfort, career success, and relationship status. But the rest, a full 40 percent, depends on how you live your life!

If you want to be happy, you're wise to use your time cultivating the inner qualities and outer activities that directly contribute to lasting happiness rather than pursuing the successes and acquisitions that are popularly regarded as the keys to well-being but actually aren't. The reason these things don't really make you happy is that you quickly habituate to improvements in life circumstances and lose the happy buzz they initially give you. For instance, you may be ecstatic about your new car for a week or two, but then you quickly start taking it for granted (or wanting a newer, bigger, shinier model). Positive psychologists call this *hedonic adaptation*.

The good news is that you can actually boost your happiness level with relatively short periods of practicing some of the exercises and involvements that positive psychologists recommend. For example, University of Pennsylvania professor Martin Seligman, one of the pioneers of the field, asked a group of severely depressed people to log on to a website each night and then recall and write down three good things that happened to them during the day. After just 15 nights, more than 90 percent had experienced relief and lifted their depression from "severe" to "mild or moderate." When combined with present-moment awareness (as cultivated in mindfulness meditation), exercises like this help cut through the habituation of hedonic adaptation and allow you to enjoy and appreciate the gifts that life brings.

Finding True Happiness with Meditation

You may be wondering how to combine all the fascinating information in this chapter into a program that you can use to actually boost your own subjective well-being. Well, lucky for you, this section offers meditations that help cultivate and enhance those qualities that positive psychologists and meditators agree contribute to lasting happiness. If you've read the earlier sections in this chapter, you know what those qualities are and how they make you happier. The rest is up to you. (If you haven't read these important sections, check them out.)

In particular, regular mindfulness meditation (see Chapter 7) makes a great foundational practice for any happiness program because it directly activates the brain centers associated with positive emotions and helps you gain perspective on the negative thoughts and feelings that may be dragging you down. Lovingkindness and compassion meditations (see Chapter 11) are scientifically proven to increase heartwarming, uplifting emotions and mental states. Positive psychologists also have found that the practice of gratitude provides a quick and measurable boost in mood. Forgiveness helps you let go of any grief and resentment from the past that may be clouding your happiness, and savoring and flow teach the joy of being in the moment. As for optimism, well, I think it speaks for itself.

If you want to reap the benefits of these meditations, choose the ones that appeal to you most, and be sure to do them regularly for an extended period of time before you assess how much they've helped you. The point is to do each meditation for its own sake, not to keep checking to see how much better you feel. And don't forget the importance of loving friends and family and an active and meaningful involvement in life. Sitting quietly in meditation is just one way to generate happiness; you also need to get up and express these positive qualities at work, at play, and in your relationships with others.

Savoring the moment

Most of the time you're racing through life, struggling to get things done, accomplish your goals, take care of your loved ones, and survive another day. In the process, you may fail to relish the little joys and epiphanies that regularly come your way — the morning sun glinting through the trees, the smile on a baby's face, the taste of a good sandwich or a fresh cup of coffee, the enthusiastic chirping of the birds, or the kind words of a friend. Every day is full of special moments like these that have the potential to add to your happiness if you only let them in.

Here's a meditation for savoring the good things in life:

1. **Choose one pleasurable activity that you normally hurry through, such as walking in nature, preparing a meal, talking with a friend, or taking a hot bath or shower.**

2. **Instead of doing the activity unconsciously, try doing it with awareness.**

Take in the pleasure and enjoyment and allow the activity to have an effect on you. Notice how you feel as you move through the activity. Savor the positive feelings like pleasure, delight, relaxation, love, and so on.

3. **If you like, you can do this once or twice a day for a week.**

   At the end of the week, take stock of how you feel. Are you happier, more optimistic, or more relaxed than before?

Fostering flow

After you've learned to pay attention to the pleasurable moments of life (refer to the preceding section), you're ready to practice completely immersing yourself in an activity until you're carried along by its energy and momentum and lose touch with time and self-consciousness. This state is called *flow*. Athletes call it "the zone."

To promote flow, follow these steps:

1. **Choose an activity that you really enjoy doing.**

   Make sure it's something that has clear goals and immediate feedback, and challenges you without evoking frustration. For example, appropriate activities include working in the garden, playing tennis, making a dress, fashioning a piece of furniture, solving a complex problem at work, or playing a video or computer game.

2. **Set aside at least an hour or two, and give your full attention to the activity. Immerse yourself completely in what you're doing.**

   Notice distractions, but don't respond to them. Stay focused on the activity throughout the designated time. (For a more complete description of the kind of mindful attention that helps foster flow, see Chapter 7.)

3. **When you're done with the activity, notice how you feel.**

   Did you find the activity more exhilarating or fulfilling than usual? Did you lose track of time or of the usual preoccupations like hunger or thirst?

Ultimately, flow isn't something you can do any more than an athlete can force himself into the zone. Flow just happens. Yet you can make flow more likely with the choice of your activities and the quality of your attention.

Developing gratitude

When you think about other people, do you dwell on the ways they've disappointed, hurt, or ignored you? When you reflect on life, do you focus on how it fails to live up to your expectations? Or do you notice instead all the many, often invisible, ways that other people provide love and support and how life circumstances foster your overall well-being? Believe it or not, you actually have the power to choose which perspective you take.

Here's an exercise that's designed to evoke gratitude in even the most unappreciative person:

1. **Begin by settling comfortably and taking a few deep breaths.**

2. **Spend a few minutes reviewing all the good things that happened to you in the past 24 hours.**

   You may recall a moment when someone — a friend, a family member, or a person on the street — treated you with love or kindness. Or you may be reminded of simple pleasures, like eating a good meal or watching an inspiring movie or taking a walk in nature. Let yourself feel and remember these moments.

3. **Reflect in the same detail on all the ways you positively contributed to the lives of others during the same 24-hour period.**

4. **Allow appreciation and gratitude to arise in your heart for these special moments.**

   If you have difficulty experiencing gratitude, rest your attention in your heart and connect with the tender place inside where you feel emotions like love and caring. Then reflect again on the good things.

5. **Reflect in the same way on the previous week.**

   Continue to breathe while you recall all the good things that happened. If negative memories come up, set them aside for now.

6. **If you have enough time, gradually extend the meditation to the past month, the past year, the past two years, and the past five.**

   Recall as much as possible. Feel and remember all the pleasant, happy, joyful moments as well as all the good things you did and all the ways you were gifted or supported by others.

7. **Allow feelings of gratitude and appreciation to well up in your heart.**

If you have plenty of time, you can extend the preceding meditation to encompass your whole life, making sure to cover the headline events and include the ways that your parents nurtured and supported you and made it possible for you to grow into the person you are today. If you have any resentment toward your parents, do the forgiveness meditation in the following section. If you'd like to make gratitude a regular part of your routine, do the first four steps each night before bed.

Gratitude exercises like this can do more than lift your mood. Psychologist Robert Emmons at the University of California at Davis found they improve physical health, raise energy levels, and relieve pain and fatigue for patients with neuromuscular disease. Those who benefited most tended to elaborate more and had a broader range of things they were grateful for.

Learning to forgive

Over the years, most people accumulate a heavy backpack full of old hurts and resentments that gradually weigh them down and limit their happiness. Instead of living in the fullness and richness of the present moment — which is where happiness happens, after all — and focusing on the good things they have (see the earlier section "Developing gratitude"), they're often trapped in the past, reliving the pain and disappointment they experienced back then.

Many people bear a special burden of guilt, shame, and anger toward themselves for the mistakes they've made and the pain they've caused others. If you're unable to shed this burden with the gratitude meditation, you can actively dissolve it with the power of forgiveness.

Follow these steps to shine the light of forgiveness on yourself and others:

1. **Begin by sitting comfortably, taking a few deep breaths, relaxing your body, and closing your eyes.**

2. **Allow images and memories of words, actions, feelings, and thoughts for which you've never forgiven yourself to float through your mind.**

   Perhaps you hurt someone you loved and drove him away, took something that didn't belong to you, or said no to an opportunity and later regretted it.

3. **Reflect on how much suffering you've caused and how much you may have suffered. Allow yourself to feel any pain or remorse.**

4. **Reflect on any lessons you may have learned and on the ways you've grown and changed since then.**

5. **Gently and wholeheartedly extend forgiveness to yourself.**

   Use words and phrases like this: "I forgive you for all the mistakes you've made and all the suffering you've caused. I forgive you for all the pain you've caused others, whether intentionally or unintentionally. I know that you've learned and grown; now it's time to move on. I forgive you! May you be happy and joyful. I take you back into my heart." (Here and elsewhere in the exercise, feel free to use your own words if you find them more resonant.)

6. **Open your heart to yourself and allow yourself to fill with love.**

   Feel the clouds around your heart dispersing.

7. **Imagine a person you love toward whom you feel some resentment.**

   Reflect on how that person may have hurt you. Reflect also on how many times you've hurt others in a similar way.

8. **Gently allow the clouds around your heart to continue dispersing as you wholeheartedly extend forgiveness to this person.**

   As you extend forgiveness to this person, use words and phrases like the following: "I forgive you for the ways that you've caused me pain, whether intentionally or unintentionally. I know that I, too, have hurt others and let them down. With my whole heart, I forgive you. May you be happy and joyful. I take you back into my heart." Feel your heart opening once again to this person.

   Remember: Here and elsewhere in this exercise, if you find that forgiveness doesn't come easily and your heart doesn't readily open, don't worry or blame yourself — you can't force yourself to forgive. You may need to welcome the painful feelings of anger, hurt, and resentment and feel them fully before you can forgive. If that's the case, you may want to work with your feelings in counseling or therapy, and then pick up the forgiveness meditation again when you feel ready. Or just do the exercise with the intention to forgive and trust that the feelings will eventually follow.

9. **Imagine someone whose forgiveness you'd like to have and gently ask for her forgiveness.**

   Use words and phrases like this: "Please forgive me for what I did or said to cause you pain, whether intentionally or unintentionally. I ask for your forgiveness. Please take me back into your heart."

10. **Imagine this person's heart opening to you and the love flowing freely back and forth between you once again.**

11. **Imagine someone toward whom you feel great resentment — someone, perhaps, whom you've excluded from your heart because of how he once hurt you.**

12. **Gently allow the clouds around your heart to disperse, and wholeheartedly extend forgiveness to this person as described in Step 8.**

13. **Reflect on all the many people toward whom you've closed your heart because of the pain they seemingly caused you.**

    Feel all the layers of resentment and pain that have built up around your heart over the years.

14. **Reflect on all the many ways that you've acted as they did.**

15. **Imagine all these people in front of you and, with your whole heart, forgive them all and ask for their forgiveness.**

    Use words and phrases like the following: "I forgive you for whatever you may have done to cause me pain, whether intentionally or unintentionally. I forgive you. Please forgive me. May we open our hearts to one another and live together in peace and harmony." Again, feel your heart opening wide and allow love to flow freely between you.

16. **Take a few moments to breathe deeply and rest your attention in your heart before getting up and going about your day.**

After you've practiced the full forgiveness meditation a few times, you can use it to extend forgiveness to particular people as the situation requires. But every time you practice forgiveness, be sure to include some for yourself.

Reflecting on life's gifts

Here's a simple meditation with a potentially powerful impact. In a study conducted by positive psychologist Martin Seligman, subjects who practiced a version of this exercise for 15 nights experienced a significant boost in their overall mood.

1. **Before you go to sleep tonight, take some time to write down three good things that happened to you during the day.**

   Describe what happened in some detail, including any good feelings you may have had at the time.

2. **Take note of what you're feeling as you write.**

   Do you notice any appreciation or gratitude arising? If not, that's fine. The point is simply to write about the good things and let the feelings take care of themselves.

3. **Practice this meditation every night for the next week.**

   Thereafter, continue the practice at least three nights a week for the next few months. If you find that it makes you happier, keep it up for as long as you like.

Choose happiness

In each moment you have a choice of where to focus your attention. Obsess about what you don't have or can't do, and your mood plummets. Reflect on what you do have and can do, and your spirit soars. Though you may be convinced that you need to worry and fret in order to survive in a ruthless, dangerous world, the opposite is actually true: The more you relax, do your best, and allow life to unfold, the more you reap the fruits of psychological and emotional well-being. Notice when your mind starts spiraling into negativity, and simply switch the channel. Practicing mindfulness meditation on a regular basis makes this exercise much easier. Notice the good things in your life. Pay attention to the beauty. Attune to the pleasurable sensations and positive emotions. Recall the joyful moments. The choice is up to you.

Cultivating optimism

Because folks are constantly anticipating and dreaming about the future, the ways they think about it have a powerful impact on their happiness levels right now. Pessimistic people tend to paint the future in shades of black and gray and envision being powerless, unsuccessful, endangered, and inept. By contrast, optimistic people imagine a future of life-affirming pastels, with endless potential for ever-increasing enjoyment and fulfillment. Whether you tend to look on the bright or the dark side, however, optimism is definitely a quality you can cultivate and nurture.

Studies have shown that imagining a particular scenario or event has the same effect on the brain as actually experiencing it. For this reason, spending time each day imagining a positive future can evoke correspondingly positive feelings like pleasure, satisfaction, accomplishment, and joy. Imagining a bright future also primes the mind to act in more meaningful and fulfilling ways.

Here's a simple meditation for cultivating optimism:

1. **Begin by settling comfortably, closing your eyes, and taking a few deep breaths.**

2. **Spend 5 minutes imagining your best possible future self.**

   Be as detailed as possible, and include every domain of life: career, relationships, family, creativity, and so on. Where are you now? Who's with you? Where are you working? What are you accomplishing and enjoying? What do you do for fun? How are you feeling?

3. **For the next 15 minutes, express your future self in writing.**

   Describe yourself and your life with as much detail as possible.

The originator of this exercise, Laura King, a psychology professor at the University of Missouri, found that participants who spent 20 minutes a day for 4 days writing a narrative description of their best possible future selves showed immediate increases in positive mood, remained happier several weeks later, and even had fewer physical ailments than those who wrote about other topics.

Chapter 17

Meditating in Everyday Life

*E*lsewhere in this book, I compare meditation to a laboratory in which you experiment with paying attention to your experience and discovering how to cultivate qualities like peace, love, and happiness. However, the discoveries you make in the controlled environment of a lab have only limited value until you can apply them to real-life situations and problems. And the skills, insights, and peaceful feelings you have on your meditation cushion won't get you far unless you do the same. In fact, the whole point of meditation is to help you live a happier, fuller, more stress-free life!

As you become more adept at being mindful during formal meditation, you naturally get better at paying mindful attention to everything you encounter, both on and off the cushion. Still, you may find it helpful to pick up a few tips on how to extend the practice of mindfulness so you can stay open, present, and attentive from moment to moment, even in the midst of challenging circumstances like driving a car in heavy traffic, running errands, doing chores, taking care of the kids, or dealing with stressful situations at work. In addition, you can find out how to use meditation to improve the quality of your family life and your intimate relationships, including the most intimate encounter of all — making love.

Being Peace with Every Step: Extending Meditation in Action

Here's a quote that expresses the spirit of meditation-in-action better than anything I could possibly say. It comes from the book *Peace Is Every Step* by the Vietnamese Buddhist monk Thich Nhat Hanh.

Every morning, when we wake up, we have twenty-four brand-new hours to live. What a precious gift! We have the capacity to live in a way that these twenty-four hours will bring peace, joy, and happiness to ourselves and others. . . . Every breath we take, every step we make, can be filled with peace, joy, and serenity. We need only to be awake and alive in the present moment.

The person who wrote these words is neither a recluse nor a Pollyanna; he's had experience practicing mindfulness in extraordinarily difficult times. During the Vietnam War, he worked tirelessly for reconciliation between the warring factions in his homeland and created and headed the Buddhist Peace Delegation to the Paris Peace Talks. For his efforts, Martin Luther King nominated him for a Nobel Peace Prize. Since then, Thich Nhat Hanh has actively taught a blend of mindful living and social responsibility, and wherever he goes he embodies the peace he espouses.

As Nhat Hanh suggests, you need to be awake and alive in the present moment. After all, it's the only moment you have. Even memories of the past and thoughts of the future occur right now, in the present. If you don't wake up and smell the flowers, taste your food, and see the light in your loved ones' eyes, you'll miss the beauty and preciousness of your life as it unfolds. Says Thich Nhat Hanh: "Each thought, each action in the sunlight of awareness becomes sacred."

On a more practical level, you can only reduce stress by getting out of your head (where all the stressful thoughts and emotions vie for your attention) and by showing up for what's happening right now. After you learn how to be present in your meditation, you need to *continue* being present again and again, moment after moment; otherwise, you'll just fall back into your old stressful habits. Besides, mindful awareness of what you're doing and experiencing can confer tremendous benefits, including the following:

- ✔ Greater focus, efficiency, and precision in what you do

- ✔ An experience of effortlessness, flow, and harmony

- ✔ Reduced stress because the mind isn't distracted by its habitual worries and concerns

- ✔ Increased enjoyment of the richness and fullness of life

- ✔ Greater availability or presence and the capacity to open your heart and be touched or affected by others

- ✔ Deeper connections with loved ones and friends

- ✔ An openness to the spiritual dimension of life

You don't have to be a Buddhist monk to practice mindfulness. You can wake up and be mindful in the midst of the most mundane activities. But you can certainly take advantage of some of the techniques and tricks that the great meditation teachers have devised, which I describe in the following sections.

Coming back to your breath

Sometimes you feel like you're just moving too quickly and dealing with too many matters at once to know how (or where) to be mindful. "Where do I place my attention," you may wonder, "when things are happening so fast?" Just as you can begin the formal practice of mindfulness meditation by counting or following your breaths (see Chapter 7), you can always return to the direct and simple experience of breathing, even in the most complicated circumstances. No matter how many other things you may be doing, you're always breathing — and the physical experience of inhaling and exhaling provides a reliable anchor for your attention in stressful times. Then, when you've begun to pay attention to your breath, you can gradually expand to include mindful awareness of your other activities.

Besides, gently paying mindful attention to your breath gradually calms your mind by shifting awareness away from your thoughts and slowing your mind down to the pace and rhythms of your body. With your mind and body in sync, you start to feel a natural ease and an inner harmony and tranquility that external circumstances can't easily disturb.

 You can begin by stopping whatever you're doing for a moment or two and tuning in to the coming and going of your breath. Your attention may be drawn to the rise and fall of your abdomen as you breathe or to the feeling of your breath as it enters and leaves your nostrils. Be mindful of these sensations for four or five breathing cycles, enjoying the simplicity and directness of the experience. When you breathe with awareness, you're consciously awake and alive in the present moment. Then resume your normal activities while continuing to be mindful of your breath. (If you find this multidimensional awareness too confusing or complicated, simply remember to come back to your breath every now and then.)

Listening to the bell of mindfulness

Monasteries traditionally use bells and gongs to remind the monks and nuns to stop whatever they're doing, drop their thoughts and daydreams, and gently return their attention to the present moment. Because you probably don't live with bells, Thich Nhat Hanh suggests that you use the recurring sounds of your environment to gently remind you to wake up and be mindful.

TRADITIONAL WISDOM

Enjoying your meal with mindful eating

Did you ever finish a meal and wonder what happened to the food? You remember enjoying it at first, and then suddenly you notice that your plate is empty and you can't recall a single bite in between. Perhaps you spent the time texting a friend or reading your e-mail or worrying about your bank account or your relationship.

Here's a meditation to help you be mindful of what you're putting into your mouth. Mindful eating not only allows you to enjoy your food as never before but it also facilitates your digestion by reducing any tension or stress you bring to the table. (Given the demands of work and family, you probably won't be able to eat as meditatively as this all the time, but you can still apply a little mindfulness to every meal, no matter how informal.) Here are the steps:

1. **Begin by disconnecting from all your electronic devices.**

   Turn off your cell phone, put your computer to sleep, shut down your tablet, and set aside your music player or PDA. Don't worry. You'll survive 10 or 20 minutes offline.

2. **Before you start eating, take a few moments to appreciate your food.**

   You may want to reflect Zen-style on the earth and the sunshine that gave life to this food and the people and effort that brought it to your table. Or you can express your thanks to God or spirit, or simply sit silently and feel grateful for what you have. If you're eating with others, you can hold hands, smile at one another, or connect in some other way.

3. **Bring your awareness to your hand as you lift the first bite of food to your lips.**

You can experiment with the custom in certain monastic traditions of eating more slowly than usual. Or just eat at your usual speed, but be as mindful as you can.

4. **Be fully aware as the first morsel of food enters your mouth and floods your taste buds with sensations.**

   Notice the tendency of the mind to judge the flavor: "It's too spicy or salty," or "It's not what I expected." Notice any emotions that may get stirred up: disappointment, relief, irritation, joy. Be aware of any ripples of pleasure or warmth or other physical sensations. Enjoy your food!

5. **If you talk while you eat, notice how the talking affects you.**

   Do certain topics cause you to tense up or give you indigestion? Does the talk take you away from the enjoyment of your meal, or can you have both?

6. **Stay mindful of each mouthful as you gradually eat your meal.**

   This step is probably the hardest because most people have a tendency to space out once they know how their food tastes. But you can continue to enjoy the taste freshly, bite after bite. If you get distracted, stop and breathe for a moment or two before starting to eat again.

7. **To facilitate your mindfulness, you may want to eat in silence every now and then.**

   Eating in silence may feel strange or uncomfortable at first, but you may find that a quiet meal can provide a nourishing respite from the pressures of life.

For example, you can set the beeper on your alarm watch or cell phone to sound every hour, and when it does, you can stop, enjoy your breathing for a minute or two, and then resume your normal activities (with greater awareness, of course). Or you can hear the mindfulness bell in the ringtone of your phone or the sound of your computer booting up in the morning or the buzzer that goes off in your car before you fasten your seatbelt. Just remember to stop, enjoy your breathing, and keep going with greater awareness and aliveness.

Even nonsounds make great reminders. Whenever you encounter a red light in traffic, for example, instead of indulging your frustration or anxiety, you can remember to tune in, breathe consciously, and let go of your tension and speed. Or you can allow moments of beauty to help you wake up — a beautiful flower, the smile on a child's face, sunlight through the window, a warm cup of tea. Then again, you can always buy a traditional meditation bell and strike it every now and then as a special reminder.

Repeating a phrase to help yourself be mindful

The Jewish tradition has special prayers for just about every occasion — from seeing a bolt of lightning to eating a piece of bread — that are designed to remind the faithful that God is constantly present. Buddhists use short verses to encourage them to come back to the unadorned simplicity of being in each moment. Christians say grace before meals, at bedtime, and on other auspicious occasions. Unlike *mantras* — words or brief phrases repeated again and again (described in Chapters 3 and 15) — these verses or prayers differ from one situation to the next and have a unique message to impart.

For example, Thich Nhat Hanh suggests silently intoning the following verse to enhance your mindfulness and turn your conscious breathing into an opportunity to relax and enjoy your life:

> Breathing in, I calm my body.
> Breathing out, I smile.
> Dwelling in the present moment,
> I know this is a wonderful moment.

Coordinate the first line with the inhalation, the second line with the exhalation, and so forth. Be sure to do what you're saying. That is, calm your body, smile to yourself (see the sidebar in this chapter "Practicing a half smile"), and appreciate the present moment. When you get the knack, you can simply say, "Calming, smiling, present moment, wonderful moment." If you don't cotton to Nhat Hanh's terminology, feel free to make up verses of your own for everyday situations like breathing, eating, bathing, working, and even talking on the phone or going to the bathroom.

Freeing yourself from the tyranny of time

Many people feel that their calendar runs their life and leaves them no room for connecting with themselves or the people they love. But you don't have to let the clock control you. You may not be able to free up your schedule, but you can definitely free up your relationship to time. Here are a few pointers for doing just that (adapted from the book *Full Catastrophe Living* by Jon Kabat-Zinn):

✔ **Remember that time is a useful convention created by the human mind to help you organize your experiences.** It has no absolute reality, as Einstein discovered. When you're enjoying yourself, time just flies by; when you're bored or in pain, minutes seem to last forever.

✔ **Live in the present moment as much as possible.** Because time is created by thought, you drop into a timeless dimension when you bypass the thinking mind and settle your attention in the here and now. As soon as you start planning for the future or regretting the past, you're immediately bound by the pressures of time once again.

✔ **Take some time to meditate each day.** Meditation teaches you how to be present and provides the most effective entree into the realm of the timeless. As Jon Kabat-Zinn puts it, "Just making the commitment to practice non-doing, to let go of striving, to be non-judgmental . . . nourishes the timeless in you."

✔ **Simplify your life.** When you fill up your life with trivial pursuits and habits that squander time, it's no wonder you don't have enough for the things that really matter to you. Take stock of what you do with your day and consider letting go of a few activities that don't feed your deeper intention to slow down and connect with yourself.

✔ **Remember that your life belongs to you.** Even though you may have a family to take care of or a job that requires your attention, keep in mind that you have the right to apportion your time as you choose. You're not cheating the other people in your life if you take a half hour for yourself each day to meditate.

Noticing how situations affect you

When you begin to expand your formal mindfulness practice from your breathing to the full range of your sensory experience (see Chapters 7 and 12), you can bring this inner awareness to your other activities as well. Instead of losing touch with yourself as you watch TV or drive your car or work at your computer, you can maintain *dual awareness,* or simultaneous awareness, of what's going on around you and of how the situation or activity affects you.

Gradually you may start to notice that driving too fast makes you tense, or that watching certain TV shows leaves you nervous or agitated, or that talking for hours on the phone saps your energy instead of enlivening you. You don't need to make any judgments or formulate any improvements based on what you discover. Just gently take note. If you're highly motivated to reap the benefits of the meditation you practice so diligently, you'll find yourself naturally moving away from situations (including habits, leisure pursuits, people, and work environments) that stress you out and gravitating to situations that support you in feeling calm, relaxed, harmonious, and connected with yourself and others.

When your suffering and stress are based on your own habitual patterns and difficult emotions (see Chapter 12), you can use dual awareness to notice your reactivity and create space inside to experience and make friends with it, instead of acting it out in relation to others.

Applying meditation to familiar activities

Anything you do or experience can provide you with an opportunity to practice mindfulness. But you may want to begin with some of your usual activities — the ones you may be doing now on automatic pilot while you daydream, space out, or obsess. The truth is, even the most routine tasks can prove enjoyable and enlivening when you do them with wholehearted care and attention. In the following sections, I list common activities with a few suggestions for infusing them with mindfulness.

Washing the dishes

If you set aside your judgments, which may insist you should be doing something more meaningful or constructive with your time, and instead simply wash the dishes — or sweep the floor or scrub the tub — you may find that you actually enjoy the activity. Feel the contours of the plates and bowls as you clean them. Notice the smell and the slipperiness of the soap, the sounds of the utensils, the satisfying feeling of removing the old food and leaving the dishes clean and ready for use.

Working at your computer

As you become engrossed in the information flashing across your screen, you may find yourself losing touch with your body and your surroundings. Pause every now and then to follow your breathing and notice how you're sitting. If you're starting to tense up and crane your head forward, gently straighten your spine (as described in Chapter 8) and relax your body. During recurring gaps in the flow of your work, come back to your body, breathe, and relax.

Taking meditation to work with you

With tight deadlines, performance reviews, high unemployment, and the constant threat of downsizing, today's highly competitive work environment places extraordinary pressures on employees and managers alike. Even practitioners of traditionally stable occupations like teaching and medicine are experiencing unprecedented work stress with the advent of standardized tests, burgeoning class sizes, computerized record-keeping, and large patient quotas. But whatever your job situation, you can reduce your stress by following these tips for meditating while you work:

✔ Each morning before you leave for work, reinforce your resolve to stay as calm and relaxed as possible. If you can, set the tone of the day by meditating, if only briefly, before you head out the door.

✔ By being mindful of your experience, you can discover the situations that really stress you out — and then avoid or change them as much as possible. Work can be demanding enough without taking on more than you can handle.

✔ Notice how your mind adds to stress. For example, it may stress you out by feeding you negative self-statements like "I'm a failure" or "I don't have what it takes." or by making you imagine that you're about to get canned, or that your boss and co-workers are plotting against you. Gently set these fabrications aside and return to paying mindful attention to whatever you're doing.

✔ Instead of hanging around the coffee machine and adding caffeine to your long list of stressors, use your breaks to meditate quietly in your office or cubicle. You'll feel more relaxed and refreshed than if you went for the joe.

✔ Have lunch with people you like or have a quiet lunch alone. You can also take a walk or do some other kind of exercise during your break. It's a great way to relieve your stress.

✔ Every hour, take a few moments to stop what you're doing, take some deep breaths, follow your breathing, and get up and stretch or walk around.

✔ Practice using a half smile to radiate well-being to yourself and your co-workers (see the sidebar in this chapter "Practicing a half smile"). When you have contact with others, do it with a warm and friendly attitude. One meditator I know reported that he single-handedly reversed the negative mood in his office by deliberately smiling and generating goodwill.

Driving your car

What could possibly be more stressful than navigating an automobile through heavy traffic? Besides the constant stop and go, you need to be aware of potential problems in every direction, any one of which could pose a threat to your safety. Yet you add to the stress of driving when you hurry to get to your destination faster than you realistically can and then get angry and impatient in the process.

As an antidote to the stress, practice mindfulness while you drive. Take a few deep breaths before you start and return to your breathing again and again as you consciously let go of tension and stress. Feel the steering wheel in your hands, the pressure of your feet against the pedals, the weight of your body against the seat. Notice any tendency to criticize other drivers, to space out, or to become angry or impatient. Pay attention to how the music or talk shows you listen to affect your mood as you drive. When you wake up and pay attention, you may be surprised to realize that you and the people around you are actually piloting these 2,000-pound hunks of plastic and steel with precious, vulnerable beings inside. And you may feel more inclined to drive mindfully and safely as a result.

Talking on the phone

As you engage in conversation, stay connected with your breathing and notice how you're affected. Do certain topics bring up anger, fear, or sadness? Do others bring up pleasure or joy? Do you become reactive or defensive? Notice also what moves or motivates you to speak. Are you attempting to influence or convince this person in some way? Do you have a hidden agenda of jealousy or resentment, or possibly a desire to be loved or appreciated? Or are you simply open and responsive to what's being said in the moment, without the overlay of past or future?

Watching TV

Just as when you work at a computer, you can easily forget you have a body when you tune in to the tube. (For more on meditation and TV, see Chapter 9.) Take a break during commercials to turn down the sound, follow your breathing, and ground your awareness in the present moment. Walk around, look out the window, connect with your family members. (Like many people, you may use food to ground you in your body while you're watching TV, but it won't work unless you're mindful of what you're eating. Besides, mindless eating has its price, as any couch potato can tell you.)

Working out

Physical exercise offers you a wonderful opportunity to shift your awareness from your mind to the simple, repetitive movements of your body. Unfortunately, many people just put on the headphones, switch on their music player, and space out.

The next time you hit the exercise equipment or attend an aerobics class, make a point of following your breathing as much as you can. Even if the routine is a challenging one, you can still keep coming back to your breath. Or simply be mindful of your body as you move — the flexing of your muscles, the contact with the equipment (or the floor), the feelings of warmth or pleasure or strain.

Attention, attention, attention!

With its emphasis on hard work and its appreciation of the ordinary, the Zen tradition has many stories that extol the benefits of mindful awareness in everyday activities. This sidebar introduces two of my favorites.

In the first story, a businessman comes to see a famous master and asks him to draw the Japanese characters that most precisely express the spirit of Zen. The master draws just one word: *attention.*

"But there must be more to Zen than this," the businessman complains.

"Yes, you're right," the master replies, and he draws the same character beneath the first: *Attention, attention.*

Now the businessman becomes angry. "You're just putting me on," he fumes, his face turning red.

Silently, the master adds a third character and shows it to his volatile guest. Now the scroll reads: *Attention, attention, attention.*

In the second story, a wandering monk arrives at a famous monastery and starts climbing the path that leads up the mountain when he notices a lettuce leaf floating down the mountain stream. "Hmm," he muses to himself, "any master who lets his disciples prepare the food so carelessly doesn't merit my time and attention."

Just as he's turning around to leave, he sees the head cook himself, robe fluttering in the breeze, hurrying down the path to retrieve the wayward leaf.

"Ah," the visiting monk thinks as he changes direction once again, "perhaps I should stop here and study for a while after all!"

Notice also what takes you away. Do you worry about your body image or obsess about your weight? Do you fantasize about your new physique and forget to be present for what's happening right now? Just notice what's occurring, and then return to your experience. You may start enjoying your body so much that you stop caring how others see it.

The Family That Meditates Together: Partners, Children, and Other Loved Ones

If you're a budding meditator, family life poses a twofold challenge. On the one hand, you may feel inclined to invite, encourage, or even coerce your loved ones to meditate with you. On the other, you may find that the people closest to you disturb your fragile, newfound peace of mind in ways that no one else can.

For example, only your spouse or partner may know the precise words that can pique your anger or evoke your hurt. And your children may have a unique capacity to try your patience or challenge your attachment to having situations be a certain way. (If you've ever tried to relax and follow your breathing while your toddler throws a tantrum or your teenager tries to explain how he crashed your car, you know what I'm talking about.)

You can definitely find ways of incorporating the formal practice of meditation into your closest relationships, but only as long as your loved ones are responsive to your efforts. Whether they have any interest in meditation or not, you can still use the ties that bind you to them as an exceptional opportunity to pay mindful attention to your habitual patterns of reacting and behaving. (For more on how to do this, see Chapter 12.) Ultimately, in fact, family life has the capacity to open your heart as no other circumstance can.

Meditating with kids

When you become enthusiastic about meditation yourself, you may want to pass on the benefits to your children (or grandchildren or godchildren or nephews and nieces). Or they may simply notice that you're spending time every day sitting quietly, and they may become interested in joining you. (Younger kids especially like to imitate just about anything their parents do.) If your children express curiosity, by all means give them *brief* instructions and invite them to meditate with you, but don't expect them to stick with it. Younger children have limited attention spans, and older ones may have other interests they find more compelling.

As you may have noticed, children under the age of 6 or 7 already spend much of their time in an altered state of wonder and delight (when they're not screaming at the top of their lungs, of course). Instead of teaching them how to meditate in some formal way, join them where they are as much as you can. Draw their attention to the little, wondrous details of life and encourage them to observe without interpretation. For instance, pick up a leaf and examine it closely with them, watch the ants on the ground, gaze together at the stars in the night sky. You can also turn meditation into a game or use imagery to engage their fertile imaginations. To protect the development of their natural capacity for curiosity and wonder, limit TV and video time, and avoid pushing them to develop their intellects too soon.

If older kids show interest in your meditation, feel free to introduce formal practices like following the breath or reciting a mantra, but keep them light and fun as much as possible — and let the kids do the practices as they feel moved, not according to some predetermined structure or deadline. Meditation will actually have its greatest impact on your children by making *you* calmer, happier, more loving, and less reactive. As they watch you change for the better, your kids may naturally be drawn to meditation because they want to reap the same benefits for themselves.

Hugging wholeheartedly

Instead of practicing formal meditation with your children, you can turn the simple, everyday act of hugging into an opportunity to breathe and be present. The next time you hug your kids, notice how you hold them. Do you tense up or keep them at a distance? Do you hold your breath, space out, or withhold your love because you're irritated or upset? Do you rush through the hug so you can get on with other "more important" things? You may be surprised by what you discover. (Of course, you may be quite happy with the way you hug, in which case feel free to ignore the rest of this sidebar!)

Instead of judging yourself, you may want to practice a different way of hugging. The next time you embrace your kids (or your partner or friends or other family members), pause while you hold them, relax your body, and breathe in and out with awareness three or four times. If you're so inclined, you can rest your awareness in your heart and consciously send them your love. (For more on opening your heart and extending love, see Chapter 11.) You may find that you enjoy hugging more and that your kids feel more loved and nurtured in the process.

Meditating with partners and family members

Like prayer, meditation can draw a family closer. (By family, I'm also referring to partners and spouses.) When you sit together in silence, even for a few minutes, you naturally attune to a deeper level of being, where differences and conflicts don't seem so important. You can also practice specific techniques in which, for example, you practice opening your hearts and sending and receiving love to and from one another. (See the sidebar later in this chapter "Connecting more deeply with a partner or friend"). If your family members are willing, you can incorporate meditative practices into your usual routine. For example, you can sit quietly together for a few moments before dinner or reflect before bed on the good things that happened during the day.

Family rituals offer a wonderful opportunity to practice mindfulness together and to connect in a deeper, more heartful way. If you invite your family members to join you as you mindfully cook a meal or work in the garden, they may begin to notice the quality of your attention and follow your lead. Of course, you can always suggest cooking or eating or working in a new and different way (you may prefer to use words like *love* and *care* rather than *mindfulness*), but your example will have a greater impact than the instructions you give. You can also practice eating meditation with your family occasionally (see the sidebar in this chapter "Enjoying your meal with mindful eating"). But be sure to keep it playful, loving, and relaxed.

Connecting more deeply with a partner or friend

If your partner knows how to meditate, you may enjoy scheduling some regular time to practice side by side. Then, if you feel adventurous and want to connect more deeply, you can experiment with the following exercise. (You can also try it with a close friend, if you like.) If your partner doesn't meditate but is open to learning how, this exercise can serve as an excellent introduction:

1. **Sit facing one another with your knees close together. Place your hands in front of you and join them with your partner's (right hands facing up, left hands facing down).**

2. **Close your eyes, take a few deep breaths, and relax as much as possible on the exhalation.**

3. **Attune yourself to your partner's breathing and gradually synchronize your inhalation and exhalation with your partner's.**

In other words, start breathing in and out together. Allow yourself to enjoy the deeper harmony and connectedness this shared rhythm evokes.

4. **After several minutes, begin to alternate your inhalations and exhalations.**

Breathe out love or light or healing energy and send it to your partner as he or she breathes it in; then breathe in the love and energy he or she sends you and take it into your heart. Continue this phase of the exercise for as long you both feel inclined. To intensify the connection, gaze with soft focus into one another's eyes and allow the love to flow back and forth through your gaze.

5. **When you feel complete, imagine the love that you've generated between you expanding to include everyone you love, ultimately enveloping and enlivening all beings everywhere.**

6. **End the meditation by bowing to one another or embracing.**

You may want to follow up with a shared massage or, if you're lovers, a hot bath or shower together or some meditative lovemaking.

Meditative lovemaking

"Why would I want to meditate while I make love?" you may wonder. "My partner and I have a great time already; what could we possibly add to the experience?" Well, I have an appealing answer for you: You can enhance your lovemaking enormously by giving it your wholehearted and undivided attention. Many people make love with their minds. They fantasize about sex not only when they're alone but when they're having sex with their partner as well. But the real lovemaking happens in the here and now, touch after touch, sensation after sensation. When you're spacing out or daydreaming, you miss the best part and then reduce your pleasure and satisfaction in the process.

People who make love meditatively report greater responsiveness and more intensely satisfying, whole-body orgasms. Men say they can last longer, and women say they can reach orgasm more frequently. Perhaps even more important is the fact that wholehearted, mindful awareness helps you infuse more love into your lovemaking, allows you to connect more deeply with your partner, and can actually transform sex into a spiritual experience.

Here are a few guidelines for making love in a meditative way. By all means, share them with your partner if he or she is interested, but remember that simply applying them as much as possible yourself can improve the quality of your sexual connection and may even entice your partner to follow your lead.

- ✔ **Connect with the love between you.** Before you make love, take a few minutes or more to connect in a heartful, loving way. You may want to gaze soulfully into one another's eyes, give one another a nurturing massage, or whisper sweet words of love. (You also can do the exercise in the sidebar "Connecting more deeply with a partner or friend.") Do whatever helps you to drop your defenses and open your heart.

- ✔ **See the Divine in your partner.** In the traditional meditative sexual practices of India and Tibet, the partners visualize one another as god and goddess, the embodiment of the divine masculine and feminine. Maybe you're not prepared to go quite so far, but you can certainly reconnect with the feelings of reverence and devotion you felt for your partner when you first fell in love.

- ✔ **Be present — and come back when you drift off.** After you've established the connection between your genitals and your heart, you can begin to touch one another lovingly with as much awareness as you can muster. When you start fantasizing or spacing out, gently return to the present moment. If unresolved feelings like resentment or hurt prevent you from connecting wholeheartedly with your partner, don't pretend. Just stop and talk things through until you reconnect.

- ✔ **Slow down and tune in.** Notice any tendency you may have to switch to automatic pilot, especially when the passion builds. Instead, slow down the pace and tune in to the full range of your sensations rather than just focusing on your genitals. You'll enjoy your lovemaking more, and you'll find that you have greater control over your energy. Be sure to tune in to your partner as well. For instance, ask how he or she wants to be touched.

- ✔ **Remember to breathe.** In the throes of passion, most people have a tendency to hold their breath. Unfortunately, this response can suppress your pleasure and hurry your climax (if you're a man) or inhibit your orgasm (if you're a woman). Conscious, mindful breathing can ground you in the present moment, relax your body, and deepen your enjoyment immeasurably.

✔ **When the energy starts to peak, stop for a few moments, breathe together, and relax.** This step may seem counterintuitive (most people tend to speed up when they get excited), but it's actually the secret doorway to a new world of sexual fulfillment. By letting go of your active, goal-directed orientation and just relaxing and breathing together, you deepen your heart connection and open yourselves to a higher frequency of pleasure, akin to what the mystics call *ecstasy*. When you feel your passion begin to wane, you can make love actively again. Feel free to stop and breathe again when your energy peaks, and then once again return to active lovemaking.

TRADITIONAL WISDOM

Practicing a half smile

If you look closely at the classical statues of the Buddha or at the faces of Renaissance madonnas, you'll notice a half smile that signifies a blend of tranquillity and joy. The Vietnamese Buddhist teacher Thich Nhat Hanh suggests that you can actually lift your mood and restore your innate happiness by smiling consciously, even when your spirits are low. "A tiny bud of a smile on our lips nourishes awareness and calms us miraculously," he writes in *Peace Is Every Step*. "It returns us to the peace we thought we had lost."

Contemporary scientific research agrees, indicating that smiling relaxes muscles throughout the body and has the same effect on the nervous system as real joy. Besides, smiling encourages others to smile and be happy.

Here are a few brief instructions for practicing the half smile that Thich Nhat Hanh recommends:

1. **Take a few moments right now to form your lips into a half smile.**

   Notice how other parts of your body respond. Does your belly relax? Does your back naturally straighten a little? Does your mood change in subtle ways? Notice also if you have any resistance to smiling when you "don't really feel like it."

2. **Maintain this half smile for at least ten minutes.**

   If your face starts to droop, just come back to the half smile. Do you notice a shift in how you act or respond to others? Do others respond to your smile by smiling back?

3. **The next time you feel your spirits sagging, practice this half smile for ten minutes or more and notice how you feel.**

Chapter 18

Using Meditation for Healing and Performance Enhancement

In This Chapter

▶ Exploring the many ways that meditation supports the healing process

▶ Meditating your way to more successful performance

*I*f you practice the basic meditations taught elsewhere in this book (especially Chapter 7), you may begin to notice that your health gradually improves (even if you think you're already healthy) and your energy and vitality increase. You may also find it easier and less stressful to do (and do effectively) the things that used to stress you out. In fact, Western researchers have corroborated the findings of traditional healers and teachers that meditation has an extraordinary capacity to help strengthen and heal your body and enhance your performance by training your mind and opening your heart. (If you don't believe me, check out the research in Chapter 4 or the detailed list of meditation benefits in Chapter 2.)

But what if you want to deal with a particular health problem, improve your tennis game, or put in a better showing at work? Does meditation have some specialized techniques to offer? Sure it does! Healers both ancient and modern have concocted some great meditations for facilitating the healing process (which you get to sample in this chapter), and in recent years sports gurus and corporate trainers have been applying the principles of meditation to enhance performance both on the field and in the office.

Elsewhere in this book, I tell you that you shouldn't be goal-oriented when you meditate. But here you get to cheat a little while applying the skills you picked up in earlier chapters — or if you haven't read any other chapters, you can pick them up here!

Meditation Has the Power to Help Heal Your Body, Too

The link between meditation and healing is a venerable one indeed. Take the world's great spiritual teachers — many were renowned for their healing abilities as well as their wisdom and compassion. Jesus, for example, first revealed his spiritual maturity by helping the lame to walk and the blind to see. The Jewish mystic known as the Baal Shem Tov had a reputation as a miracle worker and healer, and the historical Buddha is traditionally likened to a physician because the practices he taught help alleviate suffering. Even the English language reflects the sacred dimension of healing: The word *heal* derives from the same root as *whole* and *holy.*

Perhaps more important for ordinary folks like you and me, these teachers passed down special meditation techniques that enable practitioners to influence their bodily functions to an extraordinary degree. Ever hear about the yogis who stop their hearts and live for hours without any breathing or measurable metabolism? Or the Tibetan monks who generate so much internal heat that they dry wet blankets on their bodies in subzero temperatures? These people do exist, and their exceptional feats have been measured by Western researchers.

In fact, the emerging field of mind-body medicine developed in the 1970s when scientists studying the abilities of Eastern-trained meditators began to realize that the mind can have an extraordinary effect on the body — or even more precisely, that the body and the mind are inseparable. (Of course, the link between type-A behavior and heart disease dates back even earlier, to the 1960s.) More recently, researchers studying immune response have shown that the immune system and the nervous system are inextricably intertwined, and that psychological and emotional stress can suppress immune functioning and encourage the growth or spread of immune-related disorders such as cancer, AIDS, and autoimmune diseases. (For more on the mind-body connection and the health benefits of meditation, see Chapter 2.)

These days, most physicians recognize the relevance of psychological factors and the importance of relaxation and stress reduction in maintaining health. There's even a joke making the rounds in the medical field. Instead of offering the old saw about aspirin, the contemporary mind-body physician advises patients to "take two meditations and call me in the morning."

The good news is that you don't have to control your heartbeat or your metabolism to benefit from the healing power of meditation. You just have to sit still, pay attention, and practice some of the exercises provided in this section. Of course, it helps to have some basic meditation experience — which you can get by turning to Chapter 7 or listening to Track 4 — but you're welcome to begin here if you're strongly motivated and can learn as you go.

What healing really means

As I suggest earlier, healing involves returning to an intrinsic state of whole-ness and well-being that language, in its wisdom, links with the sacred. Consider the last time you got a cold, for example. When you got better, you didn't end up feeling like a different person; you just went back to being the way you were before you got sick. That's why people often say, when the cold goes away, "I finally feel like myself again!"

Meditation by its very nature provides healing of the deepest kind. The disease it helps heal is perhaps the most painful one of all: an epidemic human disor-der known as *separation* (or, even worse, *alienation*) from your own being and from other beings and things. (For more on this "disease," see Chapter 2.)

When you meditate, you heal this separation by gradually reconnecting in the here and now with your feelings, your sensate experience, and other aspects of yourself you may have previously disowned. That is, you become more whole! Most important, perhaps, you reconnect with your basic nature — *pure being* itself — which is complete and perfect just the way it is. Stephen Levine, whose numerous books have pioneered the use of meditation in heal-ing, calls this "the healing we took birth for."

The more you reconnect with your essential wholeness and well-being, the more you suffuse your body-mind with life energy and love. (As I mention in Chapter 6, the wellspring of *being* inside you is the source of all positive, life-affirming qualities and feelings.) And, as researchers have proven again and again, this life-giving energy mobilizes your body's healing resources, bol-sters your immune system, and naturally facilitates the process of repair and renewal. In other words, as you heal your separation, you contribute to the healing of your body as well.

But even if you have some chronic ailment and can never heal your body completely, you can still do the healing you were born to do. You don't have to consider yourself a failure if you don't get well (as some alternative healing approaches suggest you should). After all, you can encourage your healing with meditation, but illness is a mysterious process that you and I can't really understand. Who knows? You may be sick because you need to slow down, reevaluate your priorities, and reconnect with yourself. Like few other life cir-cumstances, illness can be a powerful messenger urging you to change your life in significant ways.

Understanding how meditation heals

Besides overcoming separation, the basic meditation practices provided in this book (especially Chapters 7 and 11) and on the accompanying CD (or in the downloadable tracks, if you're reading a digital version of this book) contribute to the healing process in a number of essential ways, which are discussed in the following sections.

Love and connectedness

As Dean Ornish, MD, reveals in his ground-breaking research (described in Chapter 11), love is more important than any other factor in the healing process, including diet and exercise. To heal your heart, he discovered, you need to open your heart — and his findings have been corroborated in studies of cancer, AIDS, and other life-threatening illnesses. By putting you in touch with the love in your heart (which, as I mention elsewhere, is not just an emotion, but a direct expression of *being* itself), meditation nourishes not only your internal organs but also your entire body-mind organism.

Relief of tension and stress

By teaching you how to relax your body and calm your mind (see Chapter 7), meditation helps you avoid getting sick in the first place by alleviating stress, a major cause of many ailments, from heart disease and stroke to gastrointestinal disorders and tension headaches. In particular, Jon Kabat-Zinn (author of the bestseller *Wherever You Go, There You Are*) has developed a stress-reduction program based on Buddhist mindfulness meditation that teaches participants not only how to reduce stress while they're meditating but also how to extend the benefits of mindfulness to every area of their lives. (For a more complete description of Kabat-Zinn's work, see Chapter 2. For research into the benefits of the approach he teaches, see Chapter 4.)

Restoring alignment and balance

Traditional healing practices such as *ayurveda* (the traditional medicine of India involving herbs and diet) and Chinese medicine, as well as more mainstream approaches like chiropractic and osteopathy, suggest that the body gets sick when it becomes unbalanced or misaligned. Meditation slows the mind to the speed of the breath, which restores balance and harmony to the body and facilitates healing. Besides, sitting up straight (see Chapter 8) aligns the spine and encourages the unimpeded flow of life-giving energy through the body, which promotes both physical and psychological well-being.

Opening and softening

If you're like many people, you tend to get impatient or upset with yourself when you're sick or hurting. You may even have strong judgments as though being ill is your fault. Unfortunately, these negative emotions may compound your suffering — and even amplify your illness — by causing you to tense up and contract. When you meditate regularly, you develop the skill of opening to your experience, however unpleasant, and softening around it instead of judging it or pushing it away.

Creating space for all your emotions

As you accept your experience in meditation, you create a welcoming environment in which your feelings can bubble up and release rather than be suppressed or acted out. (For more on meditating with challenging emotions, see Chapter 12.) Research suggests that unexpressed feelings locked in the body form focal points of tension and stress that may eventually contribute to the development of life-threatening illnesses such as cancer and heart disease. Besides, you naturally feel more enlivened — and therefore more healthy — when you can feel your feelings fully.

Harmony, joy, and well-being

Positive qualities like happiness, joy, peace, and well-being don't originate outside you in some other person or thing. Instead, they well up inside you naturally and spontaneously like water bubbling up from a spring. You simply have to create the proper internal environment, which is exactly what you do when you meditate. (Of course, you can always cultivate positive emotions like love and compassion, as I describe on the accompanying tracks and in Chapter 11.)

Western researchers have shown that these positive qualities correlate with a host of life-enhancing bodily responses, from lowered blood pressure and improved immune response to the release of natural painkillers called *beta-endorphins*. (For more on the health benefits of meditation, see Chapter 2.) As Ecclesiastes 30:5 puts it, "Gladness of heart is life to anyone; joy is what gives length of days" (*New Jerusalem Bible*).

Freedom from self-clinging and habitual patterns

Ultimately, it's the illusion (which everyone shares) of being a separate, isolated individual cut off from others and the rest of life that lies at the heart of all suffering and stress. According to the Tibetan scholar and meditation master Tulku Thondup, author of *The Healing Power of Mind,* "living in peace, free from emotional afflictions, and loosening our grip on 'self' is the ultimate medicine for both mental and physical health."

As you gradually begin to penetrate and let go of habitual patterns (which have deep roots in the body as well as the mind), you become less emotionally reactive (which reduces stress) and more positively (even joyfully) responsive to life as it unfolds. (For more on working with habitual patterns, see Chapter 12.)

Awakening to a spiritual dimension

Herbert Benson, MD, a professor at Harvard Medical School, developed the technique known as the Relaxation Response (see Chapter 2) on the basis of studies of people who repeated a simple word or phrase, known as a *mantra*. But over the years, he discovered that the more meaningful the mantra, the more effective the technique in relaxing the body and promoting healing. "If you truly believe in your personal philosophy or religious faith," he reported in *Beyond the Relaxation Response,* "you may well be capable of achieving remarkable feats of mind and body that [we] may only speculate about." In other words, you enhance the healing powers of meditation when you expand your awareness to include a spiritual dimension of being.

Meditation at the edge of life

Many teachers have written about the powerful role meditation can play in helping people bridge the chasm between life and death. In fact, some traditions, like Zen Buddhism, teach that one of the primary purposes of meditation practice is to prepare you for the ultimate transition.

Certainly, most traditions would agree that how you live helps to determine how you die. For example, if you tend to be fearful or angry in life, you're likely to be fearful or angry at death. And if you tend to be calm or loving or joyful, these qualities will probably fill your being when you die as well. Many traditions also believe that the moment of death itself can be a crucial factor in determining what happens next. (Of course, they tend to part company when it comes to describing what the next step may be!)

If you're concerned about the way you may die, you can prepare for death by using meditation to help bring more peace and harmony into your life right now. The meditations presented throughout this book teach skills that definitely come in handy when you approach the threshold between life and death.

Here are a few of the ways that meditation can help you (and those you love) die a more loving, conscious death. (*Remember:* Meditation may help make death more comfortable and less frightening, but there's no right or wrong way to do it. Everyone lives and dies in his or her own unique way.)

- **Staying present:** Needless to say, fear, regret, and other negative feelings may get magnified a thousand fold when you approach the ultimate unknown. By bringing your awareness back to your breath or some other object, you can help calm your mind and keep it from spiraling down into negativity.

- **Welcoming whatever arises:** The weeks, days, and moments leading up to death may be filled with painful sensations and difficult emotions and mind-states. When you've developed the capacity through meditation to be with your experience, whatever it may be, you're better prepared for this challenging time.

- **Opening your heart:** If you practice opening your heart to yourself and others (see Chapter 11), you'll be ready to access the love when you need it — and when could you possibly need it more? Many traditions teach that love helps bridge the chasm between this life and the next. Besides, people who die in love bestow the immeasurable legacy of love on those they leave behind.

- **Letting go:** When you keep returning to your breath or some other object of meditation, you become accustomed to letting go of your thoughts, emotions, preoccupations, likes, and dislikes — and ultimately, perhaps, even letting go of who you think you are. In Zen, they say that when you become adept at dying this way on your meditation cushion, the real death poses no problem at all. Or, as Stephen Levine puts it in *Healing into Life and Death,* "To let go of the last moment and enter wholeheartedly the next is to die into life, is to heal into death."

- **Trusting the deathless:** As you deepen your connection with *being* (as opposed to thinking or doing) through the practice of meditation, you may awaken to a spiritual or sacred dimension that infuses this life with meaning but at the same time transcends it. Whether you call this dimension true self or essential nature, God or spirit, or simply the One, you now know (rather than simply believe) that something far greater than your separate existence informs your life and survives your death. As you can imagine, this realization makes death far easier to face.

Besides preparing you to meet your own demise, meditation can teach you how to be a source of support for your loved ones and friends as they approach death. Just apply the principles listed here to the time you spend with them, either by sharing what you've discovered in your meditation (if they're open to hearing it) or by being present with them with as much love, awareness, trust, openness, and letting go as you can muster. (You can also ease their letting go by practicing the "Ahh breath" with them. To find out more about meditation and the process of dying, read *Healing into Life and Death* by Stephen Levine or *The Tibetan Book of Living and Dying* by Sogyal Rinpoche.)

Embracing the healing power of imagery

In her book *Staying Well with Guided Imagery,* psychotherapist and guided-imagery pioneer Belleruth Naparstek cites extensive research that establishes three basic principles behind the healing power of imagery. These principles help explain the effectiveness of the meditations provided in this chapter that use imagery extensively. (Incidentally, imagery may or may not involve visual images; if you're more kinesthetic or auditory, for example, you may hear or feel the "images" rather than see them.) Here are the three principles:

- ✔ **Your body responds to sensory images as though they were real.** If you're not sure what I mean, just recall the last time you had a sexual fantasy or reminisced about a vacation and had all the emotions and sensations of the actual event.

  In one study cited in Naparstek's book, 84 percent of subjects exposed to poison ivy had no reaction when, under hypnosis, they imagined the plant to be harmless. In other words, their bodies believed the images their minds evoked and didn't break out in a rash! Other studies have shown that patients can use positive imagery to measurably increase the numbers of immune response cells in their bloodstreams.

- ✔ **In the meditative state, you can heal, change, learn, and grow more rapidly.** Naparstek uses the term *altered state,* which refers (in her usage) to a calm, relaxed, but focused state of mind — precisely the state you cultivate in meditation. This principle also applies to problem-solving and performance enhancement: You can explore new behaviors, improve existing ones, and make tactical breakthroughs far more easily in a meditative state than you can in your ordinary frame of mind. (For more on meditation for performance enhancement, see the section "Meditation Can Enhance Your Performance at Work and Play" later in this chapter.)

✔ **Imagery gives you a sense of mastery in challenging circumstances, which reduces your stress and bolsters your self-esteem.** When you're struggling with a health problem or a difficult assignment at work, you may feel flustered and helpless if you believe you can't do anything to control the outcome. But if you know that you can use imagery to help your body heal or enhance your performance, you can regain your confidence and your hope in the future. Numerous studies have shown that people feel better and perform more effectively when they believe they have some control over their lives.

In addition to these principles, Naparstek adds that emotion amplifies the power of imagery. When you allow yourself to feel the images intensely as well as experience them fully in all your senses, you give them more power to heal and transform you.

Exploring six healing meditations

You don't have to do any special exercises to enjoy the health benefits of meditation. You just need to develop a consistent practice based on the instructions provided in this book (and on the accompanying tracks as well). But if you're struggling with a chronic health problem (or just want to improve your overall state of health), you may want to experiment with one or more of the meditations that follow.

You can add these meditations to your regular practice or do them exclusively for a period of time. With one exception, they use guided imagery to help you relax your body, reduce your stress, ease your suffering, enhance your sense of self-mastery, and mobilize your healing resources. (To find out more about how to use meditation to facilitate healing, read *Healing into Life and Death* by Stephen Levine or *The Healing Power of Mind* by Tulku Thondup.)

Peaceful place

Because this meditation relaxes the body quickly and easily, you can use it by itself to help facilitate healing or you can practice it as a preliminary exercise before the other healing visualizations provided in this section.

1. **Begin by sitting comfortably, closing your eyes, and taking a few deep breaths.**

2. **Imagine yourself in a safe, protected, peaceful place.**

   You may choose a place you know well (a place in nature, for example, such as a meadow, a forest, or a beach), a place you've visited once or twice before, or simply a place in your imagination.

3. **Take as much time as you need to imagine this peaceful place as vividly as you can, in all your senses.**

   Notice the colors, the shapes, the sounds, the light, the feeling of the air against your skin, the contact of your feet against the ground. Explore this special place to your heart's content.

4. **Allow yourself to rest in the feelings of comfort, safety, and tranquility this special place evokes.**

5. **Spend as much time here as you want.**

   When you're done, gradually return to the present moment and open your eyes, while continuing to enjoy the pleasant, positive feelings.

For detailed audio instructions, check out Track 12.

Inner smile

By smiling into your internal organs, you can infuse them with the healing energy of love. "In ancient China, the Taoists taught that a constant inner smile, a smile to oneself, insured health, happiness, and longevity," writes Mantak Chia in his book *Awakening Healing Energy through the Tao.* "Smiling to yourself is like basking in love: you become your own best friend."

Try the following meditation for cultivating your inner smile:

1. **Begin by closing your eyes, forming a half smile with your lips, and smiling into your eyes.**

   Feel the smile shine through your eyes. Taoists believe that relaxing the eyes calms the entire nervous system.

2. **When you feel your eyes filled with the vibrant energy of your smile, you can begin to send this energy down through your body.**

   If you're not sure how to "send energy," don't worry. Just imagine the energy moving, and it will! (Incidentally, the Taoists call this energy *chi,* as in the well-known martial arts *t'ai chi* and *chi kung,* and equate it with the life force.)

3. **Smile down into your jaw and tongue.**

   Like most people, you probably hold tension in your jaw. When your jaw relaxes, you may notice your whole body relaxing as well.

4. **Smile into your neck and throat and dissolve any tension there.**

5. **Let the relaxing energy of your smile flow down into your heart, filling it with love.**

6. **From your heart, allow the love to flow into your other internal organs in the following order, relaxing, softening, and rejuvenating them as it moves:**

   - Lungs

   - Liver (beneath your ribcage on the right side)

   - Kidneys (just below the ribcage in back, on either side of the spine)

   - Pancreas and spleen (in the center of your abdomen)

   When you finish sending love to these organs, rest your smile in your *t'an t'ien* (a point about 2 inches below your navel and about 1½ inches inside your body).

7. **Smile again into your eyes and then into your mouth.**

8. **Gather some saliva, swallow it, and allow your smile to follow it through your digestive system, spreading relaxation into your esophagus, stomach, small intestines, and colon.**

9. **Once again return your smile to your eyes and smile down the center of your spine, one vertebra at a time, until you reach your tailbone.**

   Be sure to have your back straight as you do this exercise.

10. **When you finish with your spine, rest your smile in your t'an t'ien again and notice how your body feels.**

    Rest in this feeling for a few minutes before resuming your normal activities.

When you get the knack of this exercise, you can do it in just a few minutes, if you want.

Taking your medicine

If you have an illness that requires you to take medication, you may find yourself swallowing the pills or enduring the treatments with a certain distaste, a certain judgment or aversion to being sick in the first place, as though you were somehow flawed or at fault for allowing your body to suffer. When you take your pills (or your injections) or have surgery with awareness, you can send love to your body along with the remedy and contribute immeasurably to its healing effect. (Even if you're not sick, you can take your vitamins or herbs with the same attitude.) The Sioux know this well: They call any act of love "good medicine."

1. **Begin by closing your eyes and holding the pills in your hand for a few moments.**

   Notice how they feel. Consider their weight and their texture.

2. **Consider that these pills have the power to help your body heal.**

   You may even feel some gratitude welling up in your heart. You are one of the fortunate ones: You have access to medical care and you have a health professional who prescribed these pills for you.

3. **Notice whether you feel any resistance to taking these pills.**

   You may feel fear, shame, or self-blame, for example. Allow these feelings to arise in your awareness, and meet them with kindness and compassion.

4. **Relax and soften your body as you prepare to receive these pills.**

5. **Gently and with awareness, put the pills into your mouth and wash them down with liquid.**

   Feel them moving down your throat into your stomach and radiating their healing potential there like the glow of a warm fire. Open your body to receive them.

6. **Imagine the medicine entering your bloodstream and reaching the parts that cry out for healing.**

   Send love and compassion to these parts along with the medicine.

7. **Feel the love and the medicine suffusing and healing these parts.**

   Imagine all disease and resistance dissolving. Let yourself be healed.

8. **Continue to sit quietly for a few minutes as you allow the medicine and the love to help you heal.**

By substituting the appropriate words, you can adapt this meditation for use with injections, surgery, and other necessary medical procedures.

Healing with light

Just as you can help to purify and eliminate habitual patterns by invoking the power of spiritual beings or energies (see Chapter 12), you can access the same source of power and light to help your body heal. After all, physical illness and emotional suffering are just different facets of the same basic problem, different ways you contract away from your essential wholeness and health.

Here's an exercise for directing the light to the places inside your body that cry out for healing:

1. **Begin by sitting down and meditating in your usual way for several minutes.**

   If you don't have a usual way, you can find one in Chapter 7. Or just sit quietly, take a few deep breaths, and allow your body to relax a little on each exhalation.

2. **Imagine a sphere of white light suspended about a foot above your head and slightly in front of you.**

   As you look more closely, you may notice that this sphere takes the form of a being who embodies all the positive, healing energy you need. Perhaps it's a spiritual figure like Jesus or Mother Mary or the Dalai Lama; or possibly it's a being or object from nature, such as the sun, the moon, the wind, the ocean, a tree, a flower, or a mountain.

3. **Imagine this sphere radiating light in all directions to the farthest corners of the universe.**

   As it does so, it draws the energy of all the benevolent forces that support your healing back into the sphere.

4. **Imagine this positive, healing energy shining from the sphere like the light of a thousand suns streaming down through your body.**

   Imagine the light eliminating all toxicity and stress, all disharmony and disease, and replacing them with radiance, vitality, and health. In particular, you can imagine directing this light like a beacon to all the places you know to be involved in your illness or distress. Imagine the light dissolving any contractions, replacing them with openness and ease, and flooding any weakness with power and strength.

5. **Continue to imagine this powerful, healing light infusing every cell and molecule of your being, leaving you healthy, peaceful, and strong.**

6. **Imagine this luminous sphere gradually descending into your heart, where it continues to radiate this powerful, healing light.**

7. **Imagine yourself as a luminous being with a sphere of light in your heart that constantly radiates health, harmony, peace, and vitality — first to every cell and particle of your own being and then, through you, to every other being in every direction.**

   Carry the feeling of vitality and strength that this exercise evokes throughout the rest of your day.

Ahhh breath

If you're looking for a way to support a loved one in his or her healing process, beyond buying flowers, cooking a meal, or helping with chores, you can try the partner meditation in this section, which is drawn from the work of Stephen Levine, whose many books have helped thousands of people to live (and die) with greater love and awareness. In *Healing into Life and Death,* he writes, "This is one of the simplest and most powerful exercises we know to give confidence that the ever-healed is never far away — to sense the heart we all share, the one mind of being." You can also use it to bring greater intimacy to your relationships with parents, children, partners, and friends. (If the other person feels up to it, take some time to receive the ahhh breath as well as give it.)

1. **Before you begin, describe the exercise to your partner and make sure she feels comfortable doing it with you.**

   Let her know that she can end it at any time by simply raising her arm.

2. **Begin by having the person receiving the ahhh breath lie down on the floor or a bed.**

   You sit at her side, near her torso but not touching her.

3. **Encourage the other person to relax and breathe comfortably while you observe the coming and going of her breath.**

   Now drop all verbal communication until the exercise is over.

4. **Begin to synchronize your breath with her breath.**

   When she inhales, you inhale. When she exhales, you exhale. Remain attuned to the ever-changing rhythm of her breath and adjust your own rhythm accordingly.

5. **After eight or ten breaths breathed in this way, start making the sound ahhh on the exhalation, softly and gently but audibly.**

   With each repetition, allow the sound to come from an even deeper place in your body until the ahhh originates in the bottom of your belly. Inhale together in silence, and then intone ahhh on the exhale. (Your partner doesn't have to repeat the sound.)

6. **Continue this shared meditation for as long as you both feel comfortable.**

   When you're done, take some time to talk with your partner about your experiences. This shared practice may elicit any number of responses. Some people relax more deeply than ever before. Others notice some fear of letting go or getting so close to another person. Still others glimpse a deep peace beneath all the usual turmoil and concern. Whatever you or your partner experience, you can welcome it (as much as possible) with openness and nonjudgmental acceptance.

Working with pain

Like death, pain is a complex topic that definitely deserves a chapter (or even a book) of its own. Most people never simply experience physical pain just the way it is — a set of intense physical sensations. Instead, they tend to react to their pain — to tighten and contract around it and to struggle to get rid of it — and weave a story about it that they superimpose on the experience. They say, "Why me? What did I do to deserve it?" or "I can't stand it, I won't be able to make it through." In the process, they prolong their pain and turn it into suffering. (For more on the difference between pain and suffering, see Chapter 6.)

The secret to coping with pain is to soften around it rather than resist it and to expand your awareness (and your heart) to include it rather than tighten and contract. After all, if you can't actually get rid of the pain or block it out of your mind, you may as well welcome it — and even (dare I say) make friends with it. But you can't do this readily without considerable practice, which is why the meditations taught throughout this book provide the best preparation for working with pain. (You can begin with deep relaxation as described in Chapter 7. For more suggestions on dealing with pain, see Chapter 8.)

You can begin by opening and softening in relation to the small aches and pains you experience when you sit in meditation and gradually work up to the larger pains, such as a bad headache, a sore throat, or a back spasm.

You can also do the moment-to-moment work of challenging the story your mind keeps telling you and returning to the bare sensation of the pain itself, which is inevitably more bearable than the worst-case scenario your mind fabricates. In his book *Full Catastrophe Living*, Jon Kabat-Zinn, who works with people in chronic pain at the Stress-Reduction Clinic at the University of Massachusetts Medical Center, suggests going directly into the sensations of the pain and asking yourself the question, "How bad is it right now, in this very moment?" Most of the time, he counsels, you'll find that the pain is tolerable after all.

Intense pain also has a tendency to flush out the unresolved issues and unfelt emotions of a lifetime, so don't be surprised if you need to turn to Chapter 12 for some guidance on how to work with difficult mind-states. Ultimately, pain can be a powerful teacher, forcing you to deepen your meditation and open to the present moment as never before.

Great Mother

Many meditative traditions feature an archetypal feminine figure who nurtures and heals and carries the pain of others. In the Christian tradition, she's Mary, mother of sorrows. In Buddhism, she's called Kuan Yin, who hears and responds to the cries of the world. Patterned after the good mother who loves her children unconditionally, the Great Mother can be invoked in whatever form feels most comfortable for you. She has the capacity to ease your pain with her compassion and to help you heal into wholeness.

1. **Begin by sitting comfortably, closing your eyes, and taking a few deep breaths, relaxing a little with each exhalation.**

   Allow your belly to soften.

2. **Bring your attention to your heart and notice any pain or suffering you may be holding there.**

   Gently breathe with awareness into this painful place in your heart.

3. **Imagine the presence of an infinitely compassionate feminine figure — the Great Mother.**

   Feel her arms surrounding you and holding you in her warm, supportive, nurturing embrace. You can let go completely and relax into her arms. No need to hold yourself up anymore.

4. **With each inhalation, breathe her love into your heart in the form of warm, liquid light.**

   With each exhalation, breathe out all your suffering and disease in the form of black soot, which she naturally receives and transforms into light.

5. **If you feel moved to share your pain with her in the form of words or tears, go ahead.**

   Her infinite heart is filled with compassion; she welcomes your suffering as though it were her own.

6. **Continue to surrender yourself into her arms and receive her love into your heart as you let go of your suffering and sorrow.**

   With each breath, you feel more complete, more whole, more healed. Gradually, you feel your own heart dissolve into hers.

7. **Spend as much time as you need in the presence of the Great Mother.**

   When you're done, imagine her entering you and filling you with her presence. You are the Great Mother (whether you're a man or a woman) — her heart is your heart. From this heart, you can radiate out the warm light of compassion and healing to all beings everywhere. May all beings be happy, peaceful, and free from suffering.

Making Great Waves

As I was thumbing through an old Zen text, I came across a true story that exemplifies the power of meditation for performance enhancement. It seems that a sumo wrestler named Great Waves was so powerful and adept that he could defeat even his teacher, but in public he lost both his confidence and his matches. He decided to seek out a local Zen master for guidance.

After listening to the wrestler's story, the master told him to spend the night in the temple in meditation, imagining himself to be the "great waves" of his name. "Imagine sweeping everything before you with your power," advised the master. "Then you will be the great wrestler you were destined to be."

Throughout the night, Great Waves focused his attention on the image of the powerful water. Gradually, his mind became one-pointed, and by morning he had become the indomitable ocean itself. From then on, the story concludes, no one in all of Japan could defeat him.

Meditation Can Enhance Your Performance at Work and Play

For many of the same reasons why meditation helps to facilitate healing, it also enhances performance. It relaxes your body and reduces stress and anxiety, which allows you to function more effectively. It promotes positive mind-states, such as love, joy, and well-being; and it encourages the flow of life-energy through the body, which in turn promotes self-confidence and a sense of power and effectiveness. And it awakens a deeper connection with a source of meaning and purpose, which inspires and uplifts you in whatever you do.

REMEMBER

Meditation also teaches you how to cultivate certain other qualities and skills that naturally contribute to making you better at your favorite endeavor, whether it's sports or business, gardening or studying, or simply washing the dishes or sweeping the floor. Here's a brief list of qualities and skills that you can cultivate:

✔ **Increased focus and concentration:** This one's a no-brainer: As you become adept at staying on task as you follow your breaths or recite your mantra, you can easily transfer this skill to working at your computer or playing tennis with friends. For the benefits of focus, just look at great athletes like Tiger Woods, Lance Armstrong, or Annika Sorenstam.

✔ **Minimal distractions:** This little benefit is the flip side of the preceding one: The more regularly you meditate, the more quickly distractions fade into the background as your mind settles down and becomes one-pointed. Needless to say, you work or play more effectively without a million irrelevant thoughts chattering away inside your head. As Yogi Berra once said about baseball, "How can you think and hit at the same time?"

✔ **Being in the moment, free from expectations:** Even though you may have a particular goal in mind — for example, winning the race, completing the project, landing the ball in a tiny cup 300 yards away — the paradox is that you're more likely to succeed if you set aside your expectations and keep your attention focused on the precise movements or tasks you need to execute right now. Former Los Angeles Lakers coach Phil Jackson calls it "trusting the moment."

✔ **Enhanced mental and perceptual clarity:** One of the fortuitous side effects of keeping your mind on the moment is that your senses become sharper and your mind quicker and more attuned to subtle details — which, needless to say, comes in quite handy when you're trying to do something well.

✔ **Greater endurance and longer attention span:** As you gradually increase the length of your meditations from 10 to 15 to 20 minutes or more, you gradually build your power to pay attention longer. As a result, you may find that you don't get so easily burned out or discouraged when you turn your attention to an extended work project or other demanding activity.

✔ **Flow experience:** In sports, those moments or extended periods when you feel totally in synch with your body and your surroundings are referred to as *the zone.* (In other areas of life they're called *flow.*) Time seems to slow down, feelings of well-being and enjoyment increase, you see everything clearly as (or even before) it transpires, and you know exactly what you need to do next. By cultivating your powers of concentration in meditation, you develop the ability to enter the flow, or the zone, more easily in every situation. (For more on flow, see Chapters 1 and 16.)

✔ **The capacity to see things multidimensionally:** In meditation, you practice witnessing or observing your experience without getting lost in the details. This more expanded, global awareness naturally allows you to step back and see the whole picture, which can be extraordinarily useful when you're trying to solve a problem or scope out the opposing team, or just evaluate and improve your performance. Some great athletes even report that they can see the whole game as though from above when they're playing.

✔ **Mindfulness of self-defeating behaviors:** When you expand your awareness in your meditation to include sensations and mental processes, you begin to notice repetitive patterns of thinking and feeling that cause you stress or inhibit your full self-expression (see Chapter 13). By extending this mindfulness to your performance (at work or play), you can catch self-defeating patterns and replace them with more productive, effective alternatives.

✔ **Self-acceptance and freedom from self-criticism:** Nothing dampens enthusiasm and inhibits effective performance more than the tendency most people have to put themselves down, especially under pressure. Through regular meditation, you practice accepting yourself the way you are and noticing the judgments as they arise. Then, when the going gets tough, you can use your meditation skills to gently defuse the self-criticism as you focus on doing your personal best.

✔ **Compassion and teamwork:** In his best-selling book *Sacred Hoops,* Phil Jackson describes how he forged a world-champion basketball team based on the principles and lessons he learned in his study of Zen meditation. In addition to focus, mindfulness, and the other factors listed here, Jackson emphasizes the role of compassion (which can be deliberately cultivated in meditation; see Chapter 11). "As my [meditation] practice matured," he writes, "I began to appreciate the importance of playing with an open heart. Love is the force that ignites the spirit and binds teams together."

Besides the benefits of a regular meditation practice listed here, you can also do meditations that are specifically designed to improve performance. In particular, you can use guided imagery to help you create a positive mind-state and rehearse performances before they occur. (For more on guided imagery, see the section "The healing power of imagery" earlier in this chapter.) In her book *Staying Well with Guided Imagery,* Belleruth Naparstek calls the first kind of guided imagery *feeling-state imagery* and the second *end-state imagery.* (In the sidebar "Making Great Waves" earlier in this chapter, the sumo wrestler uses a third, called *metaphoric imagery,* which actually incorporates elements of the other two.)

You've no doubt read about the Olympic and professional athletes who use both feeling and end-state imagery in their training regimens. In the following two sections, you have an opportunity to practice first a generic feeling-state performance meditation and then a meditation designed to help you execute your performance successfully.

Enjoying past success

The following meditation relaxes your body, lifts your spirits, and puts you in a positive frame of mind for an upcoming performance. If possible, begin practicing it several days or a week or more before the performance so you have ample time to prepare.

1. **Begin by doing the "Peaceful place" meditation described earlier in this chapter.**

   Or you can just sit comfortably, close your eyes, and take a few deep breaths, relaxing a little on each exhalation. Spend several minutes breathing and relaxing in this way.

2. **Recall a time when you successfully completed the same or a similar performance.**

If you've never done anything like this before, just remember a time when you did something especially well and successfully.

3. **Take some time to remember this successful performance as vividly and with as much sensory detail as you possibly can.**

   Where were you? What were you wearing? What exactly were you doing? How did your body feel? Who else was there? What kinds of feelings did this successful performance evoke?

4. **When you're fully immersed in the memory, and your positive feelings reach their peak, find a physical gesture that underscores these feelings.**

   For example, you may touch two fingers together or rest your hand on your belly.

5. **Gradually let go of the memory, return to ordinary consciousness, and open your eyes.**

6. **Practice this meditation several times between now and the actual performance, each time repeating the physical gesture.**

7. **As you begin the actual performance, close your eyes for a moment and repeat the physical gesture.**

   You'll be amazed to discover that the positive feelings return in a flash.

Rehearsing peak performance

It's one thing to be in a positive frame of mind when you perform, but it's quite another to know exactly what you're doing. When you're feeling relaxed, you can apply the principles of meditation to fine-tune your performance before-hand so you're peaking when you step up to the proverbial plate.

Here's a meditation similar to the exercises athletes use. To quote Jack Nicklaus from his book *Golf My Way:* "I never hit a shot, not even in practice, without a very sharp, in-focus picture of it in my head." Be sure to give yourself plenty of time to practice before the actual performance.

1. **Begin by doing the "Peaceful place" meditation described earlier in this chapter.**

   Or you can just sit comfortably, close your eyes, and take a few deep breaths, relaxing a little on each exhalation. Spend several minutes breathing and relaxing in this way.

2. **Imagine yourself executing your performance perfectly from beginning to end.**

   Imagine it as vividly and with as much sensory detail as you possibly can. If you're rehearsing a tennis match, for example, feel the racket in your hand and your shoes against the court; feel your arm lifting, reaching back, and arcing forward as you serve; feel the contact of the ball against the racket; and so on.

Studies have shown that kinesthetic rehearsals (in which you feel your body going through the motions) are nearly as effective as actual practice in improving performance in sports and other physical activities. If you're rehearsing a presentation at work, imagine standing in front of the group, speaking articulately and cogently, getting the important points across, and so on.

3. **Include a feeling-state dimension by noticing how good you feel as you move through the performance.**

   You may feel exhilaration, excitement, power, or enjoyment. If you notice any fear or apprehension, pause for a moment, take a few deep breaths, do whatever you usually do to allay your fear, and then resume your rehearsal.

4. **Take as much time as you need to imagine yourself executing the performance perfectly.**

   If you notice any mistakes, stop and correct them and then repeat the performance correctly. At first, your rehearsal may take as long as the actual performance. After you've clarified all the details, you can abbreviate subsequent rehearsals if you have only limited time.

5. **Be sure to practice this exercise at least several times before the actual performance.**

   Immediately before the performance, stop for a moment, close your eyes, and run through an abbreviated rehearsal.

Enjoying the dance of yes

Take ten minutes to notice the subtle (and not-so-subtle) ways your mind keeps saying *no* to life — suppressing your feelings and impulses, judging or even rejecting other people, refusing to accept the way things actually are. For example, you may feel sadness arising but push it away and refuse to feel it. Or you may look in the mirror but edit what you see, either by criticizing yourself for your appearance or refusing to see your imperfections. Or perhaps you close your heart to your loved ones because they don't live up to your expectations.

You may be amazed to discover how much energy your mind consumes by refusing to accept what's actually happening right in front of you. Instead, for the next ten minutes, just say

yes. Whatever you experience, whomever you meet, however life presents itself to you, notice your tendency to resist or deny and instead say yes. Yes to your feelings, yes to your partner or your kids, yes to your body and your face, yes to your life. As much as possible, keep an open, spacious, attentive mind. Of course, you're welcome to change what you don't like, but take a moment to say yes to it first.

You may be so accustomed to saying no that you don't know how to say yes at first. So feel free to experiment. Repeating the word *yes* to yourself can help get you started. Maybe you'll end up enjoying the dance of yes so much that you extend it to every area of your life. Yes, yes, yes!

Part V
The Part of Tens

The 5th Wave   By Rich Tennant

"Here's a tip – if you hear yourself snoring, you're meditating too deeply."

In this part . . .

You find quick answers and brief meditations. The next time you're stumped when Aunt Jenny or Cousin Dave asks a question about meditation or wants you to prove it may be good for what ails them; the next time you come up with a few questions yourself; the next time you're in the mood to meditate but don't want to thumb through the rest of this book, check out the gems in this part.

Chapter 19

Ten Commonly Asked Questions about Meditation

In This Chapter

▶ Discovering answers to your most pressing meditation questions

▶ Finding out more about the basics of meditation

*W*hen most folks first consider taking up the practice of meditation, they usually have a few questions they want to have answered — and when they get started, they come up with a few more. If you have questions, you've come to the right place. In this chapter, I provide some brief answers to ten of the most popular meditation questions. For more detailed answers, check out the rest of this book.

Will Meditation Make Me Too Relaxed to Succeed at Work or School?

In the old days, people used to associate meditation with impractical alternative lifestyles, and they feared they might morph into a laid-back hippie or navel-gazing yogi if they dared to sit quietly for a few minutes. Fortunately, times have changed, and everywhere you look you can find articles touting the scientifically proven benefits of meditation. The fact is that meditation teaches you how to focus your mind and minimize distractions so you can actually get things done more effectively. Besides, when you're tense, you can't do anything particularly well. Luckily, meditation helps you relax your body and reduce your stress so you can make better (and more enjoyable) use of your time.

As I explain in more detail in Chapter 1, most meditation practices are a blend of concentration and receptive awareness. With concentration, you discover how to stabilize your attention on a particular object, such as your breath or some other bodily sensation. Eventually, you can extend this concentration to work or sports or any other activity. In fact, psychologists have a word for the total absorption that comes with intense concentration; they call it *flow,* a state of mind in which time slows down, distractions fall away, and activity becomes effortless and supremely enjoyable.

With receptive awareness, you practice expanding your attention to include the full range of your experiences, both inner and outer. The two together — concentration and receptive awareness — combine to create the kind of relaxed alertness you see in great performers, athletes, and martial artists. Now, you couldn't accuse them of being spaced out or ineffectual, could you?

How Can I Find the Time to Meditate in My Busy Schedule?

Ah yes, the perennial issue: time! Well, the great thing about meditation is that it doesn't really take all that much time. As soon as you pick up the basics (by reading this book, of course), you can begin by practicing for five or ten minutes each day. Mornings are generally best, at least to start. You may want to sandwich a little quiet time between brushing your teeth and taking a shower. Or if you're an early bird, you can enjoy the precious moments of stillness before the rest of the family wakes up.

Whatever time slot works best for you, the most important thing is to meditate regularly — every day if possible, give or take a day here or there (and some time to sleep late on Sundays). The reason for this recommendation is not to turn you into an automaton, but rather to give you an opportunity to enjoy the wonderful benefits of meditation, such as reduced stress and greater focus. Like lifting weights or practicing a musical instrument, meditation doesn't really have an impact unless you keep it up and keep it regular.

As you meditate consistently over the days and weeks, you may begin to notice little changes in your life, such as moments of ease or peace or harmony you may not have experienced since childhood, if ever. And the more you benefit from your meditation practice, the more you're going to feel motivated to carve out the time (and perhaps even extend the niche from 10 minutes to 15 or 20).

Can I Meditate in a Chair or Lying Down Instead of Cross-Legged on the Floor?

Yes. you can meditate in many different positions. Traditional meditation postures include sitting, standing, walking, lying down, and moving in particular patterns (for example, t'ai chi or Sufi dancing). Basically, any position that you can comfortably sustain is appropriate for meditation. (To find a posture that works for you, check out Chapter 8.) Of course, lying down has its downside: You're more likely to fall asleep. So you may have to make a special effort (without getting tense about it, that is) to stay alert and focused. For obvious reasons, you're better off lying on a mat or carpet rather than on your bed!

More important than whether you sit, lie, or stand for meditation is what you do with your back. Slumping forward or tilting to the side so your body fights against gravity may eventually prove painful and make it difficult to sustain your practice over weeks and months. Instead, you can get into the habit of extending your spine (as explained in Chapter 8), which contributes to good posture in your other activities as well.

What Should I Do about the Restlessness or Discomfort I Feel while Meditating?

You may find it comforting to realize that you're not alone if you feel restless or uncomfortable when meditating. Everyone experiences agitation or discomfort in his or her meditation from time to time (or even often). In fact, meditation acts like a mirror that reflects you back to you. Believe it or not, that's one of its virtues. When you stop your busy life for a few minutes and sit quietly, you may suddenly notice the nervous energy and frenzied thinking that have been stressing you out. Welcome to the world of meditation!

Initially, meditation involves focusing your attention on some object (like your breathing or a word or phrase known as a *mantra*) and gently bringing your attention back like a mischievous puppy whenever it wanders off. (For basic meditation instructions, see Chapter 7 or listen to Track 4.) Gradually, you may notice that your restlessness and discomfort begin to settle down by themselves.

When your concentration deepens, you can expand your awareness to include first your sensations and then your thoughts and emotions. At this stage, you can begin to explore, make friends with, and ultimately accept your restlessness and discomfort. Though this process may not be an easy one, it has broad implications because it teaches you the resilience and peace of mind to accept unavoidable difficulties in every area of your life. (For more on making friends with your experience, see Chapter 12.)

What Should I Do if I Keep Falling Asleep while I Meditate?

Like restlessness, sleepiness is a common roadblock on the journey of meditation. (For more on roadblocks, see Chapter 13.) Even the great meditators of the past reported struggling with sleep. Some of them even devised extreme measures for staying awake, such as tying their hair to the ceiling or meditating on the edge of a cliff. Talk about determination!

Ordinary folks like you and me have the option of using gentler means to keep ourselves awake and alert while meditating. First, you may want to explore the sleepiness a little. Where do you experience it in your body? Is it just mental dullness, or are you physically tired as well? Perhaps you should be napping rather than meditating!

If you decide to keep going, you can try opening your eyes wide and sitting up as straight as possible to rouse your energy. If you still feel sleepy, splash some cold water on your face or try meditating while standing or walking. In any case, sleepiness doesn't necessarily have to prevent you from meditating. After all, sleepy meditation is better than no meditation at all.

How Do I Know if I'm Meditating the Right Way?

This question reflects the goal-oriented perfectionist in you who monitors your activities to make sure you're doing them right. The great thing about meditation is that you can't do it wrong, short of not doing it at all. (In fact, it's the perfectionist that causes most of your stress. And the point of meditation is to reduce stress, not intensify it.)

When you meditate, set aside the perfectionist as much as you can and keep gently returning to your focus in the here and now. For detailed meditation instructions, check out the other chapters in this book, especially Chapter 7. Or you can listen to Track 4.

The experiences that may arise as you meditate — sleepiness, busy thoughts, physical discomfort, restlessness, deep emotion — don't indicate that you're going astray. Quite the contrary; they're the grist for the mill of your meditation, the old habits and patterns that get transformed as you deepen your practice. (For more on transforming old patterns, see Chapter 12.)

As for knowing when your meditation is "working," you probably won't notice any flashing lights or sudden jolts of energy. Instead, you may recognize subtler shifts. For example, your friends or loved ones may remark that you seem less irritable or stressed out than before. Or you may find that you're less reactive in difficult situations. Again, don't look for results, or, like the proverbial watched pot, your meditation may never boil. Just trust in the process and let the changes take care of themselves.

Can I Meditate while I'm Driving My Car or Sitting at My Computer?

Although you can't practice formal meditation while you're engaged in ordinary activities, you can practice doing things meditatively. (For more on how to meditate in everyday life, see Chapter 17.) During your daily periods of silent meditation, you discover how to stay present as much as possible amidst the welter of distracting thoughts, emotions, and sensations. Then, when you slip behind the wheel of your car or sit down in front of your computer, you can apply at least some of the same mindful, attentive presence to negotiate rush-hour traffic or prepare a report. You'll find that you accomplish the activity with less effort and strain and enjoy yourself more.

It's like practicing a sport such as tennis. First, you need to work on your backhand again and again. Then, when you get into a match with a friend, you know exactly what to do, even though the situation is more challenging and complex.

Do I Have to Give Up My Religious Beliefs to Meditate?

Definitely not. You can apply the basic principles and techniques of meditation (as taught in this book and on the accompanying tracks) to any spiritual or religious tradition or orientation. In fact, many people find that meditation methods with Eastern roots actually deepen their connection to their own Western faith by supplementing prayer and belief with some direct experience of the love and presence of God.

Meditation simply involves pausing in your busy life, taking a few deep breaths, sitting quietly, and turning your attention inward. What you discover is not Zen or Sufi or Hindu, but *you* — complete with all your beliefs, affiliations, and personality traits!

What Should I Do if My Loved Ones Don't Support My Meditation Practice?

If your loved ones are openly antagonistic, you may need to meditate on the sly or with an established group or class outside your home. But if they're merely resistant or tend to interrupt you at inopportune moments or demand your attention when you're just about to get quiet, you may want to talk with them and explain your interest in meditation. Reassure them that you don't love them any less just because you're spending some time in silence each day. Show them this book — or even lend them a copy so they can read about meditation for themselves. After you've been practicing for a while, they may begin to notice that you're more enjoyable to be around — more relaxed, more attentive, less distracted and stressed out — and their resistance may gradually melt away. Who knows? One day they may decide to join you and give meditation a try themselves.

Can Meditation Actually Improve My Health?

Yes, meditation can make you healthier! Researchers have published hundreds of studies investigating the health benefits of meditation, and the results consistently indicate that people who meditate regularly have better health than those who don't. (For more on meditation research, see Chapter 4. For a summary of the health benefits of meditation, see Chapter 2.)

By bringing your mind and body into harmony and increasing your overall level of peace, relaxation, and well-being, regular meditation facilitates the release of life-enhancing chemicals into the bloodstream and bolsters the immune response. You can also practice specific techniques developed over the centuries by the great meditators of the past (and adapted for contemporary Westerners) that are especially designed to stimulate the healing process. (To find out more about meditation and healing, check out Chapter 18.)

Chapter 20

Ten Favorite All-Purpose Meditations

. . . .

In This Chapter

▶ Getting basic instruction in mindfulness, mantra, and lovingkindness meditations

▶ Using meditation for healing, grounding, and inner peace

. . . .

*H*ere are ten of my all-time favorite meditations, drawn from the pages of this book. I've chosen them not only because I enjoy them but also because they provide a range of different practices for you to sample — from elaborate visualizations to basic mindfulness techniques. (For more on mindfulness, see Chapter 7.) Feel free to experiment with these meditations straight off the page, if you're so inclined. With regular practice, they offer a taste of the meditative experience. If you start hungering for the whole meal, go ahead and thumb through the rest of the book.

Practicing Relaxation

To reduce your stress and reap the other benefits of relaxation, try practicing this simple exercise for 15 or 20 minutes each day. Known as the *relaxation response,* it was developed in the 1970s by Herbert Benson, MD, a professor at Harvard Medical School, based on research into the benefits of Transcendental Meditation (TM).

1. **Find a spot where you can sit quietly and undisturbed.**

   For more on creating an environment that's conducive to meditation, see Chapter 9.

2. **Sit in a position that you can comfortably maintain for the duration of your meditation.**

For a complete discussion of sitting posture in meditation, including diagrams, see Chapter 8.

3. **Choose an object to concentrate on.**

   This "object" can be a visual symbol (such as a geometric shape) or a special syllable, word, or phrase, known as a *mantra,* that you repeat again and again. Objects with deep personal or spiritual meaning are especially effective. As much as possible, keep your attention focused on this object; when you get distracted, come back to your focus. (If your object is internal, close your eyes.)

   For more on mantras, see Chapters 3 and 14. For guidance in practicing mantra meditation, listen to Track 2.

4. **Maintain a receptive attitude.**

   Let thoughts, images, and feelings pass through without trying to hold or interpret them. Resist the temptation to evaluate your progress; just gently bring your attention back when it wanders.

With regular practice, you may gradually begin to notice that your body is more relaxed and your mind is more peaceful. These are just a few of the many benefits of meditation.

Following Your Breath

Drawn from the mindfulness tradition of Buddhism, this basic meditation practice develops concentration and uses the breath to teach you how to stay present from moment to moment, no matter where you are or what you may be doing.

For more-complete instructions (and more about mindfulness), see Chapter 7. Or you can also listen to Track 4.

1. **Begin by finding a comfortable sitting position that you can hold for 10 or 15 minutes.**

   Take a few deep breaths and exhale slowly. Without trying to control your breath in any way, allow it to find its own natural depth and rhythm. Always breathe through your nose (unless you can't for some reason).

2. **Allow your attention to focus either on the sensation of your breath coming and going through your nostrils or on the rising and falling of your belly as you breathe.**

Although you're welcome to alternate your focus from one session to the next, sticking with a single focus for the entire meditation is best. Eventually, you're better off using the same focus each time you meditate.

3. **Give your full attention to the coming and going of your breath.**

   Pay attention to your breath the way a mother tracks the movements of her young child: lovingly yet persistently, softly yet precisely, and with relaxed yet focused awareness.

4. **When you realize that your mind has wandered off and you're engrossed in planning, thinking, or daydreaming, gently but firmly bring your mind back to your breath.**

   Thoughts and images will almost certainly continue to skitter and swirl through your mind as you meditate, but don't worry. Just patiently and persistently keep coming back to your breath. If you find it virtually impossible to follow your breath, you may want to begin with counting your breaths (see Chapter 7).

5. **Continue this simple (but not easy!) exercise for the duration of your meditation.**

   With repeated practice, you may find that your mind settles down more quickly and that you're more present and focused in other areas of your life as well.

Walking Meditation

If you don't feel like sitting still, you can try meditating while you walk. (For guidance in walking meditation, listen to Track 6 on your CD.) A time-honored technique that's practiced in monasteries and meditation centers throughout the world, walking meditation is a great way to discover how to translate the focus you learn on your cushion or chair to the ordinary world of movement and activity. If the weather allows, by all means walk outside. Or you can just walk back and forth in your house, if you like.

1. **Begin by walking at your usual pace, following your breath as you walk.**

2. **Coordinate your breathing with your walking.**

   For example, you can take three steps for each inhalation and three steps for each exhalation. If you want to change the speed of your walking, just change the number of steps per breath. But maintain the same pace each time you walk. (If your inhalations and exhalations are different lengths, just adapt your walking accordingly.)

3. **In addition to your breathing, be aware of your feet and legs as you lift and move them.**

Notice the contact of your feet with the ground or floor. Gaze ahead of you, with your eyes lowered at a 45-degree angle. If you find it too complicated to follow your breathing and be aware of your feet at the same time, just choose one focus or the other and stick with it. Be relaxed, easy, and comfortable as you walk.

4. **Enjoy your steady, mindful walking for as long as you want.**

If your attention wanders or you start to hurry, gently bring your attention back to your walking.

Mindful Eating

Did you ever finish a meal and wonder what happened to the food? Well, here's a meditation for paying attention to what you're putting into your mouth. Not only will you enjoy your food as never before, but mindful eating will facilitate your digestion by reducing the tension or stress you bring to the table. (You probably won't want to eat as meditatively as this all the time, but you can still apply a little mindfulness to every meal, no matter how informal.)

1. **Before you begin eating, take a few moments to appreciate your food.**

You may want to reflect on the earth and the sunshine that gave life to this food and the people and effort that brought it to your table. Or you can express your thanks to God or spirit. Or you can simply sit silently and feel grateful for what you have. If you're eating with others, you may want to hold hands, smile at one another, or connect in some other way.

2. **Bring your awareness to your hand as you lift the first bite of food to your lips.**

You can experiment with the custom in certain monastic traditions of eating more slowly than usual. Or just eat at your usual speed, but be as mindful as you can.

3. **Be fully aware as the first morsel of food enters your mouth and floods your taste buds with sensations.**

Notice the tendency of your mind to judge the flavor: "It's too spicy or salty" or "It's not what I expected." Notice any emotions that get stirred up: disappointment, relief, irritation, or joy. Be aware of any ripples of pleasure or warmth or other physical sensations. Enjoy your food!

4. **If you talk while you eat, notice how the talking affects you.**

Do certain topics cause you to tense up or give you indigestion? Does the talk take you away from the enjoyment of your meal, or can you have both?

5. **Stay mindful of each mouthful as you gradually eat your meal.**

This step is probably the hardest because most people have a tendency to space out when they know how their food tastes. But you can continue to enjoy the taste freshly, bite after bite. (If you get distracted, stop and breathe for a moment or two before starting to eat again.)

Cultivating Lovingkindness

This meditation helps you open your heart and initiate a flow of unconditional love (also known as *lovingkindness*) to yourself and others. You may want to begin with five or ten minutes of some basic meditation, such as the relaxation response or following your breath, to deepen and stabilize your concentration.

For a more complete version of this meditation, turn to Chapter 11, or listen to Track 7.

1. **Begin by closing your eyes, taking a few deep breaths, and relaxing your body.**

2. **Remember a time when you felt deeply loved.**

   Spend a few minutes dwelling on this memory and allowing your heart to respond. Notice the gratitude and love that arise for the person who loved you.

3. **Allow these loving feelings to overflow and gradually suffuse your whole being.**

   Allow yourself to be filled with love. You may also want to express the wishes and intentions that underlie this love. For example, you may say to yourself, as the Buddhists do, "May I be happy. May I be peaceful. May I be free from suffering." Feel free to use whatever words seem right for you. As the recipient, be sure to take in the love as well as express it.

4. **When you feel complete with yourself for now, imagine extending this lovingkindness to a loved one or dear friend, using similar words to express your intentions.**

   Don't hurry. As you extend the love, allow yourself to feel it as much as you can, rather than merely imagine it.

5. **Extend this lovingkindness from your heart to all your loved ones and friends.**

   Again, take your time.

6. **Extend this lovingkindness to all people and all beings everywhere.**

   May all beings be happy. May all beings be peaceful. May all beings be free from suffering.

Softening Your Belly

Stephen Levine, an American meditation teacher and author of a number of excellent books on healing with awareness, counsels that the state of your belly reflects the state of your heart. By consciously softening your belly again and again, you can let go and open to the tender feelings in your heart.

1. **Begin by sitting comfortably and taking a few deep breaths.**

2. **Allow your awareness to settle into your body.**

3. **Allow your awareness to descend to your belly as you gently soften this area of your body.**

   Consciously let go of any tension or holding.

4. **Allow your breath to enter your belly.**

   When you inhale, your belly rises. When you exhale, your belly falls.

5. **With each breath, continue to soften your belly.**

   Let go of any anger, fear, pain, or unresolved grief you may be holding in your belly.

6. **As you continue to soften your belly, notice how your heart responds.**

7. **After five minutes or longer of this soft-belly meditation, open your eyes and go about your day.**

   Every now and then, check in with your belly. If you notice that you're tensing it again, gently breathe and soften.

Healing with Light

Many meditation traditions suggest that physical illness and emotional suffering are just different facets of the same basic problem. They're just different ways we contract away from our essential wholeness and health. Here's an exercise for directing the life-giving power of light to the places inside your body and mind that cry out for healing:

1. **Begin by sitting down and meditating in your usual way for several minutes.**

   If you don't have a usual way, you can find one in Chapter 7. Or simply sit quietly, close your eyes, and take a few slow, deep breaths, relaxing a little on each exhalation.

2. **Imagine a luminous sphere of white light suspended about a foot above your head and slightly in front of you.**

   Like a sun, this sphere embodies and radiates all the positive, healing, harmonious qualities you most want to manifest in your life right now. (You may want to be specific at first, such as imagining strength, clarity, peace, and love; eventually, though, you can just flash on the light.) If you find it helpful, you can imagine a spiritual being such as Jesus or Buddha in place of (or inside) the sphere.

3. **Imagine yourself soaking up all these qualities with the healing light as though you were sunbathing.**

4. **Imagine this sphere drawing to itself the energy of all the benevolent forces in the universe that support your growth and evolution.**

5. **Visualize this positive, healing energy shining from the sphere like the light of a thousand suns streaming down through your body and mind.**

   Imagine the energy eliminating all negativity and tension, darkness and depression, worry and anxiety; and replacing them with radiance, vitality, peace, and all the other positive qualities you seek.

6. **Continue to imagine this powerful, healing light flooding every cell and molecule of your being, dissolving any contractions and stuck places you may be aware of, and leaving you clean, clear, and calm.**

7. **Visualize this luminous sphere gradually descending into your heart, where it continues to radiate this powerful light.**

8. **Imagine yourself as a luminous being with a sphere of light in your heart that constantly radiates clarity, harmony, and purity — first to every cell and particle of your own being and then, through you, to every other being in every direction.**

You can carry the feelings and images this exercise evokes throughout the rest of your day.

Grounding into the Earth

When you're feeling scattered or spaced out and you've lost touch with your connection to the earthly plane of existence, you may find it helpful to use the following meditation to ground you.

For detailed instructions, listen to Track 10 on the CD.

1. **Begin by sitting quietly, closing your eyes, and taking a few slow, deep breaths.**

If possible, sit on the ground, with your back relatively straight (see Chapter 8 for more on sitting positions).

2. **Focus your awareness on your lower abdomen, at a point about 2 inches below your navel and 1½ inches inside your body.**

Martial artists call this area the *t'an t'ien* (or *hara*) and believe it's a focal point for life energy, or *chi*. Explore this area with mindful attention, noticing how it feels.

3. **Direct your breath into this area, expanding it when you inhale and contracting it when you exhale.**

Consciously and deliberately breathe into your t'an t'ien for five minutes or more, allowing your awareness and your energy to concentrate there. Notice how your center of gravity shifts from the upper part of your body to your t'an t'ien.

4. **Continuing to breathe with your t'an t'ien, imagine that you're a tree with roots that go deep into the earth.**

Feel and visualize these roots originating in the t'an t'ien and growing down through the base of your spine into the ground, spreading through the soil as far down as you can imagine.

5. **Feel and visualize these roots drawing energy up from the earth into your t'an t'ien on the inhalation and feel the energy spreading down through the roots on the exhalation.**

Continue to feel and visualize this circulation of energy — up on the inhale, down on the exhale — for five or ten minutes.

6. **When your t'an t'ien feels charged and strong, you can get up and go about your day.**

   Every now and then, remind yourself to breathe with your belly again for a minute or two.

Practicing a Half Smile

The Vietnamese Buddhist teacher Thich Nhat Hanh says you can actually shift your mood and restore your innate happiness by smiling consciously, even when your spirits are low. Contemporary scientific research agrees, indicating that smiling relaxes hundreds of facial muscles and has the same effect on the nervous system as real joy. Besides, smiling encourages others to smile and be happy as well.

1. **Take a few moments to form your lips into a half smile.**

   Notice how other parts of your body respond. Does your belly relax? Does your back naturally straighten a little? Does your mood change in subtle ways? Notice also if you have any resistance to smiling when "you don't really feel like it."

2. **Hold this half smile for at least ten minutes as you engage in ordinary activities.**

   Do you notice a shift in how you act or respond to others? Do others respond to your smile by smiling back?

3. **The next time you feel your spirits sagging, practice this half smile for at least half an hour and notice how you feel.**

Peaceful Place

This simple meditation relaxes the body quickly and easily and can be used to help facilitate healing. It's also a kind of inner monastery or refuge that you can escape to when you're feeling threatened, unsafe, or stressed out.

For guidance in imagining a peaceful place, listen to Track 12.

1. **Begin by sitting comfortably, closing your eyes, and taking a few deep breaths.**

2. **Imagine yourself in a safe, protected, peaceful place.**

   It may be a place you know well (a place in nature, for example, like a meadow, a forest, or a beach), a place you've visited once or twice before, or simply a place in your imagination.

3. **Take as much time as you need to imagine this peaceful place as vividly as you can, in all your senses.**

   Notice the colors, the shapes, the sounds, the light, the feeling of the air against your skin, and the contact of your feet against the ground. Explore this special place to your heart's content.

4. **Allow yourself to rest in the feelings of comfort, safety, and tranquility this special place evokes.**

5. **Spend as much time here as you want.**

   When you're done, gradually return to the present moment and open your eyes, while continuing to enjoy the pleasant, positive feelings this exercise evoked.

Part VI
Appendixes

The 5th Wave   By Rich Tennant

"I've been meditating as hard as I can and nothing happens."

In this part . . .

If this book whets your appetite for further inspiration and instruction, here you'll find an annotated list of resources to sustain you. You can find organizations and centers specializing in a variety of techniques and spiritual orientations, as well as books by some of the best contemporary meditation teachers, both Eastern and Western.

You'll also find an appendix that explains how to use the CD. Included is a list of the CD's tracks so you can easily find the meditation you're looking for.

Appendix A

Meditation Resources

• •

*A*fter you dig into this book, you may have a hankering to hook up with other people who meditate, do some in-depth training, check out other styles and approaches, or read books on particular aspects of meditation. So here's a listing of organizations and centers and a brief, annotated bibliography of some good meditation books to complement this one.

Organizations and Centers

With the growing popularity of meditation, centers and organizations devoted to the practice have sprung up in every major city in North America and in plenty of small towns as well! At the same time, increasingly persuasive research into meditation's many benefits has introduced the practice into the venerable halls of medical centers and universities. Needless to say, I couldn't possibly list every meditation venue in these pages. So I offer you an annotated catalogue of major national organizations and representative centers. If an organization appeals to you, contact it directly for more information.

If you just want something nearby and don't particularly care about style or affiliation, use your favorite Internet search engine to look for the word *meditation* along with your general location or the nearest city. Or you can consult your local phone book or alternative newspaper or periodical.

Meditation instruction from some of these organizations comes packaged with a set of spiritual beliefs that may or may not interest you. Also, some organizations offer free instruction, whereas others charge for the opportunity. Finally, although most have been providing meditation instruction for many years (or even decades), I haven't personally checked them out, so I can't offer my double-your-money-back satisfaction guarantee.

Jewish, Christian, and Sufi meditation

The World Community for Christian Meditation
Web: www.wccm-usa.org

> Dedicated to the practice of Christian meditation as taught by John Main, a Benedictine monk who rediscovered the "pure prayer" (mantra recitation) of the desert fathers, this organization boasts more than a 1,000 local groups in more than 40 countries worldwide — and you don't have to be a Catholic (or even a Christian!) to join.

Chochmat HaLev
2215 Prince St.
Berkeley, CA 94705
Phone: 510-704-9687
E-mail: frontdesk@chochmat.org
Web: www.chochmat.org

> Specializing in Jewish "meditation and spirituality training and practice," this organization offers classes and year-long intensive programs, and hosts regular conferences that draw well-known leaders in the Jewish meditation renaissance, including rabbis Rami Shapiro, David Cooper, and Zalman Schachter.

International Association of Sufism
14 Commercial Blvd., Suite 101
Novato, CA 94949
Phone: 415-382-7834
E-mail: ias@ias.org
Web: www.ias.org

> Established to introduce Sufism to the public and to foster dialogue between different Sufi schools, this ecumenical organization publishes a quarterly journal, *Sufism: An Inquiry,* and sponsors the annual Sufi Symposium that features Sufi teachers from around the world. If you want to find out more about Sufi meditation, its website is a great place to start.

Hindu and Yoga meditation

Self-Realization Fellowship
3880 San Rafael Ave.
Los Angeles, CA 90065-3219
Phone: 323-225-2471
Web: www.yogananda-srf.org

Founded in 1920 to further the teachings of the Hindu spiritual teacher
Paramahansa Yogananda, the Self-Realization Fellowship teaches Kriya
Yoga, a set of "scientific techniques of concentration and meditation that
lead to a deepening interior peace and awareness of God's presence."
The organization has meditation and retreat centers around the world.

Kripalu Center for Yoga and Health
Box 793
Lenox, MA 01240
Phone: 800-741-7353
Web: www.kripalu.org

Kripalu Center
P.O. Box 309
Stockbridge, MA 01262
Phone: 866-200-5203

Located in the Berkshire Mountains, this "spiritual retreat and program
center" offers classes and workshops focusing on yoga, holistic health,
and spiritual development. Because it draws teachers from a variety of
different disciplines, Kripalu is a good place to begin exploring yoga-
based meditation practices.

Yogaville Ashram and Integral Yoga Institutes
Route 1, Box 1720
Buckingham, VA 23921
Phone: 800-858-9642
E-mail: iyi@yogaville.org
Web: www.yogaville.org

Satchidananda Ashram – Yogaville
108 Yogaville Way
Buckingham, VA 23921

Established by Swami Satchidananda (the bearded sage who gave the
invocation at Woodstock in 1969), Yogaville offers traditional meditation
and hatha yoga through its community and retreat facility in Virginia,
through Integral Yoga Institutes worldwide, and through an extensive
network of yoga teachers and centers.

SYDA Foundation (Siddha Yoga)
P.O. Box 600
371 Brickman Road
South Fallsburg, NY 12779-0600
Phone: 845-434-2000
E-mail: info@siddhayoga.org
Web: www.siddhayoga.org

This organization offers initiation into Siddha Yoga meditation, a devotional practice designed to awaken the fire of divinity within. Founded by the Indian guru Swami Muktananda and currently headed by his female successor, Swami Chidvilasananda, SYDA boasts six ashrams (in the United States, England, and Australia) and more than 600 centers worldwide.

Vedanta Society of Southern California
1946 Vedanta Place
Hollywood, CA 90068
Phone: 323-465-7114
E-mail: info@vedanta.org
Web: www.vedanta.org

Based on the teachings of the 19th-century Indian sage Ramakrishna and his successors, the Vedanta Society offers an integrated approach to realizing the divinity within, including meditation, devotion, insight into the oneness of God and all creation, and selfless service. It features 16 independent centers in the United States, Europe, and South America.

The Transcendental Meditation Program
Maharishi Foundation USA
1100 N. 4th Street, Suite 128
Fairfield, IA 52556
Phone: 888-532-7686
Web: www.tm.org

Perhaps the best known of all the meditation organizations (the Beatles popularized it in the 1970s), Transcendental Meditation is also the most expensive, with brief introductory courses costing many hundreds of dollars. But proponents claim that the technique is far superior to any other and therefore well worth the price of instruction. If you call the number listed, you'll be connected automatically to the nearest Maharishi Vedic University, school, or center.

Zen meditation

San Francisco Zen Center
300 Page St.
San Francisco, CA 94102
Phone: 415-863-3136
E-mail: ccoffice@sfzc.org
Web: www.sfzc.org

Founded in the 1960s by Zen master Shunryu Suzuki (see *Zen Mind, Beginner's Mind* in the "Books" section later in this appendix) and popularized in the '70s by *The Tassajara Bread Book* by resident monk Ed Brown, this organization offers traditional Zen meditation instruction and retreats at its city center and also at Green Gulch Zen Farm in nearby Marin County. (For intensive training, seasoned practitioners head to Tassajara Zen Mountain Center, a monastery in the wilderness near Big Sur, California.)

Buddhist Society for Compassionate Wisdom
1710 West Cornelia Ave.
Chicago, IL 60657
Phone: 773-528-8685
E-mail: chicago@zenbuddhisttemple.org
Web: www.zenbuddhisttemple.org

Located in a former Pentecostal church, this center offers meditation instruction to the general public, provides a supportive community for ongoing practice, and hosts monastic training for monks and nuns. Founder and teacher Ven. Samu Sunim, a Korean Zen master, also leads centers in Toronto, Ann Arbor, Mexico City, and New York City.

Zen Mountain Monastery
P.O. Box 197
Mt. Tremper, NY 12457
Phone: 845-688-2228
E-mail: zmmtrain@mro.org
Web: www.mro.org/zmm

Set in the scenic Catskill Mountains, this traditional Zen center offers meditation instruction, ongoing practice, and intensive retreats; and hosts programs on Zen and related topics, including the arts, the environment, and academic studies. The center also features affiliate centers in Vermont, New York City, and New Zealand.

Tibetan Buddhist meditation

Tergar Meditation Community
810 S. 1st St., Suite 200
Minneapolis, MN 55343
Phone: (952) 232-0633
E-mail: info@tergar.org
Web: tergar.org

Under the guidance of Yongey Mingyur Rinpoche, a well-known Tibetan Buddhist meditation master and best-selling author, the Tergar community of meditation centers offers weekly meditation and study groups as well as regular seminars on meditation and the core principles of the Buddhist path.

Shambhala International
1084 Tower Rd.
Halifax, Nova Scotia
B3H 2Y5, Canada
Phone: 902-425-4275
Web: www.shambhala.org

Founded in the early 1970s by Chogyam Trungpa Rinpoche, an Oxford-educated Tibetan meditation master who articulated the traditional teachings for his Western audience in a fresh and accessible way, Shambhala features more than 100 meditation centers worldwide (including six rural retreats) and North America's only Buddhist-inspired accredited college, Naropa Institute in Boulder, Colorado.

Insight meditation (Vipassana)

Spirit Rock Meditation Center
P.O. Box 169
Woodacre, CA 94973
Phone: 415-488-0164
Web: www.spiritrock.org

Based on traditional Buddhist mindfulness practices as taught in Southeast Asia (commonly known as *Vipassana,* or insight meditation), Spirit Rock offers a variety of practice options, from basic instruction and weekly meditation groups to intensive retreats of ten days or longer. An active family program provides practice opportunities for parents and children, and special events are offered for the LGBT community and people of color. Teachers from Spirit Rock (who are Westerners) lead retreats throughout the United States.

Insight Meditation Society
1230 Pleasant St.
Barre, MA 01005
Phone: 978-355-4378
E-mail: rc@dharma.org
Web: www.dharma.org

Founded in 1975 by Westerners trained in Southeast Asia, Insight Meditation Society, which is located in rural Massachusetts, offers intensive insight meditation (Vipassana) practice, including both short- and long-term retreats led by Western teachers. Features an annual three-month Vipassana course and regular retreats focusing on the cultivation of lovingkindness.

Vipassana Meditation Center
386 Colrain-Shelburne Rd.
Shelburne, MA 01370
Phone: 413-625-2160
E-mail: info@dhara.dhamma.org
Web: www.dhara.dhamma.org/ns

Affiliated with more than 30 sister centers and many associations in 35 countries worldwide, the Vipassana Meditation Center (VMC) conducts intensive silent retreats in the tradition of the Indian Vipassana teacher S. N. Goenka. Retreats are free of charge; expenses are covered by previous participants who wish to give others the same opportunity. Contact VMC at www.dhamma.org for a retreat schedule or an affiliate group near you.

Other organizations

Mindfulness-Based Stress-Reduction Clinic
Center for Mindfulness in Medicine, Health Care, and Society
University of Massachusetts Medical School
55 Lake Avenue North
Worcester, MA 01655
Phone: 508-856-2656
E-mail: mindfulness@umassmed.edu
Web: www.umassmed.edu/cfm/stress

Founded by Jon Kabat-Zinn, author of *Wherever You Go, There You Are,* the clinic teaches mindfulness-based stress reduction (MBSR) in an eight-week nonresidential format. The Center for Mindfulness also offers a professional training program and sponsors research into the benefits of mindfulness. Visit the clinic's website to find an MBSR program or teacher near you.

Dr. Dean Ornish's Program for Reversing Heart Disease
Preventive Medicine Research Institute
900 Bridgeway
Sausalito, CA 94965
Phone: 800-775-7674
Web: www.ornish.com

This ground-breaking meditation-based program is now being offered in hospitals throughout the United States. Contact Preventive Medicine Research Institute for the name of the program nearest you or for information about its week-long residential retreats.

Books

Meditation books abound, as a quick browse on the Internet will attest. However, none, in my humble estimation, is as comprehensive or as user-friendly as this one. But just in case you want to check out some others, this section provides a brief annotated list of some of my favorite titles. Many focus on one particular technique or tradition, and others emphasize the application of meditation for healing, peak performance, or spiritual development. Several aren't really meditation books at all. Instead, they're prolonged explorations of related themes like enlightenment and Buddhism.

Buddhism For Dummies, 2nd Edition, by Jonathan Landaw, Stephan Bodian, and Gudrun Bühnemann (Wiley)

> Unlike most other religions, Buddhism focuses on practice rather than doctrine, and this comprehensive, user-friendly introduction shows how the tradition evolved in Asia and eventually brought its emphasis on mindful attention in the present moment to an eager Western audience. It includes chapters that explain Buddhist meditation, trace a typical day in the life of a Buddhist in different traditions, and clarify key Buddhist concepts like karma and enlightenment.

Christian Meditation: Experiencing the Presence of God, by James Finley (HarperSanFrancisco)

> From a spiritual counselor who studied with Catholic contemplative Thomas Merton comes this clear introduction to using meditation as a way to connect with the God around you. Defining meditation as a "form of prayerful reflection, using thoughts and images," the author explores some of the major themes of Christian meditation. He emphasizes the importance of inhabiting your body in order to gain insight into the true meaning of the Incarnation and the value of meditating on the *tiune* (three-part) nature of God.

Dr. Dean Ornish's Program for Reversing Heart Disease, by Dean Ornish, M.D. (Ivy Books)

> Though meditation is only one aspect of the Ornish program (along with yoga, exercise, low-fat diet, and group support), this ground-breaking book is a must-read for heart patients and their families — and a sobering reminder for overachievers and other type-A personalities. The simple but powerful message: To heal your heart, you have to open your heart.

Healing into Life and Death, by Stephen Levine (Anchor/Doubleday)

> The author, who trained and taught extensively with Elisabeth Kübler-Ross, has pioneered an approach to serious illness and dying that applies

insights and techniques drawn from the Buddhist tradition. This lucid, heartful book is designed to help bring love and healing to the most challenging and painful life circumstances.

The Healing Power of Mind: Simple Meditation Exercises for Health, Well-Being, and Enlightenment, by Tulku Thondup (Shambhala)

A skillful distillation of Buddhist teachings on healing by a Tibetan meditation master and scholar, this eminently readable book offers not only a wealth of basic healing practices but also deep insights into the nature of mind and the true source of suffering.

Jewish Meditation Practices for Everyday Life: Awakening Your Heart, Connecting with God, by Jeff Roth (Jewish Lights Publishing)

Deeply rooted in Jewish tradition yet informed by the teachings and practices of Buddhism, this little book presents accessible techniques that foster the development of both wisdom and compassion. The author is founder and director of the Awakened Heart Project for Contemplative Judaism.

Joyful Wisdom:Embracing Change and Finding Freedom, by Yongey Mingyur Rinpoche and Eric Swanson (Harmony)

Written by an accomplished Tibetan meditation master and a *New York Times* bestselling author, this eminently accessible book explores the roots of anxiety and other disturbing emotions and offers meditations for facing them directly, befriending them, and transforming them into stepping stones to greater wisdom, clarity, and joy.

Lovingkindness: The Revolutionary Art of Happiness, by Sharon Salzberg (Shambhala)

Written by a founding teacher at the Insight Meditation Society in Barre, Massachusetts, this book provides a series of exercises for increasing your happiness and peace of mind by cultivating the heart qualities of lovingkindess, equanimity, compassion, generosity, and sympathetic joy.

The Meditative Mind: The Varieties of Meditative Experience, by Daniel Goleman (Tarcher/Putnam)

By the author of the *New York Times* bestseller *Emotional Intelligence,* this book explores the psychology of meditation, including a detailed description of the inner terrain that meditators may encounter, and provides a helpful overview of different approaches to meditation, from Hindu and Buddhist to Sufi, Jewish, and Christian. Be prepared for some rather complex spiritual terms and ideas.

A Path with Heart: A Guide through the Perils and Promises of Spiritual Life, by Jack Kornfield (Bantam)

> Based on the author's experience as a Buddhist meditator and meditation teacher for more than 40 years, this book provides a detailed roadmap for the spiritual journey that can be applied to any tradition. Filled with the wise counsel and touching stories that have made Kornfield such a popular presenter at growth centers and conferences.

Peace Is Every Step: The Path of Mindfulness in Everyday Life, by Thich Nhat Hanh (Bantam)

> By the Vietnamese Buddhist monk who was nominated for a Nobel Peace Prize by Martin Luther King, this gentle, compassionate book teaches how to extend the practice of mindful awareness to every moment of life. Filled with inspiring examples and informed by the author's commitment to social justice and ecological awareness.

The Power of Now: A Guide to Spiritual Enlightenment, by Eckhart Tolle (New World Library)

> As its name implies, this national bestseller guides you on the journey of realizing your timeless spiritual nature by becoming more fully present and embodied in "the Now." Offered by a contemporary teacher who has clearly walked his own talk, the words have a spiritual authority that invites you beyond words to the direct experience to which meditation points. Highly recommended.

Sacred Hoops: Spiritual Lessons of a Hardwood Warrior, by Phil Jackson (Hyperion)

> Written by the former coach of the Chicago Bulls, this fascinating autobiography tells how Jackson used the skills and principles he learned in the practice of Zen meditation to forge a world-champion basketball team. A must-read for sports fans!

The Tibetan Book of Living and Dying, by Sogyal Rinpoche (HarperCollins)

> Although this book transmits the traditional Tibetan Buddhist teachings about death, dying, and rebirth (which you may or may not find appealing), it's also filled with heartwarming stories and powerful practices that can be applied not only to help with the dying process, but also to bring more love and compassion into your life right now!

The Way of a Pilgrim, translated by Olga Savin (Shambhala, 2001)

> First made popular in the West by J. D. Salinger, this little book tells the true story of a simple 19th-century Russian peasant who wanders the countryside reciting the Jesus prayer ("Lord Jesus Christ, have mercy on me!") and discovering love and joy wherever he goes. An inspiring tale of the power of Christian meditation.

Wherever You Go, There You Are: Mindfulness Meditation in Everyday Life, by Jon Kabat-Zinn (Hyperion, 2005)

> Written by the originator of Mindfulness-Based Stress Reduction (MBSR), a popular eight-week training in meditation and mindful living, this warm-hearted, lyrical book teaches you how to wake up to the beauty and richness of each moment through the practice of mindfulness. Short chapters and personal anecdotes make this great bedside reading!

Zen Mind, Beginner's Mind, by Shunryu Suzuki (Shambhala, 2011)

> Not an instruction manual, exactly, but a prolonged meditation on the nature of meditation (and life) by one of the best-loved Zen masters of modern times, this book seamlessly weaves together profound insights and practical guidance. A spiritual classic that is also eminently accessible.

Appendix B

About the CD

This CD contains two informational tacks and ten different guided meditations to help you get started in your quest for better health, less stress, more happiness, and all the other benefits that meditation provides. As you listen to each meditation, remember to breathe, focus, and relax. And remember that practice makes perfect! Meditate daily if you can.

You can play the CD on your home stereo system or in your car's CD player. Or, if you prefer, you can play the CD on your computer.

Note: If you are using a digital or enhanced digital version of this book, this appendix does not apply. Please go to http://booksupport.wiley.com for access to the additional content.

Using the CD

To play the CD in your home stereo, car stereo, or similar device, simply treat it as you would any other audio CD.

When using the CD with your home computer, you'll find digital audio files in MP3 format that you can easily transfer to a digital music player such as an iPod.

What You'll Find on the CD

The CD consists of the following audio tracks:

Track 1	Introduction (3:39)
Track 2	Meditation: It's Easier than You Think (2:22)
Track 3	Tuning In to Your Body (5:23)
Track 4	Basic Mindfulness Meditation (7:55)
Track 5	Finding a Sitting Posture That Works for You (3:28)

Track 6	Walking Meditation (3:27)
Track 7	Lovingkindness Meditation (10:12)
Track 8	Transforming Suffering with Compassion (8:06)
Track 9	Replacing Negative Patterns with Positive Energy (6:44)
Track 10	Grounding Meditation (5:55)
Track 11	Consulting the Guru inside You (6:35)
Track 12	Peaceful Place (4:47)

Customer Care

If you have trouble with the audio CD, please call Wiley Product Technical Support at 800-762-2974. Outside the United States, call 317-572-3993. You can also contact Wiley Product Technical Support at http://support.wiley.com. Wiley will provide technical support only for installation and other general quality control items. For technical support on the applications themselves, consult the program's vendor or author.

To place additional orders or to request information about other Wiley products, please call 877-762-2974.

Index

Apple & Mac

iPad 2 For Dummies,
3rd Edition
978-1-118-17679-5

iPhone 4S For Dummies,
4th Edition
978-1-118-03671-6

iPod touch For Dummies,
3rd Edition
978-1-118-12960-9

Mac OS X Lion
For Dummies
978-1-118-02205-4

Blogging & Social Media

CityVille For Dummies
978-1-118-08337-6

Facebook For Dummies,
4th Edition
978-1-118-09562-1

Mom Blogging
For Dummies
978-1-118-03843-7

Twitter For Dummies,
2nd Edition
978-0-470-76879-2

WordPress For Dummies,
4th Edition
978-1-118-07342-1

Business

Cash Flow For Dummies
978-1-118-01850-7

Investing For Dummies,
6th Edition
978-0-470-90545-6

Job Searching with Social
Media For Dummies
978-0-470-93072-4

QuickBooks 2012
For Dummies
978-1-118-09120-3

Resumes For Dummies,
6th Edition
978-0-470-87361-8

Starting an Etsy Business
For Dummies
978-0-470-93067-0

Cooking & Entertaining

Cooking Basics
For Dummies, 4th Edition
978-0-470-91388-8

Wine For Dummies,
4th Edition
978-0-470-04579-4

Diet & Nutrition

Kettlebells For Dummies
978-0-470-59929-7

Nutrition For Dummies,
5th Edition
978-0-470-93231-5

Restaurant Calorie Counter
For Dummies,
2nd Edition
978-0-470-64405-8

Digital Photography

Digital SLR Cameras &
Photography For Dummies,
4th Edition
978-1-118-14489-3

Digital SLR Settings
& Shortcuts
For Dummies
978-0-470-91763-3

Photoshop Elements 10
For Dummies
978-1-118-10742-3

Gardening

Gardening Basics
For Dummies
978-0-470-03749-2

Vegetable Gardening
For Dummies,
2nd Edition
978-0-470-49870-5

Green/Sustainable

Raising Chickens
For Dummies
978-0-470-46544-8

Green Cleaning
For Dummies
978-0-470-39106-8

Health

Diabetes For Dummies,
3rd Edition
978-0-470-27086-8

Food Allergies
For Dummies
978-0-470-09584-3

Living Gluten-Free
For Dummies,
2nd Edition
978-0-470-58589-4

Hobbies

Beekeeping
For Dummies,
2nd Edition
978-0-470-43065-1

Chess For Dummies,
3rd Edition
978-1-118-01695-4

Drawing For Dummies,
2nd Edition
978-0-470-61842-4

eBay For Dummies,
7th Edition
978-1-118-09806-6

Knitting For Dummies,
2nd Edition
978-0-470-28747-7

Language &
Foreign Language

English Grammar
For Dummies,
2nd Edition
978-0-470-54664-2

French For Dummies,
2nd Edition
978-1-118-00464-7

German For Dummies,
2nd Edition
978-0-470-90101-4

Spanish Essentials
For Dummies
978-0-470-63751-7

Spanish For Dummies,
2nd Edition
978-0-470-87855-2

Available wherever books are sold. For more information or to order direct: U.S. customers visit www.dummies.com or call 1-877-762-2974.
U.K. customers visit www.wileyeurope.com or call (0) 1243 843291. Canadian customers visit www.wiley.ca or call 1-800-567-4797.

Connect with us online at www.facebook.com/fordummies or @fordummies

Math & Science

Algebra I For Dummies,
2nd Edition
978-0-470-55964-2

Biology For Dummies,
2nd Edition
978-0-470-59875-7

Chemistry For Dummies,
2nd Edition
978-1-1180-0730-3

Geometry For Dummies,
2nd Edition
978-0-470-08946-0

Pre-Algebra Essentials
For Dummies
978-0-470-61838-7

Microsoft Office

Excel 2010 For Dummies
978-0-470-48953-6

Office 2010 All-in-One
For Dummies
978-0-470-49748-7

Office 2011 for Mac
For Dummies
978-0-470-87869-9

Word 2010
For Dummies
978-0-470-48772-3

Music

Guitar For Dummies,
2nd Edition
978-0-7645-9904-0

Clarinet For Dummies
978-0-470-58477-4

iPod & iTunes
For Dummies,
9th Edition
978-1-118-13060-5

Pets

Cats For Dummies,
2nd Edition
978-0-7645-5275-5

Dogs All-in One
For Dummies
978-0470-52978-2

Saltwater Aquariums
For Dummies
978-0-470-06805-2

Religion & Inspiration

The Bible For Dummies
978-0-7645-5296-0

Catholicism For Dummies,
2nd Edition
978-1-118-07778-8

Spirituality For Dummies,
2nd Edition
978-0-470-19142-2

Self-Help & Relationships

Happiness For Dummies
978-0-470-28171-0

Overcoming Anxiety
For Dummies,
2nd Edition
978-0-470-57441-6

Seniors

Crosswords For Seniors
For Dummies
978-0-470-49157-7

iPad 2 For Seniors
For Dummies, 3rd Edition
978-1-118-17678-8

Laptops & Tablets
For Seniors For Dummies,
2nd Edition
978-1-118-09596-6

Smartphones & Tablets

BlackBerry For Dummies,
5th Edition
978-1-118-10035-6

Droid X2 For Dummies
978-1-118-14864-8

HTC ThunderBolt
For Dummies
978-1-118-07601-9

MOTOROLA XOOM
For Dummies
978-1-118-08835-7

Sports

Basketball For Dummies,
3rd Edition
978-1-118-07374-2

Football For Dummies,
2nd Edition
978-1-118-01261-1

Golf For Dummies,
4th Edition
978-0-470-88279-5

Test Prep

ACT For Dummies,
5th Edition
978-1-118-01259-8

ASVAB For Dummies,
3rd Edition
978-0-470-63760-9

The GRE Test For
Dummies, 7th Edition
978-0-470-00919-2

Police Officer Exam
For Dummies
978-0-470-88724-0

Series 7 Exam
For Dummies
978-0-470-09932-2

Web Development

HTML, CSS, & XHTML
For Dummies, 7th Edition
978-0-470-91659-9

Drupal For Dummies,
2nd Edition
978-1-118-08348-2

Windows 7

Windows 7
For Dummies
978-0-470-49743-2

Windows 7
For Dummies,
Book + DVD Bundle
978-0-470-52398-8

Windows 7 All-in-One
For Dummies
978-0-470-48763-1

Available wherever books are sold. For more information or to order direct: U.S. customers visit www.dummies.com or call 1-877-762-2974.
U.K. customers visit www.wileyeurope.com or call (0) 1243 843291. Canadian customers visit www.wiley.ca or call 1-800-567-4797.
Connect with us online at www.facebook.com/fordummies or @fordummies